A CULTURAL HISTORY OF WORK

Volume 4

A Cultural History of Work (6 vols.)

Winner of the 2020 PROSE Award for Multivolume Reference/Humanities

A Cultural History of Work
General Editors: Deborah Simonton and Anne Montenach

Volume 1
A Cultural History of Work in Antiquity
Edited by Ephraim Lytle

Volume 2
A Cultural History of Work in the Medieval Age
Edited by Valerie L. Garver

Volume 3
A Cultural History of Work in the Early Modern Age
Edited by Bert De Munck and Thomas Max Safley

Volume 4
A Cultural History of Work in the Age of Enlightenment
Edited by Deborah Simonton and Anne Montenach

Volume 5
A Cultural History of Work in the Age of Empire
Edited by Victoria E. Thompson

Volume 6
A Cultural History of Work in the Modern Age
Edited by Daniel J. Walkowitz

A CULTURAL HISTORY OF WORK

IN THE AGE OF ENLIGHTENMENT

Edited by Deborah Simonton and Anne Montenach

BLOOMSBURY ACADEMIC
LONDON • NEW YORK • OXFORD • NEW DELHI • SYDNEY

BLOOMSBURY ACADEMIC
Bloomsbury Publishing Plc
50 Bedford Square, London, WC1B 3DP, UK
1385 Broadway, New York, NY 10018, USA
29 Earlsfort Terrace, Dublin 2, Ireland

BLOOMSBURY and the Diana logo are trademarks of Bloomsbury Publishing Plc

First published in Great Britain 2018
This edition published in Great Britain, 2021

Copyright © Bloomsbury Publishing, 2018

Anne Montenach and Deborah Simonton have asserted their right under the Copyright, Designs and Patents Act, 1988, to be identified as Editor of this work.

Cover image © ACTIVE MUSEUM / Alamy Stock Photo

All rights reserved. No part of this publication may be reproduced or transmitted in any form or by any means, electronic or mechanical, including photocopying, recording, or any information storage or retrieval system, without prior permission in writing from the publishers.

A catalogue record for this book is available from the British Library.

A catalog record for this book is available from the Library of Congress.

ISBN: HB: 978-1-4742-4482-4
        PB: 978-1-3502-7884-4
        Set: 978-1-4742-4503-6

Series: The Cultural Histories Series

Typeset by Integra Software Services Pvt. Ltd.
Printed and bound in Great Britain

To find out more about our authors and books visit www.bloomsbury.com and sign up for our newsletters.

CONTENTS

List of Figures vi
General Editors' Preface x
Contributors xii

Introduction 1
Deborah Simonton

1   The Economy of Work 19
    Carmen Sarasúa

2   Picturing Work 39
    Christiana Payne

3   Work and Workplaces 61
    Emma Hart

4   Workplace Cultures 77
    Janine Lanza

5   Work, Skill, and Technology 95
    Leonard N. Rosenband

6   Work and Mobility 113
    Eleonora Canepari

7   Work and Society 131
    Kyle T. Bulthuis

8   The Political Culture of Work 151
    Bert De Munck

9   Work and Leisure 169
    Emma Griffin

Notes 185
Further Readings 215
Index 225

LIST OF FIGURES

INTRODUCTION

I.1 "Typefoundry." Denis Diderot and Jean le Rond d'Alembert, *Encyclopédie, ou dictionnaire raisonné des sciences, des arts et des métiers,* 1751–72. — 7

I.2 Niccoló Schiavonetti, *New Mackrel, New Mackrel,* Plate V. In the series *The Cries of London* by Niccoló Schiavonetti, after Francis Wheatley's painting. New Haven, CT, Yale Center for British Art, Paul Mellon Collection. — 11

CHAPTER ONE

1.1 Francisco de Goya, *La era o Verano* (The Threshing Ground or Summer), 1786. Madrid, Museo del Prado. Photo: Artepics / Alamy Stock Photo. — 20

1.2 Joseph Vernet, *Vue d'une partie du Port et de la ville de Bordeaux, prise du côté des Salinières,* 1759. Paris, Musée National de la Marine. — 22

1.3 Francisco de Goya, *La tormenta de nieve o Invierno* (The Snowstorm or Winter), 1786. Madrid, Museo del Prado. Photo: DeAgostini / Getty Images. — 25

1.4 Francis Wheatley, *The Return from the Market.* © Leeds Museums and Art Galleries (Temple Newsam House) UK / Bridgeman Images. — 27

1.5 Pietro Longhi, *Portrait of a Venetian Family with a Manservant Serving Coffee,* c. 1752. Amsterdam, Rijksmuseum. — 28

1.6 *Soierie. Tirage de la soie et Plan du Tour de Piémont,* "Silkmaking," Plate I. In Denis Diderot and Jean le Rond d'Alembert, *Encyclopédie, ou dictionnaire raisonné des sciences, des arts et des métiers,* 1751–72. — 30

1.7 Joseph Gabriel Rosetti, *The Workers' Workshop, Factory of Indian Cotton Fabric Founded by the Wetter Brothers in Orange,* 1764. Orange, France, Musée municipal. — 35

CHAPTER TWO

2.1 Giacomo Ceruti, *Women Working on Pillow Lace (The Sewing School),* 1720s. Photo: ART Collection / Alamy Stock Photo. — 41

2.2 Jean-Baptiste-Siméon Chardin, *The Young Schoolmistress,* c. 1736. London, National Gallery. — 43

2.3 William Hogarth, *The Fellow 'Prentices at their Looms, Industry and Idleness,* Plate I, 1747. — 44

LIST OF FIGURES vii

2.4 Agostino Brunias, *Market Day, Roseau, Dominica*, c. 1780. New Haven, CT, Yale Center for British Art.   46

2.5 Léonard Defrance, *Interior of a Foundry*, 1789. Liverpool, Walker Art Gallery.   48

2.6 Joseph Wright of Derby, *The Blacksmith's Shop*, 1771. New Haven, CT, Yale Center for British Art.   50

2.7 George Stubbs, *Reapers*, 1795. New Haven, CT, Yale Center for British Art.   52

2.8 Henry Morland, *A Laundry Maid Ironing*, c. 1765–82. London, Tate Britain.   54

2.9 John Singleton Copley, *Portrait of Mr. and Mrs. Thomas Mifflin*, 1773. Philadelphia Museum of Art, 125th Anniversary Acquisition. Bequest of Mrs. Esther F. Wistar.   57

2.10 Johann Zoffany, *John Cuff*, 1772. Royal Collection Trust.   58

CHAPTER THREE

3.1 *Candlemakers' Workshop*. In Denis Diderot and Jean le Rond d'Alembert, *Encyclopédie, ou dictionnaire raisonné des sciences, des arts et des métiers*, 1751–72. Courtesy of the Wellcome Trust.   65

3.2 Balthazar Nebot, *Fishmonger's Stall*, 1737. New Haven, CT, Yale Center for British Art, Paul Mellon Collection.   68

3.3 Anne Claude Caylus, *Bundled Firewood Seller*, 1746. *Études prises dans le bas peuple ou les Cris de Paris*: Cotterets, after Edme Bouchardon. New York, Metropolitan Museum of Art, www.metmuseum.org.   71

3.4 Benjamin Henry Latrobe, *An Overseer Doing His Duty near Fredericksburg, Virginia*, c. 1798. Baltimore, Maryland Historical society.   74

CHAPTER FOUR

4.1 William Henry Pyne, *Poulterer's Shop*, n.d. New Haven, CT, Yale Center for British Art, Paul Mellon Collection.   78

4.2 William Hincks, *Representing Winding, Warping with a new improved Warping Mill, and Weaving*, Plate VII, 1791. London, British Library.   81

4.3 John Varley, *Norwich*, n.d. New Haven, CT, Yale Center for British Art, Paul Mellon Collection.   84

4.4 Anthony Cardon, *Do You Want any Matches?* Plate IV. In the series *The Cries of London*, 1794, after Francis Wheatley. New Haven, CT, Yale Center for British Art, Paul Mellon Collection.   87

4.5 John Raphael Smith, *The Slave Trade*, 1791, after George Morland. New Haven, CT, Yale Center for British Art, Paul Mellon Collection.   90

4.6 Juan Patricio Morlete Ruiz, *Hold Yourself Suspended in Midair*, X. In *Spaniard and Return Backwards* (De español y torna atrás, tente en el aire), c. 1760. Los Angeles, LACMA.   92

CHAPTER FIVE

5.1 *Papeterie*, Plate X (Details of skills and tools of papermaking). In Denis Diderot and Jean le Rond d'Alembert, *Encyclopédie, ou dictionnaire raisonné des sciences, des arts et des métiers*, vol. 5, 1751–2. 100

5.2 *Papeterie*, Plate XII (Drying). In Denis Diderot and Jean le Rond d'Alembert, *Encyclopédie, ou dictionnaire raisonné des sciences, des arts et des métiers*, vol. 5, 1751–72. 103

5.3 *Marine*, Plate VIII (Shipyard). In Denis Diderot and Jean le Rond d'Alembert, *Encyclopédie, ou dictionnaire raisonné des sciences, des arts et des métiers*, vol. 7, 1751–72 109

CHAPTER SIX

6.1 "Porters from the town of Venice." In Cesare Vecellio, *Costumes anciens et modernes, Habiti antichi et moderni di tutto il Mondo di Cesare Vecellio*, Paris, 1860. 122

6.2 "The bureau of wet nurses in Paris—wet nurses waiting to be selected." In William Sams, *A Tour through Paris*, 1822–4. Courtesy of Wellcome Library no. 17481i. 123

6.3 Giuseppe Vasi, *Piazza Montanara*, etching. In *Sulle magnificenze di Roma Antica e Moderna*, vol. II, 1752. 124

6.4 Simon Guillain, *Vende Quadri*, after Annibale Carracci. In *Le Arti di Bologna*, 1646. 127

CHAPTER SEVEN

7.1 William Hogarth, *The Industrious 'Prentice Grown Rich, and Sheriff of London*, Plate VIII, and *The Idle 'Prentice Betrayed by a Prostitute*, Plate IX. Both in *Industry and Idleness*, 1747. New Haven, CT, Yale Center for British Art, Yale University Art Gallery Collection. 134

7.2 Thomas Rowlandson, *Hot Spice Gingerbread All Hot*, n.d. New Haven, CT, Yale Centre for British Art, Paul Mellon Collection. 137

7.3 Julien Fatou, *Jacques Necker*, after 1785, after Joseph Siffred Suplessis; Jean Langlois, *John Law*, early eighteenth century, after Jean Hubert. Both London, National Portrait Gallery; Jacobus Houbraken, *Robert Walpole*, 1st Earl of Oxford, 1746, after Arthur Pond. New Haven, CT, Yale Center for British Art, Paul Mellon Collection. 140

7.4 *Paysan et Paysanne des environs de Trieste en Austrie* (Male and female peasants from Trieste, Austria). In Jacques Grasset de Saint-Sauveur, *Encyclopedie des Voyages*, Paris, 1796. Los Angeles, LACMA. 143

CHAPTER EIGHT

8.1 Tinsmith. In Jan and Caspar Luyken, *Het Menselyk Bedryf. Vertoond in 100 Verbeeldingen van Ambachten, Konsten, Hanteeringen en Bedryven, met Versen*, Amsterdam, 1694. 155

8.2 William Hogarth, *The Industrious 'Prentice a Favourite, and entrusted by his Master*, Plate IV. In *Industry and Idleness*, 1747. 162

8.3 Coat of arms of the Antwerp blacksmiths, Plate XVII 2, and the Antwerp butchers, Plate XVII 9. Both in P. Génard, *Armorial des institutions communales d'Anvers*. 163

8.4 *Epinglier*, Plate II (Pin Making), Engraving of Deferht based upon a design of Goussier. In Denis Diderot and Jean le Rond d'Alembert, *Encyclopédie, ou dictionnaire raisonné des sciences, des arts et des métiers*, vol. 5, 1751–72. 165

8.5 Gabriel Smith (1724–83) (Printmaker) and John Linnell (1729–96) (Designer), *A new Book of Ornaments useful for Silversmiths*, 1755. London, British Museum. © Victoria & Albert Museum, London. 166

CHAPTER NINE

9.1 Bull-baiting. In Henry Alken, *The National Sports of Great Britain ... with Descriptions, in English and French*, 1823. 179

9.2 *Rural Sports. Cudgel Playing*. In *The Sporting Magazine; or, Monthly Calendar of the Transactions of the Turf, the Chace, and Every Other Diversion Interesting to the Man of Pleasure, Enterprize, and Spirit*, 1799. 180

9.3 David Teniers the Younger, *Landscape with Peasants Playing Bowls Outside an Inn*, c. 1660. Los Angeles, LACMA. 181

9.4 Etienne Jeaurat (1699–1789), *Carnival in the streets of Paris*, 1757. Paris, Musée Carnavalet. Photo: DeAgostini / Getty Images. 182

9.5 *Celebrations at Lille in honour of the birth of the Dauphin*, 1781. Paris Bibliotheque des Arts Decoratifs, Archives Charmet. Photo: Bridgeman Images. 183

GENERAL EDITORS' PREFACE

Issues around work and the workplace seem to be having a renaissance and are no longer embedded solely in the discourses around Marxism and labor movements. Similarly, new and fresh research has been taking place around guilds, skill, control, and gender issues. *A Cultural History of Work* takes an approach that focuses on culture in order to explore the subtleties of the character and dynamics of work and the people and relationships involved in working and the workplace in a theoretically holistic way to bring together disparate historical traditions and historiographical approaches. The aim and scope of *A Cultural History of Work* is to offer a comprehensive survey of the social and cultural construction of work across six historical periods. This approach that focuses on the *cultural* history of work provides an opportunity to explore the dynamics of work and the people and relationships involved in working and the workplace, helping to rethink boundaries and the issues of work. This is not an "economic" history of work, but a cultural one. Of course, we talk about economics, but the fundamental concept is to explain the ways in which work was situated in and influenced cultural dynamics of the western world. It is a key contribution to the process of rethinking boundaries and issues of work.

A Cultural History of Work draws on "the western world." Contributors approached their chapters with a great deal of freedom, drawing on their specific expertise in national and regional histories, but throughout the thirty-six chapters that make up the series, they have tried to embrace the "West." The series does not intend to "cover" all of western culture, or even all of Europe and North America. Authors instead have aimed at *representing* the broad trends and nuances of the culture of work from antiquity to the present. Thus *A Cultural History of Work* concentrates on the central themes in western work, with some sensitivity to areas we know less about.

This is a work of scholarly reference designed to provide scholars and students with a detailed, nuanced overview. Each contribution has been written as an original chapter presenting an *overview* of a theme in a period, but each also includes a wide range of case material and has a particular thrust or point of view (or points of view) informing the organization of the piece. The series is structured into six time periods—though historians will always quibble about what these periods mean and will blur the edges. That is part of the process of understanding the past. And time does not have the same meaning across regions, much less countries or continents. Each volume covers a long period of time and a broad geography that can and will introduce a range of variables. Each volume uses the same chapter titles so that readers can read on a theme across volumes, or read through a period exploring the range of themes and nuances that each volume presents. There are also overlaps within volumes and across them that enrich the discussion.

The editorial decision to study work rather than labor is suggestive of a broader, more encompassing field of study that lends itself more readily to different periods. For example, in particular it is more appropriate to use should be work for periods such as antiquity and the Middle Ages because labor looks in one sense as an eighteenth-

or nineteenth-century concept. English is rather unusual in having two words whose meanings overlap considerably, but are not identical. For example, there is only one word in French, *travail*, like *Arbeit* in German, *arbejde* in Danish/Swedish/Norwegian, *lavoro* in Italian. Some other languages tend to have one primary word also, for example, *trabajo* in Spanish, though there are other usable words. From a definitional point of view we can argue that *labor* means the use of mental or physical capacities/faculties, so it implies suffering and difficulty, whereas *work* has to do with the simple act or fact of doing something/the activity/the action in progress. From the point of view of the political economy, *labor* seems to refer to the Marxist discourse; *work* is more pragmatic and less laden with cultural overtones. So, work describes the parameters of this project while *labor* is one aspect of it, which is more important in the nineteenth and twentieth centuries, and to a lesser extent in the eighteenth. Thus we argue *work* seems more neutral and general and therefore more applicable across time.

Moving from the world of antiquity and into the twenty-first century, the culture of work has shifted considerably as technologies, organizations, and locations have changed. Workplace relations have also undergone transformations from small-scale and familial settings to large-scale and potentially less personal environments. And yet, the world of work remains complex with great variations between national cultures, political and economic approaches to managing the fields of work, and especially in the ways that people have negotiated their own spaces and places within them. Work retains many meanings from the simple need to survive to senses of deep satisfaction for the character of the job and the creativity one can achieve. It may be valued for the income or wealth it can generate; conversely, some choose to work less and on their own terms. Part-time, job-sharing, self-employment, and the IT revolution have offered different routes for some people. Workers can, however, remain tied to an employer and though nominally slavery does not exist in the West, there are those, such as sweated immigrant workshops, and live-in domestic workers, who may feel that little has changed. *The Cultural History of Work* traces and explores many of these routes and their implications for people and their cultural experience of work.

CONTRIBUTORS

Kyle T. Bulthuis is Assistant Professor of early American history at Utah State University, USA. He is the author of *Four Steeples over the City Streets: Religion and Society in New York's Early Republic Congregations* (2014), an analysis of the relationship between religious experience and social change in the antebellum United States. His current project, *Equiano's Generation*, is a social-historical study of the first generation of black authors in the British Atlantic world.

Eleonora Canepari obtained her PhD in History at the University of Turin, Italy, in 2006 and at the École des Hautes Études en Sciences Sociales, Paris, France in 2012. Her research focuses on urban mobility during the seventeenth century. She has been Marie Curie postdoctoral fellow at the Centre de Recherches Historiques (Centre National de la Recherche Scientifique, Paris), Gerda Henkel fellow at the University of Oxford, and member of the Centre for Reformation and Renaissance Studies (University of Toronto). She currently holds a "Rising Star" packaged chair from the Fondation A*Midex Aix Marseille Université, CNRS, TELEMME, Aix-en-Provence, France, and is Principal Investigator of the project *Settling in Motion: Mobility and the Making of the Urban Space (16th–18th c)*. Her most recent publication (with B. Mesini and S. Mourlane) is *Mobilhommes* (2016).

Bert De Munck is Professor at the Department of History at the University of Antwerp, Belgium, teaching "Early Modern History," "History and social theory," and "Heritage and public history." He is a member of the Centre for Urban History, Antwerp, and has published on craft guilds and apprenticeship, civil society, migration, conceptual approaches to urban history, and the "repertoires of evaluation" regarding skills and products. Currently, he is the Director of the interdisciplinary Urban Studies Institute and the international Scientific Research Community (WOG) "Urban Agency: The Historical Fabrication of the City as an Object of Study" project.

Emma Griffin is Professor of Cultural History at the University of East Anglia, England. She obtained her PhD at the University of Cambridge, England, in 2001 and has since published widely in the field of British social and cultural history in the eighteenth and nineteenth centuries. Her most recent book is *Liberty's Dawn: A People's History of the Industrial Revolution* (2013). She is currently working on family living standards in Victorian Britain.

Emma Hart is Senior Lecturer in Modern History at the University of St. Andrews, Scotland. She is a historian of the early modern British Atlantic world, specializing in urban history, material culture, and the built environment. She is the author of *Building Charleston: Town and Society in the Eighteenth-Century British Atlantic World* (2010). Her current project is a spatial history of the early American marketplace. Her work has also appeared in *Urban History*, the *William and Mary Quarterly*, and the *Journal of Southern History*.

Janine Lanza is a historian of early Modern France whose research deals with gender, law, and work. She is the author of *From Wives to Widows in Early Modern Paris: Gender, Economy and Law* (2007). Her current research project examines changes in early modern French civil law and the ways in which it shaped both business formation and gender roles in Parisian artisanal households.

Anne Montenach is Professor of Early Modern History at Aix-Marseille University, Aix Marseille Université, CNRS, TELEMME, Aix-en-Provence, France. She obtained her PhD at the European University Institute, Florence, Italy, published as *L'économie du quotidien: Espaces et pratiques du commerce alimentaire à Lyon au XVIIe siècle* (2009). Following research on the early modern urban economy, with a special emphasis on informal circulations and exchange, she has turned to working on female economic territories in early modern Europe, both illicit and legitimate. She has co edited (with Deborah Simonton) *Gender in the European Town: Female Agency in the Urban Economy, 1640–1830* (2013), (with Marjo Kaartinen) *Luxury and Gender in European Towns, 1700–1914* (2014), and *The Routledge History Handbook of Gender and the Urban Experience* (2017).

Christiana Payne is Professor of History of Art at Oxford Brookes University, England. Her publications include *Toil and Plenty: Images of the Agricultural Landscape in England, 1780–1890* (1993), *Where the Sea meets the Land: Artists on the Coast in Nineteenth-Century Britain* (2007), *John Brett, Pre-Raphaelite Landscape Painter* (2010), and *Silent Witnesses: Trees in British Art, 1760–1870* (2017).

Leonard N. Rosenband is Professor Emeritus of History at Utah State University. He is the author of *Papermaking in Eighteenth-Century France: Management, Labor, and Revolution at the Montgolfier Mill, 1761-1805* (2000), which appeared in French translation in 2005. He has coedited two books and published numerous articles, including "Comparing Combination Acts: French and English Papermaking in the Age of Revolution," *Social History* (2004), and "The Industrious Revolution: A Concept Too Many?" *International Labor and Working Class History* (2016). He is currently completing a book entitled *The Cosmopolitanism of the Industrial Revolution: Papermaking in England and France, 1650-1850*.

Carmen Sarasúa is Professor of Economic History at Universitat Autònoma de Barcelona, Spain. She obtained her PhD in History at the European University Institute, Florence, Italy, and her MA in Labor Economics at the New School for Social Research, New York, USA, as a Fulbright scholar. She has published extensively on the Spanish labor market in the eighteenth to twentieth centuries, the working lives of families, women's labor force participation and its relationship to economic growth, and the long-term transformation of the occupational structure. She is Associate Editor of *Feminist Economics* and a member of the Editorial Board of *Continuity and Change*. In 2016/7 she was Visiting Fellow of All Souls College, Oxford, England.

Deborah Simonton is Associate Professor *Emerita* of British History at the University of Southern Denmark, Fellow of the Royal Historical Society, UK, and Visiting Professor at the University of Turku, Finland. She has a long-standing interest in gender, skill, and identity. Her publications include *A History of European Women's Work* (1998) and *Women in European Culture and Society* (2010) with a companion sourcebook, and she is editor of *Routledge History of Women in Europe* (2006). She leads the Gender in the European Town Network, is General Editor of *The Routledge History Handbook of Gender and the Urban Experience* (2017), and has co edited (with Anne Montenach) *Female Agency in the Urban Economy: 1640–1830* (2013), (with Anne Montenach and Marjo Kaartinen) *Luxury and Gender in the Modern Urban Economy* (2014), and (with Hannu Salmi) *Catastrophe, Gender and Urban Experience* (2017).

Introduction

DEBORAH SIMONTON

The world in which European men and women operated from the mid-seventeenth century was built on a legacy of intellectual, economic, and religious change. The Age of the Enlightenment represented a major shift in the western mind-set. It was an organic phenomenon, building on the new rationalism of the revolution in scientific ideas of the seventeenth century. Through numerous publications, including the *Encyclopédie* and the *Encyclopaedia Britannica*, letters, articles, conversations, and dialogues, philosophers and theorists challenged many of the assumptions of the European old regime, and contributed to forging the ideas which shape our own world. Using a scientific approach, it was grounded in a fundamental belief in the importance of the human mind and the ability of people to think and reason. In the late seventeenth century, Newton had attempted to resolve the conflict between human reason and the world of God, marking a significant shift from the conception that the world could only be understood by revealed religion. God was not dismissed but became the first Cause, the Great Mechanic, or even the Watchmaker. Newton suggested that the world was governed by natural laws which were intelligible and reasonable; once discovered, these immutable and axiomatic laws of Reason would be acknowledged as just and right by all. By the laws of Nature, man's world was illuminated, as Pope wrote:

Nature and Nature's laws lay hid in night:
God said, *"Let Newton be!"* and all was light![1]

Writers such as Voltaire, Adam Smith, Thomas Reid, Montesquieu, Diderot, Condorcet, Jefferson, and D'Alembert, among others, argued in favor of sweeping away institutions based on tradition rather than reason, such as the rejection of divine-right monarchies and the myth and superstition of formal religion. The Enlightenment according to Voltaire encompassed the autonomy of reason, a belief in perfectibility and progress, a confidence in the ability to discover causality. It sought the "scientific principles" that governed nature, man, and society, and coupled that search with an assault on authority and a disgust with nationalism.

The Enlightenment enshrined the idea of "inalienable" human rights, the "Rights of Man," which would contribute to political shifts, such as the American and French revolutions and the idea of constitutional democracy. The Rights of Woman were more ambiguous and while the Enlightenment opened new ways of thinking about women, the language was far less liberating. There was no coherent feminist agenda in the *Encyclopédie*; the philosophes were influenced by an ingrained sense of female inferiority to the male, and they frequently ignored the question of women's inequality or attacked women as representatives of social classes they wished to condemn. Authors such as Olympe de Gouges and Mary Wollstonecraft and some male contemporaries insisted on women's equality in Reason and thus on the Rights of Woman stemming from the same first principles. Wollstonecraft took up the attack against socially constructed female intelligence in the *Vindication of the Rights of Woman*, 1791–2. Given the same education as men, she expected women to achieve equal virtue; she challenged society and specifically men to provide such an education and see if women did not become better, wiser, and free.[2] They were not the dominant voices, however, and a view of the female that stressed sexual difference and a domestic role for women tended to set the agenda. Even though the reality of plebeian life created alternative preconditions for female activity, authors, deriving ideas from their own largely middle-class experiences and expectations, applied many of the same definitions and values universally. While in one sense the image of women was highly classed, its transference to all women denied class difference. The assumption was that all women desired to remain away from the contamination of the public world.

Enlightenment thought was double-edged in that it redefined and placed new limits on women and their activities, and the theoretical justification derived from the belief in Nature and natural laws was very powerful. But it also established the groundwork for later developments including education and a belief in human rights that would eventually bring improved opportunities to women. In this context, it is worth noting that the key Enlightenment writers were almost all male, and the Rights of Man were clearly about men—and men like themselves; Rousseau made this explicit in his *Discourse on Inequality*: "It is of man that I have to speak; and the question I am investigating shows me that it is to men that I must address myself."[3]

Contemporaries recognized that something new was afoot, conveying the sense of light as a beacon in the new mind-set. It encompassed most of the western world in the discourse through the sharing of ideas and intellectual curiosity. In North America, for example, Benjamin Franklin and Thomas Jefferson espoused and wrote on many of the same themes. Use of terms such as *les Lumières* in France and *Aufklärung* in the German states marked this perception. The common English term, Enlightenment, in fact was coined in the early nineteenth century, but it too reflected the sense that a new light illuminated the world, freeing people from the dark days of the retrograde past. The world we see in the early decades of the eighteenth century was a world of diversity, with regional variations that overlay differences based on wealth and education. The philosophers saw themselves as a cosmopolitan solidarity of enlightened intellectuals, and as David Hume argued, philosophy was conducted as conversation and exchange. In several important ways, the period was one of flux and fundamental change. Philosophically the Enlightenment and Scientific Revolution revised people's view of the construction of the universe, their mind-set, and relations between men, as well as between men and women. Coming together with such socially far-reaching changes were economic and demographic changes which were to make Europe after Napoleon (1815) very different from Europe after the Peace of Westphalia (1648).

ENLIGHTENMENT AND WORK

The Enlightenment also led to revised ideas about work together with new social attitudes towards work and workers.[4] The "Physiocrats," or *économistes*, as they called themselves, saw natural economic and moral laws as the basis for the economy and they employed scientific modes of thinking to economic reform, as with Quesnay's *Tableau économique* (1758). They attacked mercantilism for its excessive regulation, but also because they valorized land and agriculture as the basis of the economy and as the sole producers of wealth. Though they fell out of favor, and indeed were attacked by Adam Smith and others, their essentially *laissez-faire* approach remained key to economic thinking. Turgot, although not a Physiocrat, drew on their critique of regulation when promoting abolition of the guilds in France in 1776.

Coupled with dynamism in the economy, and the rise of the middling orders including merchants and highly skilled artisans, work was more frequently perceived positively as a commodity and as a source of social respectability.[5] The right to work and the notion of personal identity came together in the minds of thinkers and workers. Workers' legitimacy as social subjects was fundamental to this shift. For example, the critique of apprenticeship, which resulted in the repeal of the English Elizabethan Statute of Artificers in 1814, was partly the result of a critique of the subordinate status that was fundamental to indentured labor. Adam Smith argued that the independent worker, unconstrained by guilds and apprenticeship legislation, was far more conducive to industry.[6] A fundamental shift in thinking took place so that work was increasingly perceived as an abstract value that was the producer of wealth, with John Locke arguing in 1690 that "Labour makes the far greatest value of things we enjoy in this world."[7] His argument promoted the concept that labor was the "unquestionable Property of the Labourer, no man but he can have a right to what that is once joyned to," a valuation used by guildsmen and women throughout Europe.[8] David Hume at mid-century argued that "Everything in the world is purchased by labour," while Adam Smith, in 1776, saw the labor value of goods as their only real worth: "It is their real price; money is their nominal price only ... The labourer is rich or poor, is well or ill rewarded, in proportion to the real, not to the nominal price of his labour."[9] They shared much with the French reformers of the time, especially Turgot who argued that "God, by giving men needs and making them dependent upon ... labor, has made the right of labor the property of all men, and that property is primary, the most sacred and the most imprescriptible of all."[10] His adherence to the abolition of privilege and arbitrary restraints thus echoed key precepts of the Enlightenment. He argued that guild regulations were contrary to a healthy economy with their "bizarre arrangements, tyrannical and contrary to humanity and good manners ... conceived by greed." Indeed, the "spirit of monopoly ... has been able to even exclude women from trades most appropriate to their sex."[11] The Encyclopedists glorified work and illustrated the volumes with plates which idealize work and the workplace. Labor was no longer seen as a penance, but as a source of individual and social satisfaction and, under the influence of liberalism, as a source of wealth, a factor creating prosperity.[12]

Recent historiography on work has interrogated the gendered division of labor and addressed the question of how the boundaries between men's and women's work were redefined and renegotiated, particularly in the context of increasing capitalist activity.[13] Indeed, the concepts of work and gender were related, and as work came to be increasingly defined as "paid work" much of what women did was defined as "not work," thus excluding a wide range of predominantly female activities in the household and for the family such as cooking, cleaning, and care giving. Other aspects of women's unpaid work also became invisible as labor market activities and men came to be increasingly seen as male breadwinners, with implications for pay and normative images of workers, especially in the next centuries.[14] The eighteenth century was one of transition as many people still retained work in kind, for barter and exchange, and as timekeeping and location of work remained flexible.

TRADE, MERCANTILISM, AND COLONIZATION

The eighteenth century, and especially the last half, was a period of economic expansion, which was intrinsically linked to growing marketplaces at home and abroad. Trade was an important element of the changes which took place. Long-distance and local commerce, wholesale and retail trade, generated new markets, demand for goods, and provided the networks to introduce new goods and a better distribution system. Mercantilist empires saw some of their greatest growth during the period, capitalizing on the exploration and colonization of the previous two centuries and the expansion of economic markets that accompanied it. The European states continued to colonize and develop important trading links with Africa, the Americas, India, and Southeast Asia. The Caribbean represented a microcosm of European expansion with the Spanish, French, Dutch, English/British, and even Danes setting up colonies and trading networks. In 1700, approximately 250,000 Europeans and Africans were living in what would become the United States. In 1775, there were approximately 2.5 million. Much of the increase was owing to immigration: the forced migration of enslaved Africans, and the more willing migration of English, Scots and Germans.

Commercial interests, rather than territorial ambition, dictated the growth of the early British Empire; a poor country, the English were neither missionaries nor colonists, unlike the Spaniards and Portuguese, but traders. Only in the seventeenth century did they recognize the advantages of settler colonies starting with the lucrative exploitation of produce from the West Indies. The union of England with Scotland as Great Britain in 1707 effectively created the largest free trade area then in existence, just as the new union's overseas possessions were expanding. Precious metals, gems, and commodities such as sugar, indigo, spices, especially pepper, silks, china, and salt had been obtainable from India and Southeast Asia since the sixteenth century. This fostered the new luxuries of Europe that helped to fuel the consumer revolution. The Atlantic economy was based not only on trade between colonies and the metropole, but also on a triangular trade between Europe, the west coast of Africa where slaves were acquired, and then to the Caribbean and the American South, ultimately returning to the metropole with sugar, rum, tobacco, and cotton. The use of plantations was a key element in creating new workplaces. They also represented new workplace power structures. Many of these workplaces were no longer home-based, guilds never gained a foothold in North America and intensive black slavery came to dominate many of the largely rural and agricultural spaces. Britain's prosperity was bound up with the slave trade until it became illegal in 1807, by which time the empire had ceased to be dependent upon it as other forms of commerce had become more profitable, and Britain was starting to emerge as the leading industrial nation.

Expanding trade and communication networks had a significant impact on agriculture, the most significant sector of the economy. Eighteenth-century agriculture was largely subsistence, geared to feeding the owners and workers of the land on which production took place, although surpluses fed the upper classes and cities. Reliance on largely traditional methods severely limited its productive capacity, as did simple tools, methods, and constraints on the amount of land used at any one time. Poor transportation made specialization local, and regions failed to take full advantage of the specialization for which their soil and climate was most suited. It was low-yield agriculture for a population which was essentially poor and subject to food crises.

However, growing market opportunities made specialization feasible, helping to move agriculture from a subsistence basis. In England and the Netherlands, most noted for agricultural improvement in the seventeenth and eighteenth centuries, this was fundamental.

Barter between grain and animal husbandry areas, both locally and further afield, increased. They traded not only basic foodstuffs, but products such as wine, tobacco, cotton, and silk were part of an increase in cash crops and a more integrated European agricultural system. Europeans also turned to newer crops from America and Asia, such as maize, rice, and potatoes to supplement diets. At the same time innovative landholders introduced new methods, beginning in seventeenth-century Netherlands and spreading initially to Flanders and neighboring parts of Germany, as well as to Norfolk in England. Throughout Europe, a decreasing reliance on grain affected the nature of agrarian organization. Southwest France, northern Spain, Portugal, and northern Italy adopted maize while rice became prominent in Valencia, Italy, and southern and central Europe. The new crops were significant in cushioning Europe from harvest disasters because they could be grown on land which was unsuited to grain production and could produce much higher yields. Growing crops for local consumption released grain for trade, thus fuelling the trade cycle.[15]

Demographic pressure promoted efficient methods of food production and increasingly insured that marginal land was farmed. In eastern Europe, large-scale "colonization" into Hungary and the Ukraine brought fertile land into cultivation, some of which had been used previously only for animal husbandry. Throughout Europe, internal migrations of people to areas of uncultivated land cleared wastes or altered the use of land already in the agrarian system. A large local labor force assisted land reclamation and improvement projects and facilitated intensive techniques of cultivation.

TOWNS AND GUILDS

Urban growth was partly generated by more efficient agricultural systems which released labor from the countryside. In 1700, high proportions of the population worked directly in agriculture or in subsidiary trades dependent upon it. Probably 85 to 90 percent of the French population were rural peasants in 1789, and it was not less in any other major continental country, although only 75 percent of the British remained in the countryside. In British America, only about 5 percent lived in urban areas, as colonists spread themselves across the landscape, already thinly occupied by Native Americans. Many towns remained small, while increased urbanization largely came in the first half of the nineteenth century. However, some regions and specific towns saw a dramatic increase. Capital cities, such as Paris, Rome, and London, grew dramatically, and so did many transport and trade centers. Britain witnessed what has been called a provincial "urban renaissance," and the growth and shift in work and leisure activities was also marked in other continental centers.[16] In North America, Boston was the largest town but with only 5,000 people; by 1775, New York and Philadelphia had grown to 25,000 each.[17] This largely rural economy witnessed changes in craft and industrial organization that were reflected in the working lives of men and women. Patterns of working overlapped so that people could work for themselves and for others, for wages, piece rates, barter, or accommodation. They were primarily involved in small-scale operations, in both towns and the countryside, although larger concerns existed. In several industries, larger workplaces emerged and with them more division of labor and specialization. Key to work patterns and experience were shifts in economic practices and especially in manufacture and commerce.

Few barriers separated town from country, industry and trade from farming, or industrial workers from agricultural laborers. The countryside produced much of the labor for the towns, particularly female domestic servants, and there was a constant movement of people between them. Agriculture and industry were often combined and many early industries were sited in rural areas, while much of industry and trade relied on agricultural products. Indeed, industry and commerce which were not related to the agricultural sector were "small islands of economic difference in a sea of agricultural effort."[18] While the late eighteenth century was a period of self-sustained economic growth, the effect and significance of changes in industrial organization by the end of the century must not be overemphasized. The population was still predominantly rural in 1801, and agriculture continued to be the largest single employer. Industrial and agricultural development was still substantially unmechanized, relying on large numbers of unskilled workers. Industrial organization continued to center on the small workshop and rural trades throughout much of Europe. Likewise, regional variations and increasing geographical specialization affected the pattern and structure of working.

However, many towns across northern Europe experienced rapid growth together with changing attitudes towards commerce and the mercantilism that shaped the production, sale, and distribution of goods. Indeed, in many places urban life shifted its physical, cultural, and economic patterns while a growing mercantile community overlaid the older guild-based tradition and reshaped the urban world in the context of business and commerce. In the second half of the century, the commercial classes virtually controlled many urban centers through corporate structures that protected trades, maintained quality, and regulated the workplace and through it the community. The system linked economic, social, and political roles in explicit and implicit ways with important ramifications for rank, status, and gender.

In towns, workshops were most closely associated with guild structure and guild regulations regarding labor, prices, and status. Before the French Revolution, urban craft guilds were chartered privileged bodies, *corporations*, which exercised a recognized monopoly over the practice of a trade in a specific region. Regardless of size, they represented the interests of their members—typically, but not always, men—while protecting society from inferior goods and disorderly workers. They also granted status in the economy and society to members through the structure of the organizations and their links to politics and manhood. Guilds were built on an ideal of quality, craft, and largely reciprocal male relationships. Shifting economies meant that guilds remained stronger in central Europe than western Europe, stronger in western Europe than in Britain. In the American colonies, they were virtually nonexistent.[19] Workplaces were remarkably diverse, as was the character of work and the skill and strength required; relations between workers, employers, and clients were also highly varied. The system was not a monolithic whole as is often assumed.

Guild-based traditions were increasingly under threat, and effectively the eighteenth century sounded their death knell. They were clearly under attack for what was seen as their role in hampering progress. They had become even more exclusive, reluctant to admit men to mastership, and even more jealously guarded their privileges. While their overt concern was to retain their standing, protect their skill, and prevent "dishonorable" men from encroaching on their privileges and guild honor, the threats operated as a strong motive to control and restrict the role of women. At the same time, therefore, women's position within the guilds became even more vulnerable. Nevertheless, women were central to many family workshops and supported the guilds with their skills and work, usually without guild membership. Geraldine Sheridan's exploration of images related to the *Encyclopédie* and *Descriptions des arts et métiers* suggests that women's participation in the artisanal trades was more extensive than we would think from written records alone. They are shown performing both highly skilled and physically demanding tasks (Figure I.1).[20] Indeed in limited places, women formed their own guilds, claiming many of the privileges, rights, and ethos encapsulated in the guild system.[21]

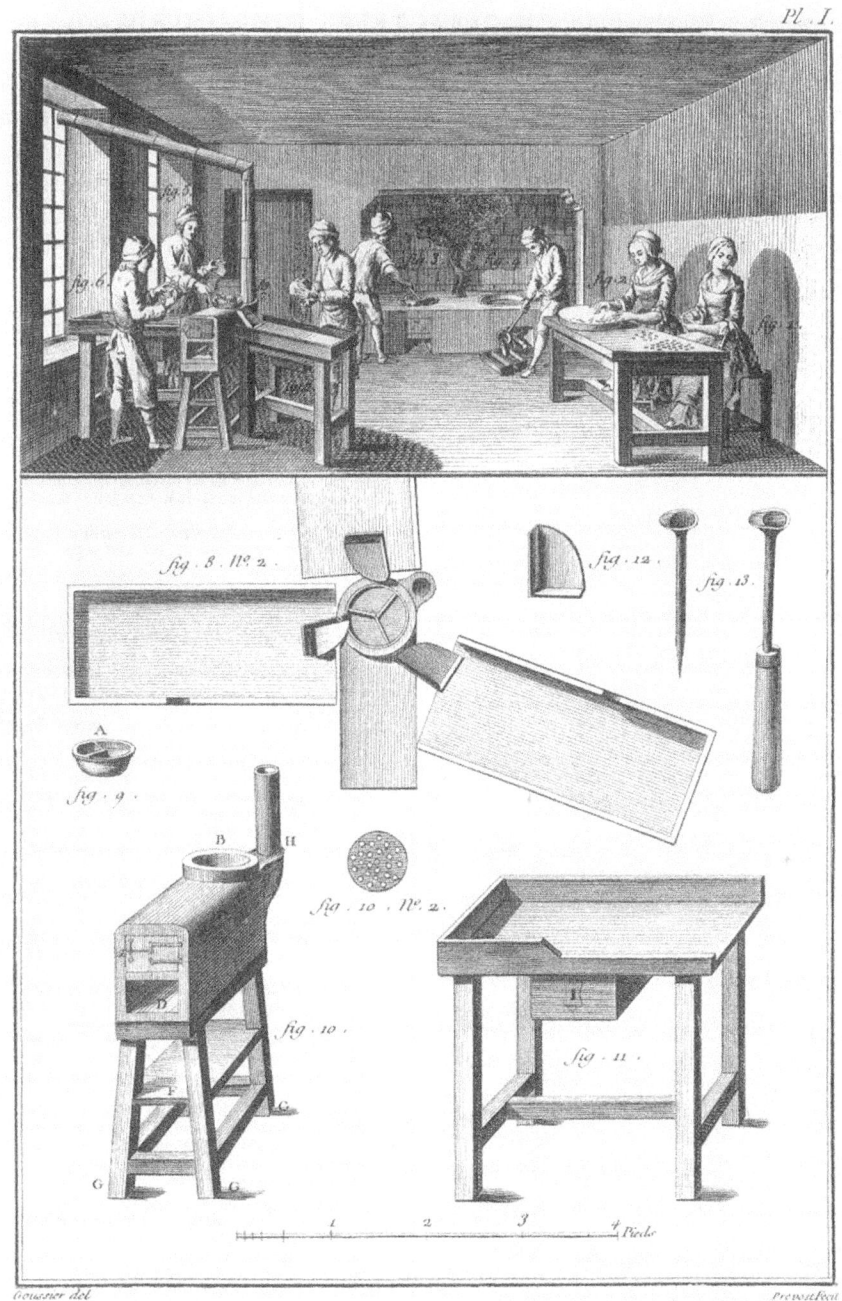

FIGURE I.1 "Typefoundry." In Denis Diderot and Jean le Rond d'Alembert, *Encyclopédie, ou dictionnaire raisonné des sciences, des arts et métiers*, 1751–72.

With such restrictive labor practices, and as merchants took control of some of the productive process instead of masters, they looked for alternative sources of labor and for ways to bypass the guilds. Adam Smith famously argued against the guilds, and especially apprenticeship, on economic grounds as a restrictive practice. Smith saw it as a fallacy that apprenticeship produced a skilled and industrious workforce. The thrust of his attack was precisely that few trades required extensive skills to practice them.[22] Enlightenment thought, echoing Turgot, figured in the legal dissolution of the guild system in Spain where guilds' reluctance to hire girls in textile manufacturing was a central battle of the war. Thus claims that guilds continued to obstruct the entrance of women contributed to the dissolution of the guilds, which European governments implemented from the last decades of the eighteenth century. Guilds also have been accused by historians as restricting technical innovation, and they were certainly vigilant in preserving their access to markets, raw materials, and even production techniques.[23] Yet many people saw guilds as organizers of town economies, as a force for social stability and feared that their abolition would herald the emergence of an unregulated proletariat. Thus the abolition of guilds caused a great deal of anxiety despite their weakening role in the economy.

INDUSTRIAL DEVELOPMENT

One of the key changes in the economy was the shift in the relative importance between agricultural and industrial activity. Industrial development can usefully be described as comprising three general patterns: the family workshop, dispersed manufacture, and compact-site manufacture.[24] Family workshops could be any site where an artisan worked with family and perhaps one or two journeymen. Located in both town and country, they were small-scale and not far removed from the homestead, if at all. Dispersed manufacture consisted of scattered workshops whose labor and production were controlled by a merchant-manufacturer. This was the typical British "putting-out system" or the Germanic *Verlagsystem* controlled by the merchant or *Verleger*. These two forms of manufacturing existed side by side throughout the eighteenth century. As cottage industries, work was based on the cottage and the worker could be both artisan and peasant.

The rapid increase in rural dispersed manufactures was a driving force in the significant growth in manufacturing which occurred in the eighteenth century. Fernand Braudel calls this a primitive form of concentration and regrouping, which effectively yoked together the town and country.[25] Located in agricultural areas with easy access to local urban or international markets, they usually required more organization and larger capitalization, especially supplies of materials, than small-scale handicrafts. They drew on underutilized rural labor, especially women, in areas near to relatively cheap food. The system would prove to be durable, lasting well after other modes of manufacture had become dominant, because of the networks and urban–rural links they forged. The phenomenon was not limited to rural Europe. Not only did the "putting-out" system operate in towns, it also transferred to North America, where together with fewer institutional restrictions on women's work, it meant that, for American women, the shift between different types of work was less complicated.[26] This system of production gave rise to proto industrial theory and its notion of familial organization of the labor force and household economy, which are discussed in the section "Proto industrialization and industriousness" below.

Although small-scale industry was prominent during the period, large-scale industry was not unheard of, often in tandem with small-scale industrial processes. Manufactories, or *manufactures* in France, developed in the finishing stages of textile production where merchants could control final processes such as fulling, scribbling, printing, and dying. Other operations where technical or economic needs of the industry required concentration also generated large sites, such as shipyards, iron works, sugar and tobacco processing, papermaking, and ceramics. Additionally, manufactures were established and maintained by the state for political or economic ends. The support and privileges of the state were often necessary because larger industries usually were not profit-making in the short term and individuals were unable or unwilling to take the risks required. For example, in Bavaria, except for the long-established glass industry, state manufactures had an average life of thirty-six years.[27] Where concentration involved industries with high demand, or resolved bottlenecks in production, or with well-established trading networks, their success was far more likely.

Braudel argues that large-scale industries tended initially to be *concentrated* rather than *centralized* because the first step brought together workers and the stages of production on one site. It was a further development to bring together the entrepreneur's capital and commercial organization. These concentrated enterprises were not factories but agglomerations of workers, often linked to a large rural workforce working under the putting-out system. Most did not develop into factories. Some like the Van Robais textile works employed upwards of 1,800 workers at Abbeville, France, and probably another 10,000 in the countryside. In the Austrian Netherlands, in 1764, "one of the most economically advanced areas of Europe," enterprises with forty-five workers were exceptionally large.[28] Private enterprise accounted for more centralized production from about the mid-century as sources of finance and newer organizational practices developed, accompanied by a shift in production as newer forms of power were developed, utilizing cheaper coal and applying steam to production. And yet, these latter developments only began to exert influence at the end of the eighteenth century and industrial enterprises using power-driven machinery on any considerable scale were rare.

A recurring theme was the variety of organizational patterns which operated, sometimes in competition, sometimes complementarily, within the industrial landscape. Coexistence was a key feature of eighteenth-century industrial development. The establishment of large firms was accompanied by a proliferation of small producing units and the continued growth of outwork. Cottage, workshop, and neophyte factory organization existed side by side throughout the period. With them came different interpersonal relationships between co workers, managers, masters, and owners. Gender was a factor in the organization of work and arguably a key factor in new work organizations that emerged around gender-based divisions of labor, which reinterpreted the gendered segregation of the workforce.

The transformation of manufacturing had no uniform effect on the location of waged labor. Despite dramatic changes brought by large-scale workshops and early factories, it disguises the fact that factories never were the major form of work, much of which continued to center on workshops. Indeed, local small-scale workshops might not be very different from households in terms of work and time discipline. Throughout the century across Europe, men and women continued to work primarily in their own homes, on land, or in workshops virtually contiguous to their home. They continued to work in others' homes as servants and laborers. Thus, for most people, separation of home from work was relatively insignificant during this period, although the relationship between them became considerably more complex. The separation of home and work, however, carries cultural ideological resonances. As waged employment became properly work for men, and family maintenance, housework, and childcare as the proper province for women, an ideological separation of home and work then took place. While this was first generated as a bourgeois ideal, actual changes in the location of work supported it. Yet it is important to ask how such ideology contributed to the way those changes took place, and specifically the impact on the organization and understanding of work.

Probably more critical was the decline and contraction in some industries, such as woollen worsted in East Anglia, England, which removed employment from some areas completely, forcing people to move to keep work or to change their work altogether. It could lead to permanent or temporary migration of individuals and whole families, as in the Pays de Caux region in France where the opportunities of factory spinning, which was more lucrative than farming, led whole families to move to Rouen.[29] Both men and women were prominent as migrants, but the character of their flows varied. Men were involved in travel locally and overseas for work, as seasonal migrants, often providing much needed labor, such as in the building industries. Some such migration was temporary and some permanent; other migrations were "repeating" in that having worked for a time they returned to their home place, making a tour seasonally or when income required it. The migration of single women was a noteworthy feature of the rural–urban nexus, as many travelled both short and long distances often for service. Once in towns and having gained experience and knowledge of the urban workplace, they also shifted jobs, sometimes moving into other jobs temporarily, other times moving back and forth between various opportunities.[30] For example, Anne Auvray alternated between working as a servant and working as a seamstress in Bayeux at the beginning of the century.[31] They also might remain in the place they had entered, move on, or return to the home place. Married women also left home to work, either locally or at longer distances. Sometimes they migrated temporarily with children or as a part of family migration, such as those who sought work in the early factories. The demand for labor in both industry and services in eighteenth-century Europe, meant that many peasant families became dependent on migration. The eighteenth-century world was not a settled stable place, and in the various forms of mobility, local, regional, and international, the idea of belonging was highly mediated.

Concentrating on large-scale trade, industry and guilds tends to overlook the growth of local commerce, and especially urban-based trade in commodities and foodstuffs to feed local markets. Food especially was in high demand as populations grew and towns developed around commercial and industrial interests. Long chains of provision from farm to mouth required organized working practices to successfully deliver the goods (Figure I.2). The lack of government regulation and guilds in British America fostered the development of lengthy supply chains that ran from rural producers to urban marketplaces. The same lack of regulation enabled wives and daughters to work in any aspect of many trades, making, selling, and supervising indentured and enslaved workers. Notable is the mixture of workers and power relationships. In Lyon, France, women also played significant roles, and Italian traveller Sebastien Locatelli commented that women were "the principal employees, they kept the double-entry ledgers, handled sales, attracted customers, politely displayed their merchandises, collected and guarded the money."[32] Across the western world, men and women owned, managed, and worked in shops of all sizes, with a myriad of structures and power relationships. Some were guild trades, others not; some were both manufacturing and retail, others not. Indeed, there was no clear distinction between "those who bought and sold" and those who "made" things. However, the top of the mercantile trades increasingly distinguished between "makers" and "sellers." Contemporary John Gibson commented: "The inhabitants of Burghs … are divided into

FIGURE I.2 Niccoló Schiavonetti, *New Mackrel, New Mackrel*, Plate V. In the series *The Cries of London* by Niccoló Schiavonetti, after Francis Wheatley's painting. New Haven, CT, Yale Center for British Art, Paul Mellon Collection.

two ranks, viz. merchants and tradesmen; by merchants are to be understood all those who buy and sell; tradesmen means mechanics of every denomination … and a difference between the merchants and trades rank very early established."[33] For those further down the trade chain, such distinctions were less important, and across the retail worlds, men and women worked at all levels from owner or manager to worker, servant, or employee.

Historians of the medieval and early modern European economy have traditionally concentrated on the legalities underpinning economic activity, as shown, for instance, by the large body of work dealing with the corporate system in this period.³⁴ However, the world of work included a variety of strategies existing alongside and threaded through the "formal" economy. Olwen Hufton's "economy of expedients" is well known.³⁵ Recently, however, historians have taken a greater interest in the wide spectrum of activities existing beyond the regulated and legal economy, revealing that irregular practices were a structural characteristic of early modern economies.³⁶

THE MEANINGS OF WORK

There is a long tradition which sees work as part of a discussion about the structures and contributions of different groups of work and occupations to the economy. It is linked to economic growth, or decline; to shifting economic structures; and to industrial development including mechanization and the emergence of factories on a small and large scale. However, *A Cultural History of Work* takes a different approach, studying work and the workplace from the perspective of their cultural meanings. Explicitly it asks, what meaning did work have in sociocultural terms?

Guildsmen and women claimed a sense of honor and status from their work, a status that they saw as stemming from their skill and expertise. While aspects of Enlightenment ideology and shifting economic pragmatism undercut the corporate system that underpinned this, it remained the case that many of its ideals and language continued to permeate the world of work throughout the next century. While workplace relations changed, people continued to value ideas of honor, hierarchy, and status in their conception of work and their place in it. Yet one of the forces challenging the guilds were workers who were not part of that system and who believed they were entitled to work, and indeed that they had the ability to do so. The increasing number of wage-earners escaped the control of masters and they progressively fostered the emergence of an intellectual and political discourse in which the right to work was inherent to each individual rather than a privilege granted by a political entity. As Clare Crowston points out, while many French seamstresses supported the guild system, after the abolition of corporations in 1776, in Clermont-Ferrand, France, they proudly declared themselves free of guild control and resisted tailors' attempts to bring them into their corporation; women in England and Italy similarly resisted guild pressures.³⁷ The voice of one such resister makes clear her belief in her entitlement to her business. In Oxford, "Ann *****" advertised, "the Mercer's (but much more properly the Merciless Company) threatening me with immediate Distress, if I do no leave off my Business or purchase a Freedom of the Company, which would cost about 20£; a Sum almost equal to the whole I possess, and which money they would most probably ... [spend] in luxurious Entertainments."³⁸ As more people were increasingly wage-reliant, the waged economy reshaped employer–employee relations as it reshaped workplace practices. As populations and towns grew, the non guild workforce clearly overwhelmed the system and some towns never became guild strongholds, like Birmingham where small workshops and large manufactories such as the Boulton and Watt Soho Works employed these workers, even recruiting abroad, demonstrating their right to employ whomever they liked.

Notions of skill were fundamental to eighteenth-century conceptions of work, and they carried with them ideas about place, status, and gender. For skilled artisans it was about power, standing, and position both in the workplace and in society and it was usually linked to masculinity. Division of labor is not neutral. It is constructed around clusters of ideas related to tools, skills, and, crucially, gender. Segregation and separate spaces are one way to claim specific jobs and tools for men, but deeply embedded notions of gender and skill are fundamental to how work is perceived, shared, and divided. Gendered notions of place and work are, of course, variable over both time and space. Different cultures at different times redefined them as other factors, such as demography, technology, and economic structure, came into play. Notions of skill were used to redefine working practices and affected both unskilled workers and most women's position in the labor force. It also affected how work was divided and access to work.

Rarely did women and men do exactly the same work, since the operation of gender and division of labor ensured different tasks. This is also linked to a perception of female labor as cheap, casual, part-time, and "ancillary." The range of activities that women engaged in were still perceived as additional—add-ons, by-employments, and therefore casual. This had an important impact on wages, since their earnings were seen as "pin money," and it also depressed wages for women who were not contributing to a family pot. Thus ideas about married women influenced the wage levels for single women. Seen as members of a family economy, women theoretically did not need to earn wages sufficient to support a household. Adam Smith's classic description of textiles illustrates the view that women's work did not add value:

> three or four spinners, at least, are necessary in order to keep one weaver in constant employment; and more than four-fifths of the whole quantity of labour necessary for the preparation of linen cloth is employed in that of linen yarn ... It is not by the sale of their work, but by that of the complete work of the weavers, that our great master manufacturers make their profits.[39]

Certainly, the idea that women functioned only within a family economy is flawed since numerous women operated throughout the economy in ways which, while compatible with family needs, were not necessarily based on family work, or even a shared location of work.

Division of labor is often a practical and common way to divide tasks between men, women, and children. However, it was also a means of keeping the best work for workers with most standing and power, usually skilled men. They may, indeed, have been the best to carry out many tasks, but ideas about skill and gender inflected the way work was distributed and coded. Skill could be defined in terms of strength, training, intelligence, custom, and control. It also related to the idea of "mysteries" of a trade that had to be understood, which could be less about skill and more about "how things were done," and usually these were not to be shared with women and non guild men. French workers spoke about work in a personal way, respecting each other as *le plus fort* or *le plus gros*, thus ascribing the quality of the work to the worth of the individual.[40]

Thus training, and this usually meant apprenticeship in the Old World, was intrinsically linked to skill, and as it followed the male life cycle, it also was tied closely to masculinity. Women's training was regarded as inferior while their "abilities" were seen as "natural," for example, nimble fingers. These explanations became more important as men sought to protect their position in circumstances that meant that their work status was threatened and with it their personal status and value. Thus it became important to define skill and status not only vis-à-vis men who were "poachers," but also in relation to women. Guilds' protection of what they saw as their interests was not explicitly gender-based. At the same time, identification of women with dishonorable work such as domestic production, the recurrent notion of women as casual labor, and a growing sense of hostility to women's work contributed to the imposition of specific restrictions against women. Thus the increasingly closed world of the guild began to use gender as a fundamental determinant of work roles and their valuation.[41]

The rewards of work, especially hard work, carried with it specific valorization in the Protestant world. Many new industries attracted Protestants, whose creed fostered labor and work, lack of excess, and a recognition of personal effort and merit. These traits helped many "dissenters" nurture their businesses and permeated much of the economic culture of the time, such that workers themselves adopted many of the ethics of hard work and enterprise. Diligence was reinforced by moralists, and William Hogarth specifically appears in several chapters in this volume with his distinctive moral tale of *Industry and Idleness*. The twelve plates celebrate "industriousness," by representing the contrasting fortunes of two young apprentices, an industrious worker who reaps a series of rewards, eventually becoming Lord Mayor of London, and a lazy one whose idleness leads to theft, murder, and eventually the gallows. In America, where many early settlers brought a deep-seated protestant work ethic with them, Benjamin Franklin, printer, inventor, and author, echoed this in aphorisms that extolled moderation, thrift, honesty, and hard work as keys to worldly success. The work ethic of the Protestant countries is apparent in the imagery of work, also, where the moral value of work colors many paintings and prints of the century. The rewards of hard work, however, were more apparent in British North America, removed from the more densely populated and restrictive societies of the countries many had left behind.

PROTO INDUSTRIALIZATION AND INDUSTRIOUSNESS

Historians elaborated the dispersed industries of the putting-out or *Verleger* system as "proto industrialization," first by Franklin Mendels in his study on the Flemish linen industry.[42] Proto industrialization as a concept described the dynamism of "pre-industrial industry" which explains and analyzes the route to factory industry and/or full-blown industrial capitalism. Hans Medick characterized proto industrialization as "the close association between household production based on the family economy on the one hand, and the capitalist organization of trade, putting-out and marketing of the product on the other."[43] He argued that the family economy of the agrarian peasantry, based on land and inheritance, underwent fundamental change in its motivation and function to become the family economy of the proto industrial cottage worker. The essential elements were the interrelationship between family structure and patterns of economic development, strategies for survival employed by the family unit, the implications for division of labor, and the relationships within the family or household which are mediated by economic concerns.

The model and ensuing debate engendered a range of research which fruitfully opened up the history of work and pushed the boundaries in important ways.[44] Two positive results are that though localized studies made generalization difficult, they greatly expanded our understanding of the largely uncharted geography of European enterprise. At the same time, they marked the level of change that had already taken place, dispelling the notion that industrialization took place in a static economy.[45] Proto industrialization adequately captured the range of domestic industry and suggested the array of industrial skills available for use in more mechanized and centralized settings. But it remains too narrow to describe the world of work and the range of factors that influenced family or individual decision-making. It is also too bold as an explanation of industrial development. Most proto industrial regions did not evolve into industrialization; nor did rural industry have a uniform, measurable impact on the demographic behavior of the population, that is, earlier marriages, increased fertility, and population growth. Studies by Jürgen Schlumbohm on Osnabrück and Gay Gullickson of the Caux region in France demonstrated that family production decisions and division of labor could readily deviate from a model based on price and economic considerations. The family balancing act went beyond production and consumption, and took in a range of variables such as labor, leisure, marital, and industrial activities.[46] Proto industrialization, then, raised important issues about economic development, family participation, the role of rural communities, gender relations, affections, and household formation. Ultimately, proto industrial literature provided us with new and invaluable elements to understand how "work before the factory" was organized.

Proto industrialization implied that more workers had been brought into the workforce and described new patterns of working. Starting from the different perspective of growth in consumption and demand for goods, Jan de Vries maintained that there was, in fact, an "industrious revolution" in which a substantial increase in the desire for new consumer goods preceded the Industrial Revolution, inducing people to work more.[47] He argued that between 1650 and 1850, "a growing number of households acted to reallocate their productive resources [and time] in ways that increased both the supply of market-oriented money-earning activities and the demand for goods offered in the marketplace."[48] De Vries wished to "place the familiar 'revolutionary' events [i.e. the 'Industrial Revolution'] in the broader context."[49] Deborah Valenze called his thesis "a paradigm-shifting notion," in which

> Gone is the familiar parade of British inventions, which had borne the weight of explanation for European industrial expansion ... Gone, too, is the argument that crucial changes necessary for "takeoff" occurred in the late eighteenth century ... With the evaporation of a particular form of British exceptionalism has come a changed focus for inquiry from the supply to the demand side of the picture.[50]

De Vries' assertion links to the proto industrialization debates as well as to the literature on the "consumer revolution," postulated in the seminal work in 1982 by Neil McKendrick, John Brewer, and J. H. Plumb. Since then a copious and vigorous literature on consumption has developed, which has refined, interrogated, and challenged their controversial notions of "consumer society," "consumer revolution," and "mass consumption."[51] Maxine Berg, who has worked on both production and consumption, further explored the economy of "semi-luxury," fashionable consumer goods during the eighteenth century.[52] Her methodology resulted in a more holistic approach, acknowledging the importance of invention as well as imitation, and recognizing the role of middling classes in promoting and stimulating not only demand for these goods but consequently driving forward production. Her juxtaposition of multiple historiographies, especially linked the grand narratives of the Industrial Revolution to the consumer one, and her identification of the importance of global connections in understanding eighteenth-century consumption were vital to the debate on industry and consumption.

As with all bold ideas, de Vries has been challenged on several points. John Komlos reminds us that food and hunger preoccupied most people, not acquisition of new consumables, and the debate about working people's wages and income has tended to argue a decline in living standards and wages.[53] De Vries' response to this problem was to argue that wives and children increased their participation in the labor force by increasing the number of days worked annually and by increasing the intensity of work. This is a key weakness of the argument, simply because the evidence is not there to support it. Michael Kwass conceded that the "pull of new clusters of goods ... drew men, women and children of the middling sort into the labour market," but like others questions the impact on the vast majority of the working poor. As Elise van Nederveen Meerkerk has shown, many were working harder to scrape by, "rather than to increase their consumption."[54] We need to know whether an increase in aggregate employment actually existed, especially of women and children, seen as the "underemployed," or whether workers decided to work longer hours. We also need to know whether households made decisions based on utility and whether they did indeed increase labor in order to consume more—especially whether the new goods drove their considerations. The standard view is that all people worked as much as they could to keep body and soul together, in households as well as those not part of a "family economy." Valenze argues that at this point de Vries becomes "at times, pointlessly polemical" and focuses "on the ambiguous way in which families combined effort and pay packets to achieve efficiency in consumption."[55] Workers were more likely to spend extra money on better quality necessities, and as prices rose rapidly towards the end of the century, people probably worked more to stay in place.

Not all people willingly chose to work harder to consume more goods, and work and leisure were more fluid for independent workers, that is, those with the discretion to make choices about their pace of work. Cultural difference played out in that, for example, among North American indigenous peoples selective consumption was embraced as part of their spiritual development. Religious moralists also remained concerned with the conundrum in the Protestant ethic in which hard work reaped rewards, while overconsumption could be seen as sinful. Workers in many trades, whether in guilds or as independent labor, often preferred traditional rights of drink and days off to more pay. A variety of work calculations informed working practices, some taking more leisure when trade was good and pay rates were high, while those with families may have made a different calculation. Thus different workers made very different decisions when confronted with the same set of circumstances.

Central to de Vries' argument is the use and allocation of time.[56] In 1967, E. P. Thompson argued that perceptions of time shifted appreciably after the fourteenth century, paralleling the development of watches and timepieces.[57] As David Landes demonstrated, pocket watches quickly became a coveted possession of every social class. European watch production rose from the tens of thousands per year at the time of the pocket globe's introduction in 1697, to nearly 400,000 per year in the last quarter of the eighteenth century.[58] Many eighteenth-century families that periodically found basic subsistence to be beyond their financial reach nonetheless possessed clocks and pocket watches. Certainly, clock ownership increased, and even if owning a timepiece was a mark of esteem and prestige, their increasing possession suggests also a growing awareness of synchronized time. Dorothy George argued that laborers and artisans frequently possessed silver watches—interestingly more as investment; something that could be pawned when needed.[59] Lorna Weatherill's study of English consumer behavior shows a measurable growth from 9 percent to 34 percent between 1675 and 1725. Breaking this down by occupational groups reveals a class hierarchy in clock ownership, not surprisingly, with 51 percent of gentry but 17 percent of craftsmen owning clocks, while innkeepers, victuallers (30 percent) and shopkeepers (25 percent) fell between these two groups.[60]

Thompson's key questions were to what extent did timekeeping shape labor discipline and did the transition to an industrial economy entail a restructuring of working habits. How far did it influence the inward apprehension of time for working people? He argues that in preindustrial communities where there was less demarcation between life and work, people relied on "natural" rhythms to dictate their timing of work. The work pattern was one of alternate bouts of intense labor and of idleness, wherever people were in control of their own working lives.[61] Henri Lefebvre made the distinction between "cyclical time"—arising from changing seasonal occupations in agriculture—and the "linear time" of urban, industrial organization, while Lucien Febvre distinguished between "lived" time and "measured" time.[62] Thompson was interested in the distinction between task-oriented work and time-disciplined work, arguing that the question of task-orientation becomes far more complex when labor is employed. The so-called family economy of small farmers or putting-out workers contained a mix of division of labor, task-orientated work, and externally imposed deadlines, which might not be hourly or based on clock time, but nevertheless constituted measured time.

As long as manufacturing remained largely small scale and without urgent need for synchronization, task-orientation still existed and reflected irregular work patterns. Thompson argues, in fact, that women's work was the most task-oriented of all, operating within "an imperfect sense of time" which is imbedded in a premodern world in which "task-orientation" in relation to the "natural work-rhythms" operated instead of time-discipline. This tends to undervalue women's work and their strategies.[63] Like men, they endured the time-discipline imposed on domestic industries by market dates, raw material delivery times, and putting-out networks—a discipline greatly amplified by the intensification of labor driving down piece rates. Both single and married women, whether working at home, in workshops, or small factories, were increasingly tied to forms of work that structured the use of their time, rather than fitting in between other tasks of domestic life. Yet acceptance of the irregularity of labor patterns before the arrival of large-scale industry tends to blur the experience of many workers. Already in the eighteenth century, some large-scale units existed, such as the abovementioned Robais textile works, while at Etruria, England, Wedgwood introduced regular work times and the first recorded system of clocking-in.[64] Many retail shops already worked to "opening hours." Aberdeen council, in Scotland, announced in the *Aberdeen Journal* in 1781 that shops were to close at 9:00 p.m.[65]

Timekeeping was associated with industriousness, signalling an elision between a stable and hardworking society and the need to "keep time." To entrepreneurs, enterprising farmers, reformers, and those accustomed to working to the clock, task-oriented time appeared wasteful and lacking in urgency, indeed "lazy." To many entrepreneurs, time had already become money; indeed, Benjamin Franklin notably pronounced "Time is money," in 1748.[66] The concern with industriousness was apparent in the strictures for schools, especially parish and charity schools. Proponents of schooling argued that instruction in reading, catechism, manners, and some form of work would teach children their place in society, making them more devout, modest, and industrious. Catherine Cappe, English educator, claimed: "My object has not been to teach dogmas and opinions, but to form the lower class to habits of industry and virtue."[67] If religion and morality were fundamental to education for the laboring orders, "habits of industry" were integral to the process. And timekeeping was one of these, with the day for both teachers and "scholars" laid out meticulously in school regulations. Similarly, Rev. J. Clayton offered the following in his *Advice to the Friendly Poor*, in 1755: "If the sluggard hides his hands in his bosom, rather than applies them to work; if he spends his Time in Sauntring, impairs his Constitution by Laziness, and dulls his Spirit by Indolence [then he can expect only poverty as his reward]."[68] In Philadelphia, Franklin put his spin on it:

Early to bed, and early to rise,
Makes a man healthy, wealthy, and wise.[69]

Thus Enlightenment ideas and burgeoning entrepreneurship colluded to improve efficiency and output. Hogarth's prints valorized hard work, and when workers were depicted resting rather than working, it was as an acceptable period of rest in the midst of working. Timekeeping, industry, and hard work were important, but there was a social acceptance of relaxation that found its way into pastoral imagery and literature, as long as it was not indolence.

Competing views of leisure underpinned Enlightenment worlds.[70] In the context of an increasingly time-controlled society, or one that was more industrious, there is a sense that workers did not play. In contrast, in the minds of commentators such as Arthur Young, they played too much. Jacques-Louis Ménétra's description of his journeyman's "tour de France," between 1757 and 1764, shows that space and time for leisure was part and parcel of the worker's concept of time. "Since it was the sunny season we went with my friends to what are called *guinguettes*. Holidays and Sundays we went to dance in front of the castle and most of the other days we played tennis with the people of the house or we went for a walk to see the local festivals."[71] Although people often worked long hours of physical labor, they also mixed work with leisure. Orthodox areas might celebrate between eighty and one hundred holidays a year, while Catholic areas honored slightly fewer, and Protestants made up for lost saints' days by resurrecting secular holidays such as May Day. Where workers had some control over their labor, they still might mark Saint Monday but with awareness of due dates and the need to feed oneself and potentially to contribute to a household.

In many respects the age of Enlightenment acted as a transition from older systems based on privilege, control, and embedded practices to a more open society increasingly based on merit and ability. It was an imperfect and conflicted transition, moving in multiple directions. Guild controls broke down, political and commercial systems loosened, but theoretical justifications could also bring new binding views to the field, such as the strengthening of ideology on home and domesticity for the female and work and politics for the male. Workers lost some of the protection that guilds had offered, for those who were part of the system, while opening access to "quality" and high-status work to a wider range of individuals. North America embodied the extremes of these transitions, with free workers able to make their way in a society based on ability and initiative while solidifying the ravages of the slavery system at the same time.

CHAPTER ONE

The Economy of Work

CARMEN SARASÚA

The eighteenth century was a time of economic prosperity and growth in the western world. European states profited from their colonial empires, developing an intense commercial traffic of slaves, raw materials, and finished goods. Prosperity, however, did not arrive for all, and in fact the majority of the population continued to live at subsistence level, scarcely productive and ignorant of innovations. According to available estimates of gross domestic product, growth during the century was slow and "mainly concentrated in the North Sea area," with England and the Netherlands at the forefront.[1] Even in those countries, innovations and wealth coexisted with increasing inequality and desperate poverty for most.

A main pillar of economic growth was the increase in agricultural output, documented throughout most of the western world. In parts of Europe this occurred in an intensive way, that is, with productivity increases. Output per unit of land and labor increased in what scholars have called the "agricultural revolution": "The years from c. 1750 to c. 1850 witnessed unprecedented changes in output and productivity in English agriculture, which warrant the appellation 'revolution'."[2] The Low Countries put the agricultural innovations in practice first during the seventeenth century. A combination of diffusion of new crops of American origin, such as potatoes and corn; of technical innovations in plows, seed drills, and other tools; of institutional changes such as the enclosure of common lands; of new cultivation techniques, such as continuous crop rotation, allowed for an intensification in agricultural production and in livestock farming, which in turn allowed for heavy manuring and more productive lands. Selective breeding programs permitted an increase in the production of meat, wool, and milk, which together with an expansion in demand from the cities made livestock farming increasingly productive.

In other parts of Europe, however, the increase in agricultural output was more limited and occurred in an extensive way. In the Mediterranean countries, environmental conditions prevented any large increase in output, and agriculture continued to center on cereals, vines, and olive trees, with modest increases in crop diversification, including rice, potatoes, flax, hemp, and silk. *The Harvest*, by Goya, painted in 1787, vividly shows the most important moment of the agricultural year for most peasants in eighteenth-century Europe (Figure. 1.1). Peasants' lives centered around the harvest, which marked the peak season of labor demand, was the main source of families' income, and determined marriages and births.

In connection with the increasing food supply, the eighteenth century was also a period of demographic transformation. The population of Europe grew from around 110 million to about 190 million. This growth has been explained as a result of the combination of

FIGURE 1.1 Francisco de Goya, *La era o Verano* (The Threshing Ground or Summer), 1786. Madrid, Museo del Prado. Photo: Artepics / Alamy Stock Photo.

increasing fertility, because women had children earlier, and decreasing mortality. In different ways both fertility and mortality reflected the improvement in living conditions because "marriage was sensitive to economic circumstances."[3] Mortality, on the other hand, was reduced thanks to famines becoming less frequent and plagues less endemic. England was at the forefront of this growth. Following the union with Scotland in 1707, the British population stood at about 6.5 million; a century later it had reached 15.75 million.

Economic prosperity and population growth also occurred in the American colonies, particularly in the coastal areas where a new middle class of merchants, tax collectors, ship builders, and bureaucrats developed. Mexico City grew from 70,000 people in 1753 to 113,000 in 1790, most of them Indians and *mestizos*. The city of New York expanded from 2,500 in 1740, of which 20 percent were black slaves, to 96,000 in 1810, becoming the leading US city after independence, ahead of Boston and Philadelphia.

The relationship between population growth and food was a concern of eighteenth-century society and the subject of Thomas Robert Malthus's *An Essay on the Principle of Population* (1798), one of the first books that can be defined as belonging to the new subject of economics. Malthus argued that an increase in a nation's food production in fact improved people's well-being, but the improvement was temporary since it also led to population growth, which in turn restored the original per capita production level. In other words, mankind had a propensity to utilize abundance for population growth rather than for maintaining a high standard of living. The Malthusian trap means that improvements in a society's standard of living are unsustainable because of the resultant population growth. Writing before the "agricultural revolution," Malthus further predicted diminishing returns to agriculture because of intensive production. His work was an attempt to justify the British Corn Laws and landlords' case for an agricultural tariff. He also opposed policies to help the poor, arguing that any mechanism to redistribute rent would have negative consequences for the country's economy as a whole and for the poorer classes in particular. It shows, in any case, that eighteenth-century Europeans were aware of the changes in population and agricultural production taking place.[4]

CHANGES IN THE ORGANIZATION OF WORK

The impact of larger agricultural output on the organization of work was intense; family farming was increasingly replaced by a system of capitalist husbandry, which would eventually mean a reduction in the number of small cottagers. Most of these farm workers, now transformed into landless laborers, would have to hire themselves out as day workers, or migrate to the cities, to eventually form part of the industrial labor force ready to work for wages as the only means to sustain themselves. This was not, however, a definitive development and, in the nineteenth century, in certain regions, a process of rerualization took place, when large estates were disentailed and governments sold small plots to new farmers.

Rural manufacturing was the most characteristic form of productive organization in the century. Coined as "proto industrialization" by Franklin Mendels in his study on the Flemish linen industry, and later developed by Peter Kriedte, Hans Medick, and Jürgen Schlumbohm to explain the transition to capitalism, it was defined as the huge rise in manufactures' output for export markets that took place in the countryside, making it possible for family cottages to complement their income from agricultural labor.[5] Decades of research have concluded that most proto industrial regions did not become industrialized; nor has a clear impact on the demographic behavior of the population— that is, earlier marriages, increased fertility, and population growth—as a result of rural industry been found in all cases. Yet, by focusing on the eighteenth century, proto industrial literature has provided us with new and invaluable insights for understanding how "work before the factory" was organized.

Urban growth was another characteristic feature of the period, connected to population growth and the agricultural revolution that allowed more nonagricultural workers to be fed. Capital cities reflected the expanding powers and functions of the state and its bureaucracies, and became the scenes of urban reforms and costly building programs that included not only palaces, parks, and theaters, but also hospitals, bridges, and factories. Urban growth both reflected and fuelled the new employment opportunities that attracted peasants, particularly young girls and boys. The cities that grew fastest were the port cities, with London, already the largest in the western world at the beginning of the century, reaching a population of one million by 1800, followed by Paris with nearly 600,000 inhabitants. Naples, the largest Italian city, had a population of about 320,000. Bristol and Liverpool, in England, and Amsterdam, in the Low Countries, also grew rapidly owing to colonial trade. In 1703, Peter the Great founded Saint Petersburg, moving the Russian capital there to gain a seaport to expand Russian maritime trade. Bordeaux is a good example of a port city that flourished thanks to overseas trade. By the second half of the eighteenth century, it controlled 40 percent of France's colonial traffic, exporting textiles, re exporting slaves, and importing huge quantities of sugar produced in the West Indies. Figure 1.2 belongs to the series *Les ports de France*, a collection of eighteen paintings commissioned by Louis XV in 1753 to show off France's maritime and commercial might.

Whether living conditions were worse or better in the cities than in the countryside is debatable. Certainly, in the eighteenth century an urban penalty existed in Europe, given the unsanitary conditions and lack of proper housing, together with the large numbers of people flocking to the cities. Cities became a trap during times of plague and epidemics, as Daniel Defoe vividly described in *A Journal of the Plague Year*, having survived the devastating pestilence that afflicted London in 1665.[6] City dwellers

FIGURE 1.2 Joseph Vernet, *Vue d'une partie du Port et de la ville de Bordeaux, prise du côté des Salinières*, 1759. Paris, Musée National de la Marine.

were particularly vulnerable during times of famine and war, owing to their dependence on food arriving from the countryside. Yet, as we shall see, the "urban factor" was key to economic and social modernization. It is associated with the rise in literacy, the spread of new ideas, the rise of new institutions, and eventually with the birth of democracy; the development of the market economy, both for commodities and for capital and labor; and with the structural change that paved the way for industrialization.

AN INDUSTRIOUS REVOLUTION?

In recent years, research has focused on the role that the mobilization of labor had on the century's dynamism. The old paradigms that explained the industrialization and nineteenth-century economic growth as a supply-side phenomenon have been replaced by accounts that focus on demand-side factors. Production, factories, capital, technological innovations, steam, coal, and iron have been replaced by consumption, households, income, tastes, shops, silk, coffee, and tea. Although this interpretation already appeared in Joan Thirsk's *The Development of a Consumer Society in Early Modern England*, and is generally inspired by the Keynesian aggregate demand model, Jan de Vries' model of industrious revolution connected this "consumer revolution" to changes in the supply of labor.[7] His theory has had the effect of granting new relevance to the early modern period, as the industrious revolution would have preceded the Industrial Revolution. "In England, but in fact through much North-western Europe and Colonial America, a broad range of households made decisions that increased both the supply of marketed commodities and labor and the demand for goods offered in the marketplace. This combination of changes in household behavior constituted an 'industrious revolution'."[8] According to de Vries, in the eighteenth-century western world people were working longer, in terms of both more hours per day and more days per year, as well as more years over their life course; this was surely a fundamental factor in accounting for the transformation of western economies and societies.

Although there is now considerable evidence supporting the idea that an intensification of work occurred, at least three important questions remain: whether an increase in aggregate employment actually existed, particularly of women and children, the larger part of the unemployed, or whether those already working simply decided to work longer hours; whether households made decisions based on maximizing their utility function, that is, the consumers' choice of goods and services that are most preferred; and whether the decision to increase households' labor supply was driven by the desire to consume more. On the first question, we already have evidence of the central role women and children played in the mobilization of work. In a pioneering work that studied two English localities in the late eighteenth century, Osamu Saito found participation rates of 67.5 percent among married women, and up to 82.1 percent for widowers, all in stocking knitting, lacemaking, strawplaiting, and spinning. "The combined effect of poverty and opportunity provided by the cottage industry," as well as the preference of merchants for a cheaper labor force that would allow them to maximize their profits, and their desire "to bypass traditional artisan customs and arrangements" account for the huge increase in the employment of women and children in the labor-intensive industries that developed in the eighteenth century, mostly in the countryside but also in urban centers.[9]

Research in recent years has reconstructed women and men's participation rates, which was previously seen as impossible owing to a lack of sources for the prestatistical period.[10] Sources are being found across Europe that, in fact, allow for a quantification of the women, men, and children in paid work. Women's participation rates in paid employment were much higher than previously thought, because the sources on which earlier research relied suffered from a huge under-recording of women's work. For example, in examining the labor market of Torino, Beatrice Zucca compared the number of women declaring they had a job in the 1802 Napoleonic census with the registers of the Ospedale di Carità, the main charitable institution of the city, where around 15,000 people asked for relief in the three decades between 1762 and 1792. Records of charitable institutions are excellent sources for the urban occupational structure, since, because they oversaw charity relief, men's and women's work was carefully recorded to evaluate their real needs. According to the Napoleonic census, women's participation rate in Torino was 33.3 percent, while the hospital's registers showed 63.2 percent of women had a paid occupation. Even more interestingly, while according to the census married women had a lower participation rate, compared to unmarried women and widows, the hospital's registers recorded the opposite situation: 73.3 percent of married women had a paid job. Married women's paid work, in fact, was particularly under-recorded in eighteenth-century sources. Although the notion of the male breadwinner was formally elaborated during the nineteenth century, "comparison between a conventional source (the Napoleonic census) and an alternative source (the registers of the Ospedale di Carità) reveals that the idea of a household economy based on the sole or main breadwinner—male or female—was already well established in the eighteenth century."[11]

My own work on inland Spain using the householders' declarations for the *Ensenada cadaster*, a large-scale census and statistical investigation conducted in the Castilian Kingdom in 1749, shows rates of up to 82.7 percent in small- and medium-size localities specializing in textile manufactures (lace, stockings, ribbons, esparto grass makers, and so on), and whenever men declared their wives' occupations. In northern Castile, rates were 66 percent for women, mostly dedicated to textile manufactures.[12] For that same period, an average participation rate for women of 45.1 percent has been estimated for several Dutch towns, mostly concentrated in the textile and retailing sectors:[13]

> changing consumption and specialization patterns increased opportunities for married women in retailing. For instance, the share of women, and especially married women, in the sale of coffee and tea rose markedly in eighteenth-century Leiden ... women formed 80 per cent of all coffee and tea sellers, and the percentage of married women among them rose from over 60 to almost 80 per cent ... compared to industrial crafts, institutional (corporate) restrictions on women were limited in the retail sector.[14]

To know whether the industrious revolution incentivized an expanding supply of labor, not only with people working longer hours but also with new people, particularly women, becoming wage-workers, we need to understand more about the preindustrial organization of work. Traditional sources obscure women's work, and erroneous models can be constructed if this is not considered.

> Changes in the terms and conditions of women's work, and in particular the increased visibility of waged labour in factories and workshops, should not be identified with an increase in aggregate employment. Thus, part of de Vries' "industrious" revolution, in which women abandoned subsistence production for waged employment to boost income and facilitate the purchase of new desirable market commodities, might also be a mirage created by changes in the types of work undertaken.[15]

Work on family farms, the most common type of work done by women and children before the eighteenth century, is also the one that was more easily hidden. The increased opportunities in retailing that Dutch women enjoyed paralleled those in the booming textile manufactures described across Europe. The new visibility of women's work may thus be reflecting more than an increase in the total supply of labor but rather a structural change in labor in which women, we now know, were at the forefront.

A second issue with the industrious revolution model refers to the decision-making process of households. To what extent did decisions on work/leisure and consumption reflect the shared preferences of the household members? The little work done on this question, such as Nancy Folbre's on colonial North America, shows that families were not egalitarian working or consumption units.[16] Still little is known about transfers of resources and rents that took place within households. Men's expenditure on alcoholic beverages, tobacco, prostitution, and gambling, all of which increased during the century alongside mobility and urbanization, could diminish a significant part of the family budget, including income earned by women and children, a practice that questions the income-pooling model with which family economies are usually explained.[17] Unequal income pooling paralleled the unequal intra-household allocation of resources, as reflected not only in the expenditure in goods but also in services such as medical attention, leisure activities, and education.

Finally, there is the question of the reason for working harder. A new culture of work developed during the century but was consuming more, and new goods, what drove workers to work harder? Was the rise in new consumption a major European phenomenon, involving the working classes as well? Evidence suggests that in most countries, if not all, peasants were unable to choose between leisure and consumption. Income generated by the growing participation in the labor market was used by peasant and urban workers to cover other more pressing needs than exotic consumption goods: not only to pay for food and clothing, at ever-increasing prices, particularly for those who had moved to the cities, but also to pay their debts, taxes, and rising land and housing rents. In any case, it is true that new opportunities for social mobility explain the many initiatives, across Europe, to move up the social ladder; households, for example, borrowed money or saved to buy or rent new plots or cattle or open a shop. Historians have put forward various theories to try to account for the rise in consumption, pointing to the role played by wages as incentives that allowed workers to access and consume goods which previously had been limited to a minority.

Evidence of working time is fragmented. Fixed capital was still a very small part of the productive system, with most trades remaining labor-intensive. Labor-saving machinery and devices started to develop only in the last decades of the century. Together with new patterns of divisions of labor, they would eventually transform how work was done, allowing for clear increases in labor productivity. But, in general, labor productivity remained very low during the century. Figure 1.3, *La tormenta de nieve o Invierno* (The

FIGURE 1.3 Francisco de Goya, *La tormenta de nieve o Invierno* (The Snowstorm or Winter), 1786. Madrid, Museo del Prado. Photo: DeAgostini / Getty Images.

Snowstorm or Winter), by Goya, which shows a group of men transporting a slaughtered pig through a snowstorm, illustrates well this low labor productivity, in this case of transportation, done by foot with the help of a donkey. As in the case of cloth washing, "the hardest, most unpleasant profession," as Spanish statesman Gaspar Melchor de Jovellanos put it, it reminds us that, in the eighteenth century, labor was still about loading heavy weights; suffering extreme cold, heat, and humidity; contact with all kinds of dirt; breathing polluted air; and having all kinds of accidents and sickness, that in many cases left workers crippled forever, often as girls and boys, unable to work and dependent upon charity.[18]

Research on the organization of work suggests that three main developments can be identified. First, there were the new forms of work for the rural population, across Europe and to a large extent in the colonies, combining agriculture, husbandry, dairy production, and commercial activities. The new economic possibilities that became available to peasants through the rise in demand were recreated by enlightened writer Félix Maria Samaniego (1745–1801) in his version of the classic tale of the milkmaid, told by Jean de La Fontaine (1621–95) in the seventeenth century, who in turn had taken it from Aesop, and which became immensely popular in the eighteenth century.

> A milkmaid took the pitcher to the market on her head … the happy milkmaid marched alone, and said to herself: "Selling this milk will give me so much money, and with this money I want to buy a basket of eggs, to produce one hundred chickens … With the amount obtained from the sale of so many chicken I will buy a pig; with acorn, bran, cabbage, chestnut it will get fat without limit … I will make good money out of it without a doubt; I will buy a robust cow and a calf …" Lost in her thoughts she jumped in such a violent way that the pitcher fell. Poor milkmaid! Goodbye milk, money, eggs, chickens, pig, cow and calf. (See Figure 1.4)

The tale introduces an actor surely well known at the time: the peasant "ambitious of a better or more prosperous fortune." This perfect example of "Rational Economic Woman" is planning a business consisting of producing for the market, selling goods at market prices, and reinvesting the money earned in additional sources of earnings. The tale is also significant in revealing the growth of local markets. "A commercial revolution did take place in eighteenth-century Europe: not in the glamorous long-distance expeditions to exotic lands, but in the seemingly mundane business of regional exchange and local shop-keeping."[19]

But what was surely the most important feature of the organization of work was the increasingly widespread manufacturing sector, particularly in textile goods. It was important in quantitative terms, most likely involving hundreds of thousands of workers across Europe, and important for its connections with industrialization. The proto industrial theory developed by Mendels and others in the 1970s saw rural industry as a precursor of factory industrialization. Rural industry did not always evolve into industrialization, nor did it have impact on demographics in the way the model predicted. But seeing Europe as a large rural workshop remains a key contribution to our understanding of the economy of this century. As Maxine Berg argued: "It is now apparent that the eighteenth-century economy was much more industrial than once thought." This vision has been obscured until recently because most of this work took place as domestic rural manufacture: "Dramatic changes brought by factory working in some areas obscures the fact that it never was the major occupation and that much industrial organization continued to centre on workshops."[20]

Finally, seasonal and temporary migrations acted as an intermediate mechanism between countryside and cities, and across economic sectors and occupations, allowing people to

FIGURE 1.4 Francis Wheatley, *The Return from the Market*. © Leeds Museums and Art Galleries (Temple Newsam House), UK / Bridgeman Images.

move from peak agricultural seasons to mining, rural manufactures, transportation, and service. Mobility became, in fact, a very eighteenth-century phenomenon, as institutional ties preventing or impeding it began to disappear. It was a resource the poor increasingly relied on, and what led Olwen Hufton and others after her to define the economy of the poor as "an economy of makeshifts."[21] The occupational structure in the cities was different from that in the country. Except for industrial cities such as Lyon, France, which had become the principal urban center of silk production, the main occupation in eighteenth-century cities was domestic service (see Figure 1.5).[22] The sector reached its peak in this century, declining in relative terms from the first decades of the nineteenth century, when alternative occupations for men in industry, mining, and the building sectors started to increase. It is also the period when domestic service transformed from a mostly male to a mostly female occupation. Supply and demand factors accounted for the importance of this sector: not only in demand, with the middle classes imitating elite lifestyles, but also in supply, as hundreds of thousands of girls and boys were ready to look for a master to work for. Domestic service was an occupation but also a room, food, shoes, legal protection, a social identity, and a site of core social relationships. It is important to consider all the functions performed by domestic service to understand its crucial importance in the eighteenth-century economy.

FIGURE 1.5 Pietro Longhi, *Portrait of a Venetian Family with a Manservant Serving Coffee*, c. 1752. Amsterdam, Rijksmuseum.

CHANGING IDEAS OF WORK AND WORKERS

"Economic change in all periods depends, more than most economists think, on what people believe."[23] Economic changes brought about new ideas. But there is little doubt that economic and demographic changes were also, and perhaps largely, the result of new ideas. Although the importance of ideas has long been recognized as central to modern economic growth, in the form of a scientific or technological revolution prior to the Industrial Revolution, their role has been recently reclaimed by the works of Joel Mokyr, for whom European Enlightenment was pivotal in the propulsion of economic growth in the nineteenth century. Mokyr goes beyond ideas as the origin of new institutions: "What mattered was not only what people believed about social contracts, political pluralism, religious tolerance, human rights and so on, but also what they believed about the relationship about humans and their physical environment and role of what they called 'useful knowledge' to improve material wellbeing."[24]

One of these fundamental cultural changes was the new social attitude towards work and workers. Changes in the organization of work and the increasing economic dynamism brought about a new positive attitude in favor of work not only as a source of income, but, most importantly, and new, *as a source of social respectability and identity*. Most importantly, because the new social place of workers, their increasing legitimacy as social subjects, would soon decisively contribute to the erosion of the *ancien régime*.

As the impact of Diderot and D'Alembert's monumental *Encyclopédie* (1751–72; see Figure 1.6) has been described:

> Although it is doubtful whether the many artisans, technicians, or labourers whose work and presence and interspersed throughout the *Encyclopédie* actually read it, the recognition of their work as equal to that of intellectuals, clerics, and rulers prepared the terrain for demands for increased representation. Thus the *Encyclopédie* served to recognize and galvanize a new power base, ultimately contributing to the destruction of old values and the creation of new ones.[25]

One of the sources of this change in the way Europeans perceived work and workers was the experience of overseas colonization. Breaking "virgin" lands became a metaphor of work that granted newcomers political and economic rights through citizenship and land ownership.[26] This is what the first school of economic thought, the Physiocrats, and particularly François Quesnay (1694–1774) and Richard Cantillon (1680–1734) defended from France. Unlike what mercantilist theory claimed in the first half of the century, agricultural labor was the only activity producing a net product; all other economic activities simply transformed it. Crucial to notice here is the difference between land and agricultural work; it was only *work put into the land* that created wealth, and farmers, in Europe or in the colonies, were the foundation of the social body.

WAGE WORK: MORALLY SUPERIOR, ECONOMICALLY EFFICIENT

The eighteenth century saw the birth of economic thought, primarily centered on the question of labor. "The primacy of labour as a factor of production in the mercantilists' intellectual schema, together with the pervasive problem of pauperism throughout much of Europe, produced a body of policy-oriented economic literature that because of its dual emphasis on the problems of poverty and unemployment can be considered the beginning

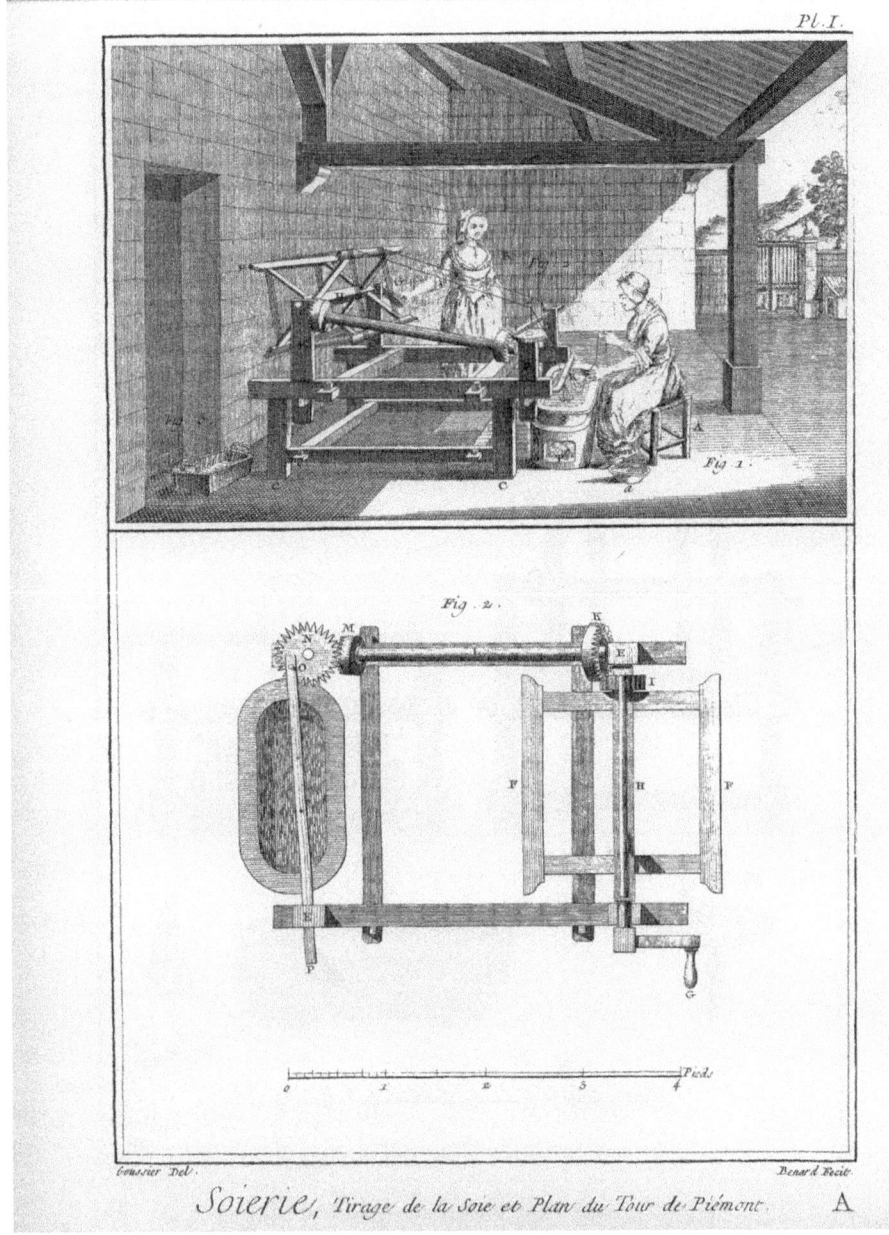

FIGURE 1.6 *Soierie. Tirage de la soie et Plan du Tour de Piémont*, "Silkmaking," Plate I. In Denis Diderot and Jean le Rond d'Alembert, *Encyclopédie, ou dictionnaire raisonné des sciences, des arts et des métiers*, 1751–72.

of modern labor economics."[27] The physiocratic idea of *laissez-faire*, later developed by Adam Smith as the invisible hand, was an explicit defense of the market, and included a new vision of work as "free work," as opposed to nonmarket forms of labor. Free labor, that is, labor freely contracted in the market in exchange for a wage, was morally superior to, and economically more efficient than, servant and slave labor. "Work done by slaves ... is in the end the dearest of any. A person who can acquire no property, can have no other interest but to eat as much, and to labor as little as possible."[28] This idea of market work as morally superior, socially more convenient, and economically more efficient would be fundamental in establishing new more favorable institutional frameworks that allowed labor markets to develop and the supply of labor to expand, two central requisites for economic growth.

Innovative thinking about work came not only from economists. The two political movements that have largely shaped contemporary societies and economies, antislavery and women´s rights, were both born in the last decades of the eighteenth century, and both defined having a paid occupation as a basic economic and political right and a central component of becoming a citizen. It is in fact remarkable that eighteenth-century defenders of women's rights drew a parallel between their situation and that of slaves. This was the result of early feminists coming from the abolitionist movement, like the North American Abigail Adams (1744–1818). In fact, denouncing women's, and particularly married women's, "slavery" was commonplace in the writings of eighteenth-century feminists. In 1786, Josefa Amar y Borbón published her *Discurso en defensa del talento de las mujeres y otros cargos en que se emplean los hombres* (Speech in defense of the talent of women and other positions in which men employ themselves): "Not content with having reserved for themselves the employments, the honours, the profits, in a word, everything that could inspire the efforts of their wakeful hours, men have dispossessed women even of the pleasure that results from having an enlightened mind. Women are born and raised in absolute ignorance."[29] In her 1791 *Déclaration des droits de la femme et de la citoyenne*, Olympe de Gouges claimed:

> all Female and all Male citizens, being equal in law, must be equally entitled to all public honours, positions and employment according to their capacities and with no other distinctions than those based solely on talent and virtue ... woman shares all the labour, all the hard tasks; she should therefore have an equal share of positions, employment, responsibilities, honours and professions.[30]

Mary Wollstonecraft also paralleled women's economic and legal situation with slavery in her 1792 *A Vindication of the Rights of Woman*. But neither slaves nor women had the legal or political capacity to reform institutions. It was through the support of a few white middle-class men, moved by egalitarian ideas, that male and female slaves and "free" women were eventually granted economic and political rights.

Thinking of all individuals (not yet citizens) as holding the right to work for a wage and making work respectable and wages desirable were all elements of the eighteenth-century formation of a large supply of labor. Advocates of middle-class women's right to have a paid occupation explicitly used the argument of the respectability of paid work to defend this right as moral. As Louis-Sébastien Mercier argued:

> Business of various kinds, they might likewise pursue, if they were educated in a more orderly manner, which might save many from common and legal prostitution. Women would not then marry for a support ... The few employments open to women, so far, from being liberal, are menial ... How much more respectable is the woman who earns her own bread by fulfilling any duty, than the most accomplished beauty![31]

Cultural and institutional factors had as much relevance as economic factors in this process. But the decisive transformation would take place at the factory, as Adam Smith argued:

This great increase of the quantity of work, which, in consequence of the division of labour, the same number of people are capable of performing, is owing to three different circumstances; first, to the increase of dexterity in every particular workman; secondly, to the saving of the time which is commonly lost in passing from one species of work to another; and lastly, to the invention of a great number of machines which facilitate and abridge labour, and enable one man to do the work of many.[32]

CHANGING POLICIES: THE ENLIGHTENED AGENDA FOR ECONOMIC GROWTH

State intervention in economic activity was widespread and systematic in most of eighteenth-century Europe. Absolutist states became central actors of economic policy. In the context of deep changes in the trade positions of European countries, the expansion of industrial activity became a central goal of the economic agenda, which governments pursued through protectionist legislation and subsidies to private and public institutions. Increase of industrial output was intended to increase fiscal revenues and, as an import-substitution policy, to reduce commercial deficits. State support to industrial modernization took several forms. In Italy, Spain, Sweden, Saxony, Bohemia, and France this encouragement occurred through the establishment of royal factories, mostly devoted to the fabrication of luxury goods such as porcelain, tapestries, silk, and crystal to replace imported goods, but also to meet the internal demand for linen, wool, and cotton textiles. Through royal factories, enlightened states aimed at diffusing foreign innovations and hiring foreign technicians, but they were in general a failed attempt to promote industrialization "from the top," incurring huge deficits and failing to substitute imports.

Two aspects of state intervention had a special relation with work: the programs of institutional reforms aimed at expanding the supply of labor, and the antipoverty policies. The two were intended as means to achieve economic growth, not in the modern sense, as a means to improve living standards for society as a whole, but with the intention of supporting and financing the military and competition for colonial power. As they embarked upon costly wars, and public deficits grew exponentially, European states needed new taxpayers and new taxable wealth. The two interventions were also closely related, as the policies to deal with the poor were in fact public efforts to transform the populace into "citizens useful to the republic."

Poverty was not an eighteenth-century novelty; instead, for most of the population, it had been the norm for centuries. What was new was that poor people were more plentiful, more mobile, more visible, and more dangerous. Population growth had increased the numbers of the poor. The loosening of feudal ties had facilitated their migration to the cities in search of a master to serve or begging opportunities. Across Europe, thousands of children were abandoned at the doors of churches or foundling hospitals that became more numerous across the continent.

As poverty and unemployment intensified throughout Europe, they became favorite subjects for reformists.[33] An interesting development in the new ideas on work was the criticism expressed by English travellers throughout Catholic countries, where almsgiving was a widespread and respected practice. They were horrified at the long queues of poor at the doors of churches and monasteries, waiting for some food or money. They should be working instead! In fact, a new climate against begging swelled across Europe. The new idea of the poor as idle, and of poverty as the deserved consequence of idleness, had profound implications in policy terms; a variety of measures to enforce work developed, with varied success, with the English Poor Laws surely as the most developed institutional attempt to solve the problem. Work was promoted by the authorities as the best means to avoid poverty and thus the political risks associated with the increasing number of beggars in the cities. To promote work, states went from presenting work as morally superior to the enforced reclusion of beggars in workhouses. In many countries, antibeggar legislation was enacted. In France, begging was defined as "absolutely opposed to the current order of society ... Begging and indigence have been replaced by this active and working poverty that only makes the true wealth of the peoples, and that deserves all the attention and protection from the wise governments, because what produces is more important than what the epicurean who only consumes."[34]

EXPANDING THE SUPPLY OF CHEAP LABOR

The central means to expand labor supply, which eventually became a key aspect of the labor agenda of enlightened reformists across Europe, was the increase in women's participation in the labor force. This occurred for two reasons: because wages paid to women were much lower than those of men's, thereby employing women would reduce productive costs and make industry more competitive; and because women's increased participation in manufacturing would permit male workers to be "reallocated" to agriculture, public works, and the army. In fact, the new interest in workers and the goal of promoting a new work organization included as one of its key elements a notion of gender-based division of work, a redefinition of the gender segregation of the labor market. In 1774, Spanish minister Pedro Rodríguez de Campomanes, prime minister under Carlos III and one of the principal ideologists of the enlightened reforms, had advocated rural manufactures in his highly publicized *Discurso sobre el fomento de la industria popular*. This was a win-win solution, as it permitted an increase in the country's industrial production while at the same time maintaining the population in the countryside, avoiding the social troubles of proletarization and keeping wages low. Peasant families had no need to put a high price on the manufactures fabricated by their women and children in their "spare time." Plenty of descriptions show how well women did by combining agriculture and manufactures. In Majorca, the local enlightened society was pleased to claim in 1798: "Women who go out to work in the fields, after they retire themselves at night to their houses, they spin at the spindle until they go to bed."[35]

The developments that led to the legal dissolution of the guild system were also part of the enlightened labor agenda. In Spain, the goal of recovering the country's manufactures, the convenience of reducing the trade deficit, and the need to facilitate people's access to cheap consumption goods led reformists to advocate a reorganization of the labor market that would start by taking men out of textile manufactures. Campomanes had already identified the problem in the 1770s, when discussing the high price of textiles in Madrid. "A weaver of ordinary cloth makes more than 10 *reales* per day," which is caused "for two reasons: the short number of weavers, who have their clients imploring them," and the rise in the price of fabrics, and the fact "that this operation is performed by men," for which there is no reason, because in northern Spain "women are the ones who weave the cloth." Men should, then, be replaced by women, because these "will be happy to make five *reales* per day instead of 10, now paid to the male weavers. I must insist that public administration is obliged to employ women in this and similar works, and the way to achieve it is teaching girls and not men."[36]

The central battle of this war was to be fought against the institution that had the monopoly of technical knowledge, the guilds, which excluded women from the manufactures of luxury goods. Despite repeated admonitions, the Guild of Silk Cord-makers of the city of Valencia made the government furious in 1779 by its resistance to accepting girls being taught silk-reeling techniques.

> My Council, having noticed how harmful it was for the fomentation of industry ... the exclusions of women established by some of their Ordinances from the works which are more proper and suitable to their sex than to men's, who for their robustness and strength seemed more appropriately applicable to agriculture, the armies and navy; and having present the fact that the Guild of Silk Cord-makers, *Passementerie* and Button Makers of the City of Valencia has attempted to prevent a School to teach the Girls all the relative to the industry of cord-making be established ... We order: that with no pretext you prevent, obstruct, or by the guilds or other people be prevented or hindered, the teaching to women and girls of all those works and artefacts that are proper for their sex, and that they can freely sell, by themselves or on their own account, the manufactures they make.[37]

The fact that guilds continued to obstruct the entrance of women into several trades was one of the main reasons for their dissolution, which European governments implemented in the final decades of the eighteenth century (see Figure 1.7).

Preindustrial textile manufactures were labor-intensive. This explains the interest in reducing labor costs, and replacing male workers with women was the simplest and easiest way of doing so. In Spain, the average daily wage for unskilled male workers was 4 or 4.5 *reales*, while by working at looms at home, women and girls could make 1 or 1.5 *reales* per day. In the face of increasing foreign competition, manufacturers and merchants in other countries were doing the same. In Bologna's "silk district," while the sector of dyed silks entered crisis, white silks remained competitive "partly through agreements among manufacturers and also by taking on women and children as workers in order to reduce costs."[38]

The gender re segregation of the labor market included prohibitions on women occupying certain jobs or entering certain sectors—for instance, proscriptions against women joining gangs of harvesters that departed in late spring from Galicia. Migrations to Andalusia and Castile for harvest every year attracted some 25,000 to 30,000 young women and men, and were the main source of income for the inland areas, without access to fisheries. Women's participation in this flow of migration, which seemingly amounted to a third of it, became a matter of deep concern for authorities during the eighteenth century. In an attempt to put an end to it, prohibitive measures were consecutively reenacted.[39] In 1736, emigration of women harvesters to Castile was forbidden in Spain. In 1748, jail sentences or the confiscation of property for those contravening the prohibition were announced. In 1754, an order from the administrative authority of Galicia revealed that women were emigrating dressed in men's clothing:

> That no gang boss nor other person who goes to the works of Castile takes any woman, under penalty of twenty *ducados* for each one taken, and of ten years of jail in one of the presidiums of Africa; that no husband, father, brother, or relative or master, permits his wife, daughters, sisters, relatives or servants who are under his custody, to go to such works, under the same penalty; that justices and officials be vigilant in the observance of this and let it immediately be known when any woman from their parish is missing, and take and place an embargo on the properties of the person under whose custody she is

THE ECONOMY OF WORK   35

FIGURE 1.7 Joseph Gabriel Rosetti, *The Workers' Workshop, Factory of Indian Cotton Fabric Founded by the Wetter Brothers in Orange*, 1764. Orange, France, Musée municipal.

... in cases of women being found going to the work dressed in men's clothes, besides the said penalties, she and the man taking her must be punished by public shaming.[40]

Despite the endless regulations to prevent women from migrating to Castile "in men's gangs," they continued to do so, since they needed the money and had few other opportunities in their villages to earn it. Scholars talk of "endless announcements in all the parishes" and a "female exodus."

As has been seen, women and men's "proper places," what we call today the gender segregation of labor, were, in the eighteenth century (like today), concerned with wages. The entire first age of political economy was devoted to justifying the convenience and correctness of low wages, wages sufficient just to allow workers' subsistence. This ideological product was fundamentally useful because at that moment labor-intensive industries were booming, and industrialists needed to employ thousands of workers. The fact that they could find cheap workers, allowing them to keep production costs low and firms competitive, and the fact that paying workers very little was morally respectable and economically efficient, clearly had much to do with the eighteenth century being the period that paved the way for the success of industrialization.

Nominal wages (in kind or monetary) were low before the eighteenth century owing to several factors: in the first place, the political weakness of urban workers. New workers were no longer part of the guild system, but unions had not yet developed. Competition between workers was growing, owing to population growth and increasing mobility in Europe and between colonies. But increasing mobility was also a chance for workers to escape poor working conditions, even serfdom and slavery. Workers, women and men, tried to escape such conditions by embarking for the colonies or moving to cities, although the former came with a cost that many could not afford. Second, technical problems accompanied the production process. Constant interruptions left industrial production poorly organized: demand for agricultural work was still heavily seasonal, at least in Mediterranean countries; but activity was also interrupted for part of the year in industry, mining, building, and transportation. The arrival of raw materials from overseas markets was sporadic, with many arriving in bad condition, shaping the work rhythm and making wages uneven. Finally, the transformation of the internal composition of the labor force affected income. The huge presence of women and children, alongside the transformation in gross domestic product and occupational structure, partially accounts for the fall in labor costs. Children and young women often worked only for food. For instance, in the second part of the century, across most of Europe, the wages of hand spinners appear to have decreased, leaving thousands of women near destitute.

Thus, rather than increasing nominal wages, it was the supplementary income of different family members, particularly children and women, that allowed households and families to cope with rising prices and enabled them to increase their purchasing capacity. In recent years, economic historians have focused on changes in the organization of work as the key factor in accounting for the eighteenth-century increased work effort, paving the way for the intense growth seen in the nineteenth century, with productivity increases in the industrial sector. This thesis revisits the birth of the industrial factory and the role work played in it. According to Robert Allen's "High Wage Economy (HWE)" thesis, the Industrial Revolution first occurred in Britain because the high costs of labor relative to capital and fuel motivated the development and adoption of labor-saving techniques, which included the spinning jenny. Allen's thesis is founded on the work of Craig Muldrew, among other scholars, which expounded increasing wages of hand spinners. More recent work by Jane Humphries, Jacob Weisdorf, and Benjamin Schneider has contested the Allen–Muldrew's HWE thesis, providing new evidence of hand spinning as a low-income, low-productivity occupation, and claiming that "mechanisation, especially the development of the factory, was motivated by the desire to use cheaper child and female labour in a way that ensured discipline and quality control."[41]

New evidence is needed on eighteenth-century nominal wages from a micro perspective, to better understand labor demand and to what extent low labor costs accounted for the success of the first industrial enterprises. Yet we should always take into account the local and sectoral patterns of gender segregation of labor because women, men, and children were not always easily replaceable, even before institutional barriers to substitution developed, such as unionization. Nominal wages are of course needed, together with prices of basic goods, to better understand people's standard of living.

CONCLUSION: PAVING THE WAY FOR THE MODERN ECONOMY

"The difference in natural talents in different men is, in reality, much less than we are aware of; and the very different genius which appears to distinguish men of different professions, when grown up to maturity, is not upon many occasions so much the cause, as the effect of the division of labour."[42] One of the most attractive and intriguing aspects of the age of Enlightenment are the incredibly modern opinions and ideas that some of the women and men who lived in this period sustained. For people who had been born and raised and were living in *ancien régime* societies, organized at the level of the legal institution of estates (*estratums*), enlightened ideas of equality, freedom, and individual rights were not only progressive but revolutionary. Scholars have already identified the contradictions and limitations of enlightened thinkers. The idea that the differences between individuals are *not the cause but the consequence of* the division of labor shows an extraordinary modernity, with implications that Adam Smith was surely far from foreseeing. Custom and education form people, not Nature. The division of labor is the result of the social (political) organization, and not divinely ordained. This simple idea had the potential to change everything, as in fact it did.

The eighteenth century came to a close amid an unprecedented rise in the prominence of the poor in Europe. They were not only the majority population but their increasing concentration in the cities lent them a new visibility, converting them into a political risk. The rapid growth in the urban population explains the increasing dependence on the food produced in the countryside. And the poor, increasingly discontent at their position, tolerated poor harvests, food scarcity, and rising prices with difficulty. The growing unrest of workers would eventually be the final impetus for the French Revolution in 1789, which symbolically closed the century in historic terms, having been preceded by countless food riots across Europe in the decades before.

The political and ideological innovations that developed during the eighteenth century were connected to the new institutional framework implemented in the first half of the nineteenth century, intended to pave the way for economic growth and the consolidation of the market economy. In Sweden, like elsewhere in Europe, "each occupation and sector in the economy had been protected against competition and interference. At the beginning of the nineteenth century, however, reforms and deregulation created property rights in land and forests, loosened old restrictions which had inhibited the free flow of goods and labor both within the country and as far as exports were concerned."[43] The new ideas diffused during the eighteenth century inspired new institutions and formed the basis of the new "rules of the game," not, however, without fierce opposition from the privileged classes and from the poor. Labor, transformed into a commodity, was at the center of these changes. The difficult transition to the "free flow of labour" would, to a large extent, define the historical development of the century that followed.

ACKNOWLEDGMENTS

I would like to thank the volume editors for their comments and Christiana Payne for suggesting the inclusion of Figures 1.4 and 1.6.

CHAPTER TWO

Picturing Work

CHRISTIANA PAYNE

The Enlightenment concept of work was a highly positive one. Traditionally, the biblical designation of labor as the curse of Adam reinforced the aristocratic notion that work was degrading, and saw workers as deserving their place at the bottom of the social hierarchy. But this way of thinking was gradually giving way to a new perception of work as valuable in itself, and hence of workers as useful citizens. In his influential work *Two Treatises of Government* (1689), John Locke argued that labor is the true source of property rights; nearly a century later, Adam Smith in *The Wealth of Nations* (1776) reinforced the positive view of work by asserting that labor is the source of all wealth. Voltaire summed up the new attitude to work succinctly in his novel *Candide* (1759) when he declared that work was the answer to the three major problems of life: boredom, vice and poverty. At the end of the novel, after many adventures, the characters meet a "good old man" who is living a life of perfect contentment. Candide observes that he must have a vast estate, and the old man replies: "Only twenty acres ... my children help me to farm it, and we find that the work banishes those three great evils, boredom, vice, and poverty." As a result of this meeting, Candide and his companions decide that they should stop arguing about philosophical questions and get down to cultivating their garden. The men take up field-work and carpentry, the women take care of the cooking, the sewing, and the laundry. Candide has been reunited with the love of his life, and at first this is very much a mixed blessing, as she has become unattractive and headstrong, but the women settle down under the influence of honest labor:

> There was no denying that Cunégonde was decidedly ugly, but she soon made excellent pastry. Pacquette was clever at embroidery, and the old woman took care of the linen. No one refused to work, not even Brother Giroflée, who was a good carpenter, and thus became an honest man.[1]

The problem of the evil in the world was thus solved at a stroke—although, of course, one cannot be sure whether Voltaire was being entirely serious or merely ironic in offering such a simple solution.

Eighteenth-century visual images of work and workers are generally attractive, portraying work in the way that Voltaire presents it: a wholesome occupation, beneficial both to the individual and to society in general. The illustration of processes in the French *Encyclopédie* helped to stimulate a widespread sense of work as a spectacle, worthy of being observed either in person or through paintings. Elite patrons both commissioned genre depictions of people at work and, on occasion, chose to be represented as involved in useful work themselves. Gender distinctions are important in images, as they are in

Candide. Muscular, heroic male laborers and women employed in peaceful domestic occupations begin to proliferate in art. In addition, a broadly Protestant insistence on the moral value of work colors many paintings and prints in this period. Across Europe and the Americas, the rise of the middle class and the development of industrialization favored a recognition of the value of work and its role in creating prosperity. It is only towards the end of the period that we find in art a consciousness of the darker side of industrialization and the consequent exploitation and degradation of the worker.

Visual images are important sources of information on work practices and processes, but they need to be used carefully. What they tell us is not necessarily how things were but how people thought they should be. Often, they provide evidence of the attitudes and values of their time, rather than of what actually happened in the past. A painting that seems to illustrate work or workers may turn out, on closer investigation, to be a representation of a myth or allegory. In other cases, it may become clear that an interest in work was not the main priority of the artist, his or her patron, or their wider public. An apparent interest in the early phases of the Industrial Revolution, for example, might take second place to a concern with dramatic effects of light and shade. A depiction of a woman worker—or even of a child street seller—could be little more than an excuse for titillation and erotic allure. Paintings that seem to show a new sympathy for the working classes may turn out to be about the charitable efforts of the wealthy, either spurring them on to greater efforts or encouraging self-congratulation and complacency. The most interesting and sophisticated images work on several different levels, depending on who is looking at them, either in their own time or across the centuries.

WORK IN MYTH AND ALLEGORY

In the seventeenth century, a new interest in modern, non elite life transformed art. Genre scenes and landscapes became popular with collectors, especially in the Netherlands, and artists influenced by Michelangelo Merisi da Caravaggio (1571–1610) occasionally produced large-scale paintings in which everyday work is prominent. Usually, however, when work was depicted on a larger scale there was a justification for its appearance within mythology, biblical history, or allegory. Nicolas Poussin's *Summer* (1660–4) is one of a series of four seasons that the artist painted towards the end of his life for the duc de Richelieu.[2] *Summer* shows laborers harvesting wheat in the fields: women are working alongside men, cutting the crop with a sickle and binding it into sheaves. However, its official subject is the story of Ruth and Boaz from the book of Ruth in the Bible: the work goes on in the background, but the foreground shows Ruth asking Boaz if she can glean in his fields. Similarly, Diego Velázquez's *The Spinners* (c. 1657) is not simply a representation of women in a tapestry workshop, as it used to be thought, but a complex allegory relating to the mythological story of the contest between Arachne and the goddess Athena.[3] In both paintings, however, work processes are clearly shown. Velázquez's three women are, respectively, carding, winding, and spinning wool. Less convincingly, Poussin shows his laborers carrying sheaves of wheat to a threshing floor, apparently on the side of the field, where horses are threshing it.

At about the same time, the Le Nain brothers painted *The Forge* (1640s), a depiction of a blacksmith at work, with his family gathered around him.[4] This, too, may be a disguised mythological subject, a modernized version of the story of the goddess Venus at the forge of Vulcan. However, the figures are represented with great dignity and tenderness: the blacksmith and his wife look directly at the observer, with thoughtful and intelligent expressions. Not surprisingly, the painting has been seen as marking a new recognition of the essential humanity of ordinary people. Part of the appeal of the subject, however, lay in its dramatic chiaroscuro. Caravaggio and his followers were adept at portraying figures illuminated by artificial light sources, firelight, or candlelight, and it could be argued that the artists were primarily interested in the play of light upon the features of their humble protagonists, hence the attention devoted to the features and expressions on the faces.

A more sustained study of the faces of the poor is found in the work of the Italian artist Giacomo Ceruti (1697–1767). His painting *Women Working on Pillow Lace (The Sewing School)* (Figure 2.1) is one of a group of some fifteen large paintings that were probably made for the noble Avogadro family of Brescia in the 1720s, and are now known as the Padernello cycle. Art historians have noted the somber melancholy tone and starkly realistic style of Ceruti's work. In this example, a group of young women are making pillow lace in the cramped conditions of a bare, unfurnished room, with no windows. The young women are well-dressed, but their expressions suggest fatigue and melancholy, slightly relieved by the presence of a girl in the center who reads to them as they work. Three of the figures look directly at the viewer as if challenging or inviting our sympathy, while one girl, to the right of the center, seems not to be working and may be ill or disabled. It is not hard to imagine that they are orphans, forced to labor in an institutional setting, listening to a reading that is morally improving rather than entertaining. Other paintings in the same cycle depict beggars, and it is likely that they are connected with

FIGURE 2.1 Giacomo Ceruti, *Women Working on Pillow Lace (The Sewing School)*, 1720s. Photo: ART Collection / Alamy Stock Photo.

the charitable works considered appropriate for a noble family.⁵ Even this painting is not a straightforward depiction of work: the subject of the sewing school could also have an allegorical meaning. It appears to have been developed from paintings by Bernhard Keil (1624–87), a Danish artist who worked in northern Italy and was known as Monsù Bernardo. He repeatedly treated the subject of sewing as an allegory of the senses of touch and sight. As with the Le Nain brothers' *Forge*, however, Ceruti's approach is strongly suggestive of a new sympathy with working people.

WORK IN GENRE PAINTING

On a smaller scale, many seventeenth-century genre paintings depicted people at work. Although much of the Dutch and Flemish genre is concerned with leisure—the tavern scene, the village merrymaking, for example—there are also significant numbers of paintings showing craftsmen in their workshops, or women engaged in domestic tasks in the home. As Christopher Brown has argued, Calvinism meant that a high moral value was placed on the practical benefits of work. A very popular set of prints, *Het Menselijk Bedrijf* (*The Work of Men*; see Figure 8.1), was issued in 1694 by Jan and Caspar Luyken. They showed one hundred occupations, mainly involving men, though women appear in some of the plates, each one accompanied by religious verses. Painters took up similar themes, depicting men as fishermen, tailors, cobblers, knife grinders, and weavers, while women are shown preparing fruit, making pancakes, ironing, sewing, and spinning.⁶ The paintings of women at work are especially celebrated today. Johannes Vermeer's *Milkmaid* (c. 1660), Caspar Netscher's *Lacemaker* (1662), and Nicolaes Maes' *A Woman Scraping Parsnips* (1655) have a serenity and harmony that could lull the most ardent feminist into a belief that domestic work is a sacred duty.⁷ These paintings have a strong contemplative element, and children are often included in such scenes, demonstrating how mundane tasks can educate and create a bond with the next generation.

This aspect of the depiction of women's work was developed further by Jean-Baptiste-Siméon Chardin (1699–1779) in eighteenth-century France. His paintings of servants and mothers give a new dignity to everyday occupations. Unlike his flamboyant contemporary François Boucher (1703–70), who specialized in paintings of nude nymphs and goddesses, Chardin demonstrates a reserved, almost puritanical, approach to the depiction of women. In Chardin's work, they are well covered up, not consciously alluring, often lost in reverie, suggesting a capacity for thought even in the lowly servant class. Sometimes there is a hint that this reverie is erotically charged, as in *The Cellar Boy* and *The Scullery Maid* (1736 and 1738, respectively), designed to face one another as companion pieces. When prints of Chardin's works were sold, verses—added by the engravers—would occasionally draw attention to such possibilities.⁸ The overwhelming impression given by his work, however, is of the satisfaction to be found in labor.

Chardin's early paintings show servants at work: *The Kitchen Maid* (1738) is scraping vegetables and depositing them in a dish of very clean water, but her thoughts are elsewhere as she holds her knife suspended over a turnip and looks into the distance.⁹ *The Young Schoolmistress* (Figure 2.2) may be a servant, an older sister, or a young mother. The painting celebrates the importance of education, a favorite Enlightenment theme, but does so with a suggestion, in the expression on the older girl's face, that teaching a child to read may be frustrating as well as enjoyable. The theme of education occurs so often in Chardin's work that one can only assume that his reverence for the task was sincerely felt. However, the engraver Nicolas-Bernard Lépicié (1735–84) encouraged a very different

FIGURE 2.2 Jean-Baptiste-Siméon Chardin, *The Young Schoolmistress*, c. 1736. London, National Gallery. Required credit: © The National Gallery, London, Bequeathed by Mrs Edith Cragg, as part of the John Webb Bequest, 1925.

interpretation when he added an inscription to his print of the painting. "If this charming child," he wrote, "takes on so well the serious air and imposing manner of a schoolmistress, may one not think that pretence and artifice come to the fair sex no later than birth." The inscription subverts the whole idea of a young woman being engaged in valuable work, representing her instead as one practicing arts which will later enable her to flirt with men.

From the 1740s, Chardin progressed to a higher level of society in the world he represented in his paintings, showing middle-class mothers gently instructing their children in embroidery or the saying of grace before a meal. *Saying Grace* and *The Industrious Mother* (1740) were given by the artist to the king, Louis XV, following their success at the Salon of 1740.[10] The women in both paintings are working on several levels: doing needlework and serving food, but also educating their sons and daughters so that they will grow up into useful, pious citizens like themselves. The creamy brushwork emphasizes the profusion of white linen, underlining the links between cleanliness and godliness. In these paintings, Chardin's attitude seems to be unambiguously approving of the educational role of mothers. It is significant that his seductive portrayals of useful and satisfying work move gradually up the social hierarchy. In the second half of the century, as we shall see, elite portraiture also adopted Voltaire's theme of work as a suitable occupation for the wealthy as well as the poor.

INDUSTRY AND IDLENESS

The importance of industriousness as a virtue in the masculine sphere was emphasized in the same decade, the 1740s, in William Hogarth's popular series of engravings *Industry and Idleness* (1747; Figure 2.3). In his announcement in the press, Hogarth declared that his series was "shewing the Advantage attending the former, and the miserable Effects of the latter."[11] This series illustrates how two apprentices can start from the same humble beginnings—but one rises to be Lord Mayor of London, while the other takes to crime and dies on the gallows. Quotations from the Bible accompany the scenes throughout. The two apprentices begin as weavers, working on large looms. The idle apprentice snoozes, while the industrious apprentice pursues his trade diligently. The message of the series as a whole is that hard work and application can take a poor child up to the apex of the social scale. Idleness, conversely, is presented as the root cause of misfortune, although in this first plate we see some of the other factors involved, notably drunkenness and promiscuity. The idle apprentice (helpfully named as Tom Idle) is accompanied by a tankard of beer, a pipe of tobacco, and an advertisement for *Moll Flanders*, while a cat, symbol of rampant sexual desire, stands on its hind legs to play with his shuttle. Meanwhile, the industrious apprentice (Francis Goodchild) attends diligently to his work. The series became very well known, being used as the basis for sermons and hung in schoolrooms.[12]

The same theme is transferred to a rural setting in George Morland's pair of paintings from around 1790, *The Comforts of Industry* and *The Miseries of Idleness*.[13] The industrious family is placed in a comfortable cottage, with plentiful food and well-maintained clothes.

FIGURE 2.3 William Hogarth, *The Fellow 'Prentices at their Looms, Industry and Idleness*, Plate I, 1747.

The wife's industry is demonstrated by the bright whiteness of her baby's dress and of her own apron, shawl, and bonnet. The idle family, meanwhile, is in a hovel, wearing tattered clothing and with little to eat. As in Hogarth's *Industry and Idleness*, the viewer is given clues to the vices that accompany idleness: the father of the idle family has a pipe, and a tankard and barrel are placed on the floor, while the mother wears a fashionable hat and patterned scarf. The implication is that the poor have only themselves to blame for their situation: with sufficient industry, they would avoid the temptations of drink and vanity and be able to rise to a higher level. Like Hogarth's series, these paintings were reproduced as prints. Reaching a wide audience and extending their influence down the social scale, such images helped to shape the later Victorian idea of the "deserving poor."

Other depictions of the rural poor in late-eighteenth-century England are less straightforwardly didactic, however. Thomas Gainsborough (1727–88) had great success in the 1770s and 1780s with his "cottage door" paintings, such as *The Cottage Door with Children Playing* (1777–8).[14] These pictures show families relaxing at the end of the day outside their cottage homes. The light is soft and the women and children look plump and healthy, so on one level these scenes are idyllic. However, the fathers of the family may be shown staggering home under a heavy burden of faggots, the cottages themselves are tumbledown, and the children's clothes are ragged. The purchasers of such paintings were usually landowners. It seems that the appeal of these paintings lay in a complex blend of sentimental envy and charitable sympathy. The purchasers could hanker after the simple life (and several did take to living in cottages at this period) but at the same time they could feel their sympathies—their sensibility—engaged by the visual evidence of poverty, and could congratulate themselves on their participation in the paternalistic charity that was an accepted part of their social position.

The visual evidence of the poverty of rural laborers was often used as a counterargument to the concerns raised by antislavery campaigners in the late eighteenth and early nineteenth centuries. Apologists for slavery argued that the slaves in the plantations were well looked after by their owner; they were, it was claimed, clothed and fed and had security, unlike many members of the poorer classes in England. The paintings of Agostino Brunias (1730–96), an Italian artist who worked in the Caribbean, depict slaves on the plantations, but he never shows them in the fields. Instead, they are shown dancing and enjoying themselves, or else in the marketplace. *Market Day, Roseau, Dominica* (Figure 2.4) shows mulatto women selling and buying cloth, while darker-skinned slaves sit in the background or in the shadows. The scene looks peaceful, prosperous, and harmonious. Brunias worked for Sir William Young, commissioner and receiver for the sale of lands in Dominica, St. Vincent, and Tobago. His patron was keen to present a favorable image of life on the islands, to encourage investment and counter antislavery propaganda, and Brunias's images were widely circulated in the form of prints.[15] The most degrading and backbreaking work of the period—cutting sugar—did not, therefore, become a subject for art.

Slaves occasionally appear in portraits of their owners, such as those of Dominique and Marguerite Deurbroucq (1753) by Pierre-Bernard Morlot. Dominique is accompanied by a boy in a silver slave-collar, holding a dog, a symbol of fidelity, while his wife is offered sugar by a young woman in an immaculate white dress and headscarf.[16] In such paintings, the health and neatness of their slaves act as a testimony to the presumed care of their master and mistress. Like the cottage door paintings, these images are ambiguous. They may reflect a real sympathy for the slaves on the part of their owners, or they may have functioned as a gratification for their vanity, demonstrating their sensibility along with their wealth.

FIGURE 2.4 Agostino Brunias, *Market Day, Roseau, Dominica*, c. 1780. New Haven, CT, Yale Center for British Art.

THE *ENCYCLOPÉDIE* AND ITS INFLUENCE

One of the most important sources of images of work in the Enlightenment was, of course, the French *Encyclopédie* (1751–72, 1777). The *Encyclopédie* includes many depictions of the mechanical arts, laid out in a diagrammatic way so that the processes can be easily understood. The authors claimed to have respect for craftsmen. As Denis Diderot put it in his article on art: "it is up to the liberal Arts to rescue the mechanical arts from the scorn where prejudice has held them for such a long time."[17] These images have been intensively studied by historians. William H. Sewell, Jr. has compared them with earlier prints and concluded that the workers are represented as "docile automatons" in an "early capitalist utopian vision."[18] Cynthia Koepp is also cynical about Diderot's apparent interest in workers and thinks that it was the machines rather than the human beings operating them that interested him.[19] More recently, Celina Fox has said that they should be judged in the context of the graphic conventions of the day, and that the figures look like manikins because of artistic shortcomings, not sociological manipulation.[20] The *Encyclopédie* plates undoubtedly reflected, and disseminated, an interest in a wide range of working practices, even if the workers themselves were not afforded a great deal of autonomy or individuality.

Geraldine Sheridan has shown that there is much information about women workers to be found in these images, and in the related set of plates, *Descriptions des arts et métiers*, published by the Académie Royale des Sciences between 1761 and 1788.[21] She has identified a corpus of around two hundred images showing women at work, including plates prepared for the *Descriptions* but never actually published. She finds that, in contrast to earlier prints, the figures are represented without caricature, sexual objectification, or Christian moralizing: "the worker is always justified, even dignified by the work itself."[22] These images suggest that women's participation in the artisanal trades was more extensive than we would think from written records alone. They are shown performing both highly skilled and physically demanding tasks.[23]

The format of the *Encyclopédie* depictions of work was taken up by two painters of genre scenes, the Swedish Pehr Hilleström (1732–1816) and the Belgian Léonard Defrance (1735–1805). Hilleström, who studied with Chardin in Paris in 1757–8, painted several pictures of industrial scenes, including *In the Anchor-Forge at Sörderfors: The Smiths Hard at Work* (1782).[24] This is an ambitious work, nearly two meters wide, with many figures in a spacious, dramatic setting. Five men stand in active, muscular poses, their arms raised and their sleeves rolled up, alternating hammer blows as they work on a huge anchor. To the side, a group of well-dressed visitors, including two women, is being shown around the forge by a man in a long blue coat, who is evidently explaining the processes to them. The man in the blue coat is the owner of the forge, Adolf Ulrik Grill, who commissioned the painting in 1782. His companions look as if they could be portraits of specific individuals, but most of the workers have their faces turned away from us. The glow of the furnaces is contrasted with large areas of shadow in the upper part of the painting.

Foundry and forge scenes were popular subjects with painters, because of the potential they offered for dramatic chiaroscuro. Léonard Defrance, a painter who took an active part in revolutionary politics, painted many scenes showing work processes, including a tannery, a tobacco factory, a coal mine, a marble quarry, a forge, a foundry, and a printing workshop. His repertoire obviously suggests an interest in work that was linked to his politics. Indeed, he was so active as a revolutionary that he took part in the destruction of Liège Cathedral in the 1790s. His paintings include a series of four scenes showing a visit to the printing press of his friend Clément Plomteux, painted around 1784, with advertisements for the works of Rousseau, Voltaire, and other philosophes on the walls.[25] In 1778, however, Defrance wrote that he had to paint "night subjects" such as foundries for his patron, the prince-bishop. This was François Charles de Velbruck, the ruler of Liège, who regarded himself as an enlightened prince.[26] The drama of industrialism is particularly evident in Defrance's *Interior of a Foundry* (Figure 2.5), in which the manipulation of the molten metal is presented as a spectacle, witnessed by a fashionable couple and a child. In nearly all Defrance's paintings of work, well-dressed gentlemen and ladies are shown visiting the scenes and taking a great interest in the processes. Unlike Hilleström's painting of the anchor-forge, however, Defrance's pictures are small—cabinet size—rather than monumental. The ladies in his paintings have particularly extravagant hats, perhaps to emphasize the contrast between frivolous fashion and honest toil. The workers, in each case, look vigorous and healthy, and, as in the *Encyclopédie* illustrations, they have little individuality.

There are similar scenes by British painters. In the same decade, the 1780s, the Scottish painter David Allan completed a series of four scenes, in oils, for the 3rd Earl of Hopetoun, showing the stages in the process of converting lead ore from his mines into lead bars.[27] In the first scene, child workers pound lumps of crude lead ore, watched by the earl and his countess. In the second, the ore is washed in a large tub. The final scenes show lead being smelted in a furnace, and then the bars are weighed, watched over by an official who makes sure that every sixth bar goes to the owner. In all four paintings, the workers are anonymous, as they are in the plates of the *Encyclopédie*. Such paintings

FIGURE 2.5 Léonard Defrance, *Interior of a Foundry*, 1789. Liverpool, Required credit: ©National Museums Liverpool, Walker Art Gallery.

demonstrated the patron's enlightened interest in the latest industrial processes, as well as providing reassurance that his workers were in good shape. The boys pounding the lead ore with paddles, for example, look as if they are playing a game, and all the figures are well-dressed. The processes are shown taking place in spacious, airy structures of wood and brick, which look tidy and well-ordered.

In late-eighteenth- and early-nineteenth-century England, the painters Paul Sandby Munn (1773–1845), Philip James de Loutherbourg (1740–1812), Julius Caesar Ibbetson (1759–1817), and J. M. W. Turner (1775–1851) all produced paintings that play on the dramatic chiaroscuro of industrial scenes. Ibbetson's watercolor of *The Iron Forge at Merthyr Tydfil* (1789) is an interior scene, comparable in format to Allan's paintings but without the well-dressed spectators.[28] Here, once again, the artist exploits the potential of the subject for drama: one of the workers casts a giant shadow on the wall, the figures being, in other respects, dwarfed by the carefully drawn machinery. Munn, de Loutherbourg, and Turner all painted industrial landscapes in Coalbrookdale the Shropshire valley in England, which became a major center for the production of iron in the eighteenth century. Turner's early oil painting *A Lime Kiln, Coalbrookdale* (c. 1797) shows the kiln by night, its flames reflected in a pond and transforming spindly trees into eerie silhouettes against the sky.[29] There is more than a hint of the damage done to the natural world by industrial pollution. De Loutherbourg's painting *Coalbrookdale by Night* (1801) depicts the Madeley Wood iron smelting furnaces in the valley, also known as Bedlam furnaces, because the noise of the processes was associated with the activities of a madhouse (the famous Bethlehem Hospital).[30] The warm glow of the furnaces is contrasted with the cold light of the moon; in the foreground, a woman and child pick their way through a landscape littered with sections of cast iron pipes and collars of monstrous proportions. The scene is reminiscent of medieval visions of hell. Munn painted a watercolor from the same viewpoint, *Bedlam Furnace, Madeley Dale, Shropshire* (1803), which shows the scene by day but against an overcast sky that contrasts with the glow of the furnaces.[31] Smoke from the coke hearths spirals into the atmosphere, merging with the dark clouds. All these paintings show effects which were a gift to artists, but their settings in landscapes raise questions about what it was actually like to live in such a place; the cottages of the workers are uncomfortably close to the foundries and it is evident that work, and noise, go on far into the night.

WORK IN THE COUNTRYSIDE: HARVESTERS AND BLACKSMITHS

Questions of individuality and of the effects of industrialization are also raised by two very famous sets of depictions of work, by Joseph Wright of Derby and George Stubbs (Figures 2.6 and 2.7). Both are set in the countryside rather than in the new industrial towns. Wright's blacksmiths' shops and iron forges led to him being hailed by Francis Klingender in 1947 as "the first professional painter directly to express the spirit of the industrial revolution," though this characterization is now seen to be problematic since the processes he depicts were not particularly new.[32] The first of these paintings, *The Blacksmith's Shop* (Figure 2.6), was exhibited and engraved in 1771. The blacksmiths are shown working by night in a ruined building, presumably a church or abbey since there is a carving of an angel on the spandrel above them. Their vigorous movements have attracted much praise. Recently, Celina Fox has written that Wright "invests these men with expressions of concentrated intelligence and monumentalizes a moment when honed skill and judgement are required to accomplish successfully as a team a complex and mutually dependent series of action," while the setting is "surely intended to emphasize the spiritual dimension of labour."[33] The muscular arms and rolled-up sleeves of the principal figures strike a new note in depictions of work, and probably influenced, directly or indirectly, many later depictions of the worker as hero, from Ford Madox Brown's *Work* (1852–65) to nineteenth-century trade union banners and twentieth-century Soviet posters.[34] The print after *The Blacksmith's Shop* may also have been known to Hilleström and Defrance, whose industrial scenes date from a decade or so later.

However, Wright's first idea for the painting, recorded in his account book, is headed "Subjects for Night Pieces," and specifies the sources of light—the bar of iron, the moon, and a candle. He does not seem to have set out to glorify work; indeed, his only specific thoughts about the figures of the blacksmiths concern an "Idle fellow." Instead, he appears to have been thinking mainly about the chiaroscuro effects and the way he can use a narrative to justify them:

> A Blacksmiths Shop—Two men forming a Bar of Iron into a horseshoe—from whence the light must proceed. An Idle fellow may stand by the Anvil, in a time killing posture, his hands in his bosom, or yawning with his hands stretched upwards, & a little twisting of the Body. Horse shoes hanging upon ye walls, and other necessary things, faintly seen being remote from the light—Out of this Room, shall be seen another, in wch. a ffarier [*sic*] may be shoeing a horse by the light of

a Candle. The horse must be sadled [sic] and a Traveller standing by The Servant may appear with his horse in his hand—on wch. may be a portmanteau—This will be an indication of an Accident having happen'd, & shew some reason for shoeing the horse by CandleLight—The Moon may appear and illumine some part of the horses if necessary.[35]

The ecclesiastical details may have been prompted primarily by Wright's desire to show the three light sources, so that a ruin was needed, and an abbey would be a plausible ruin.

FIGURE 2.6 Joseph Wright of Derby, *The Blacksmith's Shop*, 1771. New Haven, CT, Yale Center for British Art.

The old man seated to the side on the right, apparently lost in thought, may be one of the travellers who has taken shelter in the forge.

Since Klingender's time, many scholars have pointed out that blacksmith's shops are hardly indicative of the Industrial Revolution, since they had existed for centuries and the figures are using traditional methods. Two slightly later paintings by Wright depict iron forges with tilt hammers in action, but even these were not particularly new devices. Significantly, both paintings of iron forges include a figure who could be construed as an "idle fellow." There is a man with "his hands in his bosom" in the *Iron Forge* of 1772 (now in the collection of Lord Romsey), while a man slouches, with his back to the wall, in *An Iron Forge from Without* (1773).[36] Wright may have been thinking of Hogarth's industrious and idle apprentices, and intending to make a contrast between industry and idleness. It is tempting to assume that the paintings would have appealed to the rising middle classes—and the buyers of the prints may indeed have come from this section of society—but three of the four paintings were bought by the traditional aristocracy. Lord Melbourne purchased *The Blacksmith's Shop*; one of the iron forge paintings was sold to Lord Palmerston, the other to Empress Catherine the Great of Russia.[37] Catherine was a reader of the *Encyclopédie* and was keen to promote industrial development in her own country. As in the cases of the Earl of Hopetoun, François Charles de Velbruck, and Adolf Ulrik Grill, these industrial genre scenes were either commissioned or purchased after completion by patrons who were taking an active role in exploiting, or encouraging, the kinds of processes they depicted.

Workers look somewhat less heroic in the depictions of reaping and haymaking by George Stubbs (1724–1806), who is otherwise known mainly for his depictions of horses and jockeys. These paintings show traditional processes, unchanged by the agricultural and industrial revolutions, and familiar to their contemporary viewers from pastoral poetry as well as from actual observation in the countryside. In all, seven harvesting paintings by Stubbs are known: two pairs of oil paintings, dated 1783 and 1785, and three enamels, from 1794 to 1795. Stubbs also produced mezzotints, based on the first versions of the scenes, but these are rare, suggesting that they were not commercially successful. In the oil paintings, reaping and haymaking are contrasted, but it seems that the haymaking scenes were more popular, since two of the enamels are of this subject and only one of reapers.[38] These paintings are all particularly beautiful, but they have puzzled modern art historians since the workers are suspiciously clean, fashionably dressed, and apparently untouched by the dirty and strenuous aspects of their labors. They are typical of the artist, however. Stubbs was a meticulous painter and experimented with enamel colors so that he could achieve an even smoother finish for his paintings: rags, mud, and dust would have held no aesthetic appeal for him. His horses and jockeys are similarly immaculate. Stubbs gradually refined his compositions in the course of painting the series of reapers and haymakers, creating harmonious rhythms and proportional relationships that are very satisfying to the eye.

The last of the enamels, *Reapers* (Figure 2.7), has the workers lined up like characters in a play, looking respectfully towards the mounted overseer. The three male laborers are cutting the crop and setting up the sheaves, while the woman has the lighter job of making straw ropes to bind them. The placing of the church spire in the center of the composition suggests divine approval for the class relationship depicted in the painting, as well as referring to the customary thanks given to God for the harvest. Costume is carefully observed. The woman on the far left wears a splendid hat but also has arm protectors and an apron; the men wear buckled shoes and their breeches are neatly buttoned. Although

FIGURE 2.7 George Stubbs, *Reapers*, 1795. New Haven, CT, Yale Center for British Art.

they cut the wheat with a sickle, the stubble is very short, suggesting, rather, that it has been cut with a scythe. The overall effect is, therefore, contrived rather than realistic. On the other hand, the laborers have specific and contrasting features and could almost be portraits of known individuals.[39]

Several other British artists depicted agricultural workers in the fields in the closing decades of the eighteenth century, but they are often shown resting rather than working: sheltering from a storm, as in Richard Westall's *A Storm in Harvest* (1796), or enjoying a lunch break, as in Francis Wheatley's *Noon* (1799).[40] In this case, it is not idleness that is shown but an acceptable period of rest in the midst of labor. Even in the early nineteenth century, when a new vogue for naturalism and open-air study stimulated many artists to paint convincing harvest scenes, the actual work often goes on in the background, while the foreground focus is on resting groups. Peter De Wint's large *Cornfield* of 1815 is a good example of this tendency: raking, gleaning, and stacking of corn are evident in the middle and far distance, but the family group of laborers in the foreground is sitting among the sheaves eating a meal.[41] The emphasis on rest and relaxation is a traditional feature of the pastoral poetry from which many artists drew their inspiration. James Thomson's poem *The Seasons* (1746) was a particular favorite. Thomson describes haymaking and reaping, but he makes hard work sound more like play:

Before the ripen'd field the reapers stand,
In fair array; each by the lass he loves,

To bear the rougher part, and mitigate
By nameless gentle offices her toil.
At once they stop and swell the lusty sheaves;
While thro' their cheerful band the rural talk,
The rural scandal, and the rural jest,
Fly harmless, to deceive the tedious time,
And steal unfelt the sultry hours away.[42]

This passage follows on from a long hymn to the blessings of "industry," which provides "whate'er / Exalts, embellished, and renders life / Delightful" (lines 141–3).[43]

Similarly, in a less widely read poem, *The Fleece* (1757), John Dyer praised industry "which dignifies the artist, lifts the swain, / And the straw cottage to a place turns." Before the principle was stated definitively by Adam Smith, Dyer was confident that industry was the source of a nation's wealth: it is, he claimed, "chief by numbers of industrious hands / A nation's wealth is counted."[44] Both Wright's blacksmiths and Stubbs' reapers represent pleasing images of the "industrious hands" that were seen as creating national prosperity.

WOMEN AND CHILDREN AT WORK: FANCY PICTURES OF THE LATER EIGHTEENTH CENTURY

In visual depictions, women workers are often prettified and eroticized. In the later eighteenth century, paintings and prints of female street sellers, milkmaids, and domestic servants were popular as so-called "fancy pictures," and often amounted to little more than an excuse to show an attractive woman, presumably one who in real life would be sexually available to the elite patron. The most reproduced plates in Francis Wheatley's popular series *The Cries of London* (1790s) were those representing women—such as the milkmaid, the strawberry seller, the match seller, the primrose seller. As Isabelle Baudino has commented, these images deny the practical realities of women's work, removing all references to poverty and destitution. The women are shown as impeccably and elegantly dressed, with fashionable hairdos and flawless complexions.[45] They have a delicate prettiness, hardly convincing in the light of their outdoor occupation and their presence on the street, and their slender arms look incapable of carrying the loads they are depicted with—the heavy baskets of fruit or substantial milk churns. Wheatley's images are part of the long tradition of depictions of street sellers, exemplified in France by the *Cris de Paris*, studied by Vincent Milliot.[46] In Wheatley's hands, as in the *Cris de Paris*, they are given an almost explicitly erotic charge.

The same is true of many genre paintings of domestic servants. In sharp contrast to Chardin's modestly dressed servants, the young woman represented in Henry Morland's *Laundry Maid Ironing* (Figure 2.8) is clearly meant to be sexually attractive: she wears a low-cut gown, and her soft, pale hands and arms show no evidence of the redness and soreness that would have been the inevitable accompaniments of eighteenth-century methods of doing laundry. Her clothing is also, surely, too fine for a servant, though contemporary accounts make it clear that servant girls of the time—especially in wealthy households—liked to keep up with fashion. Like Wheatley's prints, this painting was very successful commercially. One of a pair, no fewer than five versions were exhibited during

FIGURE 2.8 Henry Morland, *A Laundry Maid Ironing*, c. 1765–82. London, required credit: ©Tate, London 2017.

Morland's lifetime, and the paintings were also reproduced as mezzotints in 1769.[47] The figure in the companion picture, *Lady's Maid Soaping Linen*, is even more explicitly alluring: she looks up from her work to direct an inviting glance towards the viewer, a slight smile on her pretty face.

Child workers, too, were commemorated in fancy pictures. Sir Joshua Reynolds' *Strawberry Girl* (1772–3) represents a very young girl who is selling strawberries on the street.[48] The title of the painting may imply that she is working in Strawberry Gardens, a popular leisure resort where it would have been impossible to retain her innocence for long. John Russell's pastel painting *Love Songs and Matches* (1793) is similarly ambiguous in its appeal: a beautiful young boy is holding up a love song alongside his basket of matches, wearing tattered clothes and accompanied by his begging dog.[49] For such children to have to support themselves by working in the street implies severe poverty and deprivation: they have presumably been orphaned or abandoned by their parents, and they all were too likely to be tempted into theft or prostitution.[50] It is not at all clear whether the buyer or viewer is meant to be stimulated to charitable activity by such works, or simply to find them alluring.

PORTRAITURE: MEN AND WOMEN AT WORK

The fancy pictures were not meant to be identifiable individuals, though they were often drawn from specific models. Another phenomenon of the later eighteenth century was the vogue for portraits of domestic servants. These reflect the new value placed on work, combined with an awareness of the need for loyalty. The latter was especially important at a time when revolutionary activity made employers aware of the potential dangers of having servants living in their houses: they might betray or blackmail their masters and mistresses or even (since they had control of the food supply) poison them. Giles Waterfield and Anne French note that early examples by the Swedish court painter David von Ehrenstahl (1628–98) suggest that it may be legitimate to associate likenesses of servants with the work ethic of Protestant countries.[51] Supporting evidence for this interpretation comes from the unique painting of his servants by the staunchly Protestant William Hogarth. This painting, now entitled *Heads of Six of Hogarth's Servants* (c. 1750–5), was probably made with a practical purpose in mind: to demonstrate his skills to patrons who came to his studio considering a portrait commission.[52] Nevertheless, there is no mistaking the human sympathy and understanding of individual character that it projects. Although there is no record of their names, the painting testifies to Hogarth's affection for his servants. Later in the century, there are major cycles of portraits of the servants of great houses in England. In 1783, the Duke of Dorset commissioned a set of forty-six miniature portraits of the servants at Knole, of which twenty-one now survive. The artist Arnold Almond has presented his sitters as fashionable and respectable. In the 1790s, the Yorke family at Erddig began commissioning portraits of their servants, each one accompanied by a verse composed by the master of the house. The first seven—including portraits of a gamekeeper, a blacksmith, and a housemaid—were painted by a local artist, Jon Walters of Denbigh, between 1791 and 1793, while Philip Yorke I composed the verses. The tradition continued at Erddig into the twentieth century.[53]

The portraits of elite sitters in this period also show a growing respect for the moral value of work. It was still most common for sitters to be represented as gentlemen or ladies, in fine clothes, striking a pose, and surrounded by evidence of their wealth and social position. Nevertheless, there are some notable portraits that show wealthy sitters engaged in some form of work. Authors were represented in the act of writing, such as Denis Diderot in his portrait by Louis Michel van Loo (1767); actors and actresses were shown in character, acting a part on stage.[54] The French chemist and discoverer of the role of oxygen in combustion, Antoine-Laurent de Lavoisier, was a nobleman, but he was depicted by Jacques-Louis David surrounded by instruments, including a barometer, a geometer, a water still, and a bell jar (1788).[55] He, too, is caught in the act of writing, pausing only briefly from his researches to look up at his wife, Marie-Anne Paulze Lavoisier, who was his assistant and contributed to his work.

Women were typically shown engaged in some form of needlework. Sir Joshua Reynolds' portrait of *Anne, Countess of Albemarle* shows her knotting (1757–60), while *Mary, Duchess of Richmond* (1758–60) is depicted bending over a circular tambour frame, intent on her embroidery.[56] The unidentified lady in Joseph Wright of Derby's *Portrait of a Woman* (c. 1770) proudly displays the filet lace that she has been making: she is holding two netting shuttles, and her scissors and workbag lie on the table beside her.[57] Even Madame de Pompadour, the flamboyant mistress of King Louis XV of France, was depicted working at embroidery. François-Hubert Drouais' *Madame de Pompadour at her Tambour Frame* (1763–4) shows her in the last year of her life.[58] She is wearing a lavishly embroidered dress, liberally supplied with lace, bows, and ribbons; but she is doing some form of needlework, though the angle of the frame means that we cannot see what she is making. This portrait of Madame de Pompadour is very different from the earlier pastel (1752–5) of her by Maurice Quentin de la Tour in which she is shown as a patron of the arts.[59] In Drouais' portrait, instead of amusing herself in a dilettante fashion with literature and art, she is involved in useful work, like Voltaire's Pacquette.

Such examples may well have been known to John Singleton Copley when he painted *Mr. and Mrs. Thomas Mifflin* in 1773 (Figure 2.9). This portrait of the man who was later to become the quartermaster general of the revolutionary army and the governor of Pennsylvania, with his wife, might seem to be the perfect expression of American values. The harsh lighting and direct gaze of Mrs. Mifflin suggest honesty and sincerity, while the composition implies a marriage of equals. The prominence given to the fringe loom and the accuracy with which it is portrayed demonstrate respect for the moral value of work. Nevertheless, the different roles of husband and wife, he with his book and she with her handiwork, are very much in line with the gendered division of labor expressed in the European art of the time.

Occasionally we find artists giving non elite working people the lavish attention that was normally reserved for elite portraits. Johann Zoffany's portrait of *John Cuff and his Assistant* (Figure 2.10) was painted just one year earlier than the Mifflin portrait. It was exhibited at the Royal Academy in London in 1772 entitled "An Optician, with his Attendant," and it seems that it was bought by Lord Grosvenor for the large sum of £200, passing, by the early nineteenth century, into the collection of King George III. It is remarkable in the respect it shows for the skill of the elderly John Cuff, shown here in the act of polishing a lens, perhaps for a microscope, watched by his equally elderly assistant. Cuff was renowned as a maker of optical instruments, and he was patronized by the king, who had invited him to watch the transit of Venus from his newly constructed observatory in the Old Deer Park, Richmond, England, in June 1769, and supplied him with the tools of his trade in the last years of his life. Zoffany probably painted Cuff in the year of his death, but it is not known whether the portrait is a posthumous one. It has been suggested that the artist planned the picture as a memorial to a vanishing world, the world of the preindustrial craft workshop. Certainly, these two men in their beautifully tidy workshop look like relics of the past. It is known that Cuff struggled financially in the latter years of his life as large workshops offered stiff competition, although their economies of scale were regarded as going hand in hand with a decline in quality.[60] Like the servant portraits and the depictions of industrial scenes by Hilleström, Defrance, and Allan in the 1780s, the painting celebrates the skills of the artisan, but also the implied benevolence of those who employ him.

FIGURE 2.9 John Singleton Copley, *Portrait of Mr. and Mrs. Thomas Mifflin*, 1773. Philadelphia Museum of Art. 125th Anniversary Acquisition. Bequest of Mrs. Esther F. Wistar to The Historical Society of Pennsylvania in 1900, and acquired by the Philadelphia Museum of Art by mutual agreement with the Society through the generosity of Mr. and Mrs. Fitz Eugene Dixon, Jr., and significant contributions from Stephanie S. Eglin, and other donors to the Philadelphia Museum of Art, as well as the George W. Elkins Fund and the W. P. Wilstach Fund, and through the generosity of Maxine and Howard H. Lewis to the Historical Society of Pennsylvania, 1999 Accession number EW1999-45-1.

FIGURE 2.10 Johann Zoffany, *John Cuff*, 1772. Royal Collection Trust.

CONCLUSION

Voltaire's characterization of work as the antidote to poverty, vice, and boredom finds many echoes in the visual images of the period. The interest taken in work processes, evident in the paintings by Hilleström, Defrance, Allan, Wright, and Stubbs, demonstrates the role of work as an antidote to boredom. This is further emphasized in the portraits of the wealthy engaged in some form of useful activity. The contrast between industry and idleness, a theme that is stated most explicitly by Hogarth, shows work as the enemy of vice and the remedy for poverty. Hogarth's industrious apprentice Francis Goodchild is an unconvincing stereotype, but the portrait of his servants—and the illustrations to this chapter of paintings by Ceruti, Wright, Stubbs, and Zoffany—shows that artists could also achieve a recognition of the humanity of the workers that occasionally gave them real dignity and individuality.

It would be wrong, however, to take these images as proof of a new egalitarianism. In the contexts within which the paintings were displayed, commissioned, and bought, they could act as reminders of the efforts of the wealthy rather than the poor, the factory owners rather than those who toiled in them, the benefactors rather than the recipients of charity. Ceruti's lacemakers may have functioned as a celebration of the charitable activities of its patron, just as Zoffany's portrait of Cuff was a reference to the patronage of George III. The rigid divisions of the social hierarchy and the gendered division of labor are very evident in the images. Even in paintings by the revolutionary sympathizer Defrance it is clear who are the workers and who are the elite visitors. This assertion of the social hierarchy is at its most explicit in Stubbs' *Reapers*, in which the farmer or overseer sits on his sleek horse, raised physically above his workers. The images also conform to traditional ideas about designated roles for women, whether they are shown with modesty by Chardin, Copley, and Stubbs, or as objects of sexual desire by Wheatley and Henry Morland.

The images of work produced during the later seventeenth and eighteenth centuries generally represented it in a positive light. By the end of the eighteenth century there are the first hints of a recognition of the darker side of industrial development, not only in the landscapes by Turner, Munn, and Ibbetson, but also in the images of the *Chimney Sweep* and of *London* in William Blake's *Songs of Innocence* (1794). Early in the new century, in 1804, Blake coined his memorable phrase "these dark Satanic Mills" in his *Preface to Milton: A Poem*. Although scholars argue that this phrase may refer instead to the universities or the churches of Blake's time, in popular belief it sums up the exploitative nature of early industrial development, with its attendant evils of child labor, urban overcrowding, and miserable poverty. In the nineteenth century, the worker was to become a symbol of the inhumanity of man to man, downtrodden and neglected. For the artists discussed in this chapter, however, work was a visual spectacle, well worth visiting and watching, as well as a guarantee of virtue and a route to prosperity.

CHAPTER THREE

Work and Workplaces

EMMA HART

Once upon a time, the Age of Enlightenment was considered a golden age of the workplace. Conditions in such spaces had improved over the poverty and grime of the medieval era. This was a time in which people were increasingly well-fed, and workers followed an independent and leisurely existence, striving in small workplaces that were often integrated into the family home. With the full demands of a capitalist time and wage regime not yet having taken hold, workers were not required to labor in accordance with someone else's demands. Skilled artisans took pride in their output, controlling their own work rates and laboring in spaces that were pleasant, restful, and situated in tight-knit communities. A widespread commitment to the "common good" ensured the continuity of working conditions and prices, protecting this idyllic lifestyle and preserving the small workshop or the family farm. It was only from the 1780s onwards, when conditions declined with the onset of the Industrial Revolution, that this workers' paradise was shattered by the profiteering ambitions of merchant-manufacturers and improving landed aristocrats, who cruelly severed the obligations of the moral economy to dispossess workers of independence in the name of their own personal fortunes.

This is, of course, a caricature of historical opinion about the economic and social transition that took place in the decades between 1650 and 1800. Certainly, such a chiaroscuro portrait omits the subtleties of both historical experience and current scholarship; yet it nevertheless highlights the lasting popularity of a particular narrative of early modern work.[1] This was a narrative in which workplaces, moreover, had a special part to play as a great deal of change centered on the physical relocation of workers that was part and parcel of the move from household production to factory output, from tenant farmer to field hand. The rhetoric argued that the artisan who had produced bespoke metal wares in his own forge was now reduced to repetitive waged labor in a nail factory he did not own. The tenant farmer and his family who enjoyed the protection of a patriarchal landowner were now at the mercy of a master preoccupied with "improving" his estate. Whereas the workplace had formerly been a secure, and even homely, environment, it was now a site of uncertainty, stress, and overwork.[2]

The major achievement of the last thirty years of historical scholarship, however, is that this "light to dark" narrative has been substantively challenged. Accompanying a shift to the idea of an "industrial evolution" as opposed to an industrial revolution, historians have settled on a much more complex, and contingent, story of economic change. This story incorporates not only new perspectives on the transition between the preindustrial and the industrial, but also some serious rethinking of what both states involved. The transition, historians now argue, took place over a much longer period and was patchy across different work settings. Furthermore, "preindustrial" workplaces governed by guilds, or regulated by reciprocal community relations, were not always the benign environments that scholars previously believed them to be. At the same time, an "industrialized" workplace came in many different guises—the factory only being one of them.[3] Heightened interest in the Atlantic stage of interaction has further broadened our horizons, and here we must incorporate those workplaces located in the cities, mines, and farms created by European colonists, as well as the sites inhabited by indigenous Americans.[4]

This chapter documents the nature of the workplace in this era—an era, therefore, that incorporated many changes but not one that involved a total transformation. As Keith Wrightson has highlighted in his survey of British economic life in this period, while it "bore the face of a commercial civilisation, it remained still a mixture of forms, structurally, geographically, culturally and in its congeries of social identities, shot through with ambiguities and inconsistencies."[5] People's economic lives simultaneously embraced new structures and practices while still proceeding within familiar places, hierarchies, and cherished traditions. These shifts spanned not only Europe, but across some of Europe's American colonies too. These were changes, moreover, that took place within the context of the family economy—the productive unit formed by husbands, wives, children, and other household dependents.[6]

This chapter explores these subtle changes in the physical characteristics and the location of the workplace in this era of industrial evolution and increasingly commercialized agriculture. Urban and rural spaces, as scholars from a variety of disciplinary backgrounds have shown, were not simply backdrops to working lives but were vital in shaping work practices and defining the relationship between the individual, the family, and the larger community. Although this relationship shifted dramatically for some workers, for others it altered only marginally, as did the character of their workplaces. This chapter surveys this variety by discussing a sequence of workplaces in turn, beginning with those that saw relatively incidental change and ending with labor settings that were almost entirely novel. Thus, while this story begins and ends with agricultural labor—visiting first the European farmer and last the American plantation—the narrative departs from the familiar setting of European agriculture, marked by centuries-old field boundaries and customary rights, and ends up in the tropical heat, hard labor, and deadly conditions of the Caribbean sugar plantation.

Grounding our exploration in the settings of early modern work will not only allow us to better immerse ourselves in what it was like to labor in spaces that are unfamiliar to the twenty-first-century office worker, but also to draw some conclusions about the larger forces that shaped them in the age of Enlightenment. Perhaps most importantly, the core dynamic that we will repeatedly encounter is between the family and the workspace. While in Europe economic change reconfigured certain aspects of the relationship between domestic and work settings, colonization definitively wrenched the family home from its customary position as the principal unit of production.

ON THE FARM

The vast majority of early modern Europeans and Americans lived in a rural setting. Even in the most urbanized societies of Britain and the Netherlands, no more than a third of the population lived in towns by 1800.[7] Hence, the majority of families labored in the house, in outbuildings, and in the fields to achieve a subsistence. The location of their labor depended on its purpose, and consequently, the rural workplace was heavily gendered. While men spent more time outside, women worked in and around the farmhouse, applying themselves not only to agricultural activities, but also to proto industrial tasks such as spinning, weaving, and finishing fabric.

The setting of the European family farm was itself characterized by variety, a variety that only increased with European New World expansion and the capitalization of farming that occurred (unevenly) in Europe itself. Probably the most important influence on the farming experience was the wealth of the farming family. From peasant laborer, to tenant, to yeoman, and to gentry landowner, the working environment differed significantly. These contrasts increased still further with the expansion of the Atlantic world, where tenancy continued to exist but at much lower levels than in Europe. In the "old" world, tenant farmers and rural laborers would often have to work small, nonadjacent plots of land, held on a complex array of different leases. With not enough acreage to support a family, some French peasants would labor for part of the year in Paris, returning home only for the spring sowing on their tiny plot.[8] The contrasts between these farmers and their New World brethren were enormous. Benjamin Franklin promised that immigrants to his native Pennsylvania could live in "general happy mediocrity," and even in the 1760s no more than a quarter of the colony's farmers were tenants and average farm size stood at 125 acres, easily enough to feed a family and produce a profitable surplus.[9]

Across Europe and its Atlantic colonies, elite farmers and planters enjoyed estates that stretched further than the eye could see. Henry Laurens, a South Carolinian signer of the Declaration of Independence, is an excellent case in point. Laurens owned four plantations and a town house. One of his plantations—closest to Charleston—was a genteel rural retreat, equipped with a lavish house. The other three were "slave labor camps" as Max Edelson has called them. Laurens hardly visited these places, which were supervised by white managers and designed to produce as much rice and indigo as possible. Laurens was thus a farmer, but the setting of his work barely resembled that of his tenant farmer contemporaries. Indeed, his experiences much more closely matched those of Europe's landed aristocracy, who enjoyed political influence and the *beau monde* in London and Paris, while managers and tenants cultivated their estates.[10]

Henry Laurens' absence from some of his farms was partly down to the large distances that separated them from his home base in the coastal town of Charleston. These were remote locations situated on the frontier of European colonization, and in close proximity to those indigenous Americans who already inhabited the region. The enslaved people and white managers who lived there permanently were severely isolated by their distance from the next plantation. This was a level of remoteness that was only approximately replicated in a few upland European settings; the Northumberland sheep farmer, the Highland cattle man, and the resident of the Alpine *Alm* operated in extremely rural situations that were nevertheless in closer reach of a village. Elsewhere, however, the capitalization of farming and decreasing farm size—at least in countries without primogeniture—meant that farms became significantly less remote. Around large cities, the ring of market gardens became ever larger as greater quantities of food were required to feed inhabitants. Already by the middle of the eighteenth century, sophisticated networks had developed linking Kent, "the garden of England," to London. Kentish boatmen doubled as middlemen and creditors, connecting produce and grain farmers with the London merchants who distributed the food to the capital's residents.[11]

However, it would be erroneous to assess the settings of early modern farm work using the yardstick of agriculture—fields, orchards, and pastures—alone. In the first instance, women's work often took place around and inside the farmhouse, and often did not involve laboring outdoors for long periods of time. Indeed, field work was considered unsuitable for European women, while during the seventeenth century the presence of enslaved African women in American fields was already becoming a key indicator of their inferior status. Instead, European women often combined work in the dairy, or the chicken coop, with industrial production of cloth, yarn, or lace.[12] Across the early modern era, the relationship between these aspects of women's work and their function within the broader farm economy has prompted much historical debate. Debates concerning the nature and larger economic impact of this process have been lengthy and complex, but when it comes to the issue of the workplace, the consequences are quite clear, and are again gendered. The introduction of the option of putting-out work turned the farm house also into a place of production—of spinning, weaving, and finishing, and even of assembling clocks and making straw hats. For the most part, this shift did not represent a process by which women were "freed" from the drudgery of heavy agricultural labor. Rather, it represented a gradual reallocation of labor resources in the farming family; one that kept women working in and around the house. As part of this reallocation of family labor resources, women often had a limited choice as to whether to engage in proto industrial work or to stick with their agricultural tasks. Officials returned single women in the Black Forest (southwest Germany) who went to work for wages as spinners in other people's homes to their family home or told them to marry. Women's work in the weaving industry, moreover, was heavily regulated by the guild masters of the New Draperies guild. In northern France, female householders' clothmaking activities were dictated by the vicissitudes of the rural economy.[13] Once again, the American setting does provide some contrast here. As Adrienne Hood has shown, proto industrial cloth production on Pennsylvania's farms transferred across the Atlantic, but since weaving was still profitable men dominated cloth production. This, along with the absence of institutions that sought to keep women firmly in their place, meant that for American farm women the shift between different types of work was less complicated.[14] However, enduring European gender conventions ensured that the woman farm manager was as yet a fictional character.

In sum, in the rural workplace the age of Enlightenment saw subtle shifts in character as a result of enclosure, marketization of agriculture, imperial expansion, and proto industrialization. For many of the families who occupied these rural spaces, though, these changes were more a game of "musical chairs" rather than a fundamental workplace revolution. The family endured as the main unit of labor, except in certain parts of the New World. Commercialization affected the setting of the farm—consolidating it and making it smaller or larger—but it did not fundamentally shift gender roles within the family unit. Indeed, it was in the farming family that we can most clearly detect the logic of Jan de Vries' industrious revolution, a revolution in which more people worked for wages, resulting in a resource reallocation that nevertheless took place in a setting that remained fundamentally similar.

IN THE ARTISAN WORKSHOP

As tethered as rural folk were to their farm houses and fields, which formed both a productive household unit and a family home, urban manufacturers were tied to their workbenches and workshops, which were also more often than not attached to their family residence. Indeed, historians have frequently illustrated the contrast between rural and urban work by placing the farmer and artisan in opposition to each other. Where the farmer was more likely to remain part of a subsistence economy, his work changing according to a seasonal rhythm, the artisan more quickly became drawn into the urban capitalist economy, living in a monetized society and working for profit. However, just as farm work became connected to proto industrialization as the farmhouse turned manufactory, so the relationship between home and work became more expansive in the city, where early industrialization and a consumer economy ushered in change. Some artisans like Nehemiah Wallington, the Godly City of London turner who wrote copiously about his religion and work, still labored in a small shop attached to their family home, with perhaps an apprentice or two to assist them, and a wife at the counter out front, selling bespoke and ready-made products (Figure 3.1).[15] Yet this situation became rarer, especially in the English-speaking world. There, while home and work did not become completely separated, the relationship between the two became considerably more complex as artisans created new types of workshop economies to produce consumer goods, and to incorporate innovative production methods and exotic materials into their wares.

The division of labor in the pinmaking industry, so famously described by Adam Smith in his *Wealth of Nations*, was not so widespread in the eighteenth century, but in the urban factories of the leading industrialists, new production techniques and increased outputs were achieved through innovative workplace design.[16] A good case in point were the "factories" established by leading makers of the new decorative ceramics and metal wares that cluttered the mantelpiece of many an elite and middling drawing room by the end of the eighteenth century. The industrial work–living complexes established by English entrepreneurs such as Josiah Wedgwood and Matthew Boulton during the 1760s significantly reconfigured the relationship between the worker, the family, and the workplace. Their newly built compounds included a large central building—in the style of Boulton's Soho Works, which stood at the edge of Birmingham. Within this edifice, workers applied themselves to all aspects of production, sending out large quantities

FIGURE 3.1 *Candlemakers' Workshop*. In Denis Diderot and Jean le Rond d'Alembert, *Encyclopédie, ou dictionnaire raisonné des sciences, des arts et des métiers*, 1751–72. Courtesy of the Wellcome Trust.

of standardized decorative wares for domestic and overseas consumption. Wedgwood's Etruria, completed in 1769, also incorporated housing for his employees. In favoring this arrangement, the potter pioneered the industrial village that would be replicated elsewhere across a variety of industries—New Lanark near Glasgow being one of the earliest examples.[17]

Such workplace arrangements remained rather extraordinary before 1800, however. As John Smail has documented among the cloth workers of Halifax, England, even when the scale of production started to increase at the beginning of the eighteenth century, the process of leaving behind an artisanal culture, in which the family home and members of that family were the basis of production, was slow and hesitating.[18] Those weavers who owned more than one loom and were involved in putting out cloth to cottagers for production still shared neighborhoods, and accommodated looms and spinning wheels within their homes, in the same way as their poorer counterparts. In Sweden, iron production was not increased by the construction of factories but by the more intensive supervision of peasants, who remained the commodity's principal manufacturers until the nineteenth century.[19]

Thus the 1700s witnessed the emergence of a wider range of relationships among work, family, and home when it came to industrial production. The sheer variety of these connections has been a chief discovery of historians of the last decades who have argued for the Industrial Revolution as a slower and more contingent process. Between the poles of Josiah Wedgwood and the Swedish ironmaking peasant, historians therefore now recognize various configurations of workshop networks, in which small producers worked together from homes and small factories scattered throughout towns. In Birmingham, Boulton's Soho Works was an unusual landmark in an industrial landscape that otherwise consisted of networks of workshops, linked together by the cooperation of master artisans in different branches of metal working trades to produce large quantities of buttons and "toys." Similar networks sprang up among London cabinet makers and Sheffield cutlers, while also transferring on a smaller scale to Britain's American colonies.[20] In France, meanwhile, the silk industry of Lyon functioned using a comparable structure. Silk masters presided over thousands of waged workers, who labored in their homes in the various tasks required to produce the fabric for which the city was so renowned.[21] While these workplaces did not completely represent a break between the home, family, and work, they nevertheless were part of a gradual process in which manufacturing inched away from a domestic setting and into a purely industrial one.

Almost without exception, the workers affected by these changes were wealthier male artisans and their families, who succeeded in building up capital and becoming employers of multiple journeymen and laborers. Often these men came from families who could afford to pay the higher fees demanded by those tradesmen working in industries with a high profit potential. As such, these changes in the industrial workplace were strongly structured by both gender and class. Single women were confined to less profitable trades, such as millinery and haberdashery, or were recruited as waged laborers in the emerging cotton industry. The increasing number of retail shops offering these consumer durables and groceries for sale added to the gendered character of urban workplaces. As Daniel Defoe argued, in his *Complete English Tradesman*, it was advisable for wives to know their husband's business so that they could continue in trade if disaster befell the spouse. However, the era witnessed the emergence of a rhetoric arguing that the shop was not a respectable place for women to be seen at work. Indeed, Defoe wrote, "it would be ridiculous for the women to appear" as workers in the shops of most traders who sold consumer goods, including drapers, mercers, and booksellers. Nevertheless, women still frequently defied such efforts to keep them out of the shop, remaining a vital presence in retailing spaces during this era.[22]

Such considerations, however, were peripheral to poorer families working in the emerging luxury trades that were commonly subject to the whims of fashion. Often, such workers struggled to find a consistent market for their products and slipped into debt. As Julie Hardwick has shown in her study of poor working families in the French cities of Lyon and Nantes, the creditors were often the cause of family breakdown, swooping in to claim unpaid bills, bringing business to a halt, and forcing marginal families out of their home and workplace into total destitution.[23] Thus, in the urban workshop economy, a continuing entanglement between house and workshop increasingly signified poverty in working cultures where success translated into the separation of these key units.

WORKING TO SUPPLY THE URBAN MARKETPLACE

These burgeoning workshop economies were partly responsible for the urban growth that characterized many societies across the early modern western world. Among the most urbanized nations were Britain and the Netherlands, where around 30 percent of people lived in towns by 1800. City life was also transplanted to the New World, with New York, Mexico City, and Rio de Janeiro among the major emerging conurbations of this era. While manufacturing occupied one segment of the urban population, feeding the town's inhabitants preoccupied a second major group of people, who traded in the marketplace. In these commercial spaces, retailers gathered to sell food and manufactures that they had raised, grown, or cooked either within the city limits or in the surrounding countryside (Figure 3.2). As cities grew, markets became larger and more specialized. In addition to drawing their stock from the city and its immediate hinterland, they began to suck ever larger swathes of the surrounding countryside into their commercial vortex.

Overall, therefore, supplying the urban market demanded a large variety of tasks carried out in a kaleidoscope of settings. At the end of the supply chain stood the retailer, staffing their market stall from the early morning on market days in all weathers, ready to welcome customers from the sounding of the bell that signalled the official opening of trade. This stall, though surrounded by others and in a space that was customarily set aside for retail, could still be ephemeral in character, consisting of only a portable table and a canvas awning. A fortunate few were protected from the elements by market hall structures, but for the most part such permanent buildings did not appear until the nineteenth century.[24] Dotted throughout and around the city were the spaces in which retailers, as well as wholesalers, prepared the provisions on the stallholder's table for sale. Some of these spaces, namely the places in which animals and their by-products were processed by butchers, tanners, and tallow chandlers, were extremely unpleasant. Surrounded by blood, entrails, skins, and the often poisonous substances used to turn hides into leather, or fat into candles, workers dismembered animals to extract every last profitable gram. Given the mess created by these processes, urban authorities were keen to confine slaughtering to clearly delineated spaces within the city. For the most part, they were not successful in moving them off private property and into a single, public slaughterhouse. Rather, efforts were directed at closely regulating butchers' yards. Meanwhile, regulatory edicts directed at the premises used by bakers to produce the daily loaf for urban inhabitants were just as thorough-going, if focused on the fire hazard as opposed to the risk of dangerous miasmas. Baking was not generally a profitable trade,

FIGURE 3.2 Balthazar Nebot, *Fishmonger's Stall*, 1737. New Haven, CT, Yale Center for British Art, Paul Mellon Collection.

meaning that hot ovens were often situated in cramped neighborhoods built up with flammable wooden buildings.[25]

Growing vegetables, or producing milk, butter, and eggs for sale in the town marketplace, was obviously a far less bloody affair, and the market gardens around many towns and cities provided a clue to travellers that they were nearing a town, as well as the workplace of those who labored in these semi-rural spaces to produce the fruit, vegetables, and dairy products that were offered in the "green" markets of towns. As cities expanded, gardens moved beyond the town limits; yet the impossibility of transporting produce quickly to markets until the advent of the railway kept them within easy reach of the marketplace.

The experiences of these traders and producers in both urban and suburban workplaces were structured by three key variables—gender, wealth, and the power of local guilds. Wealthy butchers in British America took advantage of a complete absence of government regulation to create supply chains that ran all the way from rural grazing lands to suburban fattening pastures and finally to the urban marketplace. In Charleston, South Carolina, it was not unusual for one man to deploy the labor of enslaved Africans and white servants in marshalling animals all the way from field to plate. The free white butcher had become a maestro of the market, moving with ease between rural and urban market spaces, while slaves and servants staffed the key links in the chain. Without guild regulations, wives and daughters could work in any aspect of the trade, and there is evidence that they retailed meat, butchered it, and supervised enslaved butchers. In Europe, wealthier and larger families used gendered divisions of labor also to operate multiple elements of the supply chain. As Danielle van den Heuvel has shown, in Dutch market gardening on suburban farms, families used the labor of all to cultivate produce that was then moved to the urban market by husbands and sold in the marketplace by wives and daughters. Likewise, butchers sold meat in the guild market hall, while their wives sold offal and processed meats in a designated space opposite.[26]

Moving between a familiar array of workplaces in which urban marketplace and suburban market gardens smoothly connected was not the experience of everyone, however. Opportunities for single women in the provisioning economy were variable. As Janine Lanza has shown, Parisian widows frequently ran the businesses of their deceased husbands, despite the criticism of male commentators.[27] Some women traded on the margins of the marketplace, literally standing near the official stalls but not at them. Although such women were making a living in a commerce defined by men as illegitimate, they were nevertheless an essential link in the chain of urban provisioning.[28] Others were limited in the choice of provisions they might retail by factors beyond their control, such as the level of family dominance of supply chains and the regulations set by retailing guilds.

What is more, during the eighteenth century increasing commercialization dislodged the importance of familiar and customary spaces that had long been hotspots of the provisioning trade. As Sydney Watts has discovered, Paris's traditional cattle markets at Sceaux and Poissy, where city butchers met cattle merchants to purchase stock, became quieter as tax farmers introduced ever more rigorous duty collection. Instead, the parties met illegally, in suburban pastures owned by the merchant middlemen. With ever more cattle and sheep coming through these markets, from even greater distances, this shift meant that the customary spaces of trade on Paris's periphery consistently lost importance.[29]

Nevertheless, the early modern period did not see a universal or dramatic reconfiguration in the types of spaces frequented by those involved in the urban provisioning trades. Fairs, marketplaces, and suburban farms remained woven together in a familiar economic relationship. The way in which individuals moved through these spaces continued to be shaped principally by their gender, family status, and the local regulatory regime. Likewise, the relationship between home and the workplace remained as detached in 1800 as it had been in 1650. Yet, in particular locations and in certain trades, established patterns were beginning to give way to new configurations that were dictated by the profit motive, and the desire of those involved in feeding growing urban populations to take full advantage of the economies of scale that came with the rise of the city in western life.

ROAMING FAR AND WIDE: THE "MOBILE" WORKPLACE ON LAND AND SEA

The workplaces we have explored so far were all fixed in space, if not precisely in time. While peering into them has thus revealed a level of mobility that was undoubtedly increasing in this age of European imperialism and industrialization, their occupants still frequented a repertoire of spaces that existed in relatively close proximity to one another. Yet there were some types of work that, in this expanding western world, acquired an unprecedented level of mobility.[30] There had always been some groups of workers who had no main location of employment but instead wandered far and wide in their quest to make a living—strolling players, chapbook sellers, merchant sailors, and shepherds are a few occupations that come to mind. What was remarkable about the post-1650 era, however, was that the number of people engaged in these professions rose significantly, and the area across which they roamed increased also. This section will examine these "mobile" workplaces, explaining how Atlantic imperialism made them different from earlier eras.

The most ubiquitous mobile worker was the peddler. Across Europe, peddlers had long played an important role in the distribution of all types of goods, from books to cloth and trinkets. The continued importance of peddlers manifested itself in a sustained ambivalence towards them, stemming from the absence of an identifiable or fixed position in the local community (Figure 3.3). In the Netherlands, the more "strange" the itinerant trader, the heavier the justice meted out to them for disobeying the regulations of resident guilds. While local peddlers were subject to having their goods randomly, and sometimes illegally, seized, they escaped fines, and eventually had their wares returned. Jewish peddlers coming from farther afield and obviously of different religion and ethnicity, on the other hand, endured large fines if they dared to encroach on the territory of local retailing guilds.[31] In Britain, peddlers were identified as the source of disorder throughout the eighteenth century, with newspapers railing against them as wandering villains who set up temporary stalls in town inns so that they might undermine the business of the "resident trader."[32] The rising contingent of shop owners viewed themselves as the very antithesis of the peddler, whom they consistently sought to undermine by supporting government legislation that made peddling licenses extremely costly.[33]

However, the commercialization of European societies, and their New World possessions, put the itinerates' enemies on the back foot. As we have already seen, greater agricultural commercialization spawned a significant number of middlemen, travelling factors who orchestrated the supply of foodstuffs. Commercial agents also became more common in industry, as manufacturers sent out salesmen on regional circuits in an effort to increase standing orders for their products, the so-called "Manchester men."[34] However, the mobility of certain workers increased most markedly with Europe's New World expansion. From the 1600s onwards, men (and sometimes women) roved across the eastern reaches of the North American continent trading European manufactured goods and alcohol for the natural bounty of the forests and plains, mostly in the form of animal skins and peltry. This trade was entirely a product of the European invasion of the American continent, and as such it translated into a completely new workplace for its participants. There were many parallels between the types of peddlers and itinerant traders who roved across Europe, not least in the frequently hostile reaction of governing authorities to their presence.

FIGURE 3.3 Anne Claude Caylus, *Bundled Firewood Seller*, 1746. *Études prises dans le bas peuple ou les Cris de Paris: Cotterets*, after Edme Bouchardon. New York, Metropolitan Museum of Art, www.metmuseum.org.

Nevertheless, the environment in which these "Indian traders" found themselves was both unfamiliar and challenging. Their workplace was more expansive than any encountered in the Old World. In addition, dangerous wildlife and impassable terrain were a feature of almost every journey into the "backcountry" to the trading posts that sprang up in Native American towns such as Kaskaskia and Detroit, or European forts such as Fort Pitt and Fort Augusta. As they struggled along unfamiliar paths and rivers with their packs and canoes loaded with goods, these traders lived at the frontier of an international trade that operated with little regard for the communal or customary values that still had purchase in the Old World. It was every man, or woman, for themselves as they roamed beyond the reach of any fixed marketplace or governmental authority. In such an environment, opportunities unfolded for any person who could both survive and negotiate the complex intercultural character of this itinerant trade. Extraordinary individuals emerged, like Sally Ainse, a Native American woman separated from a *métis* husband who in the 1760s relocated her family from Philadelphia to the Great Lakes. There, Ainse roved the region by canoe, using the small fur-trading post of Detroit as her base. Lending money, trading furs for rum and European manufactures, while also dealing in local provisions such as wood, Ainse sustained herself and her children for almost forty years.[35]

Essential to the supply of these traders were the merchant fleets that gathered and transported European manufactures, enslaved Africans, and Asian products to (and around) the New World. Protecting these merchant fleets from the depredations of competing nations were large naval forces. Put together, this increased seaborne traffic added up to an astonishing rise in the number of boats circulating around the Atlantic, connecting it to the Indian Ocean and to the Pacific. And, of course, more boats needed more sailors, who knew no fixed workplace other than on board and at sea—a unique "wooden world" where the rules of land-based society had little currency. Given the dramatic rise in the number of sailors during the age of Enlightenment, this group has proved to be of particular fascination to recent historians, who have often used their biographies and experiences to document rising mobility and the emergence of "global" lives.[36]

Some of these seafaring itinerants were merchant seamen, who would invariably have a "home" port in which resided their family, or many families, as some contemporaries joked. Yet levels of mobility increased to a degree where a sailor might spend most of his career operating on an Atlantic, if not global, scale. African seafarers, such as Olaudah Equiano (1745–97), used this mobility to evade those ports in unfree societies that might attempt to re enslave them. Equiano escaped a period of slavery in Virginia when he was purchased by a sea captain, and eventually became free altogether and joined the antislavery movement in London, where he settled down.[37] Even among white sailors extreme itinerancy presented issues that had not been previously faced in societies that had not historically harbored such circulation and movement of workers. Hence, immediately after the American Revolution, the young nation's sailors created US citizenship as they pleaded with the government for passports that would confirm their nationality as they travelled around the Atlantic and found themselves in danger of being taken for Europeans, and thus pressed into their navies.[38]

As scholars have recently recognized, the number and variety of peddlers operating in Europe increased during the eighteenth century in response to the growth of consumer societies, and the desire of people located in the countryside to access the array of products they offered. This, however, was only the leading edge of a much larger expansion in the "mobile" workplace. With widespread European colonization well underway by 1700, the number of individuals who left their communities to become traders or sailors increased exponentially. For these people—mostly men but in some circumstances women—this translated into a dramatic shift in the character of their workplace, which was no longer a familiar locale in which family and working life combined, but could now be an oceangoing vessel, a canoe, a turnpike, or a forest path that required traversing if that work was to sustain them.

THE INDUSTRIAL PLANTATION COMPLEX

However, this "frontier" of European settlement moved ever further westwards and took over all the Caribbean by the middle of the eighteenth century. Europeans' hunger for land was seemingly insatiable, as not only were precious metals and gems discovered buried in the mountainous regions of South America, but settlers realized that the soil and the climate could support the growth of exotic commodities such as sugar, indigo, tobacco, cotton, and rice. As we explore the new types of working environment created by this colonial exploitation, we come full circle. Many of these workplaces were rural and agricultural in character, and combined early levels of industrialization with the cultivation of crops. Here, however, the comparison with the family farm or the market garden ends. Instead, we find ourselves in a dramatically different environment, in which race played the key role in determining where people would work and what their experiences would be. We end up in the heart of the horror that was racial slavery and hence in the most commercialized workplaces of the Enlightenment era—caught in a contradiction between "progress" and "savagery" that even contemporaries, such as Abbé Raynal and Hector St. John Crèvecoeur, recognized.[39]

Historians of New World slavery are universally agreed on the fact that, for the enslaved African on the plantation, and indeed the master or mistress who owned them, the crop under cultivation specifically contributed to the character of their working environment. With cotton only becoming a major product in the 1790s, it was sugar, tobacco, and rice that the labor of the enslaved mainly produced. Of these three crops, the tobacco plantation was often the smallest enterprise, resembling a European farm more than the classic image of industrial agriculture that came to dominate in the nineteenth century. As with all plantations, the workplaces and living spaces of blacks and whites were carefully distinguished. Enslaved Africans lived in separate "cabins" at some distance from the owner's house, though always observable from that house. Most slaves' workplace was the open fields, where they were charged with the tedious and often exhausting labor of cultivating and processing tobacco. Africans cleared fields, planted seedlings in hand-fashioned mounds of earth, and spent hours picking pests from the leaves of the growing plant. After harvest, these leaves needed to be bundled and hung for drying before they were packed into barrels. The Chesapeake's extreme climate meant that the enslaved often worked in unbearably hot and humid conditions. Slave "drivers" stood over gangs of workers, pushing them on with a whipping if they showed signs of slowing down (Figure 3.4).[40]

On rice plantations, the working conditions were comparably awful, if not a step worse. Rice, of course, is grown in flooded paddies, meaning that enslaved Africans often found themselves waist-deep in mud and water. What is more, much of the work needed to construct drainage systems that could flood fields on demand was carried out during the winter months when, since South Carolina and Georgia were subtropical, temperatures could dip below freezing. During the rice harvest, Africans worked to separate the rice from the husk by pounding and winnowing. Machines to perform this work started to appear in the later eighteenth century, but were far from common. Breaking the rice during the winnowing process would devalue the crop and result in a severe whipping for the individual thought to be responsible. Many of the most intensive rice plantations were situated far from the luxury and comfort of Charleston and were staffed not by the actual owner (who lived in a genteel townhouse) but by an overseer or manager. Slave and manager alike lived in ramshackle, wooden accommodation, with minimal access to any of the comforts of life. Indeed, the owner of multiple plantations and founding father Henry Laurens sent slaves who "misbehaved" to these "labor camps" as a punishment for their actions.[41]

FIGURE 3.4 Benjamin Henry Latrobe, *An Overseer Doing His Duty near Fredericksburg, Virginia*, c. 1798. Baltimore, Maryland Historical society.

However, most Africans in the New World worked to produce sugar after they had arrived on these French, British, Spanish, Portuguese, Dutch, and Danish plantations following their sale into chattel labor from their African homelands. The vast majority of Africans arrived on these plantations because they had been purchased to replace slaves who had died as a result of hard labor, poor diet, and tropical disease. While the enslaved population of the North American mainland became self-sustaining by the end of the eighteenth century, this was never achieved from the Caribbean southwards. The sugar plantation was a brutal agricultural machine that consumed lives as it demanded relentless labor in a tropical climate. Enslaved Africans had no choice other than to devote themselves to the cultivation, harvest, and processing of sugar cane. Working, like their Chesapeake brethren, in gangs, slaves were driven relentlessly to produce the highest quality sugar possible. On many of the largest plantations, where hundreds were employed, the cane was processed in situ. So, if a slave was not cutting cane with dangerously sharp machetes in the hot and humid fields, he or she was stuck in the sweltering heat, stirring boiling vats of cane juice until it crystalized. Nevertheless, the sugar they produced lined the pockets of absentee planters and fuelled the consumer economy that sponsored the change in workplaces that affected almost all the different individuals we have looked at.[42]

As a workplace, the plantation completely severed the customary relationship between the family home and labor and established a new, and unsettling, one. The enslaved family was at once the foundation of any black sense of community and subjected to disruption by the demands of profiteering and violent white masters. From the assemblage of traumatized men, women, and children that found themselves on the plantation, Africans did their best to create supportive family groupings—not as an industrious household but as a bulwark against the unceasing demands of commercial agriculture. Rather than lightly reconfiguring the relationship between family and workplace, commercialization thus completely shattered them as the demands of sugar, rice, and tobacco sent enslaved Africans to an early grave, or saw them sold away from kinfolk at the will of masters thinking only of profit.

CONCLUSION

Surveying these workplaces in the age of Enlightenment has principally illustrated how, with a growing body of historical research into Atlantic imperialism and changing perceptions of the Industrial Revolution, we can now appreciate the vast range of workplace experiences that characterized this commercializing age. Some patterns emerge in the increased variety of workplaces, and even as a greater number of permutations evolved between the worker and the workplace, the "family economy" nevertheless continued as the dominant unit of production. However, within this framework, specific types of work harbored certain trends adding up to a widely varying amount of change. On the family farm, workplaces changed little as working roles shifted within existing settings. In the urban industrial context, and in the New World plantation complex, however, there were much more dramatic shifts. There, as western capitalism expanded, fuelled by the age of empires, some workplaces became dramatically detached from the domestic setting, relocating workers into an early factory setting or the miserable fields of plantation agriculture. From the enlightened order of Boulton's Soho Works to the brutal efficiency of the Jamaican sugar plantation, the drive to make money reorganized workplaces that stood at the heart of new working cultures. How workers experienced the effects of this reconfiguration entirely depended on their gender, class, and, increasingly, on their race. Working conditions had always been partly determined by social difference; yet as the age of Enlightenment became the age of empire, such differences came to shape workplaces more decisively than ever before.

CHAPTER FOUR

Workplace Cultures

JANINE LANZA

In western Europe, the period from 1650 to 1800 was a time of rapid transition in economic production and organization, a set of changes generally described by the term the Industrial Revolution. Among the many changes set into motion were shifts in the norms and practices of workplace culture, that is, the ways that workers understood and shaped their work environments. In western Europe, the model established by artisanal production remained dominant, even while the relationships, pay, and labor of workers changed in response to deskilling, routinization, and an influx of rural workers to urban centers. In part the continued influence of artisanal culture reflected the enduring prestige of artisanal work and workers, long considered the elite of working people. Artisans, in the popular imagination if not always in practice, enjoyed a level of independence and self-rule that most other workers did not. However, by the eighteenth century the changes in the broader economy exerted a larger and larger impact on workers' lives, and, by extension, their behavior and practices in the workplace.

In light of the shift towards more industrialized production, and the use of fewer skilled and well-paid workers in shops and factories, one of the underlying dynamics of the workplace became more evident, namely the tension between employers and employees over what we might think of as the appropriation of effort in the workplace. One of the overarching dynamics of all workplaces was the struggle over how much and how hard and on whose behalf workers exerted themselves. Employers in all instances sought to extract as much labor as possible from their subordinates, in order to maximize their profits. Employees, whether journeymen, hired hands, servants, or slaves, aimed to exert as much control as possible over the pace and output of their labor. It was the continual mediation of this tension, the constant negotiation of this relationship, which informed how that workplace culture developed. Workers behaved in the workplace in ways that tried to push back against the fundamentally asymmetric relationship employment thrust upon them. Whether those workers started from a position of relative strength, such as skilled artisans who had portable and valuable skills, or from a position of nearly complete abjection, as did slaves who used the few cracks in their bondage to shape their work environment, all workers pushed to define the terms of their laboring lives in the face of employers who wished to define the terms of work themselves (Figure 4.1).

FIGURE 4.1 William Henry Pyne, *Poulterer's Shop*, n.d. New Haven, CT, Yale Center for British Art, Paul Mellon Collection.

GUILDS AND THE ARTISANAL IDEAL

Due to the relative privilege artisans enjoyed—the shared culture imparted by their training and their superior pay and working conditions in comparison to transient, unskilled, or unfree laborers—they had the opportunity to develop a more coherent and established workplace culture. Artisans, despite the ways their workplaces were being destabilized by economic shifts discussed in the section "The Guild Model in Operation" below, retained a sense of shared identity and traditions in ways that less privileged workers such as unskilled laborers, peasants, women, and enslaved populations were not able to develop. That said, other groups of workers did create cultures of labor that helped them to manage and make sense of their work environments. When examining workplace culture, it is useful to draw attention to the ways in which, even while workers of all kinds shared certain assumptions about the culture of working, they were in fact a vastly heterogeneous group. The starkest division was between free and unfree labor; gender and skill also shaped the kinds of shared identities and practices available to different workers. Economic changes, social hierarchy, legal status, and geographic location all influenced workplace culture.

The impact of artisanal culture was more evident in some European countries—such as France and Germany—and less apparent in others. Nonetheless, an initial examination of the workplace in this era begins with an understanding of ways guilds organized and created meaning in working spaces. In some ways, this idealized standard of workplace culture provided a measure of stability for skilled workers who were seeing other aspects of their working lives, such as wages, tasks, level of responsibility, and interpersonal relations, change dramatically. The shift in workplace organization and relationships in response to growing consolidation and mechanization in the workplace had not yet, in the eighteenth century, radically changed the culture of the artisanal workplace. Although workers were finding their relations to their employers, their jobs, and their co workers changed, the importance of honor, hierarchy, and status remained largely in place through the end of the eighteenth century. These categories of organization and appraisal were drawn from the artisanal workshop, and although artisanal modes of production were being pushed aside as mechanization and industrialization took greater hold, first and most noticeably in Britain and then in France and elsewhere in continental Europe, artisanal ways of making sense of relations and values in the workplace remained in place throughout this period. Well into the nineteenth century, the language used in the workplaces of skilled laborers visualized an idealized artisanal past.[1] Even as mechanization drove forward, practices and attitudes drawn from guild structures continued to influence not only production but also organization and interaction in industrializing workplaces.[2] As all workers—skilled, unskilled, male, female—found themselves in rapidly changing work conditions, they all drew upon aspects of artisanal culture to make sense of their environments.

For a first example of a developed and coherent workplace culture, we need to examine the spaces occupied by skilled, generally guild-centered, labor. Before delving into the assumptions and practices that undergirded artisanal production, two points are worth making. First, artisanal work was highly diverse. Workers under the umbrella of the guild system performed a vast array of tasks, from the brute effort of forging iron or tanning leather to the delicate work of tooling watch works or creating delicacies from puff pastry.[3] Second, in addition to the diversity of skill and strength needed to perform the array of tasks undertaken in artisanal enterprises, the relations among workers, employers, and clients differed considerably from workplace to workplace. In some small enterprises master artisans, workers who had acquired the title of a master of his trade and the right to own his independent business, worked with just a few other employees to fabricate goods to sell. In other shops, masters oversaw large commercial enterprises and occupied themselves with keeping accounts and supervising their workers.[4] While it is crucial to keep this diversity in mind in thinking about workplace culture, whether in a large or small enterprise, skilled workers shared certain assumptions about relations in the shop, the ways shops should be managed, and how work should be valued and rewarded. For the most part these assumptions were drawn from the institution of the guild. Further, in many ways skilled workers, especially those in livery companies or guilds, were seen as setting the benchmark for workplace culture that other workers could emulate, aspire to, or reject.[5]

The guild existed in two dimensions in the early modern period: first, as an idealized set of norms and, second, as a messy functioning institution. Ideally, the guild established not only the kinds of work to be performed in the shop but also the relations among workers and between a worker and master. This normative ideology prized harmony and hierarchy above all else. The idealized vision of life in the artisanal workshop imagined the master as a paternal figure, a benevolent overseer to journeymen and apprentices (hired hands used as cheap labor to help the master save on wages, called *alloués* in Paris, did not enter into this fancy) who looked up to their master as a mentor, model, and father figure.[6] In this labor utopia, all the denizens of the shop knew their places and harmony reigned. Any conflict between workers was settled by the master whom they trusted; grievances against masters were settled equitably by the guild. To a great extent, this vision of artisanal culture derived not only from the statutes, generated by guild leaders and officials, but also from other writings and representations coming from leadership.[7]

This utopia, of course, never truly existed. As the research of numerous historians has demonstrated, the culture of the workshop was the culture of conflict.[8] There were multiple sources of discord, ranging from the structural economic changes that accelerated in the eighteenth century and made work more precarious and competitive to the increasingly closed nature of guild leadership that provided fewer and fewer places as masters and officers to aspiring craftsmen. The family-based nature of many craft enterprises also served to create a sense of an institution closed to newcomers. Further, in addition to controlling production, "distribution and supply were [also] dominated by the livery companies [guilds]."[9] Whether it was owing to frustrations over lack of economic opportunity or over an inability to enter what seemed like a closed caste of actors, in the early modern period the guilds experienced a great deal of conflict.

Despite the frustrations provoked by guilds, as institutions they existed for several reasons and they served several constituencies. On the most straightforward level, they organized skilled production in early modern European cities and granted financial privileges to their members (Figure 4.2). Guilds attempted to create economic monopolies and restrict competition, thereby increasing the value of guild membership. These institutions also controlled the supply and movement of workers, with masters and guild officers employing regulations to assert control over potentially unruly workers. In this endeavor they, with the support of the corporation, set wages for workers and required workers to conform to a system of work permits regarding changing employers and other conditions that limited worker autonomy. Affiliation with a corporation also, crucially, provided a sense of honor and distinction to members and granted status and identity to them as well. Most of these advantages accrued primarily to guild masters who benefited from the regulations and limits guilds placed on production and trade of certain goods. However, skilled workers who labored in artisanal shops also gained from their affiliation with these associations. Their wages, while kept low by the concerted efforts of guild masters, were higher than those earned by unskilled laborers or those working outside of the guild system.[10]

Guilds served other, noneconomic functions, connected not to the regulation and organization of work but to the shared ties of their members. Guilds provided social support to their members in various forms. Members of these corporations were often members of religious associations, which held services on important feast days and other civic holidays.[11] These religious fraternities also organized and attended funerals of fellow guild members. Guilds offered charity to indigent members or their families as well, providing a modest safety net.[12] Together, these elements contributed to the ways guilds and their members functioned internally and in society at large. Part of this process was creating a sense of a shared culture that provided a framework for performing these

FIGURE 4.2 William Hincks, R*epresenting Winding, Warping with a new improved Warping Mill, and Weaving*, Plate VII, 1791. London, British Library.

functions. Artisanal culture, the ways artisans did things, how they understood their society and their places in it, their values and goals, attempted to bind together the sometimes contradictory economic and social functions of the guilds.

THE GUILD MODEL IN OPERATION

In examining how statutes, organization, and expectations worked together in lived experience, we can begin with the most famous extant example of artisan cultural practices, namely Robert Darnton's cat massacre. This well-known incident lays out several perspectives on understanding early modern work culture. In the telling, the workers in M. Jacques Vincent's print shop were bedeviled by cats, including the mistress's cat, La Grise, a spoiled beast that disturbed the printers day and night with its caterwauling and spoiled demeanor. In a fit of crabbiness, the workers in M. Vincent's enterprise beat the cats that were tormenting them, including the mistress' favorite. They then held a trial for the corpse of La Grise and, after hearing the evidence and pronouncing the cat's guilt, strung up the corpses of La Grise and several other cats in the master's courtyard.[13]

The veracity of this tale has been questioned by historians but whether printers' apprentices and journeymen actually killed and tried a cat in this fashion precisely as told is less important than the glimpse into the artisanal workplace it provides. The author of this vignette, Nicolas Contat, worked as a printer for several decades and included the story of La Grise as part of an autobiographical account of his life as a printer and foreman.[14] Two issues stand out in his description: the constant presence of strife and conflict in the workplace and the emphasis placed on hierarchy and standing. According to Contat, the master treated his apprentices abysmally: "they slept in a filthy, freezing room, rose before dawn, ran errands all day while dodging insults from the journeymen and abuse from the master, and received nothing but slops to eat."[15] The journeymen took out their frustrations at their master on the apprentices who had no recourse as the lowliest denizens of the shop. The issues of hierarchy, respect, and conflict intertwined in the atmosphere of this business.[16]

These issues emerged in the early modern period across other European countries. While Darnton's account of trouble in this print shop is most complete, in Germany, Britain, and Italy similar conflicts cropped up over similar issues—namely concerns over respect for guild hierarchy in the workshop and the willingness of artisanal workers to fight to enforce the guild norms that they considered advantageous. In 1665, artisans in Lübeck took to the streets over the course of several days to protest the hiring of "illicit" workers by merchants looking to save money on wages. The artisans also damaged and destroyed tools and work completed by this unlawful workforce.[17] Artisanal workers in seventeenth-century London and eighteenth-century Turin participated in similar actions, resisting their masters for denying them fair pay, treating them disrespectfully, and not abiding by guild regulations that were meant to protect workers.[18]

These conflicts and actions that began with issues in the workshop but spilled out into the street and demanded the attention of civil authority came from several sources of conflict that framed them and that strongly shaped workplace culture in the early modern period. These responses and actions took place against the trajectory of profound economic changes, changes that were making artisanal workers more financially insecure. Increasingly, artisanal production was characterized by instability and change, transformations that shaped workers' conditions of labor and emotional responses. The early modern economy in much of early modern western Europe was marked by a rapid acceleration of consumption and production of consumer goods. In this period, "a growing number of households acted to reallocate their productive resources ... in ways that increased both the supply of market-oriented, money-earning activities and the demand for goods offered in the marketplace."[19] The response by master artisans to this increasing demand was one based on the idea of "constant returns to scale," that is, the expansion of production by subcontracting and putting-out, rather than by centralizing and rationalizing assembly of goods. What this meant was that masters added and subtracted workers—either journeymen or temporary laborers—as orders waxed and waned. For artisans, this response to fluctuating demand brought about insecurity since "labour could be added to or reduced by the employer without difficulty to expand or contract the volume of output in response to demand."[20]

This kind of uncertain labor and production market created anxiety among masters but more markedly among journeymen. No longer anchored to the idea that apprenticeship led to journeymanship led to mastership, artisanal workers became more economically insecure and less attached to official ideas and definitions of guild membership. In this climate, where guild membership was becoming increasingly elusive for many journeymen and apprentices, marginalized workers could find it more difficult to reconcile the values and culture espoused by the guilds with the market-oriented thinking that increasingly governed workplaces.[21] Added to the increasing economic turmoil resulting from greater market volatility was the problem that even available masterships increasingly benefited sons and sons-in-law of masters.[22] Artisanal families used their membership in the guilds to benefit themselves, and in the process shut down the promise of guild membership for those who went through the socialization offered by guilds. Apprentices and journeymen increasingly saw a future where they would be permanent employees of masters, without the possibility of moving into mastership themselves. This development within the guilds, coupled with the destabilizing shifts in the broader economy, created a sense of detachment from the traditional promise of the guilds, one that manifested itself specifically in artisan disputes and more generally in the fractious tenor of communication and interaction in the shop.

These transformations in the economy did not mesh especially well with official guild structures, and guild discourse did not respond to these changes. The guild model envisioned a process wherein workers moved from apprenticeship to journeymanship to mastership in a span of time suited to the requirements of the trade. For drapers in Paris the journey could take as few as three years; for weavers in seventeenth-century London it was seven years.[23] What made these training periods tolerable for aspirants was the implicit promise that they would eventually be admitted as full guild members. Even as guild statutes and practices were revised and reissued, this vision of guild life as a structured passage to mastership was not altered, nor were economic shifts acknowledged. Once skilled workers became masters they could marry and establish a family, set up and run a business, and generally take on the status of an independent and honorable member of society. The reality of guild life, in the seventeenth and eighteenth centuries, and perhaps always, did not correspond to this ideal. For those waiting to settle down and take on these new roles of husband, father, and head of an enterprise, the clear trend of scarcer prospects was not reassuring. Guilds offered fewer opportunities to advance from rank to rank, a narrowing of opportunity that meshed with the more insecure footing workers experienced in an economic marketplace that chased consumer demand through hiring and firing at need. The often violent ways that workers responded to their supervisors in part reflected their disillusionment and anger over their deteriorating work prospects but also their refusal to kowtow to a hierarchy that promised what it could not deliver. Instead of a ladder to advancement, guild hierarchy was about enforcing honor and obeisance for the benefit of those on top, while hiding behind the language of order and tradition.

Despite the language of inclusion and membership found in much that is written on behalf of guilds, on the most basic level, guilds were institutions of economic organization functioning in a shifting landscape. They served as one way to sort workers into distinct groups and grant privileges and status to some while withholding those benefits from others. While purporting to label workers according to the labor they performed, guilds simultaneously created a collective identity for their members "through erecting and maintaining boundaries between an imagined 'us' and 'them'."[24] This creation of boundaries dovetailed with the larger hierarchal character of early modern European society where identity was relational and thus rooted in "a subjective experience of difference."[25] People knew who they were and how they fit into their society in relation to others. Members of a guild, in addition to enjoying the right to engage in a particular segment of the skilled economy, belonged to a group that could claim certain privileges and that lifted members above outsiders. While all work was seen as debasing to some extent, unskilled workers, *gens sans état*, were the most reviled of all. Workers affiliated with the guilds, whether as apprentices, journeymen, or masters, all took pride in and benefited from their status, in the fact that they had a position in the social hierarchy that lifted them above those who merely labored as they could for their daily bread. While workers in the guild system bemoaned their loss of status, other workers could only wish to have the stability, status, and developed traditions of skilled laborers.

THE "UNSKILLED" WORKER

During this era, it was increasingly difficult for unskilled workers and day laborers to eke out even a precarious living on the strength of their backs and arms. For unskilled workers in growing cities, the location of work and the employer changed often, providing them with little footing to create ties to one another or to a workplace culture. The unskilled labor market relied most often on hiring workers by the day with no promise of continued employment or skill development. As Haim Burstin explains "one of the characteristics of such [unskilled] labour is its fluctuation among employment, unemployment, and semi-indigence."[26] Given this precariousness and the absence of organizing institutions for unskilled workers, the shared culture was based less on the work done or the location of that work than on other commonalities. The constant search for work created a sense of solidarity and shared struggle (Figure 4.3).

FIGURE 4.3 John Varley, *Norwich*, n.d. New Haven, CT, Yale Center for British Art, Paul Mellon Collection.

One common trait that many unskilled workers shared was the status of being a migrant. In the early modern era, many European cities were growing dramatically as displaced rural laborers sought employment in cities where industrial production bespoke greater demand for workers. As in other growing European cities, unskilled workers in eighteenth-century Antwerp were often migrants, drawn by the growing demand for labor in this burgeoning port city.[27] Throughout the early modern period, migration shaped the practices and cultures of unskilled workers. Rather than relying on a stable workplace, unskilled laborers relied on other like workers who came from their home regions, who could be counted on to provide information about jobs and affordable housing, as well as news from home. The struggle to earn a living shaped the ability to create a workplace culture, pushing laborers to move beyond the workplace in their creation of networks of aid.[28] The culture of unskilled work was also shaped by the need for poor relief. As many historians have shown, unskilled work often did not provide adequate pay to support workers, especially if they had families.[29] Even when multiple family members sold their labor they still needed external support to get by. Knowledge of where to seek food, shelter, and indigent medical care bonded poorly paid day laborers as they all sought to survive on meager wages.[30]

In examining the myriad factors that shaped workplace culture, alongside skill, gender was an important determinant. Both women and men labored to sustain themselves and their families. Nonetheless, most occupations in the premodern era were segregated by gender, with men dominating skilled work and women being relegated either to less-skilled occupations or to those deemed suitable for women such as sewing, provisioning, or textile production. And when men and women worked as unskilled laborers, men earned higher wages for their efforts. Part of the reason women were not considered equal to men in the workplace had to do with assumptions about the family economy. While this concept has been sharply questioned by historians, nonetheless it expresses the justification used to pay women less, namely that they were part of the larger economic unit of the family and therefore did not need to earn wages sufficient to support an entire household.[31] This assumption, along with other timeless notions about female capability, helped to place women in positions subordinate to men.

Consequently, virtually all guild statutes excluded women from membership (although widows did have important responsibilities in guilds) and even erased the extremely important roles women played in the workplace. Fundamentally, masculinity was central to guild ideology. That said, in terms of the daily functioning of artisanal businesses, women's labor was crucial. Wives, daughters, and daughters-in-law formed the backbone of the workforce; a master could rely on these workers to show up and work hard, assumptions he could not always make about his other employees. Even hired female workers benefited a master's business, as he could pay them much less than the men he employed.[32] It is not clear precisely how this formal expression of inferiority affected women's sense of their role in the workplace. One clue resides in the behavior of widows and wives of masters. Guild regulations in France offered the widow of a master craftsman the possibility of taking over the family enterprise and running it in her husband's stead.[33] In large numbers widows took on that role, many successfully running complex and successful enterprises. Similarly, wives of master craftsmen readily acted when their husbands were away. The wives of Parisian guild masters paid bills, made complaints to the police, and oversaw production in the shop without the slightest hesitation. And officials from the guild or city government recognized a wife's right to act on behalf of the business. When Angélique Letûmier's husband, a master pastry maker, left her in charge of his shop, a worker began to quarrel with her. Letûmier requested that a police commissioner come to the shop so she could lodge a complaint against the apprentice who "raised his hand to her and refused to obey."[34] In his notes, the commissioner wrote that he reprimanded the apprentice and ordered him to heed his mistress. These actions suggest that while women were formally absent in guild regulations, they were integral parts of guild life, and enjoyed a sense of identity and belonging based on their work in family businesses. The ways that wives and widows stepped into male roles suggest that they understood and could function in the workplace culture of the artisanal shop.

While women who were members of families formed a large segment of the female workforce, widowed and single working women faced specific challenges. Widows who had the resources to run a family business solo did not have to face the prospect of poverty, but many widows and other women living without men battled daily poverty. Some of their poverty was brought on by the vastly inferior wages women earned, but it was also difficult to maintain a household on the wages of one adult. Just as with migrants, these impoverished female workers tended to cluster and share knowledge with one another. Widows and other single female workers often shared lodging, splitting the costs of rent, heat, and light.[35] Such expediencies both allowed impoverished women to survive and created a sense of community that may have superseded a sense of belonging that might have developed in the workplace. Since women were often marginalized in the spaces where they labored, the sense of solidarity created elsewhere, as with migrants, provided them with meaning (Figure 4.4).

The other similarity between the kind of shared culture women and migrants created is linked to the use of social services. Just as migrants shared information about sources of relief, whether that be food or shelter or other assistance, women too shared information about sources of relief. Parishes often specifically devoted resources to poor women—widows and mothers with children. A record of one Parisian parish's distribution of aid gives an idea of the help offered and criteria used by religious institutions that sought to assist poor women. Despite the title of the register, "Les Pauvres Veuves" (poor widows), the parish of Sainte-Marguerite in Paris offered food aid, work supplies, and even cash to widows and mothers. The presence of work supplies, such as cloth, wood, and thread, suggests that, for women in particular, labor was often accompanied by poverty; they needed to supplement their wages with food and goods from this religious charity.[36] The register does not specify the ages or situations of the women the parish helped, but the presence of both mothers and childless women (some widows and some not) suggests that working women were widely recognized as living in poverty despite their marital or family status.

UNFREE LABOR AND THEIR WORKPLACES

We have moved from the most developed and autonomous expressions of workplace culture in artisanal shops and other sites of skilled labor such as retail shops, foundries, and mines, to unskilled workers who created a sense of meaning for their work lives under much more difficult circumstances than skilled laborers, to women who were obliged to make the most of roles created for men, roles that explicitly excluded them, with women squeezing autonomy and meaning out of restriction. As we move in concentric circles from more to less autonomous, we arrive at the space of unfree labor, whether that was indentured servants working under the terms of constraining contracts or slaves, for whom no contract, law, or practice offered autonomy or dignity. These groups of workers nonetheless created a sense of meaning for their work and the spaces

FIGURE 4.4 Anthony Cardon, *Do You Want any Matches?* Plate IV. In the series *The Cries of London*, 1794, after Francis Wheatley. New Haven, CT, Yale Center for British Art, Paul Mellon Collection.

in which they labored out of the scraps of independence they could gather together. Further, in terms of the broad issue discussed in the introduction to this chapter—the fundamental tension between employer and laborer over the appropriation of labor—it is by examining specifically the culture of slavery in the Americas that we see most baldly the inner workings of that dynamic.

The system of indentured servitude and slavery in the early modern period was tied to the Atlantic trade system and European colonies in the Americas. Both sources of labor were key to the profitability of Atlantic trade. Of course, the conditions of these two groups were not comparable; the unfree condition of indentured servants did not approach the complete lack of liberty of the enslaved. Nonetheless both groups of laborers worked to create a culture of work on their own terms with the resources, however meager, they had at their disposal. In the process of building the economy and culture of the Americas, the labor contributed by enslaved Africans had more lasting significance. But for many colonial settlements, particularly English ones, the system of indentured servitude came first and established some of the enduring patterns of labor culture. In the sixteenth and seventeenth centuries, in English settlements, indentured servants were almost the sole source of bound labor. Because the English did not enslave native populations in large numbers at first, as the Spanish and Portuguese did in their New World colonies, they looked to bring in huge numbers of indentured servants to help them make their fortunes.[37] Given that the early focal point of the Atlantic economy was the exploitation and movement of raw materials from colony to metropole, abundant and cheap labor was vital. Prior to being transported, many indentured servants had either been convicted criminals, opting for transportation to the Americas rather than punishment in the English judicial system, or destitute individuals with such little hope for opportunity in England that they opted for the dangerous trip across the Atlantic and a difficult stint of labor.

The systems of indentured servitude and slavery relied on the use of theoretically unfettered violence to force compliance with the demands of masters; to force laborers to acknowledge with their actions if not in their thoughts, that they were not free. The legal practices and punishments of the colonies laid bare the unfree status of these groups of people: "Convicts, indentured servants, and redemptioners were far more likely to feel the heavy hand of justice; simply being intoxicated in the presence of a magistrate or minister could result in confinement in the stocks or up to 39 lashes. [The] gentry and planter class, on the other hand, were shielded from severe corporal punishments."[38] The unfree laborer dealt with coercion and violence well beyond the corrections meted out by masters disciplining unruly journeymen and apprentices. Consequently, the kind of resistance that made up the working culture of indentured servants went well beyond the rowdy behavior masters encountered in their shops or with their servants or what employers dealt with when they hired day laborers. The violence required to hold a system of compulsory labor together called forth a much more aggressive response by workers who sought to claim any scrap of dignity and autonomy they could find. This resort to violence was likely exacerbated by the identities of indentured servants, many of whom were criminals who were transported to the Americas rather than face execution in England.[39] But even those who signed up voluntarily, looking for opportunities in the colonies that were not available in England, were subject to brutal treatment.

Given the severe consequences indentured servants faced for breaking the law, their resistance to the work regime demanded of them had to take on more subtle forms than straightforward insubordination. While journeymen might get away with "sassing" the master or even destroying property, like Darnton's printers, indentured servants did not have the same leeway. Their status evoked fear and suspicion among their masters with the punishments for transgressions reflecting that fear; outright resistance had to give way to underhanded opposition. The workplace culture of indentured servants thus relied on slowdowns, willful stupidity, and other similar acts that reduced the amount of work done but not so far that they would provoke a violent punishment by a master. In addition to these kinds of actions, the working habits of indentured servants could also be marked by more assertive means of pushing back against the demands of the master.

Indentured servants were known to use alcohol to excess; the English author Aphra Behn, in her work *The Widow Ranter*, depicted such workers as perpetually drunk and unruly.[40] This kind of resistance to masters' work demands not only limited the amount of work laborers could perform. The excessive use of alcohol caused masters to complain incessantly about lack of productivity.[41] It also offered an avenue for servants to shape their responses to their situation and to assert their will in an environment where they had few other avenues to resist the master's power.

Despite the similarities, the status of indentured servant was not nearly as degrading as that of slave. Indentured servants lacked autonomy and self-determination; they were subject to a master's will and the use of violence. But their status was temporary and they were not seen as inhabiting a clearly inferior, subordinate status in society as slaves did. One clear indication of the chasm between these two groups was the fact that indentured servants were at times given the authority to oversee slaves. In Barbados by 1685 most of the demand for indentured servants was "for the upkeep of the local militia and for the policing of slaves."[42] This demographic shift in the American colonies, from labor supplied by indentured servants to that supplied by enslaved Africans, also saw a shift in the behavior of those workers themselves. Once indentured servants, and their masters, saw themselves as hierarchically superior to slaves, the kinds of subtle resistance that marked the culture of forced labor in the colonies became less the province of indentured servants and more that of slaves. And as those transported to the colonies finished their terms of indenture, and moved past their term of enforced servitude, the lifetime bondage of enslaved Africans, the way that inescapably divided their lack of freedom from that of indentured servants, came to define slavery more and more.

As the American colonies grew both in size and in economic productivity, the demand for labor increased apace. By the beginning of the eighteenth century, the flow of indentured servants to the North American colonies had diminished substantially, in part owing to the cooling off of interest on the part of potential servants who no longer saw transport as an attractive option. But also, with the growing number of Africans transported to the Americas to be used as slave labor, masters decided that slaves were a better source of reliable and profitable labor. Indentured servants had protections under law and custom that limited how much profit masters could extract from them. In the colony of Virginia, for example, servants were entitled to "sufficient food, clothing, and shelter; a Sunday free of hard labour; and moderation in correction."[43] Legal protections for slaves were minimal and custom allowed masters nearly *carte blanche* in how they dealt with their property, including their slaves. Masters could use more violent and direct methods to discipline and coerce slaves, methods they could not employ with indentured servants.[44] Also, in contrast to the terms of service laid out for indentured labor, where masters contractually obliged themselves to provide food, clothing, shelter, and rest time, slaves could make none of those formal demands. In terms of the treatment of slaves, masters were not limited by the law—"courts seldom intervened on any African's behalf"—but by the calculus of how much mistreatment they could mete out before their slaves could no longer supply profitable labor to their owners (Figure 4.5).[45]

This transition away from indentured labor to slave labor turned not simply on matters of supply and demand but also on an emerging racial hierarchy in the American colonies. In the seventeenth century, as slavery became a larger and more profitable institution, "slaveholders explanation of their own domination generally took the form of racial ideologies."[46] As race and enslavement became ever more closely associated, the position of slaves deteriorated and the possibilities for shaping their conditions of

FIGURE 4.5 John Raphael Smith, *The Slave Trade*, 1791, after George Morland. New Haven, CT, Yale Center for British Art, Paul Mellon Collection.

work deteriorated as well. Especially as the plantation grew more common as a form of economic and social organization, race and pigment carried "a far greater weight in defining status than heretofore."[47]

For slaves, then, race became the fundamental fact of their social status. The importance of race to status was central not only in British colonies but also in areas of the New World colonized by French, Spanish, and Portuguese, despite the absence of white indentured servants outside of the anglophone colonies. But work, too, was central to how they were perceived; they were defined as enslaved largely because their labor belonged unequivocally to someone else, a facet of the slave system that is often overlooked according to Ira Berlin and Philip Morgan.[48] As in other working relationships, a central concern was the issue of how much labor could be extracted from laborers versus how much autonomy workers could exercise. The working culture of enslaved laborers revolved around their aim of working as little as they could for their masters and as much as they could for their own account. Given that their autonomy had been negated when they were cruelly sold into slavery, deciding how to allocate their time and effort to the extent possible was one of the few ways slaves could exert any self-rule. In the asymmetrical relationship wrought by the slavery system, slaves' ability to push back was much more attenuated compared to other workers. Essentially, slaves were protected almost entirely by their value to their masters rather than by legal or even moral principles. Violence against slaves was limited by a master's repugnant desire to keep his property in working order.

Despite the almost total lack of self-determination, slaves found ways to assert their autonomy and shape the terms and contours of their work culture for themselves. The slave system of course incorporated a great deal of diversity, and the rhythm of labor and relations between masters and slaves depended on the geography, agriculture, and customs of the region. Slaves in the Chesapeake engaged in a wide array of labor—"mixed agriculture, agricultural processing, iron making," and so on.[49] In contrast, many of the other colonies like Virginia and the Deep South organized labor on vast plantations that engaged in monoculture, of rice, tobacco, cotton, and other commodity crops. One of the most common ways that slaves took control of their work environment was to determine the pace of work for themselves. Commonly, masters required their enslaved workers either to work a certain amount of time per day or to carry out a certain number of tasks. The latter circumstance provided enslaved workers with more opportunity to shape their work arrangements, especially since slaves engaged in "piece work" most often were obliged to provide their own food from land provided by their masters. In these cases, such as with slaves in South Carolina who had a great deal of leeway given to them in exchange for not making material demands on their masters, slaves could manage their time and effort in ways that benefited them, at times even at the economic expense of their masters.[50]

In geographic areas where slaves were employed in the production of commodity crops such as sugar and cotton, they generally worked all day for their masters, under the demanding eye of an overseer, who gave them almost no opportunity to allocate their time or effort as they wished.[51] On these large plantations, the opportunities to exercise independence were generally far fewer than on smaller plantations. Here, the small amount of power slaves could exert over their working culture resided in the knowledge that a master was dependent on his slaves to work and to obey.[52] While the law provided the owner of enslaved workers the opportunity to use physical force against them, up to the point of inflicting death, such actions both damaged workers, rendering them less productive, and created resentment and fear, both of which naturally led slaves to hold back as much as possible when working on their master's behalf. When masters and overseers "sought to lengthen the working day, to exact heavy labour during seasonal lulls in the planting cycle, and to extend their supervision … the planters confronted slaves who were no less determined to resist what they insisted were violations of customary practice."[53] Even for such workers with almost no autonomy or self-determination, their conception of norms and custom pushed them to shape the contours of their working conditions and the culture in which they understood and performed their work.

The ramifications of the culture of work in the colonized New World, the interplay between exploitation of slave labor and the desire for autonomy by enslaved workers on the other, reverberated far beyond the balance sheets of plantations. In 1791, enslaved Africans in the French colony of Saint-Domingue (modern-day Haiti) responded to the shameful conditions of their bondage by joining in the revolutionary movement already underway in the metropole. Unlike in other New World colonies, the enslaved population in Saint-Domingue outnumbered the white population by a ratio of approximately twelve to one. These slaves engaged almost exclusively in the backbreaking work of growing sugar cane and coffee; as a result of the harshness of the labor regime, more enslaved Africans were brought into the colony than to any other colonial settlement in the New World.[54] In terms of the work culture in the French sugar colonies, they "were notorious for the demands they placed on their slaves."[55] The demographics of slavery in Saint-

Domingue meant that African slaves had other African slaves as overseers; white French men and women were thin on the ground in the French Caribbean (Figure 4.6).[56]

These characteristics of the slavery system of labor in Saint-Dominigue contributed towards the eventual independence movement. Plantations were isolated, life was brutal, and as the ideas animating the revolution in France spread to colonial settlements, the enslaved pushed for their freedom. The culture of work on French plantations nourished a sense among slaves that they had nothing to lose by exercising their will. The practice of enslaved workers to find ways to assert autonomy found its farthest expression in the emancipation movement in Saint-Domingue and other French colonial settlements. While the French National Convention abolished slavery in 1794 in part to align the practice of the revolutionary government with its ideals, by that point this gesture was simply recognizing the situation in Saint-Domingue. Napoleon tried to reinstate slavery in 1802, primarily for economic reasons, but this law did little to reimpose this system. Former slaves had effectively won their freedom, motivated by the French Revolution's rhetoric of liberty. But some of the tools needed to accomplish this task came from the conditions under which they worked; slaves bonded over the inhumane treatment they experienced, and they found ways to act outside of the stringent limitations the slave system placed upon them. The plantation, their workplace, was the birthplace of the Haitian independence movement.

FIGURE 4.6 Juan Patricio Morlete Ruiz, *Hold Yourself Suspended in Midair*, X. In *Spaniard and Return Backwards* (De español y torna atrás, tente en el aire), c. 1760. Los Angeles, LACMA.

CONCLUSION

Workplace culture is a flexible and capacious concept. Workers of varied status, skill, and autonomy have used a range of tools to shape the practices of the workplace to reflect their wishes and goals, in the face of resistance from masters and employers. This examination of workplace culture moved from the most autonomous workers, artisanal craftsmen, to the most bound, slaves, to understand some of the ways all workers understood and shaped the spaces and relationships in which they labored. It is evident that skilled men, who stood at the apex of the social structure in terms of pay, respect, and independence, had the most opportunity to define how they worked. Actions such as protests over wages and working conditions, work stoppages, and even the damaging of a master's property brought little serious retribution down on the heads of skilled workers. These actions did not stop the advance of the economic and social changes conveyed by increasing industrialization; however, they did confirm the ability of skilled, privileged workers to push back against that change. Workers without valuable skills or status, while enjoying fewer opportunities to define their work practices, still found ways to exert some autonomy as they labored. Women provide an excellent example of finding ways within systems that excluded them to participate nonetheless. Women as wives and widows made themselves indispensable to businesses and enterprises, thus harnessing necessity to open up space to act.

Even indentured servants and slaves, who did not enjoy the status of free men and women, found ways to shape their work culture. Resistance played a large part in carving out space for self-determination. Tactics taken up later by skilled and unskilled workers faced with increasing mechanization and job losses, like slowdowns, feigned ineptitude, and even outright destruction of property, were practiced by unfree workers seeking to free themselves even incrementally from the grasp of their masters. For workers of all stripes, molding the conditions, practices, and physical spaces where they labored provided them with a measure of control and autonomy. Workers used all the tools at their disposal to achieve these ambitions.

CHAPTER FIVE

Work, Skill, and Technology

LEONARD N. ROSENBAND

Pierre Montgolfier was sure he knew how to improve his trade. French paper manufacturers, he thundered, had to make "fabrication as little dependent as possible on the pains of workers on whom one can rarely count, perfect the machines that are employed in papermaking, and imitate the Dutch who substitute them for men as much as possible."[1] But even the Dutch found clockwork machines and men scarce in a broad range of trades. This chapter considers the interplay of work, skill, and technology in Europe (and its outposts) during the eighteenth century.[2] It examines the gritty, often turbulent, and always unforgiving labor of the skilled craftsmen who toiled in small urban shops and larger, concentrated sites of production. It also explores the precise tacit knowledge employed by these artisans and the afflictions that accompanied their work. Too often, the efforts of skilled men and women have been overshadowed by the application of steam power to the machinery of cotton production and its consequences. Yet for many of them, changes in the days and nights of their working lives took shape before, and apart from, the onset of large-scale mechanization. Accordingly, this chapter also probes the social and power relations that informed production in workshops large and small.

Most students first encounter the Industrial Revolution in T. S. Ashton's remarkable pamphlet book, *The Industrial Revolution, 1760–1830*. He depicted these years as a period of rapid economic growth and dynamic technological change.[3] But a sturdy scholarly consensus now emphasizes slower rates of growth and the persistence of familiar tools and techniques in most late-eighteenth-century trades.[4] As a result, consideration of economic change in the "long eighteenth century," with boundaries of 1688 and 1815, has shifted to the issues of anticipation and settings. This scholarly move returns the inquiry to a perennial question: what accounted for Britain's industrial primacy? The traditional formula was "free men, free minds, and free markets." When those answers proved too vague, a new set of more rigorous approaches emerged. We now have the "industrious revolution," the "industrial Enlightenment," and the early stirrings of the "great enrichment." On the flip side of the coin, we can also observe a variety of illiberal features, including aggressive protectionism, an interventionist Excise, anti-labor Combination Acts, and the conquest of an empire, with its staple commodities produced by slave labor.[5] Put simply, this debate now turns on the inroads that both petty and large-scale capitalism, science, and the state made in craft shops and mills, and the extent to which they remade work itself.

In 1810, George Crabbe wrote that "'Trades and Professions'—these are themes the Muse, / Left to her freedom, would forbear to choose."[6] Perhaps he was unmoved by consideration of pulleys, gears, and grease, as well as tons of output. But there is a long tradition that links meditation about work as the primal curse with concern about the tedium of idleness. An acceptable, if mechanical, definition of work is the exercise of human energy, both physical and mental, in pursuit of a productive goal, that of securing a livelihood. Yet there is little room in this understanding for the social, cultural, and political dimensions of skilled work during the Old Regime, with its characteristic blend of specialized know-how and manual prowess. This labor was fatiguing and unsentimental, with compositors or stonemasons, who often toiled ten or more hours a day, sacked as soon as they completed a pressrun or a building. But it also had its pleasures, such as fellowship in a craft community, the chance to demonstrate one's technique, and even a cleansing, cooling sweat. In its physical and emotional range, this world of work amounted to a fully realized *comédie humaine*.

In every mechanical art, skilled men labored mightily to preserve the value of their mastery. They struggled to keep their ranks thin, familial, and initiated in the customs as well as the technologies, the methods, and tools of their trades. Yet these efforts did not always yield men of a single mind-set as mechanical as the instruments and machines they used. Consider two tales from eighteenth-century print shops, one in London and one in Paris. Ever boastful, Benjamin Franklin surely failed to endear himself to his brothers in a London printing shop. The author of *Poor Richard's Almanack* sometimes "carried up and down Stairs a large Form of Types in each hand, when others carried but one in both Hands." His "constant Attendance" and abstention from Saint Monday, typically venerated by compositors and pressmen at the alehouse, "recommended [him] to the Master," but never to his fellows. When he violated yet another of his comrades' rules, the "Chapel Ghost," the guardian of their duties and liberties, exacted revenge "by mixing [his] Sorts, transposing [his] Pages, breaking [his] Matter."[7]

Across the Channel, a rather different story unfolded. There, two sleep-deprived apprentices unleashed a peculiar sort of revolt in a printing shop on the rue Saint-Séverin, probably during the 1730s. Tormented by the nightly cries of cats who lived among the print shops, the apprentices took matters into their own hands. They climbed above the master's bedchamber and howled and meowed for a week, leading the *patron* to call for the elimination of all the animals except his wife's favorite, *la grise* (the gray one). Aided by the journeymen, the apprentices beat the cats into a stupor, and then dispatched them after a mock trial. The boss' wife bellowed when she saw the dead *la grise* hanging from a noose, but what could she do? Her husband had ordered the annihilation of the animals, and he was preoccupied by the work stoppage. Apparently, the story was passed around for years, complete with burlesque-like reenactments (see also Chapter Four, where the master's role is not mentioned).[8]

The London and Parisian accounts reveal that there was more to Old Regime work than the labor itself. There were solidarities forged and ignored, power struggles won and lost, output quotas respected and broken. At every turn, artisanal toil was both collective and individual. And whether it was carried out in cramped ateliers or large workshops, it was affected by some combination of disruptive droughts, shifts in fashion, changes in state policy, technical modifications, and distant wars and blockades. Finally, and perhaps most notably, the population of western Europe grew from approximately 81.5 million to 132.9 million people from 1700 to 1820.[9] As a result, the rising real wages enjoyed by many skilled men before the Seven Years' War stagnated and often declined. In the years immediately before the French Revolution, the height of laboring men diminished slightly, a measure of tough times. Yet, in 1767, Sir James Steuart observed that "Men are forced to labour now because they are slaves to their own wants."[10] One example of this shift was the growing presence of mirrors famously detected by Daniel Roche in the working-class quarters of Paris. Was this newfound attention to appearance among the laboring poor evidence of a fresh, widespread desire for adornment? Put simply, skilled workers in their ateliers or on large worksites were buffeted by several crosscurrents, many of which were trade-specific. The Industrial Revolution emerged out of an unsettled world of work and its cultures.

GUILDS, LARGE WORKSHOPS, AND THE HOURS OF PRODUCTION

Perhaps the most familiar urban workspace in Old Regime Europe was the craftsman's shop, with a skilled master, a journeyman, and an apprentice or two turning out shoes or candlesticks, and the master's wife keeping the accounts while his daughter eyed his charges for a mate. These crowded (and complicated) working and living arrangements should not be mistaken for spheres of thoroughly independent, self-reliant artisans. Instead, the skilled residents of goldsmiths' lane and shoemakers' alley were generally members of occupational guilds. In the organic order of European societies before the French Revolution, urban craft guilds were legally privileged bodies, or *corporations*. Whether they owed their charters to a prince or an imperial city, guilds exercised a formal monopoly over the practice of a particular trade in a specific area. Whether they contained a handful or hundreds of members, they represented the interests of the guildsmen (and occasionally guildswomen) while protecting society from shoddy goods and unruly hands. Like so many facets of guild activity, this balance both kept order and stirred conflict.

In 1768, the Bavarian chancellor, Baron von Kreittmayr, complained hotly that "A dog cannot have as many fleas as the guilds have abuses."[11] Of course, to the guildsmen, these "abuses" ensured their livelihoods and amounted to essential prerogatives, ranging from mutual assistance to the right to labor with particular raw materials. But Adam Smith believed that assemblies of skilled craftsmen, "even for merriment and diversion," seldom resulted in anything other than "a conspiracy against the public, or in some contrivance to raise prices."[12] The Spanish reformer Pedro Rodríguez Campomanes declared that "nothing is more inimical to popular industry than the setting up of guilds and public charters," while the enlightened French Controller-General Turgot actually dissolved France's guilds for a time in 1776.[13] Accordingly, the utility and purposes of Europe's guilds were fiercely debated at the end of the Old Regime. They were said to exile the genuinely skilled and throttle technical innovation. Certainly, they were highly legalistic, ceaselessly suing each other over access to markets, raw materials, and even production techniques spirited from each other. The inventory of their sins and shortcomings was endless.

Nevertheless, for Europe's rulers, the guilds had their uses. The states drew revenues from them, trusted them to govern the transmission of skill from one generation to the next, and depended on them to police footloose journeymen, at a time when the man on the move was inevitably depicted as dangerous. Only the craftsmen who attained the rank of master enjoyed membership in the guilds. Collectively, the masters monitored the recruitment, training, and certification of the apprentices, who learned primarily by observation and practice during the term of their indentures. For the most part, the term of apprenticeship contracts lasted for three to seven years, when the successful youngster became a journeyman. Now the waiting commenced; many journeymen never advanced beyond this rank, and in a broad array of trades, they served as a reservoir of cheap, skilled labor. Some *compagnons* satisfied their *Wanderlust* and tramped, which offered young men a chance to refine their skills and attract financial backing. When a journeyman caught the fancy of a master's widow or daughter, or secured capital in another fashion, he might make a masterpiece (sometimes only symbolically), ascend into the company of masters, and operate his own shop.

In a small town, like the German village of Fulda, the pursuit of mastership was a face-to-face affair. In 1784, its twenty-one guilds averaged thirteen members, with a low enrolment of two furriers and a great company of sixty shoemakers.[14] At the other end of the spectrum, during the early 1720s, the 117 incorporated trades of Paris included approximately 35,000 members.[15] At times, the interests of masters and journeymen in guilds large and small overlapped, such as when they patrolled the borders of their crafts for interlopers. At other moments, the tensions that smoldered in the compact shops of Fulda were the same as those in the large trade communities of Paris. Masters and men constantly quarrelled over such matters as the amount and quality of the food or the nature of the living quarters that were the resident journeymen's due. And they squabbled restlessly about the proper duration of *une journée de travail*, a day's work. Assessing these hours can be difficult. Consider this imprecise but eloquent rendering of the hatter's day: "a man goes early and works late."[16] London's tailors labelled their slow summer hours "cucumber time," when short days meant that they subsisted on little else.[17] In printing, leather breechmaking, and other trades, a "day" represented a carefully negotiated amount of output rather than a quantum of hours. Consequently, a skilled hand might be paid for two *journées* accomplished during a single working day. There were also payments for "overwork," wages for labor on half-holidays, and compensation for "downtime," when the master or manufacturer failed to provide the expected work. Worktime and its rewards in early modern Europe were trade- and place-specific, laced with custom and hard-won. Despite its need for skilled hands, a Swiss printing house refused to hire two ailing journeymen, knowing that turning them to the road and the *hôpital* surely consigned them to their deaths.[18]

When they could find work, the skilled men of Old Regime Europe labored long hours. Parisian blacksmiths had workdays of fourteen hours, while bookbinders sweated for sixteen.[19] With such exhausting workdays, it is not surprising that every adjustment was contested. In 1735, the master joiners of Augsburg complained to the Crafts and Trades Court that their journeymen refused to rise at the customary hour of 4:00 a.m. The journeymen retorted that the masters had scrapped breakfast and the vespers meal, so what did it matter if they arrived at their workbenches a little later?[20] In 1805, it was the journeymen locksmiths of Augsburg who had their say about worktime. If their masters would allow them to rise an hour later and "improve the usual breakfast," they would work on Saint Monday.[21] This was quite the concession: English weavers were said to "play frequently all day on [Saint] Monday, and the greater part of Tuesday, and work very late on Thursday night, and frequently all night on Friday."[22]

Worktime and its management posed particular issues in the Old Regime's large workshops. These mills, sheds, and outdoor sites were distinguished from factories by the absence of power-driven machines that turned out long runs of products. Nevertheless, these concentrated structures were capital-intensive, turned on the synchronized work of flocks of skilled and unskilled labor, often produced goods in batches, and usually depended on water power. David Landes located these large workshops in brewing, ceramics, dyeing, fulling, glassmaking, metallurgy, papermaking, and tanning, as well as at certain construction sites. Deep mining and sawmills also belong on this list. Some of these large workshops were established in towns and cities. More often, these production sites were located in the countryside, along with resident workforces, beyond guild sway. On the whole, they required more energy than small shops; greater space for large products, workbenches, or stocks of raw materials; and tools and small machines that were too costly for the budget of a worker or two. Some facilities, such as tanneries and paper mills, smelled so bad that their neighbors exiled them; and others, especially arsenals, needed isolation for secrecy.[23]

If bells and whistles signalled the start and close of work at these sites, and managerial cadres watched over and integrated the skilled and unskilled labor there, the work in these structures was never quite as mechanical as the bosses desired. Successful paper production turned on timely weather, a full storeroom of old linen, accessible markets, the absence of catastrophic disruptions, and a ready supply of skilled journeymen. Few manufacturers could count on all these assets for very long. More typical were the troubled circumstances of the papermakers of Languedoc. According to a survey from 1772, a manufacturer in Le Vigan reported that one of his vats "had been idle for a long time for want of [raw] materials." A producer in Cavaillac claimed that "this mill only works for six months of the year for want of water." A papermaker in Joyeuse lamented that "these mills would work profitably if they were busy all year." But they ceased making paper for three months each year due to "droughts and inundations." The waters of the Tarn River, which "are dirty most of the time," produced "considerable unemployment" in the mills of Mazamet. Seeking relief from the onerous paper tax imposed by the Crown in 1771 and probably petitioning indirectly for state subsidies, these papermakers may have underestimated their output and production seasons. Yet it was the rash paper manufacturer who turned to one expert's estimate of a working year of three hundred days as a reliable guide for his annual profits. Instead, the producers and workers went about their daily labor, which often lasted until the pulp ran dry (Figure 5.1).[24]

In the midst of these routine interruptions of production, the influential and calculating Montgolfiers engineered particularly precise workdays punctuated by equally exact mealtimes at their mill in Annonay. A foreman sounded the bell at 3:45 a.m. and work began at 4:00 a.m., a departure from the craft convention that work should start at midnight or 1:00 a.m. The day's labor was divided into four segments, each capped by a meal, and ended at 7:00 p.m. Seasonal light mattered little in the mill, since the Montgolfiers ignored the longer summer workdays prescribed by the state in 1739. Just to be sure, they computed the exact hours of candlelight needed in their mill from mid-August to the end of April; December, for example, required six hours and forty-five minutes' worth of candles. Theirs may have been an unusually mathematized, enlightened approach to secure regular diligence and output, but it was less audacious owing to their reliance on the long-established, highly synchronized skills of their trade.[25]

Arthur Young, the caustic eighteenth-century commentator on economic affairs, claimed that "everyone but an idiot knows that the lower classes must be kept poor or they will never be industrious."[26] He was outraged that in flush times working men and women might labor less yet consume more. Thomas Pennant put it less abrasively in 1772: "Till the famine pinches they will not bestir themselves."[27] Known to scholars as "low-wage thinking," this approach dominated educated opinion in Britain and on the continent during the Old Regime, though it began to lose traction around 1750. To be sure, a few observers worried that the relatively stagnant and declining wages of the later decades of the century limited consumption and inhibited general growth. Adam

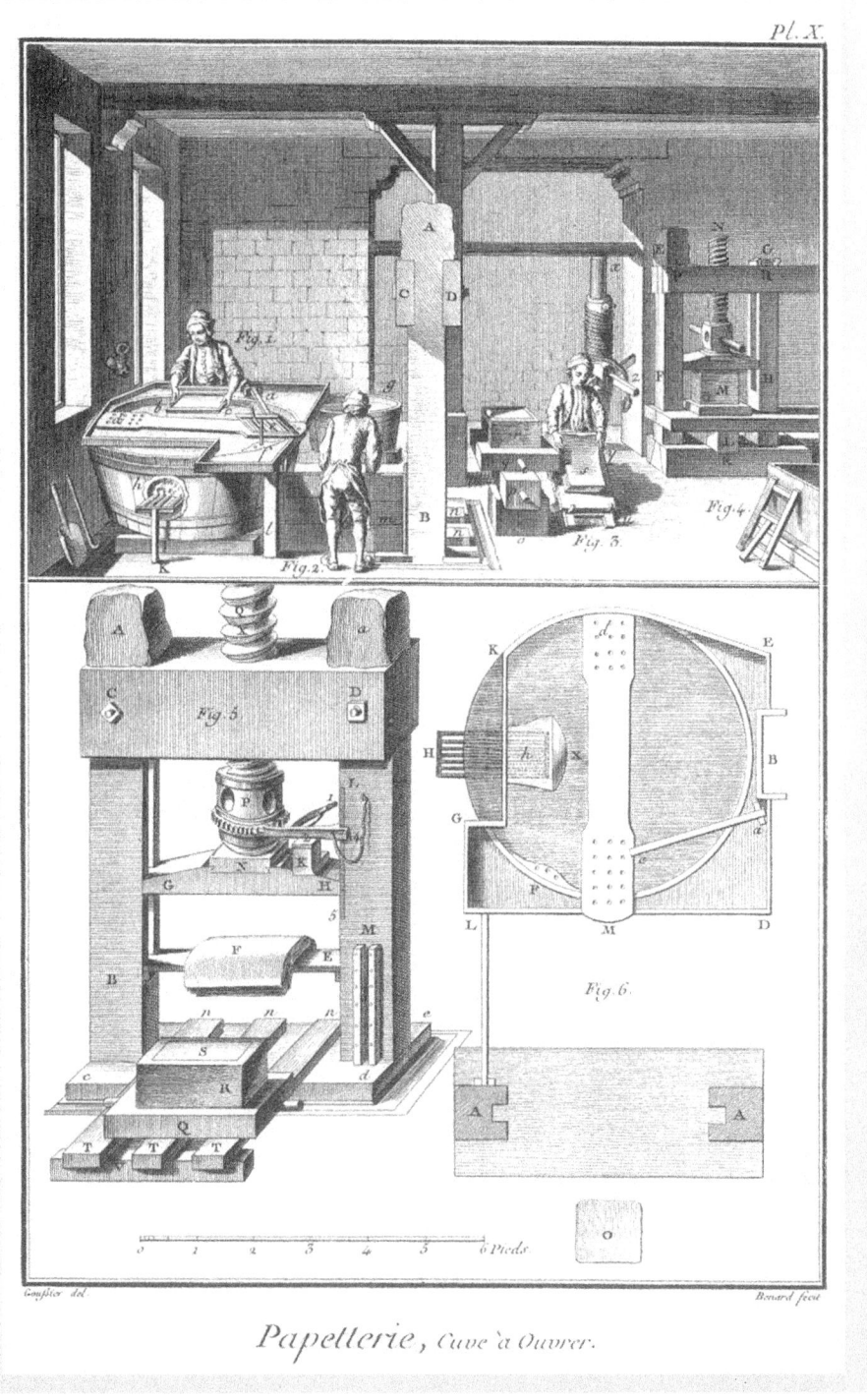

FIGURE 5.1 *Papeterie*, Plate X (Details of skills and tools of papermaking). In Denis Diderot and Jean le Rond d'Alembert, *Encyclopédie, ou dictionnaire raisonné des sciences, des arts et des métiers*, vol. 5, 1751–72.

Smith figured prominently in these ranks. He explained "that a little more plenty than ordinary may render some workmen idle, cannot well be doubted; but that it should have this effect upon the greater part, or that men in general should work better when they are ill fed than when they are well fed ... seems not very probable."[28] Thus the question arises: were skilled men (and women) laboring longer hours, and doing so with greater intensity, in the later years of the eighteenth century than previously? And if so, how did this pattern influence the coming of the Industrial Revolution?

Much of the recent debate in early modern European labor and economic history has centered on Jan de Vries' concept of the industrious revolution. Briefly, he argued that skilled and unskilled workers *chose* to labor longer hours, often more vigorously, in order to consume novel manufactured goods and imported commodities. Moreover, plebeian families increasingly found employment beyond the household to pay for these objects. As a result, men, women, and children spent increasingly more time at waged labor, and their expanding purchasing power proved decisive in stimulating large-scale industrialization. Particularly in England, northwestern Europe, and colonial America, de Vries claimed, this burgeoning consumption added a demand-side element to the familiar supply-side impulse of new machines and reconfigured production practices.[29]

De Vries' thesis has proved controversial. There is little debate that England, continental Europe, and colonial America grew richer in the eighteenth century, and that some of this wealth drifted down to the lower orders. Wants became needs, supposedly smudging the distinctions between the orders. In 1768, an anonymous memoir from Montpellier raged that: "The most vile artisan behaves as the equal of the most eminent *artiste* or anyone who practices a trade superior to his. They are indistinguishable by their expenditures, their clothes, and their houses."[30] Even shop girls now wore stockings and to the horror of their betters, might be mistaken for persons of quality. But was it really the best of times for skilled workers and their consumer appetites? Frank Trentmann has challenged this conclusion in a number of ways. First, he pointed out that in the century after the English Civil War, the laboring classes tended to spend their money on essentials, such as "better furniture," rather than "novelty items." He concluded that working hours likely lengthened in the second half of the eighteenth century, but ascribed much of this to soaring inflation (especially in food prices) and ever more competitive labor markets. And cleverly, he maintained that the purchase of more tea, candles, and sugar was less an issue of keeping up with the Joneses and more a question of workers remaining solvent by staying warm and awake while they hammered or spun later into the night.[31]

Étienne Montgolfier calculated that the skilled men in his family's mill had "an effective workday" of thirteen hours.[32] How much more of the precise work of papermaking could they perform—or wish to perform—beyond these already fatiguing hours? Not surprisingly, when the Montgolfiers introduced their pioneering program of labor discipline, they made limited changes in the "day's work." Meanwhile, skilled and unskilled hands in many trades had to work harder to meet increasing tax burdens amid the perpetual warfare of the late eighteenth century. Worse yet, the English bureau of the Excise was growing steadily more effective—and aggressive. And in France, the Catholic Church was instrumental in a considerable reduction in the number of feast days, which added more work days to the year. We still need evidence of the *precise* links between whatever new patterns of consumption emerged during the long eighteenth century and *measurable* shifts in the pace and duration of labor, in large workshops and small. Only then can we assess what was revolutionary or even *newly* "industrious" about the drives and efforts of early modern Europe's skilled hands before they were overpowered by the mechanization of their arts.

WORK AND ITS INFIRMITIES

Whether there was an industrious revolution or not, eighteenth-century essayists, master craftsmen, and manufacturers agreed that it was best for skilled workers to stay in place and stay at their jobs. Stability, said their employers, would render them more regular in their conduct and their work. Even the sunup to sundown regimen of North American slaves, improving plantation managers averred, was "morally redemptive," since it bridled the worst tendencies of these men and women while yielding profits for their owners.[33] Skilled journeymen, too, would prosper in proportion to their hours away from the road and the tavern. Of course, this perspective took no account of the conditions that ground down the workers.

Consider the environment inside an Old Regime paper mill. Depending on the season and their functions, the workshops were either cold or hot, drafty or musty, damp or dry. Throughout the year, however, these workplaces were insect-ridden, easily identifiable by their stench and, above all, choked with dust. A typical French mill housed only one production vat but consumed as many as three hundred quintals of rags every year. At the close of the seventeenth century, the Jews collecting "filthy wares," the cast-off linen that served as the base for most handmade paper, caught the eye of the physician Bernardino Ramazzini. As Jews hauled the dusty or sodden rags to Italian paper mills, he claimed they were tormented by "coughs, asthma, nausea and vertigo," the same afflictions known to plague paperworkers.[34] Red arms, missing fingernails, and rheumatism were the lot of every veteran hand in papermaking. Stooped backs often hobbled them, so skilled paperworkers sometimes traded tasks to ease the pain. In a rare concession to the human toll of papermaking in an Old Regime encyclopedia, the *Britannica* noted that the duster, a device that shook the debris from the rags before they were sorted, rendered this pitiless work "less pernicious to the [female] selectors."[35] Fortunate paperworkers were warmed by fireplaces, slept on straw mattresses, and even had stiff bedlinen. But for many, living quarters amounted to pallets in dark, airless *chambres* scattered among noxious workshops. No doubt the bosses observed that these spaces surpassed the cold ground of the open road but often just barely. Battered by long hours in the mills and long hours on the tramp when the mills shut down (as they so often did), few journeymen turned out paper once they reached the age of forty; indeed, paper workers above this age inevitably had to prove that they still handled the molds smoothly. This premature aging helps explain why journeymen fought so hard to maintain the routine quotas and elaborate custom of their trade, and thereby make clear their right to a place in it (Figure 5.2).

Old Regime gilders, Ramazzini reported, fell victim to "vertigo, asthma, and paralysis." "Very few of them reach old age," he continued, "and even when they do not die young their health is so terribly undermined that they pray for death." Makers of timepieces and other "fine work," Ramazzini explained, "incur such grave defects of vision that before they are old they become practically blind." Thus, he concluded, "of the whole body of workers those who make glass display the most prudence. When they have worked for six months … they take a vacation, and when they reach the age of forty, just when it is the right time to give up, they say farewell to their craft and spend the rest of their lives enjoying what they have laid by for their leisure and security, or else they devote themselves to work of another sort."[36] Yet it is unlikely that many glassworkers, or artisans of any stripe, enjoyed such rewarding retirements or secured other work. Surely the fate of a miner named Ralph Crawhall was more typical. He had the highest earnings at Graham's pit in the Whickham, England, colliery during two weeks in May 1742.

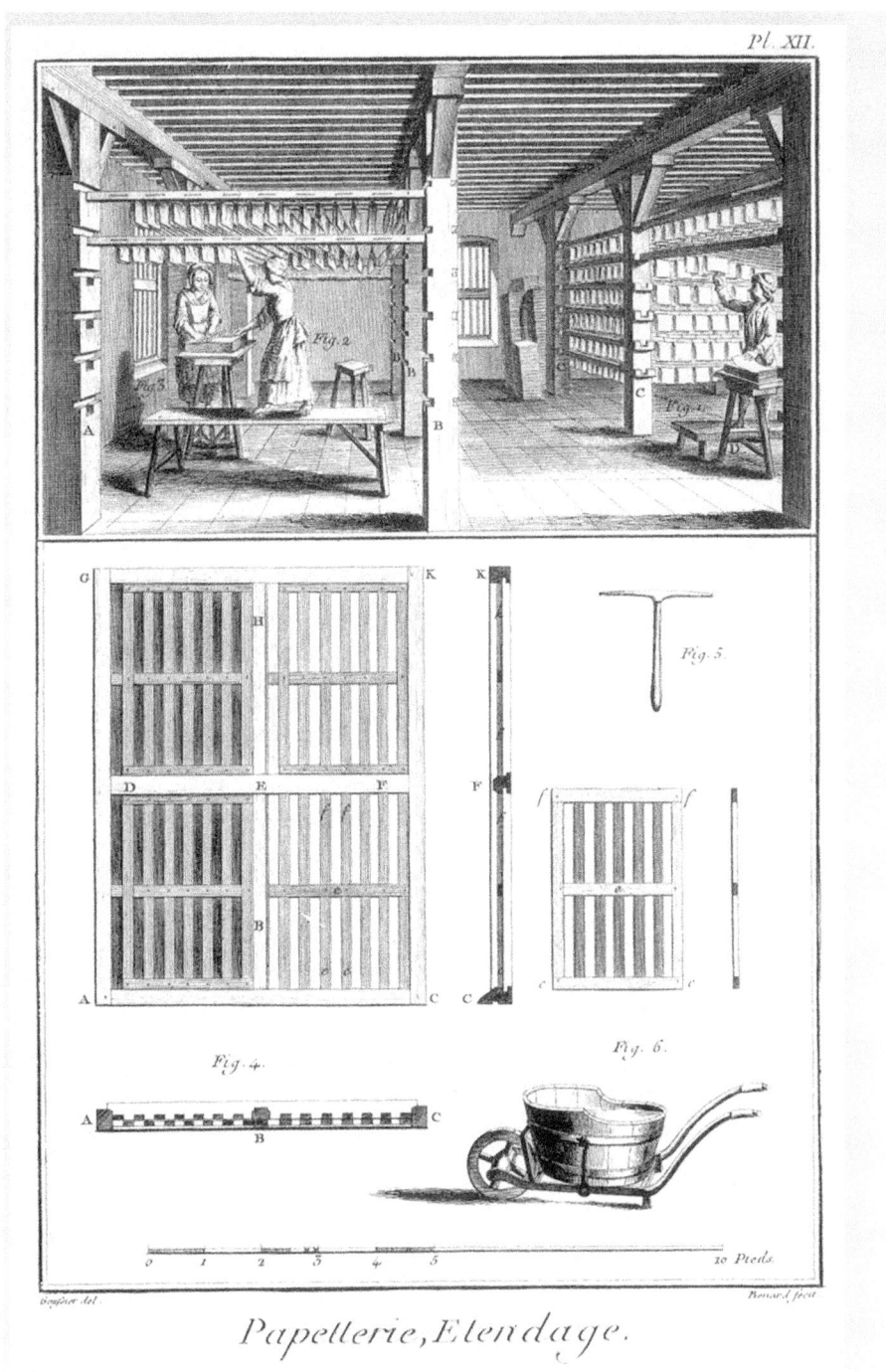

FIGURE 5.2 *Papeterie*, Plate XII (Drying). In Denis Diderot and Jean le Rond d'Alembert, *Encyclopédie, ou dictionnaire raisonné des sciences, des arts et des métiers*, vol. 5, 1751–72.

But in 1764, when he was too enfeebled to hoist his pick, his "wife and children [were] starving."[37] Small wonder, then, that Benjamin Franklin's striving and quota-busting ways frustrated his mates. They must have seen his speedy work and indifference to Saint Monday as monopolizing hours of labor that might offset lean times. In this hard-bitten world of work, the journeymen inevitably took their revenge.

CHANGES IN THE WORKS: THE GUILDS

During the last decades of the Old Regime, many master craftsmen were unable to resist challenges to their prerogatives, or to their skills themselves. The Parisian *corporation* of carpenters and cabinetmakers spoke for many craft communities when it denounced competitors outside its ranks as "disturbers of the repose of the guild."[38] They proscribed "usurpers" of every sort, such as *faux-ouvriers* (workers who had failed to make an apprenticeship or refused to play by the masters' rules), *alloués* (workers *à louer*, for hire by anyone) and *chambrelans* (illegal workers who lived and labored in dank, tiny rooms). When guildsmen located these lawbreakers, they had the authorities seize their raw materials, tools, and wares. But the number of illegal workers evidently continued to increase, and even guild masters silently subcontracted work to them. As the economies of eighteenth-century Europe expanded, the temptations of new profits opened cracks in the guild regime.

The growing penetration of large-scale capital widened these cracks. Gail Bossenga has cautioned us to avoid conflating master, a legal status, with artisan, an economic status. As international trade expanded during the Old Regime, some masters, she explained, became "big businessmen."[39] As such, they resorted to *faux-ouvriers*, and turned their fellow masters and journeymen into skilled wage-earners. After all, *les grands* needed regular output, standard products, and a certain subordination from headstrong skilled men to meet the demands of international markets. As Émile Coornaert put it, the "guilds were hostile to *le monopole* in principle; they ended up by sanctioning it."[40] If this reordering left some crafts untouched, Coornaert emphasized its growing role in the export sectors of textiles, printing, and shoemaking.

In the midst of ever more *alloués* and the intensifying capitalist transformation of their crafts, journeymen turned outside the guilds to brotherhoods of their own making for protection. These associations had long pedigrees by the eighteenth century. In the towns of the upper Rhine, for instance, the journeymen's brotherhoods, or *Gesellenvereine*, had appeared among the bakers, smiths, furriers, tailors, and shoemakers by the turn of the fifteenth century.[41] Already in 1539, the French edict of Villers-Cotterêts explicitly outlawed "any alliance or *intelligence* between journeymen, any assembly on their part for whatever cause, in short, any coalition against the masters."[42] Some journeymen's combinations represented a single trade, while others, such as the French *compagnonnages*, yoked together numerous crafts. Above all, the associations fought— often literally—for journeymen's interests. They made sure that no brother worked "under price," ensured that workers had their say in recruitment and placement, and marked the routine passages of tramping or advancement up the ladder of skill. They also defended their timeworn skills with hammers and fists against intrusions by interlopers and technological innovators. Although the brotherhoods sometimes accepted technical changes, particularly when shifts did not disturb their custom, these organizations had a conservative cast and thereby helped contribute to the ongoing outflanking of the guilds by dispersed, rural production.

Cottage manufacture is a vast topic, too long to address in detail in this chapter. It centered on the spinning of thread and weaving of textiles, as well as the production of small metalwares. It fit nicely in an era when circulating capital, such as yarn, was relatively valuable and tools and instruments, such as looms, were considerably less expensive than later machinery. And it shifted certain risks from the manufacturer to the worker; as Landes explained: "If orders fell off, the putter-out [of raw materials] had only to stop buying [finished products]."[43] The labor was performed by men, women, and children in their homes, reducing manufacturers' capital costs. Outside the guild setting, moreover, there was less chance of widespread, collective resistance to technological novelty or departures in style and fashion. In many regions, dispersed production had become a formidable competitor for the guilds.

Taken together, the pressures and practices of late-eighteenth-century production weakened the guilds. So the Crown attempted to strengthen the masters' hand against the workers in France. In 1749, Louis XV issued letters patent that prohibited *cabales* among journeymen and other workers, and required them to carry records of previous employment, the better to weed out the intransigent or those men who had run up debts with former masters. In 1781, royal letters patent again banned association among the workers and now mandated that the journeyman must possess a printed record of his employment and identity, the *livret*. Of course, the efficacy of these orders is difficult to assess, especially since journeymen were often caught carrying forged and duplicate papers after 1749.

In the corporate order of France, "personal initiative," wrote Pierre Deyon and Philippe Guignet, could only "flourish" under the stamp of state privilege and exemption. By granting the title of royal manufactory, the Crown intended to stimulate fresh approaches and infant industries, and also to free producers from shackles imposed by guilds.[44] Even guildsmen themselves petitioned princes and municipalities for exemptions from trade statutes and regulations so they could fashion their goods and govern their journeymen as they saw fit. Meanwhile, the administrators of France's economic system at the close of the Old Regime were not of a single mind about the regulatory order, including the craft guilds. According to Philippe Minard, the inspectors of manufactures fell into three camps: the old school, strict state regulators; the officials who sought a balance between regulation and the market, so that the excesses of relatively free trade and production did not undermine the quality of French goods, especially those destined for international commerce; and the deregulators who had embraced the cause of "laissez-faire, laissez-passer" and the dictates of consumer demand.[45] Such was the divided state of opinion when the Revolution erupted.

In sum, one size did not fit all in the powers and condition of Europe's guilds in 1789. Both the needs and the circumstances of their home states also mattered. In the wake of the Reformation, Sheilagh Ogilvie argued, the English crown grew hesitant about chartering guilds beyond London. "By 1600," she concluded, "even the powerful London guilds ... were increasingly unable to prevent London citizens from practicing any occupation freely." Nor were they able any longer "to regulate their own members systematically."[46] They persisted, but the repeal of the Statute of Artificers in 1813 put an effective end to the guilds, since it removed their control of apprenticeship. In 1770, Peter Leopold, later Holy Roman Emperor Leopold II, abolished the guilds of Tuscany. In the states of western Germany, however, political fragmentation continued to breathe life into these bodies. According to Robert Duplessis, the German guilds retained greater powers than elsewhere in Europe. They accounted for half the region's output in 1800, and still had the muscle to hold back technological change and corral their competition. But even here, "imperial ordinances in 1731 and 1772 gave individual states the right to end corporate monopolies and to open upcrafts to all who wanted to practice them."[47] Napoleon's occupation put an end to the trade communities of Westphalia and the Rhineland; earlier, in France itself, the d'Allarde law had abolished the guilds in March 1791. (An admirer of Turgot, d'Allarde reminisced that, in 1776, "He [Turgot] enlightened the king for a moment, and for a moment these abuses ceased to be.")[48] In June 1791, the Le Chapelier law concluded the work of eliminating the *corporations*, while also outlawing workers' "coalitions" and work stoppages. Across Europe, the guilds were in no position to stop this process.

CHANGES IN THE WORKS: CONTRIBUTIONS OF THE ENLIGHTENMENT

The "great divergence," the paradigm that centers on the growing gap between "the West and the Rest" during the eighteenth century, has generated a great deal of heat and light among historians. In recent years, the "small divergence," the new dress of the perennial debate about England's industrial primacy in the West, has joined its older sibling. Both discussions have generated fascinating research about how and why industrial capitalism and mechanization "took command." Some of the explanations have been granular, from advantages in metalworking to the relative intake of sufficient calories to complete a long day's labor. Some have emphasized big processes, like the growing "financialization" of Western economies or the increasing "commodification" of working men, women, and children.[49] And still others have accentuated culture, especially a distinctive scientific mentality in the West, with its ring of institutions and means of communication. To explore all of these issues is beyond the scope of this chapter. To get at some crucial concerns, however, we will turn to the intersections of work, skill, and the "industrial Enlightenment," primarily in large workshops from the 1760s to the early nineteenth century.

Several historians maintain that the plates in Denis Diderot and Jean le Rond d'Alembert's *Encyclopédie*, which appeared from 1762 to 1772, constituted a visual manifesto. According to these scholars, the illustrations and accompanying texts amounted to nothing less than a call to retool the mechanical arts on a rational, scientific footing. After this transformation, the production of pins or the binding of books could be done efficiently anywhere, just as scientific principles and laboratory results could be replicated anywhere. The plates offered an image of how work could be accomplished once it was freed from the burdens of place, history, and craft mystery. These mechanical utopias would be shorn of cluttered workshops, contentious negotiations between masters and men, and many of the frustrations ingrained in the lived art.[50]

In a series of learned volumes, Joel Mokyr has considered the economic history of the Encyclopedists' crusade.[51] He coined the term "industrial Enlightenment" as a shorthand for this effort, and maintained that it was the deepest wellspring of modern economic growth.[52] In practice, Mokyr's industrial Enlightenment was at once a set of institutional transformations and a campaign that exposed "tacit artisanal *savoir-faire*" and its supposedly inflexible nature to the sunlight of scientific inspection.[53] Manufacturing techniques that incorporated the most advanced understanding of "natural phenomena and regularities" would bridge the worlds of the *savant* and the *fabricant*.[54] Once this novel sort of "useful knowledge" diffused, the improvement of production and, ultimately, large-scale mechanization would inevitably follow.[55] But ever the historian as well as the economist, Mokyr recognized the limited immediate impact of the industrial Enlightenment. He allowed that "the bulk of innovation in manufacturing and agriculture before 1800 advanced without science providing indispensable inputs."[56] Instead, he ascribed these changes to "experience-driven insights, trial and error," and good fortune. The industrial Enlightenment's dramatic transformation of production technologies, Mokyr conceded, awaited the nineteenth century. That said, the Encyclopedists' program, with its zeal for a systematic ordering of production and enhanced efficiency, certainly figured in the systems of labor discipline that the Montgolfiers, Josiah Wedgwood, and Samuel Bentham designed.

CHANGES IN THE WORKS: CONCENTRATED PRODUCTION

The connections between nascent industrial capitalism and novel systems of labor discipline took shape in England as early as 1700. In that year, Ambrose Crowley penned an elaborate code for his ironworks. In Order 103, he declared that "from 5 to 8 and from 7 to 10 is fifteen hours, out of which take 1½ for breakfast, dinner, etc. There will then be thirteen and a half hours *neat* [my italics] service." Crowley also forbade "quarrelling, contention, disputes or anything foreign to my business, any way loytering."[57] His workers' time belonged to him *tout court*.

The Montgolfiers were also jealous of their journeymen's time. Making paper by hand entailed closely synchronized, delicate tasks inscribed (as we have seen) in seasonal patterns of production. Whenever the Montgolfiers or their counterparts challenged the *workers'* custom, the journeymen walked out en masse and often engaged in rolling strikes, leaving behind vatfuls of perishing pulp. In 1780, the Montgolfiers introduced a state-of-the-art device to pulverize the discarded linen that served as the fiber of their reams. At the same time, they trained a flock of youths from nearby villages who were innocent of the art of papermaking for their expanding mill. When the Montgolfiers shielded the youngsters from the veterans' ways, the journeymen stalked out of the mill—and were promptly locked out by their masters. The Montgolfiers, then, attempted to create a new sort of worker, the employee, who was both loyal to them and cut off from the journeymen. Most notably, the Montgolfiers made limited changes in the tasks of the trade, since they were not in the business of deskilling. Instead, they sought to decouple these skills from the journeymen's custom, and thereby take command over their transmission. For a time, the Montgolfiers' plan succeeded, but the workers' ways ultimately reappeared in the mill, which led Étienne Montgolfier's son-in-law to install a papermaking machine in 1822.[58]

Josiah Wedgwood wanted to "make such *machines* of the *Men* as cannot Err."[59] He recognized the difficulty of this task, and when things went badly, he "almost env[ied] many of [his] Bretheren for the simplicity of their work."[60] In 1765, he observed that his workforce was a bunch of "dilatory drunken, idle, worthless workmen." But a decade later, Wedgwood boasted that he employed "a very good sett of hands."[61] Like the Montgolfiers, he replaced venerable workers (albeit more gradually) with young men and (unlike the Montgolfiers) women inexperienced in the traditions of the potteries. He created a hierarchy of production units, as did his counterparts across the Channel. But Wedgwood alone thoroughly separated his shops, termed the "Useful Works" and the "Ornamental Works," as well as the hands that sweated inside of them. He also intensified the familiar division of labor in each shop, shaping uniquely specialized workers. This approach posed dangers for these workers, since they risked being sacked when fashion changed. As Wedgwood coolly noted, "Gold, the most precious of all metals is absolutely kicked out of doors, & our poor Gilders I believe must follow it."[62] Yet his highly trained workers were prized by other potters, and he had his hands full holding on to them. Following Karl Marx and Harry Braverman, certain economic historians would describe Wedgwood's imposition of an ever finer division of labor as an episode in the deskilling of labor at the heart of industrial capitalism.[63] According to Neil McKendrick, however, Wedgwood's plan "did not destroy skill: it limited its field of expression to a particular task, but within those limits it increased it."[64] Certainly, that skill was evident in the red- and black-ware that vastly surpassed the earlier, crude pottery of Staffordshire. But however skillful, Marx and Braverman would claim the workers' labor at narrow tasks was the measure of their slide into the ranks of the dispossessed.

Wedgwood introduced flow production in his pot-bank at Etruria, where his wares moved from the kiln to the storage room in an orderly stream. He treated his hands in the same fashion: they were to be punctual, productive, and orderly. *His* rules mattered in production, not the rule of thumb that traditionally governed the potteries. Wedgwood trained a bevy of overseers, and took special care in warning them about the everyday evasions and tricks of the trade. He prospered and the international reputation of his wares soared. He even developed an early clocking-in system, which his workers, on at least one occasion, turned against his interests. In 1772, they massed outside the pot-bank's gates to agitate for higher pay at precisely 6:30 p.m.[65]

In sum, Wedgwood never transformed his men into machines; indeed, in 1776, he lamented that his new model men "have been at play 4 days this Week, it being Burslem Wakes. I have rough'd, & smooth'd them over, & promis'd them a long Xmass, but I know it is all in vain, for Wakes's must be observ'd though the World was to end with them."[66] His schemes spread slowly through his trade, as did the Montgolfiers' designs in their industry. Lesser manufacturers likely believed that these high-end producers, with their advantages of scale, established markets, and international presence, would have succeeded without their novel programs of labor discipline.[67] But both manufacturers pointed the way to more extensive and invasive control of labor, and thereby remade the practice and setting of a maturing industrial capitalism.

As early as 1600, a fleet of administrators supervised the Venetian state shipyards, better known as the Arsenal. At least a score of clerks and bookkeepers, as well as one hundred technical and disciplinary figures, were tasked with the oversight of every facet of production. (Despite all these watchful eyes, it should be noted that both the skilled and the unskilled hands in the yards preserved their pranks, dodges, and capacity to pilfer timber and rope.) As a result of the yards' organization of production and the Republic's resources, the Arsenal's ability to turn out a considerable number of ships in a matter of months or weeks had won it widespread renown. Still, the work in these sites revolved around traditional skills, with their enduring custom and nomenclature (Figure 5.3).[68]

A very different project took form in the English naval dockyards when Samuel Bentham was appointed Inspector-General of the Naval Works in 1795. At the time he took office, the royal shipwrights were paid according to "treble days, double days, day-and-a-half, two for one, task, job, common hours, nights and 'tides'."[69] Bentham would have none of that. He had invented the panopticon popularized by his brother

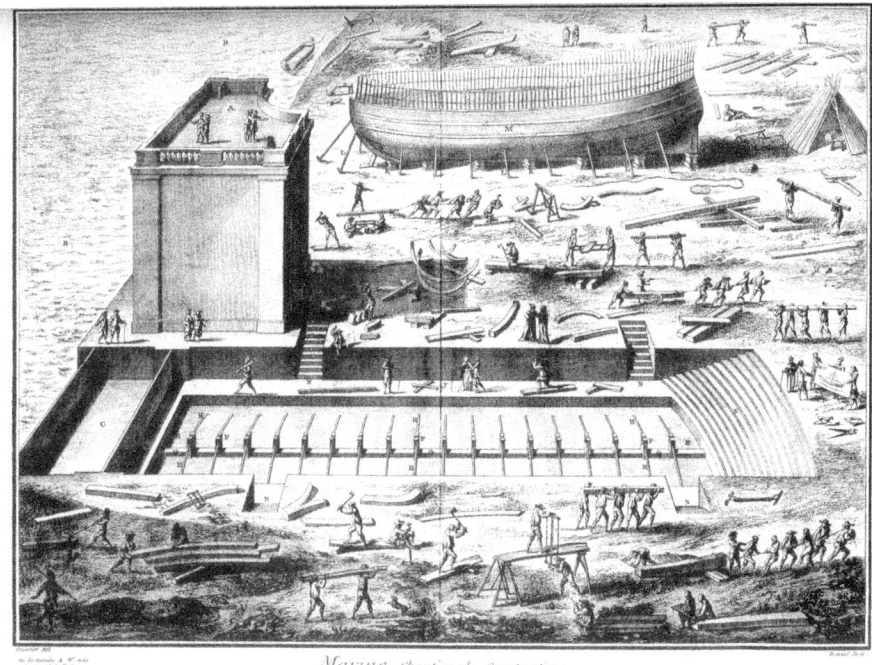

FIGURE 5.3 *Marine*, Plate VIII (Shipyard). In Denis Diderot and Jean le Rond d'Alembert, *Encyclopédie, ou dictionnaire raisonné des sciences, des arts et des métiers*, vol. 7, 1751–72.

Jeremy, and trusted in close observation, precise accounting, and managerial latitude. He was determined to undo the dockyard workers' spirit of independence by putting an end to their rule of thumb, intensifying the division of labor, and renaming the resultant tasks. As his proud widow, Maria, revealed: "He therefore began by classing the several *operations* requisite in the shaping and working up of materials of whatever kind, wholly disregarding the customary artificial arrangement according to trades."[70] No longer would the caulker's work of rendering ships watertight rest on his tacit knowledge and individual judgment. Instead, as William J. Ashworth explained, carefully guarded skills would "be illuminated, restructured and formalized" in accord with Bentham's larger system.[71] Then, Maria Bentham concluded, he would design machines that would accomplish the yards' work "independently of the need for skill or manual dexterity in the workman."[72] And so he did, in part: Bentham reorganized and sped up the refitting of ships with his "floating dam," introduced a new method for joining wood, and adopted the steam-powered sawmill for the handling of rough timber. This last innovation put a stop to the custom known as "lawful Chips," the right of journeymen to the shavings and flakes from recently worked wood, which had long justified the disappearance of much larger pieces from the dockyards.[73]

Bentham intended to drown the traditions and solidarities of the naval yards in a fresh pool of workers. "It is well known," he observed, "that an increase of the number of workpeople in any business is the most effectual bar to combinations."[74] So he turned his powers against the shipworkers' apprenticeship system. Like the Montgolfiers and

Wedgwood, Bentham dreamed of malleable, skilled men, who were innocent of the customs and combined might of the veteran hands. Though he settled for less, in many ways Bentham's reforms, like 24-hour shift work—or "INCESSANT WORK" as he scripted it—lasted longer than did those of his contemporaries.[75] Of course, his efforts rested on the enduring powers of the state rather than Wedgwood's less forceful heirs.

While Bentham, Wedgwood, the Montgolfiers, and others were experimenting with new programs of labor discipline, they were also integrating new tools and machines into their shops. Many of these devices had been invented and refined abroad; but the importation of blueprints and diagrams without experienced hands often proved futile. So improving masters and manufacturers frequently turned to men on the move, including tramping journeymen and state-sponsored industrial spies. The tacit knowledge conveyed by these migrants was instrumental in the making of industrial capitalism, as well as England's industrial primacy.

In eighteenth-century Europe, workers with diverse origins rubbed shoulders in large workshops and small. Consider the Guadalajara woollen mill, a royal enterprise in Spain. It was worked primarily by Dutch, French, English, and Irish hands, but workers there also had Italian, Polish, Prussian, and Swiss roots.[76] In the seventeenth century, it had been the English who had benefited extensively from the importation of continental know-how. The origins of the English patent system, according to Christine MacLeod, can be traced to the Crown's use of letters patent to insulate European émigrés and their techniques from the guilds. She also noted that Dutch engineers drained the fens of East Anglia, and that artisans seeking their fortunes and Huguenots seeking religious liberty improved English papermaking along with clock- and watchmaking.[77] Closing a circle, Richard Arkwright, whose water frame (patented in 1767) transformed cotton spinning into a factory industry, sought out timepiece makers to build his machines. With this invention and the virtual birth of industrial engineering at Matthew Boulton and James Watt's Soho Works, the arrow of technological and skill transfer in the seventeenth century had unequivocally reversed direction. The transformation of England into the workshop of the world drew on both native and imported work practices, skills, and technologies.

CONCLUSION

By the end of the eighteenth century, market pressures, efforts to systematize production, and state actions impinged on the customs and work practices in Europe's large and small workshops. As skills and tools at the base of artisanal cultures shifted, so did the customs that sheltered them. Skilled craftsmen spoke of their membership in "honorable" trades and employed "false workers" in dark corners of their cities; journeymen fought together for their customs and toiled alone, with little or no hope of becoming masters; and craft apprentices learned their trades by observation and doing, while pauper apprentices suffered in poorhouses, workhouses, and cotton mills. In every age, surely, such complex and even contradictory identities and experiences coexist. But this era also gave rise to the novel political radicalism of the *sans-culottes*, the Sons of Liberty, the London Corresponding Society, and the United Irishmen. In turn, the Le Chapelier law, Alien and Sedition Acts, and the British Two Acts and anti-Combination Act of 1799 challenged this radical tide. The maturation of industrial capitalism, then, did not pass through neat, Rostovian stages.[78] As E. P. Thompson taught decades ago, industrialization was—

and is—a conflicted, multidimensional process. It entailed changes in technology and skill, workplace relations and status, political pressures and forms, and much more. The "stress" of such transformations, Thompson insisted, fell upon "the whole culture."[79] And so it did around 1800, when all that had seemed solid in the Old Regime of production was already starting to melt into air.

CHAPTER SIX

Work and Mobility

ELEONORA CANEPARI

This chapter focuses on the relationship between work and mobility in western cities in the seventeenth and eighteenth centuries by exploring the multiple ways individuals managed to maintain a state of mobility while at the same time holding a professional occupation in a specific place. How was it possible to access the labor market and engage with local institutions without being permanent residents of the city? This chapter demonstrates that this kind of mobility, which was both residential and professional, was not only consistent with being inserted into the local context but also constituted a structural feature of *ancien régime* cities and played an especially crucial role in the organization of work.[1] To do so, the chapter focuses on the elements that made it possible for individuals to work in a specific place without settling down. By using the notions of "complementarities" (of mobility and local work organization) and drawing on the existing literature and the case study of Rome, the chapter demonstrates that the work of "people on the move" was actually highly integrated into local settings.

The first section defines the notion of "mobility" as a concept that includes not only migration but also the many forms of unsettledness. It is well known that mobile workers were part of urban economies, discussed in the section "Fluctuations and Mobility in Labor Markets," because of the fluctuations in demand that characterized the *ancien régime*'s economy. What is less well known, however, is how and through what means workers "on the move" could integrate into local labor markets. In the sections "Supra local Connections" and "Places, Houses, Workshops: Mobile Workers and Local Settings," the chapter explores some of these channels of access: on the one hand, supra local networks, and on the other specific elements of local settings, namely hiring places, forms of cohabitation, and guilds.

FROM MIGRATION TO MOBILITY

In this chapter, the notion of mobility is used to define a broad set of situations that have unsettledness as a common feature. The other common feature this chapter focuses on is that they are all workers. While all the sectors of the economy (both rural and urban) are taken into account, this choice excludes people who were constantly "settling in motion," such as merchants. The reason for this lies in the aim of exploring how people who were not granted fiscal exemptions and who did not have consulates and specific facilities at their disposal (for instance, the *entrepôts*) were nevertheless able to access local labor markets without settling down. While the bibliography on merchants in the city is extremely rich, few works have explored the way migrant workers of the lower classes accessed local resources other than hospitals and poor shelters.[2]

In fact, "foreigners" in early modern societies were not necessarily individuals coming from elsewhere; instead, the term applied primarily to individuals who were unsettled and lacked local ties. For this reason, this chapter uses "mobile workers" to refer not to individuals who came from outside the city and settled inside it but to those who continued being mobile, unsettled individuals such as seasonal and temporary migrants but also laborers and journeymen whose professional (and thus spatial) mobility was deeply entrenched. In doing so, this chapter falls within the framework of recent historiography on migrations in *ancien régime* societies that has profoundly transformed the notion of "foreigner." One of the main changes introduced by this body of work has been a shift from the notion of "mobility transition" to that of mobility as a commonplace experience in early modern societies. According to the concept of "mobility transition," twentieth-century modernization was the key event that produced a sharp increase in individual instances of migration as compared to premodern societies, which were stable and self-sufficient.[3] This notion of a stable early modern society in which people moved only when forced to has been called into question by the work of Jan and Leo Lucassen, who argue that high levels of mobility actually date to much earlier than the twentieth century, and that most "basic decisions by human beings—the choice of a profession or a partner—" pushed people to migrate from their places of birth or residence. Regardless of distance, people's movement often led them to other geographical environments.[4] In a recent article, they point out that the increased mobility characterizing the nineteenth century was due more to improvements in transportation than to any so-called "modernization," and concluded that "it was not the underlying structural causes of migration that changed, but rather its scale."[5] Indeed, the two historians argue that, at least in western Europe, early modern societies were driven by different kinds of migration, such as temporary and permanent, seasonal, covering short or long distances, and so forth.

Challenging the notion of a stable pre modern society—and arguing for a high incidence of early modern mobility—has inevitably cast doubt on the assumption that strangers were marginalized individuals who had "dropped out" of the social fabric. If mobility was a widespread and common experience, then foreigners were "common individuals"; they were not necessarily paupers or vagrants.[6] With this analytical shift, a completely different notion of foreigner has emerged, enriched by research carried out at the scale of the city. At this scale, scholars have mainly explored mobility in relation to processes of local integration and in the wake of the "ecological" approach pioneered by the Chicago School, which stressed the cultural differences separating groups of strangers living in a given city and viewed integration as equivalent to assimilation.[7] Drawing inspiration from Norbert Elias' monograph on Winston Parva, scholars have pointed out that, rather than natives and migrants being kept apart by inherent cultural differences, the real distinctions were created locally.[8] Indeed, being a native inhabitant of the city was not an asset in and of itself; it was an asset because it automatically meant that the individual took part in local networks. In contrast, since migration entails a reorganization of the migrant's social life and relations, foreign dwellers were obliged to establish their own networks in the arrival city—even if relations established in the arrival city and bonds maintained in the birthplace were often connected.[9] As a consequence, the real divide between foreigners and native inhabitants appears to have been the length of time they had lived in the city and their degree of local integration. Indeed, early modern cities did not distinguish between inhabitants in terms of strangers versus native dwellers but rather in terms of settled versus unsettled individuals.[10] Simona Cerutti demonstrates this change in perspective when she suggests that "foreigners" be defined as *unsettled* individuals, regardless of birthplace.[11] In other words, a foreigner is not someone who comes from another place but rather someone who has no local ties. Consequently, native inhabitants who lost their local bonds—for instance, because of temporary migration—and weakened their degree of social insertion might "become" foreigners in their own birth cities. The status of foreigner was therefore determined by the fact that an individual failed to satisfy the requirements of a specific settlement process as established by municipal authorities. These requirements included professional, residential, and familial forms of belonging: permanent residence and a job and, as in the 1580 Roman municipal statute, a man being recognized as *pater familias* and having his family with him in the same city.[12]

Accordingly, historians now consider local rootedness and a continuous, stable residence in the city as the main requirements for the urbanization process. Nevertheless, many early modern towns were characterized by a high degree of mobility among their inhabitants. In 1996, Bernard Lepetit defined these as "pluralists" or "mixed" societies whose existence and development relied heavily on migrant inflows.[13] Indeed, through all of the early modern age, cities relied on many migrants to carry out the economic activities sited there. And yet massive in-migration to towns was neither the only nor the main form of movement people enacted in early modern societies. As Lucassen and Lucassen have argued, "a high level of early modern mobility resulted largely from ubiquitous local and regional moves from parish to parish."[14] Besides internal and "international" migrations, therefore, cities also hosted a form of local or intra urban mobility which, these authors argue, accounted for the majority of individuals' relocations.[15]

The sections that follow use this notion of mobility drawn from the latest findings in historiography as a definition that applies to several situations: not only newcomers but also those workers who came to the city on a temporary basis, whether regularly or not, as well as unsettled laborers, journeymen, and other workers living in precarious conditions. How were these individuals, whose presence was characterized by the lack of strong local ties, able to find jobs and to make a living with their labor?

FLUCTUATIONS AND MOBILITY IN LABOR MARKETS

Defined by Jean-Yves Grenier as "a world of uncertainty," early modern economies were characterized by irregular production and changing levels of supply and demand.[16] Moreover, many professional activities were organized around seasonal rhythms of production. For these reasons, un- or semi skilled temporary workers were an important resource, as they could be employed according to production fluctuations. Carmen Sarasúa argues the demand for labor in both industry and services in eighteenth-century Europe, together with the labor supply, "led to an increasing dependence of peasant families on these migrations."[17] As Jan Lucassen points out, seasonal work was very widespread in western Europe from the Middle Ages: "The data available show that people were prepared to travel as much as three hundred kilometres in search of seasonal work. At the end of the *ancien régime*, it involved more than 300,000 people in a handful of important pull areas."[18] In addition, it is important to consider short-distance migrations, that is, migrations within district borders, which can be roughly estimated to have involved half a million workers. For example, temporary migrants working in the maritime sector of Scandinavian urban centers such as Copenhagen and Stockholm during the eighteenth century came both from the hinterlands of the two cities and from a series of countries (northern Germany, Finland, Norway) that formed a migratory system.¹⁹ In both cities, "the majority of the migrants could be called internal migrants in contemporary terms," that is, individuals coming from the rural maritime areas.²⁰

The incidence of seasonal workers was especially significant in the building sector; Lucassen cites the example of brick workers from the German principality of Lippe-Detmold who migrated on a seasonal basis to, for example, Germany, Scandinavia, and the Netherlands.²¹ This movement involved approximately ten thousand workers specialized in brickmaking and organized into teams of about ten men each that were employed from spring to autumn. Temporary work and the organization of laborers into gangs also characterized many activities in English cities. Donald Woodward has found that in three of the northern ports, Hull, Newcastle, and York, most urban laborers worked in gangs "doing a thousand and one varied jobs, sometimes alongside craftsmen, but often not," including handling goods brought to the quayside.²² In York, groups of specialist laborers were licensed by civic authorities: the stevedores who unloaded cargo from vessels at the wharf, and the porters who distributed it throughout the city. While laborers already living in the city met normal levels of demand, sudden surges of activity necessitated emergency measures including the hiring of extra workers from nearby villages.²³ Hull gangs were therefore "called out whenever needed," and many laborers worked for the city's institutions only a few days in the year.²⁴

The building sector was not the only one that relied on the presence of a temporary workforce. The manufacturing industry in the textile sector was also sometimes organized on a seasonal basis; indeed, manufacturing *indienne* was a seasonal affair, since bleaching and washing that took place prior to printing were not carried out in winter, as the more limited supply of water at this time impeded the use of water-powered machines. As a consequence, "when business stopped, the earnings of those involved in printing, painting, bleaching and washing also ceased."²⁵ Another sector of the preindustrial economy that relied on temporary workers was services; it is well known that temporary migration led many people to cities in search for a job in the service sector as a specific stage of the life cycle.²⁶ Women were especially likely to find employment in the "care" sector.²⁷ In her article on temporary migration in eighteenth-century Spain, Sarasúa highlights that "excluded from apprenticeship by guild regulation and social custom, women had no access to these migratory flows; instead they went into domestic service." She focuses on a migratory system that led women from the northern regions (the Cántabro valleys, and especially the Pasiego valley) to relocate to Madrid to work as wet-nurses. The mobility of women from Pasiego was temporary but, unlike seasonal labor migrations, its rhythm was dictated by "personal circumstances," that is, the birth of babies. This intensive emigration flow began in the last decades of the eighteenth century, when Pasiego women became the most popular choice for middle- and upper-class families in Madrid.²⁸

A "generally limited and highly fluctuating demand for products and services" also characterized small commodity production in central European countries during the early modern age, according to Josef Ehmer: "In nineteenth-century Europe, the largest mass occupations outside agriculture were, as a rule, not—or at least not only—weavers and miners, but shoemakers, tailors, stone masons, carpenters, and the lie, or female domestic servants."²⁹ Indeed, migration was a key mechanism for regulation of the artisanal labor market; during the eighteenth century, at least three-quarters of the journeymen population was made up of immigrants. In Vienna, only 24 percent of artisans were native inhabitants of the city. Migratory systems linked Vienna to several specific rural areas, which Ehmer defines as "areas of high density of rural artisans."[30] In these regions, the small average size of the workshops generated a surplus of young men who immigrated to the cities because they could not find employment in their home villages. In the city, some crafts, such as tailors, shoe makers, and cabinet makers, were more likely than others to employ a large number of young immigrants and therefore played a key role in attracting immigration streams from the rural areas.

A similar pattern of labor migrant employment existed in early modern Rome, with certain crafts, such as shoe makers, offering job opportunities to a population that was not necessarily made up of young men. A survey of 510 apprentices and journeymen in seventeenth- and eighteenth-century Rome has demonstrated that men aged thirty years and over accounted for the majority in some professions, such as shoe makers, bakers, and chicken breeders (*pollaiolo*). Nevertheless, men aged thirty and over did not practice only low-qualified jobs but also more skilled ones such as barber, barrel maker, keysmith, and tinsmith. Skills are not the only criterion to explain the distribution of individuals across the professions; indeed, those younger than twenty constituted the majority in occupations such as innkeeper, barber, carpenter, apothecary, and pasta maker. If the presence of young apprentices in some of these professions—barbers, apothecaries, and carpenters—was owing to the young men's willingness to acquire new skills, other occupations—such as pasta makers and innkeepers—were easily accessible jobs that did not require any specific expertise. To explain this professional distribution, therefore, it is necessary to consider other criteria such as the degree of accessibility characterizing some jobs. Inns, for example, were extremely numerous in a city where pilgrim and migrant inflows were so intense that most of the population was non-Roman. This meant that jobs opportunities were available not only to men of an age to begin an apprenticeship but also to those who were trying to make ends meet. The organization of the profession represents another relevant factor: baker and shoemaker masters needed many assistants and helpers to meet the demands of their trade.

The turnover rate was extremely high, regardless of professional status, in all age groups represented in the survey. As Daniel Roche, Michael Sonenscher, and Bronisław Geremek have demonstrated, a high rate of turnover characterized many labor markets. In her study on the Baroque economy, Renata Ago distinguishes what she calls "guaranteed" apprentices and journeymen, who worked for the same employer for many years, from the "precarious" ones whose careers were extremely mobile and who were constantly in search of employment. The sample of 510 apprentices and journeymen mentioned above is almost entirely composed of "precarious" individuals: only eight people appear in the records in more than one year. In the parish of Santa Maria ad Martyres, for instance, only 4 percent of the apprentices and journeymen recorded in 1677 were still there for the 1680 census, and 2.6 percent for the 1682 census.[31]

Intense labor migration inflows and high turnover rates have also been observed in eighteenth-century Barcelona.[32] At the end of the century, the city underwent an intense process of densification and rapid population growth, with the population tripling over seventy years thanks to immigration flows from the Pyrenean areas and central Catalonia.[33] Migrants were attracted by both the welfare system and the expanding labor market. Montserrat Carbonell-Esteller argues: "the changes in occupation, the progressive transformation of apprentices into wage earners, the appearance of the first calico factories ... as well as the growth of the service sector, allowed the influx of numerous people in search of work."[34] At the same time, however, these changes contributed to exacerbating the economic disparities within the lower classes. Indeed, the gap widened between guild members and craftsmen who did not belong to guilds, whether native inhabitants or immigrants, and a progressive process of "proletarianization" was triggered in which many apprentices were impeded from becoming masters.

The same dynamics—changes in the labor market, intense migration inflows, and the start of a "proletarianization" process—were ongoing in eighteenth-century Paris, as several scholars have pointed out.[35] The *"ville promise"* was the preferred destination for a growing population of migrant laborers from French rural areas, attracted by the possibilities the capital city offered. As Daniel Roche argues, just as in Barcelona, there was a big difference between workers who belonged to guilds, held a certain status and professional specialization, and, potentially—although this became progressively more difficult—enjoyed career advancement, and the *"gens sans état."* William J. Sewell emphasizes the same difference between the *"gens de métier"* and the *"gens de bras,"* who were deemed to be *"sans état,"* meaning unsettled, lacking in social status and occupation.[36] This group included individuals working in manufacturing and those earning a living in the service sector (day laborers, dockhands, porters, handymen, and so on). As Roche notes, the massive population of the *"gens sans état"* present in the *faubourgs* was a tangible sign of ongoing changes in the organization of work related to the development of the city's operations in the eighteenth century, operations requiring a not highly specialized workforce to perform a variety of minor and casual tasks.[37] The growth and differentiation of the Parisian population therefore led to an increase in small trades and services—a great deal of daily retail activity, production, and goods repair, often performed directly on the streets of the city.[38]

Like western Europe, several scholars have noted that the labor market of North American cities at the end of the eighteenth century was characterized by an increase in the demand for "casual labor." Some studies have emphasized that this demand, together with the freedom of individual initiatives in the colonies, opened opportunities for workers to achieve vertical mobility. Indeed, in colonial times a journeyman was conceived of as "tomorrow's master mechanic."[39] This view of vertical mobility and "fluidity" in the social structure of preindustrial North American cities has been contradicted by several scholars, however, who have demonstrated that many urban inhabitants, both native residents and migrants, lived in conditions of poverty and/or worked all their lives as salaried labourers.[40] As Jeanne Cuillier points out, "labour, beginning in the 1760s, had by the 1820s produced salaried labour as the dominant form of production relations in major urban areas."[41] Increased residential mobility—intense but short-distance—was associated with this phenomenon. Douglas L. Jones identifies the category of "transients" as "mostly poor and of lower-class origins," "moving very short distances from town to town and job to job."[42] In the city of Salem, transients listed in 1791 were working-class artisans (mostly men) and lower-class mariners and laborers. Because of the high number of single men, it is likely that transients were mainly former servants who experienced "intense poverty and physical hardship." According to Jones, transiency was different from the tramping artisans system in that it was "individualized and nonunionized"; as a consequence, he raises the question of whether Massachusetts transients were capable of travelling in search of a job, given their poor economic conditions. As the next section argues, the answer to this question lies in the supra local networks that structured and enabled the mobility of workers for short and long distances.

SUPRA LOCAL CONNECTIONS

Several authors have pointed out that one of the main assets employed by migrant workers was the supra local network based on the arrival city and place of departure, a network composed of individuals' mobility and trans local social ties. Some of these networks were regulated by institutions, as in the case of the *Wanderzwang*, or compulsory travel as a journeyman, while others were completely informal. Their common denominator was that they enabled mobile workers to access local resources and information by remaining "in motion."[43]

As Sewell observes, the fact that they were "*sans état*" meant journeymen could not create associations that enjoyed the official recognition of local authorities; for this reason, they remained unofficial, clandestine groups. As a direct consequence of not being recognized by local authorities, journeymen's associations had a supra local nature. Indeed, one of the main differences between French masters' guilds and journeymen's associations is that the former had a specific local jurisdiction whereas the latter gathered together men working in different places. In fact, while masters' titles and privileges were only valid within the city whose municipal authorities had granted them, journeymen did not have a local guild with a specific set of rights to claim and instead moved from city to city in search of jobs. Although this lack of local recognition was certainly a disadvantage for journeymen, the supra urban and multiprofessional structure of their organizations enabled them to move from place to place and to access local labor markets for short periods of time. Daniel Roche, in his commentary on the apprentice glass maker Jean-Louis Ménétra's journal, notes that these networks relied on facilities such as inns that were widespread along the migrants' itineraries. Inns were an essential part of the migratory system since they provided men not only with food and shelter, but also with information about the labor market.[44]

For central European apprentices, the same functions were provided by the *Wanderzwang* system. By offering them social contacts and material support, it constituted, according to Ehmer, part of a highly institutionalized framework. This system consisted of "a multiyear phase of circulation in which short-term stints of employment in one city or another alternated with days or weeks spent literally on the road."[45] As he emphasizes, in central Europe the *Wanderzwang* system was fully complementary to the stable and corporate organization of work thanks to a close association of spatial stability and mobility; in other words, migration was "an essential and regular component of a relatively stable social and economic order."[46] In fact, journeymen, who Ehmer defines as a "highly flexible, superregional workforce," were mainly unmarried and mobile young men; they accounted for the majority of individuals working in the artisanal labor market and thus represented the backbone of the crafts organization.[47] For these workers, mobility had become part of the group's specific culture and identity, in contrast to the lifestyle typical of masters, which was characterized by more stability.[48] Apprentices were also highly mobile workers. On the one hand, Ehmer has shown that many of them were not born in Vienna—for example, more than 50 percent in a mass trade such as the cabinet makers, and despite their young age (thirteen to eighteen), had travelled to the city from a range of places including relatively distant regions.[49] On the other hand, apprenticeship was not a phase of stability because many apprentices left their masters before the end of their training.

Another kind of supra local network was the one which, Laurence Fontaine argues, provided the foundations for the structure of peddlers' itinerant trades in the cities;

although in a different way, also in this case the network brought together settledness and mobility, arrival cities and birthplaces. In her studies on peddlers leaving the Alpine valleys for northern and southern Italy, she emphasizes that mobility sometimes represented a way to engage in local space, and a sedentary way of living was not necessarily the only objective of all migrations. Mountain migrant workers built multisituated networks that linked together different families, and this granted these itinerant vendors privileged access to information, allowing them to adapt to changing local situations from a political, religious, and economic point of view while also reducing transaction costs. In pointing out the existence of "mountain" capitalism, Fontaine has demonstrated that these networks were managed through pyramidal structures headed by entrepreneurs from the same mountains as the peddlers whose work they organized.

These workers set up a network of supra local trade from the sixteenth century onwards, and Fontaine highlights the significant role they played in processes of integration.[50] Theirs was a nonspecialized trade, since the peddlers used to sell different kinds of items according to changing urban needs and opportunities. These networks were built on two components: the existence of an extended kinship network in their places of birth and what Fontaine calls a *"quadrillage"* of the commercial space. This consisted of opening depots and shops in the arrival city, where some families from the village had succeeded in establishing an initial supply center, and in hiring a workforce from the local site giving rise to this migration flow. These networks developed thanks to the way they used the city as an "epicenter" for peddlers' immigration and itinerant trade. The link between the arrival cities and the villages where the migration originated was constituted not only by the commercial network but also by a circular mobility that villagers continued to engage in even after having completely settled in the city. Alpine valley peddlers, "even once they became *bourgeois* of a city, went on living in or going to their birthplaces on a regular basis."[51]

This finding applies not only to peddlers' migration but also to other kinds of mobility, including that of highly specialized craftsmen. In her studies on glass makers from Italy, Corine Maitte has demonstrated that the organization and characteristics of these *"migrations de savoir-faire"* were not determined by their profession itself but rather by the structure of the community in their departure place.[52] Indeed, most "Italian" glass makers came from Altare, a village in Liguria. This community lived off the exportation of both its manufactured products, which extended as far as Sicily, and its men. These migrants were highly specialized craftsmen whose mobility was organized in a seasonal pattern: for part of the year, Altare's inhabitants left the village to work in Italian cities as glassmakers; in the following period, they either came back to their village or travelled outside Italy. Maitte highlights the strong ties that this "moving" community maintained with Altare no matter the distance they travelled, and the high degree of integration between mobility and the economy of the village; managed by the guild of the village, these migrations were integrated into the local economy, for which they represented the main resource.

In early modern Rome, preserving strong ties with one's birthplace was part of a migratory pattern typical of migrants from the north of Italy (dioceses of Vercelli, Milano, Bergamo, Novara) who came to the city to either settle down or spend long periods working in workshops. These patterns relied on strong community bonds in which kinship, origins, and employment networks overlapped and enabled men and women as well as information to circulate from the arrival to the departure place and vice versa. This continuous flow allowed migrants to retain control over properties they owned in their places of origin, thanks to the mobility of members of the community network as well as specific devices such as the power of attorney.[53] The simultaneity of these kinds of migration—settlement in a city and regular trips to the birthplace and/or maintaining tight connections—played an important role in the urban labor market, since it allowed newcomers to easily and quickly find a job once they arrived in the city.[54] In these migrations, the community of origin represented the main asset for newly arrived immigrants to rely on, as it granted them access to essential urban resources such as temporary accommodation, a means of entering into the labor market, and socialization in the local professional *milieu*.[55] This was also due to the fact that, after arriving, the newcomer was often housed in the workshop (or shop) where he might serve as a factotum or apprentice while learning how to perform the job and establishing his own network of local contacts. It is also worth noting that, because of circular mobility, some individuals used to come and go from the city and thus needed to "reinsert" themselves into the local labor market more than once. This circular and "simultaneous" migratory pattern also enabled migrants to associate mobility and "settledness" in another way, by facilitating the practice of handing a workshop down to another person from within the same community. In fact, specific communities used some workshops for many years in a row (either through ownership or rent) even though the workers changed every year. In this case, we can see that people came and went from the workshop, circulating within the community network but also between city and birthplace. Of course, this does not mean that the only framework for these migrants' presence in the city was their community of origin but only that this community was an important asset for accessing urban resources in these kinds of migrations, and especially on the occasion of a migrant's first arrival.

The same connecting network characterized a specific migratory pattern: that of porters (Figure 6.1). They were usually men, even if it is worth noting that Louis Mercier also describes women porters.[56] The specificity of this labor migration lies in the fact that porters did not settle down in the arrival city, nor were they seasonal migrants. According to Raul Merzario, porters were "multi-annual" migrants; they lived in the city for several years but without seeking to settle down definitively.[57] The precariousness and temporary nature of porters' often lengthy residence in the city is demonstrated by their residential patterns: very often, their households were made up of ten to twelve men who were at the same time co residents, coworkers, and co villagers. For these workers the existence of a multisituated and dense network granted easy access to the arrival city's labor market. Therefore, in pointing out the high degree of integration between the economies of the valleys the porters came from and those of the arrival cities, Merzario emphasizes that "it is necessary to take into account the fact that migration implies two geographic and economic places," that is, the departure village and the arrival cities and towns.[58]

The same multilocal network was part of the migratory system that led Pasiego women to relocate to Madrid for work. In fact, this flow was based on constant group movements from the Pas valley to the capital city. Women moved together from their common birthplace to the city where, thanks to the shared network of information, they knew they were very likely to find employment.[59] Nevertheless, it is worth noting that in this case as well mobility was organized within the framework of a connecting network; on arriving in Madrid, Pasiego women could count on the solidarity of other women from the same valleys already living in the city and working there as itinerant vendors. The assistance of these women was especially useful for Pasiego wet-nurses to find employment in Madrid, and their meeting point was the hiring place of Santa Cruz.

FIGURE 6.1 "Porters from the town of Venice." In Cesare Vecellio, *Costumes anciens et modernes, Habiti antichi et moderni di tutto il Mondo di Cesare Vecellio*, Paris, 1860.

PLACES, HOUSES, WORKSHOPS: MOBILE WORKERS AND LOCAL SETTINGS

Besides these multisituated networks, there were other resources that enabled different kinds of workers to hold a job in the city while remaining mobile, either on a seasonal basis or engaging in "multi-annual" migration patterns or life-cycle mobility. One of these resources was the hiring place. Although personal connections were the preferred way to hire someone, seasonal workers did not always have contacts with local employers.[60] Hiring places—"*marchés aux bras*," defined by Geremek—enabled workers to transcend their lack of local knowledge and locate one of their first jobs in the city.[61]

In eighteenth-century Madrid, as described by Sarasúa, migrant Pasiego women who had not already found jobs and, consequently, lodgings used to go to the square of Santa Cruz, located in the center of the city, to meet potential employers. Santa Cruz was indeed "an outdoors labour market" that displayed newly arrived women seeking jobs for the convenience of all the inhabitants of the city: a place that a contemporary author defined as "a daily market in human flesh, one whose effect on social custom has yet to be considered."[62] For the same reasons and also to regulate labor relations between employers and wet-nurses, there was an office in eighteenth-century Paris called the *Bureau des* Nourisses *et des Recommanderesses* (Figure 6.2). The *bureau* was composed of officers and physicians in charge of the physical and moral examination of wet-nurses. As Mercier points out, this office was created in response to the intensity of the migratory stream of women coming to Paris in search of positions as wet-nurses.[63]

In early modern Rome, more than one place served as a meeting point for employer and workers. The most famous of these was the piazza Montanara (Figure 6.3), where agricultural laborers from villages of the Latium and Romagna and dioceses of L'Aquila,

FIGURE 6.2 "The bureau of wet nurses in Paris—wet nurses waiting to be selected." In William Sams, *A Tour Through Paris*, 1822–4. Courtesy of Wellcome Library no. 17481i.

FIGURE 6.3 Giuseppe Vasi, *Piazza Montanara*, etching. In *Sulle magnificenze di Roma Antica e Moderna*, vol. II, 1752.

Rieti, and Urbino gathered together in the morning to wait for *casali* and vineyard owners to hire them on a daily basis. Here the *caporali*, intermediaries between workers and land's owners, came to put together the gangs of agricultural laborers they would then supervise.

This kind of hiring process applied to those jobs already described as typical occupations of seasonal/circular/daily migrants and dependent workers: wet-nurses, agricultural laborers, journeymen bakers, and so on. For these employment sectors, hiring places were sometimes the only way to respond to a primary need faced by all newcomers to the city, namely finding a way to support themselves. Another necessity for "mobile" individuals was accommodation. For those people who did not plan to settle definitely in the arrival place, the practice of cohabitation was a useful resource that made possible their stay not only in the city but also in rural areas. For instance, seasonal brick workers from Lippe-Detmold used to share the dining and sleeping facilities provided by their employer, and at the end of the season the household costs were deducted from the gang's wages.[64]

In late-eighteenth-century Barcelona, the rapid demographic growth and pauperization of the city's population were associated with an increase in the price of accommodations which, Carbonell-Esteller argues, had the direct consequence of stimulating "different forms of co-residence and the appearance of complex households with several nuclei." Apprentices, laborers, journeymen, wage-earners, single individuals—both men and women—maids, and lodgers; all were driven to cohabitation by the need to meet the increasing costs of accommodation. Similarly, in eighteenth-century Massachusetts, most transients' households were made up of single individuals; in Essex County, the percentage ranged from fifty-two to sixty-two.[65] As Carbonell-Esteller points out, "the adoption of a certain profile of household constituted in itself a strategy for survival."[66]

A widespread residential practice was for eighteenth-century households to host non-kin, such as servants, lodgers, and apprentices; this was so common, in fact, that Michael Mitterauer stated that "the most important feature of the western family is doubtless the fact that it was not constituted by bloodlines but was a house or household community largely free of kinship ties."[67] The difference between family and co resident group has also been highlighted by Jürgen Schlumbohm writing on proto industrialization.[68] In eighteenth-century London, for example, the presence of non-kin individuals within households has been defined as one of the "very characteristics that made London unique, including the frequency of co-resident households and the high numbers of lodgers and inmates."[69] According to many scholars, urban life was characterized by internal mobility— of seasonal migrants and lodgers and also those who moved from one accommodation to another.[70] As we have mentioned before, this residential practice involved mostly migrant workers of different kinds whose number further increased with the industrialization of English cities. Jane Humphries has estimated that approximately one-fifth of English urban households between 1700 and 1860 housed at least one lodger.[71] This data is confirmed by case studies. In late-eighteenth-century Ardleigh (Essex, England), the proportion of households formed only of relatives was equal to that of those households that included lodgers.[72] These latter households have been defined by Robert Jütte as "a 'collectivity' consisting of household labourers who did not necessarily have to be related to each other."[73]

For mobile workers, the practice of cohabitation therefore represented one of the main assets enabling their temporary presence in the city. This shows that the urban setting was complementary to mobile work from the point of view of both the lodgers and those who already lived in the city. This mutual benefit has been observed in many cities. In Barcelona, "it was a key supplementary source of income to balance the family budget, as demonstrated by the incorporation of tenants, lodgers or relatives."[74] In other words, as highlighted in relation to London, it was "a beneficial arrangement for both sides of the lodging exchange and functioned as an expedient in the 'economy of makeshifts'."[75] As we know, this was especially true for women, often widows, who were particularly likely to take in lodgers, as observed in London, Rome, and Venice.[76] For Venice, Monica Chojnacka highlights a "substantial presence of women innkeeping in the city" and notes that this activity was performed in an unofficial framework; it was "an informal, off-the-record system based on capacity and demand."[77]

In this regard, the case of New York is especially interesting because this colonial city was literally built during the seventeenth and eighteenth centuries, and the formation of its housing market was closely related to the presence of labor migrants. Elizabeth Blackmar argues during the seventeenth and early eighteenth century, master craftsmen, merchants, and widows in New York City provided accommodation for "dependent members" as part of their households, either within their houses or through boarding in the neighborhood. The accommodation was provided in exchange for work. At the same time, some practices of rearrangement already existed for those "mechanics" who were not able to access their own house and who thus shared existing ones. The practice of boarding generated rent that circulated within the artisan ranks, unlike the ground rents that tied craftsmen to landowning merchants. As Blackmar underlines, boarding in New York City was at the origins of a process of adapting the houses: "internal adaptations of houses to create specialized living space for boarders not connected to household production prefigured the external separation of trade and domestic workspace and the production of housing as a commodity for a general market."[78]

The production of housing as a commodity took place during the mid-eighteenth century when commercial expansion and the modification of labor relations put an end to the household system and changed the way mobile workers sojourned in the city. Because of increasing demand for space near the port for commercial activities and of expanding production for the market, master craftsmen moved away from their shops and stopped housing dependent members. The growth of migrant inflows to the city and the decline of apprenticeship, seen by Blackmar as evidence of the demise of the household system of labor in New York City, made "transience" and "detachment" permanent conditions for dependent workers and provoked the growth of the city's wage-earning class. These processes contributed to the formation of an urban housing market, "that is, the widespread social need for domestic shelter separate from centres of production and commerce."[79]

It can therefore be argued that cohabitation and boarding point to a high level of complementarity between mobility and sedentariness. This practice was beneficial for both labor migrants and those who housed them; furthermore, this residential pattern was closely related to the formation of the urban housing market. The same integration of migrant labor and local structures is demonstrated by an analysis of guild statutes concerning the everyday running of workshops and shops. We have already seen that labor migration played a key role in the urban economy of early modern cities, because their labor markets constantly called for temporary workers.

In addition, there was a high degree of integration between workshops and itinerant vendors. It was not only the guilds, as urban bodies, that conceived of the presence of mobile labor; a part of the everyday running of the workshops and shops relied on itinerant sellers as well. Fontaine has highlighted the substantial unity of the urban economy and the non opposition between formal, recognized trades and itinerant work, especially when masters made use of peddlers in order to promote their shops by selling their merchandise throughout the city.[80] In trying to regulate itinerant sales by requiring peddlers to purchase a specific license, guild statutes describe the extent to which mobility represented a component of the everyday operation of the workshops. Some statutes reveal that workshop masters, apprentices, and journeymen used to carry out some official, recognized itinerant sales. Indeed, some chapters forbade masters from providing peddlers with merchandise to sell and underlined that only the employees of the workshops could engage in itinerant selling. For instance, the only individuals who were authorized to sell their bread on the streets were journeymen who worked in the bakeries.[81] And in the case of fishmongers, apprentices were defined as "those who will go sell the fish in the streets of Rome."[82] The practice of itinerant sales by guild members can also be seen in the statutes of service-oriented professions such as barbers, whose statute established that apprentices and journeymen employed by a master were entitled to go out and offer itinerant services around Rome, both in the streets and in private houses or rooms.[83] The same was true of carpenters, who were allowed to fix barrels and buckets in the streets of the city and in vineyards as long as they were owners of a workshop.[84] Finally, it is worth noting that this combination of workshop and itinerant selling also concerned "luxury" activities such as the goldbeaters and furriers (or painting sellers; see Figure 6.4), whose statute established that "masters are neither allowed to sell in the streets of Rome, nor to set up stalls to sell the merchandise."[85]

These examples demonstrate that some forms of itinerant selling were complementary to sedentary professional activities and represented a normal practice for those who worked in workshops, whether apprentices, journeymen, or masters. The statutes also

FIGURE 6.4 Simon Guillain, *Vende Quadri*, after Annibale Carracci. In *Le Arti di Bologna*, 1646.

allowed for mobile workers outside the guild to carry out itinerant sales, following the payment of an annual fee. This special fee was reserved to those workers who, owing to their mobility, were not full members of the guild; it was not a form of membership but rather an authorization to sell. In other words, itinerant vendors were permitted even without becoming members of the guild, but a fee had to be paid. For instance, junk dealers (*rigattieri*) had to pay six golden *scudi* in order to purchase the license, and six additional *giuli* each year in order to be part of the guild; as for the "*passeggieri*"—itinerant vendors who were forbidden to open a shop or to maintain a fixed place in the city—they were required to pay a reduced yearly fee of twelve *giuli* per year.[86] Besides the guilds' intention of retaining control over their trades, we can also interpret the imposition of a special fee as proof that guilds actually comprehended mobile work and, to some extent, authorized it. By doing so, they provided peddlers with a way of officially holding a professional occupation in urban settings and acquiring a certain form of local belonging.

CONCLUSION

The notion of complementarities would appear to represent a useful "tool" for understanding certain aspects of the relationship between mobility and work as viewed from another perspective. On the one hand, this notion stresses the "agency" of migrant workers while on the other it points out the high degree of integration between mobility and local settings. As we have seen, the shift in the notion of "foreigner," from a "drop-out" to a "normal" individual, has led scholars to give increased attention to the conditions of local insertion and the importance of local ties. The migrant workers at the center of this chapter are individuals who did not settle down in the arrival place but who rather "settled in motion," being able to continue moving around and, at the same time, integrate into a local setting.

In western Europe and North America, the eighteenth century has been viewed by many scholars as a period of changes in the labor markets of many cities, such as Barcelona, Paris, Vienna, and Salem (Massachusetts) for instance. The increase in salaried labor, differentiation of the urban population, and demand for casual labor are hypothesized to have functioned as trigger factors giving rise to a "proletarianization" process involving many "transient" individuals who migrated in response to the growing needs of eighteenth-century cities and their inhabitants. In some cases, migrant workers came from the same region/district as their arrival places, acting as "internal" migrants, for example in Stockholm and Copenhagen; in other cases, they travelled long distances. In all instances, mobility was made possible by the existence of supra local networks linking the departure village to the arrival place. Despite the variety of contexts, such as Alpine peddlers, highly skilled glass makers from Altare, tramping artisans in central Europe, and food vendors in Rome, these networks played a key role in the migration process. Indeed, they organized the migration from the village and enabled people to live in a dimension of simultaneity—a *double horizon* that could be an asset for migrants in accessing both systems of resources.

The existence of supra local networks provides evidence of complementarity between mobility and (temporary) settlement, which was locally enabled by certain structures and facilities. Hiring places, for instance, were typical spaces in many cities, such as Madrid, Rome, Paris, and so on, that granted migrants without strong local ties access to the city's labor market. The same can be said of housing, which reveals the high degree of integration between the mobility of migrant workers and the residential practices of "settled" inhabitants. In many cities, such as Barcelona, Rome, and New York, the practice of cohabitation offered both accommodations for migrant workers and supplementary income for a precarious population, especially widows. In New York City, for example, this process was at the origins of a radical transformation of residential practices. Finally, local guilds displayed the same pattern of complementarity; as in the case of Rome, itinerant sales were part of the everyday running of the workshop.

By emphasizing the role played by migrant networks and the ways mobile workers (temporarily) integrated into local settings, it is possible to glean a more complete understanding of the complex relationship between mobility and work, transcending a limited rejection versus acceptance perspective by putting the accent on individual agency and the continuities between mobility and settlement.

CHAPTER SEVEN

Work and Society

KYLE T. BULTHUIS

The age of Enlightenment proved to be an important transitional era in the relationship of work to society throughout the western world. In broad lines, work moved from being integrative and holistic to being more segmented and set apart. Community activities that blended work with relaxation and amusement gave way to a more regimented experience that separated work from leisure, and a more atomized structure in which individual workers represented themselves in a contractual relationship with an employer rather than as part of a family, village, or society in a series of reciprocal relationships. Households grew less inclusive and smaller, pointing to a future era where the nuclear family, and ultimately the individual, was the source of all legally recognized labor in a free market. Underlying these developments was a separation of work from play; a general increase in individual consumption, and connecting such consumption to leisure, created new patterns for and meanings of work.

That was the larger transformation, on an international level and which lasted centuries. Individuals and families, making their way through macroeconomic conditions across the century ranging from falling wages to rising prices, from famines to wars to work shortages to wage surpluses, most likely paid little heed to how their efforts fit with the larger trends. Yet elites, government officials, intellectuals, and community leaders did attempt to address such questions. Their efforts and interactions with laborers from all walks of society reflected two fundamental visions in perceiving the role of work in society, what might be considered the traditional and the revolutionary positions. These two positions lay independent of one's supposed progressivism in political or religious matters, and concerned mostly conceptions of economy, society, and individual human goodness (or not). A variety of individuals, many within the rationally educated and enlightened camp, ultimately accepted traditional views of work alongside strange bedfellows of clergy and peasantry; others who clung to confessional religion or remained suspicious of reforms in the political realm nonetheless adopted revolutionary positions regarding the economy that connected them to philosophers and so-called anarchists.[1]

Those promoting the most radical changes did so from a vantage point that had already witnessed major social, economic, or political rifts to the traditional fabric of everyday life. In Europe, Britain and the Netherlands were the central sites of the new vision of growth, as were the Anglo colonies of the Western Hemisphere, founded upon shifting alternative visions of what a proper society should look like. Elites in states surrounding these also advocated for changes but had varying levels of success and influence. Outside of this comparatively narrow Atlantic corridor, variations of the traditional view remained in a much stronger position.

THE TRADITIONAL VIEW

The traditional view of society, so regarded from its roots in a medieval and renaissance heritage, held it to be innately hierarchical. A great chain of being connected God to the lesser beings of his creation, from angels to humans to beasts. Within the human realm some individuals were naturally given to rule, and others to be ruled; some were wealthy, others poor. The doctrine of original sin bound all individuals and emphasized limits for all individuals and social groups. Those who overstepped their place, and upset the proper order of things, would necessarily cause disruptions for all around them, and bring malady upon themselves.[2]

Assumptions about economic growth undergirded this social picture. Observers of production and consumption typically considered economics to be a zero-sum game. Economies might grow extensively when populations increased: more individuals producing, and consuming what others produced, led to a larger economy but not one with any greater intensity or efficiency. Indeed, larger economies built by growing populations were more unwieldy and susceptible to disruption when catastrophes such as famines and wars struck. The eighteenth century bore these assumptions out for most of Europe. Few famines and comparatively few wars affected the eighteenth-century population, so economies generally improved. But in rural France, the Italian states, many of the German states, and the Iberian nations of Spain and Portugal most growth simply manifested as more hands growing food and feeding more mouths. In France and Italy, population density meant that agriculture grew intensively rather than extensively, and per capita economies shrank. In parts of eastern Europe, the German states, and Spain, movement into comparatively empty frontiers allowed for modest overall growth. But in all these regions economics remained, at its core, a zero-sum game.[3]

Thomas Malthus, an English cleric, was among the most perceptive observers of the demographic dynamic. His influential work *An Essay on the Principle of Population* first appeared in 1798, and it accurately described the position of most preindustrial, agriculturally based economies. Malthus noted that an economy growing extensively would eventually collapse in famine, as populations would outstrip agricultural supply. Neoclassical economists have since criticized Malthus for his inability to observe increases in economic and agricultural efficiency, but such critics often fail to note that Malthus's work was descriptively accurate for most of the eighteenth century, even if it failed to be predictively so in the nineteenth.[4]

In most of Europe outside England and the Low Countries, agriculture often remained bound to traditional forms of medieval work structures. Such forms were strained in practice but the cultural significance of them remained, shaping actions in the workplace for all levels of society. Serfs in eastern Europe, peasants in central and western Europe, and poor agriculturalists in western Europe all tended to cling to customary habits for work patterns. Living a near-subsistence existence, most such poorer workers remained suspicious of innovations. Villagers generally held pasturelands in common, worked fields that adjoined each other, and joined in common feast days and celebrations interspersed throughout the calendar. Most fought against noble attempts to increase fees and taxes but also generally resisted measures that might improve productivity, for failed innovation could spell death.[5]

Landed nobles (and landowning gentry, particularly in Britain) had traditionally avoided labor per se. Administration of the estates was a gentlemanly pursuit and even if it involved some level of mental and physical effort was not, for many, categorized within the world of work. Drawing from classical Greek and Roman models in which patricians avoided labor, and interpreting the biblical Fall equating work with the curse of sin, many nobles practiced conspicuous consumption, amassed large debts, but showed little interest in improving their estates. A significant number of them congregated in regional or national capitals, seeking and dispensing patronage in the form of bureaucratic offices and military commissions.[6] This admittedly exaggerated picture, since revised significantly in recent decades, illustrates the ideal type that more conservative social theorists embraced.

In the context of flat economic growth, poverty was an ever-present condition, something that both Bible and nature had appeared to demonstrate. The great order of being presumed both wealthy and poor. But because a number of individuals clearly did improve their economic positions in the eighteenth century, what scarcity meant for the poor, or rather, what scarcity meant about how elites thought about the poor, could take different forms. On the one hand, some concluded that the poor became so in part because they had not practiced the values of thrift and industry. In a world of scarcity, those who worked the hardest deserved the spoils. These observers, such as many intellectual proponents of the American or French revolutions, could be considered liberal in the sense that they attacked the right of hereditary aristocracies to continue to control property by virtue of birth. But they could hardly champion the lower orders, whose tendencies toward ignorance, idleness, and stupidity—coupled often with lasciviousness, addiction, or other vice—rendered them undeserving of any additional favor. Those who worked hard, and practiced thrift and industry, generally deserved the (slightly) larger slice of the pie that they had acquired.

Eighteenth-century satirists often reflected this view, which praised work as a key to success. William Hogarth, one of the chief popular printers of the age in Britain, produced prints that exemplified the assumption that the vices of the lower orders continued to entrap them in poverty. Among these was the twelve-plate series *Industry and Idleness*, which displays the paths of two young apprentices, one who works hard and reaps a series of rewards, eventually becoming Lord Mayor of London, and the other whose idleness leads to theft, murder, and eventually the gallows. Meaningful productive work was the key to a well-functioning society (Figure 7.1). Benjamin Franklin of Philadelphia, founding father and successful printer of *Poor Richard's Almanac*, often repeated simple maxims that praised moderation, thrift, honesty, and hard work as keys to worldly success. Simple statements such as "At the working man's house hunger looks in but dares not enter" and "God gives all things to industry" suggest that the fault for poverty lay with those who remained poor. Good morals and habits trumped misfortune, for, as Franklin allowed Poor Richard to note, "Diligence is the mother of good luck."[7]

On the other hand, economic pessimists could also point to scarcity as a reason that there would always be poor, and that even given the presence of vices among them, there were many poor who were virtuous, and comparatively innocent of the pains that they suffered. Jonathan Swift's 1729 satire *A Modest Proposal for Preventing the Children of Poor People from Being a Burden to Their Parents or Country, and for Making Them Beneficial to the Publick* also reflects the traditional view. His bombastic narrator calls for Irish children to be prepared as meals for the wealthy, thus solving problems of Irish overpopulation and poverty, and demonstrating the ridiculous conclusion to modern uses of rational reform. In one fell swoop, then, Swift created sympathy for the poor and scorn upon those who offered too-quick condemnation of and too-easy solutions for them.[8] Furthermore, middling and even wealthy individuals, virtuous and hardworking, sometimes found fortune impoverished them owing to no clear fault of their own. Clerks, schoolteachers, and ministers in the anglophone world, all in respectable employment,

FIGURE 7.1 William Hogarth, *The Industrious 'Prentice Grown Rich, and Sheriff of London*, Plate VIII, and *The Idle 'Prentice Betrayed by a Prostitute*, Plate IX. In *Industry and Idleness*, 1747. New Haven, CT, Yale Center for British Art, Yale University Art Gallery Collection.

were often paid poorly and a short step from ruin. Sudden deaths, although rarer than in previous centuries, suddenly created widows and orphans, or ended family lineages and fortunes, for elites as well as for commoners. The overall vision presented suggested that conceptions of original sin, which held as constant for all major Christian traditions, Protestant or Catholic, warned against too much hubris in individual plans.

TRADITIONAL APPROACHES TO POVERTY, GUILDS, AND HOUSEHOLDS

Poor relief in the western world throughout the late medieval and early modern periods had been tied to the local community and church. Individuals fallen upon hard times could appeal to local authorities who would presumably know them and their circumstances, and determine what, if any, aid they might be worthy of. Charity was often given "outdoors," as gifts in kind of food or fuel. As steady demographic growth put strains upon the system, authorities increasingly weighed claims according to worthiness, with dependent individuals such as widows, orphans, the infirm, and the aged more clearly deserving of aid than others. In many European towns, and in the North American colonies, poor relief was linked to residence. Strangers to a town who claimed another place of origin would face being "warned out" rather than be given alms. In this practice, poor relief enforced community lines and identities, and a traditional sense of tribe and location. This was true throughout the West, although some scholars have suggested the impulse of the Catholic Counter-Reformation rendered poor relief more extensive and wide-ranging in nation-states such as Spain, Portugal, France, and Italy, when compared to Protestant states.[9]

The reality of growing numbers of poor in an expanding eighteenth century, particularly in urban sites, forced officials to rely upon a variety of forms, including nontraditional means, in alleviating poverty. Particularly difficult were seasonal inflows from the rhythms of the economy, or sudden emergencies forged through adverse weather, war, or other catastrophes. Centralized states began to take over more poor relief duties from private and church-run organizations. This did not necessarily entail increased secularization, for religious individuals and bodies remained involved in distributing charity. Further, most states throughout the era maintained a Protestant or Catholic identity that retained a de facto connection to religious practice in the distribution of relief. In addition, in rural and smaller town locations, scale dictated that traditional means of relief—either quick dispensation of funds or food, or taking in the poor in individual private homes—remained preferable.[10]

Two other institutions—guilds and family households—offered a brake on innovations in the century, keeping labor within a more traditional understanding and setting. Ultimately, the status of guilds in any given town or region, or industry, depended as much on structural conditions of trade, resources, and governance as the efforts of the masters, laborers, or populace. In general, increased competition on an international level weakened guild regulations and limits, but the artisan ideal pushed back to enforce a general understanding of skilled, quality labor as desirable, and that well-managed trades were crucial components of social cohesion. When strong, guilds could establish a monopoly in production in a given industry. Masters within a guild setting were leading laborers in the town, on par with leading professionals and merchants. The guild ideals of quality craftsmanship, reciprocal relationships (framed in the vocabularies of masculinity and patriarchy), and customary benefits dominated their ideals of work. The assumptions of the guild as a central component of a well-functioning society undergirded this vision, which remained stronger in central Europe than western Europe, stronger in western Europe than in Britain, and stronger in Britain than in the American colonies.[11]

Specific industries could vary considerably, however. Guild masters in prosperous industries, such as jewelery or cabinet making, might ascend to become leading citizens of their cities and appear more professional or elite than laboring. By contrast, guilds with lower barriers to entry and greater competition, such as shoemaking, tailoring, or weaving, forced many masters into poverty. In Italy, where growth was slow, Carlo Poni's evaluation of Bolognese shoe makers reveals fault lines between urban and rural workers, and between guild masters and trade masters, that suggest hardships in a saturated environment. Masses of journeymen in those trades, and others, evinced a solidarity that pushed against innovations that threatened their well-being, as Leonard Rosenband's consideration of the traditions of paper makers at the Montgolfier mill reveals.[12]

Finally, the traditional vision of the world included the household as its primary base. Households consisting of nuclear family units, extended family members, apprentice and journeymen laborers, and associated kin, friends, or employees, were the primary units in western economies. These units participated in economies of money and credit, yet remained somewhat independent of them through forms of patronage and barter. Women took on major roles in the protection and production of the household. Women of the elite often found work in managing their households; in the eighteenth-century, satirists often belittled such labors as frivolous consumption but the increased revenues and consumption demands of eighteenth-century aristocracy belied such a claim. Elite couples worked in partnership to further their family fortunes by managing agricultural estates, speculating in new financial ventures, and marrying off children and other relatives in kinship networks that promised to extend their social capital. Rosemary O'Day's studies on the 1st Duchess of Chandos reveal the complicated negotiations that elite women undertook in attempting to expand their households' respective influences.[13]

Women of the middling orders often worked alongside their husbands in various household economies, and in many cases successfully continued businesses after the man's death. Economic observers may have overlooked many women's activities on behalf of the household, viewing them as unproductive, because they lay ostensibly outside the monetary and credit markets, but the reality was that women's management of servants or children was a de facto organization of labor. Their expenditures in kitchen, drawing room, or bedroom required control over costs. And their work in garden, barn, or workshop was integral to the functioning of the household economy, which often aided the movement of any goods to the money and credit markets that innovators recognized as "real" economic activity.[14]

Women participated throughout the economy to a greater extent than an initial glance at traditional records currently suggests. Their position, however, in a legal sense supplementary to their husbands' work, suggested they functioned outside the newer, contractual-based economy in a more traditional arrangement, and as such their presence is not as prominent in the historical record. The activities of widows, too, who managed significant estates and businesses, even expanding on and transforming what their husbands left them, often have been poorly documented with records stunted and unkept, or lost to indifferent heirs or antiquarians who assumed female inferiority. Deborah Simonton's study of Margaret Morice in Aberdeen reveals a woman who successfully maintained her family business in the baking trades after her husband's death, even though few papers related to her estate remain. Laboring women of the lower orders could also work alongside their husbands in smaller affairs. Young women especially might be employed as domestic servants to wealthier families (Figure 7.2).[15]

FIGURE 7.2 Thomas Rowlandson, *Hot Spice Gingerbread All Hot*, n.d. New Haven, CT, Yale Centre for British Art, Paul Mellon Collection.

Women stood out uniquely, although infamously, in the profession of prostitution. The sex trade appears to have increased with the growth of urban centers, as the anonymity offered by cities allowed more men to seek illicit contacts among a large and varied female population in cities such as London and Paris, but even in smaller towns or in provincial centers such as New York, as Timothy Gilfoyle has revealed. The traditional view of humanity held, of course, that prostitution was a horrible vice; Hogarth appears yet again as the chief interpreter of the evils of prostitution in a series of prints titled *A Harlot's Progress*. But observers also offered consolation and pity for the most tragic cases caught in the sex trade; London's Magdalene House, founded in 1758 for women wishing to evade prostitution, suggests that observers recognized that prostitution was not simply a sin to be condemned. In his 1722 novel *Moll Flanders*, Daniel Defoe paints an incredible image of a thoroughly immoral heroine whom he nonetheless portrays sympathetically, especially as the vicissitudes of fortune as much as immorality marked her life course. The case of an apparent rise in prostitution suggests that traditional views were strained by realities of eighteenth-century life.[16] A series of revolutionary views regarding work in society also reflect such changes.

THE REVOLUTIONARY VIEW

The traditional vision of human sinfulness and of the limits of opportunity in a stagnant economy remained strong, even among those intellectuals who embraced newer, rational visions of the world. All was toil and work, and the best one might be able to hope for would be, as Voltaire concluded in *Candide*, to tend one's garden. Yet in that reference, Voltaire heralded another movement that offered a garden not as a simple retreat but rather as a fount of new possibilities. Toiling in one's garden offered a new way to examine the economy. The intellectual movement of physiocracy in France was among the first to examine economies with rational, scientific models. Physiocrats, the most prominent figure of which was François Quesnay, were influenced by John Locke's position that labor was a necessary condition in establishing ownership of property and that labor was what created and added value to any given property. Physiocrats, however, limited the labor theory of value to those who worked the soil, believing economic growth to be possible, but only in the realm of agricultural output. All other laborers, from artisans to shopkeepers, bankers to merchants, belonged to a sterile class. Aristocrats and wealthy landowners of all stripes were to some degree necessary as owners and *rentiers* but were not the driving force of economic growth. Yet such an opinion, though rooted in the soil, was hardly traditional in affirming the peasantry, for Physiocrats held that scientific applications drove agricultural output.[17]

Just as Thomas Malthus's position reflected a general description of preindustrial agricultural society, physiocracy reflected the reality and evidence of an agricultural revolution that occurred through the eighteenth century, especially in Britain. Indeed, the French thinkers behind the movement appear to have promoted it to goad their nation into greater reforms, as French farmers remained far more isolated and traditional in their agricultural practices than their British counterparts. Increasingly scientific and commercial applications to land usage—ranging from more intensive fertilization, to more complicated crop rotation, to the invention and refinement of new tools—created a surge in agricultural output that helped spur population growth. Physiocrats also championed free international markets as a means to rationalize production across national lines. Ultimately, though, peasants in central Europe, smallholders throughout the West, and elites who managed their lands all had their hands full with the traditional seasonal rhythms of their work, and found little time to actively apply physiocratic dictates. Physiocracy was therefore not prescriptively widespread, and in different places where physiocratic theory won a free trade in grain, such as France and Spain in the 1760s, popular backlash led to the dismantling of their reforms. Physiocracy, however, found influence in the American colonies among elites who brandished republican political theories. Most prominent among them was Thomas Jefferson, the most idealistic and Enlightenment-steeped of the British colonial leaders for independence.[18]

Through the course of the century, another set of assumptions came to reject both the hard limits of economic pessimists and the narrow-based agrarianism of the Physiocrats. The movement embodied a general belief that economic growth was possible, although supporters ranged from those who favored government financing of debt and spending through tax revenues, and those who promoted a more *laissez-faire* model of a "hands-off" government approach to economic activity. Ironically often labelled today as conservatives, such theorists were the great economic innovators of the eighteenth century. At the level of the nation-state, government financiers increasingly used debt as a tool for economic growth, funding projects and the general protection of their mercantile interests. The traditional view largely condemned debt for the individual, but innovative financiers argued that the nation-state should use debt as a tool rather than bemoan it as a moral failing. Such politicians served as lightning rods in public discourse, attracting a lot of attention, much of it negative. But the results were effective, indicated perhaps by the way in which such policies were reproduced. John Law's innovations in public debt in 1710s France, although ultimately disastrous, paralleled Robert Walpole's policies in 1730s Britain. Walpole's efforts found similarities with Jacques Necker's work in France in the 1780s, and Alexander Hamilton's in the United States in the 1790s (Figure 7.3).[19] The increased centralization of state authority led to greater government oversight over several types of work. Guild conflicts within and between industries and regions often led to greater government powers, as Carlo Poni's study of eighteenth-century Italian shoe makers suggests; the ultimate victors in disputes between laborers and small businessmen were bureaucrats and lawyers. Government attempts to create freer trade in selected industries could cripple some industries at home.[20]

Some innovators recognized the possibilities of economic growth but rejected increased central authority in fomenting it. The Scottish philosopher and economist Adam Smith has gained the most prominent place as harbinger of the new vision, but just as Malthus and the Physiocrats reflected rather than predicted reality, so did Smith reflect the world he knew in his 1776 *Wealth of Nations*. Smith's emphasis on the division of labor and the primacy of the consumer in determining the flow of goods, reflected the economic development of Britain in the eighteenth century. Guilds had been broken in most towns, and entrepreneurial merchants and managers had reorganized labor in industries as varied as textiles and pottery to great effect. The growing consumption of small cottage households in the Midlands, England, and in the American colonies, helped spur production in the British economy.

One example of an early and unique expression of this new world for individual consumers is a satirical poem by Bernard Mandeville, titled "The Fable of the Bees," which first appeared in full in 1714. It depicts a fictional hive, set to symbolize the human world. The bees labor, as bees do. But they also labor in order to consume. When the bees are granted by their Maker the ability to rest, to not strive, and to not consume, the hive goes entirely to hell. Only in consuming and desiring and in selfish private acquisition

FIGURE 7.3 Julien Fatou, *Jacques Necker*, After 1785, after Joseph Siffred Suplessis; Jean Langlois, *John Law*, early eighteenth century, after Jean Hubert. Both London, National Portrait Gallery; Jacobus Houbraken, *Robert Walpole*, 1st Earl of Oxford, 1746, after Arthur Pond. New Haven, CT, Yale Center for British Art, Paul Mellon Collection.

does the hive prosper: the drive to consume led to the drive to work, which led to a prosperous harmonious society. Subtitled "Private Vices, Public Benefits," Mandeville's poem scandalized churchmen and intellectuals. By connecting luxury to labor, Mandeville

FIGURE 7.3 (*Continued*)

mixed vice and virtue, a combination that did not readily fit with the idealists who promoted consistent idealistic visions of their fully functioning mental worlds.[21]

Despite general horror from moralists and clergy, Mandeville's praise of consumption augured for a generally increasing consumption over the eighteenth century for many individuals, across classes. The steady increase in consumption of new goods came to be seen as increasingly acceptable, especially as it gained new proponents who did not state the position as baldly as Mandeville had. By the end of the century, the vision that consumption was no vice came to be cloaked in sentimentality and ethics, through the works of Francis Hutcheson and Adam Smith. With Smith's famous passage, "It is not

FIGURE 7.3 (*Continued*)

from the benevolence of the butcher, the brewer, or the baker that we expect our dinner, but from their regard to their own interest," the ideal of public benevolence from private vices reached its fullest articulation.²²

Not all individuals willingly elected to work harder to consume more goods. Conspicuous objectors included Native American groups in North America, who viewed selective consumption in part as an opportunity for spiritual development and in part as exchanges that furthered kinship networks and built alliances. Journeymen in a number of skilled trades preferred the traditional rights of drink, ritual, and days off to increased pay; such opposition helped spur factory owners and business managers to pursue greater mechanization. Evidence in Spain and Italy suggests that in some communities poorer laborers worked less when wages were high, forgoing the increased income in order to gain more leisure time (Figure 7.4). And religious moralists of all stripes, whether religious sectarians or enlightened agnostics, remained uneasy at calls to enjoy the benefits of material wealth. Yet, in the most commercialized countries, particularly Britain and the

FIGURE 7.4 *Paysan et Paysanne des environs de Trieste en Austrie* (Male and female peasants from Trieste, Austria). In Jacques Grasset de Saint-Sauveur, *Encyclopedie des Voyages*, Paris, 1796. Los Angeles, LACMA.

Netherlands, the increase in consumption appears to have grown steadily despite such opposition.[23]

Accompanying the new vision of consumption were new ideas about types of valuable work. The professions of law and medicine emerged in this century as increasingly codified and bureaucratized undertakings. Even as guilds faltered, professionals' club-type organizations held off challenges from individuals without the same education and training which they held to be essential for proper practice. Lawyers were the leading politicians for independence in the American Revolution and the most prominent occupation in most towns within the Third Estate at the time of the French Revolution. Doctors made strides to shut out popular practitioners who had not been trained formally, including female midwives and common cunning folk.[24]

The increased use of credit in many markets also made some consider investment and speculation to be not simply gambling, or idle play, but rather forms of estate management. Elite families, particularly, whose household arrangements included the economic preservation of estates through purchases, political patronage, and wise management, also now included diversification of their holdings, in part with monetary speculation and the advancement of credit. Because both the professions and the worlds of finance drew those of higher birth as well as more middling types, such efforts were largely accepted as legitimate forms of work, even though they had traditionally lain outside what constituted labor. In Britain, especially, the line between noble birth and wealthy pursuit blurred, especially as a large gentry class managed to increase their estate holdings and successfully invest in new shipping and manufacturing ventures.[25]

The newer vision of economic growth outlined the beginnings of change regarding poor relief and debt. The possibility of ruin for the middling and upper sorts, individuals who gambled and lost to fortune, eroded some of the traditional views that attributed success to virtue and failure to vice. In the most commercialized economies, laws began to reflect a consideration of risk and debt not on a moral plane but on a business plane. Bankruptcy proceedings were softened and allowed individuals to make additional runs at success, without the stigma of moral failure attached to it. Laws concerning debtors' prison also relaxed. Creditors did not do so from some moral change of heart, however, but from expediency. It became clear that ancient bankruptcy laws and proceedings proved to be ineffective in gathering results or capital for those who were owed. Rather, the rationalization of debt and credit suggests a revolution that viewed money increasingly instrumentally.[26]

Enlightenment thought, moreover, developed a sentimentality that recognized pain and suffering in other creatures, both human and animal. In such a setting, pain was not simply a reflection of God's will but a hardship to be avoided where possible. And insofar as there was a duty, it was to reduce such pain inflicted upon other beings. Such an impulse lay behind the vision of institutions designed to alleviate poverty. The charity schools might promise that hardworking pupils could gain tools that might uplift them from devastation. Poorhouses, workhouses, and hospitals promised to be temporary inconveniences that would lead, ultimately, to more pleasant ends.[27]

Not all was positive in this new vision, however. If poverty was mutable, and vice conquerable, then theorists and business managers reasoned that the proper discipline and management of laborers could engineer new and favorable results. Enlightenment theorists joined with business owners to consider ways to improve efficiency and output. These included systematic attempts to control laborers, whether by eliminating inefficient traditional customary privileges, increasing marginal output of hours or exertion. And while pain was to be avoided, the new theorists recognized it could still be a useful tool, in training the new cogs of the economy to work properly.

Nontraditional means of poor relief in this century entailed institution building, often through private subscription but also public–private alliances. These included charity schools, hospitals, asylums, orphanages, and workhouses. Expensive to maintain and boasting inconsistent and questionable results, these new institutions offered glimpses of a new type of world of reform, one that augured possibilities of economic growth, and, conceivably, of the possible goodness, or even mutability, of human nature. Limited to larger urban centers, especially cities such as London, they represented the future of reform.

This expansive vision also involved the inclusion of women and children as laborers, groups previously considered belonging to the worthy poor and not requiring compulsion to work. Scholars dispute the main causes for this new economic development—some suggest the lower wages were a cost-saving venture, others suggest employers sought more controllable or pliable subjects in their factories. On a macroeconomic level, political figures and theorists alike sought to compel work from formerly unproductive populations in an attempt to create productive subjects and to expand the tax base for the benefit of the royal coffers. The coercion embedded in the new systems led to unrest throughout the century. The Esquilache Riots in Spain, in 1766, involved criticisms of liberalized agricultural policies that led to higher food prices; another grievance concerned government attempts to ban traditional Spanish dress of wide-brimmed hats and large capes for the purposes of retaining money for domestic coffers. The rioters gained some minor concessions, although the Spanish Crown continued its liberalization policies. The Spitalfields Riots in London, about the same time, involved weavers whose pay was increasingly dictated by merchants who had undercut their efforts.[28]

CHATTEL SLAVERY AND REVOLUTIONARY FORMS OF LABOR

Elite attempts at efficiency translated directly into colonial agricultural economies, particularly in the form of slave labor.[29] Slavery represented a way to circumvent traditional labor forces. Socially and legally dead, chattel slaves could be controlled, and managed, to maximize profits. In the colonial setting of the Western Hemisphere, labor continued to be transformed by the continual influx of slaves from West and Central Africa. The transatlantic slave trade accelerated in the eighteenth century, with half of the approximately twelve million slaves transported in the Middle Passage arriving in those hundred years. Slave plantations in the mainland colonies, West Indies, and Latin America (especially Brazil) continued to grow, driven by the continued integration of cash crops into the world economy. Chattel slavery explicitly recognized slaves as property by law, in which they suffered a full social death. Historian Ira Berlin has deemed such societies in which chattel slavery was central to economic output "slave societies," to distinguish them from "societies with slaves," in which the nature and extent of slavery did not shape all social institutions.

A few plantation owners viewed themselves as Roman patricians, above work and toil, but the everyday working of their worlds required new methods of supervision and discipline. The full framing of slavery as a premodern institution would not occur until the next century; in the eighteenth century, plantation owners were organizational modernizers. Historian Justin Roberts has demonstrated how Jamaican plantation owners imposed Enlightenment discipline on their charges, borrowing from the same theories that economists and entrepreneurs had devised for manufacturing laborers. These included attempts at increased work output and efficiency. Political leaders in slave societies regulated all aspects of slave life, restricting the use of musical instruments, forbidding groups congregating after-dark or other specified times, and requiring special clothing or marking. Recalcitrant or rebelling slaves were subject to punishments not generally inflicted upon the laboring population in Europe, including castration, limb removal, and execution by drawn-out torture, including starvation and burning at the stake.[30]

For their part, slaves in plantations did not simply accept work as a given. Slave rebellions rocked New York City in 1711 and 1741, and South Carolina in 1739. Jamaica witnessed a century-long slave rebellion, with runaway slaves, deemed Maroons, enforcing concessions from authorities and gaining a legally recognized status in the island's mountainous backcountry. In the Chesapeake region, a more balanced sex ratio and a healthier climate, coupled with the comparatively lighter work of tobacco cultivation compared to that of sugar or rice, led to a self-sustaining slave population, a first in the New World. This region also witnessed slave populations growing their own food outside of mandated work times.[31] In the following century, Adam Smith's foundational ideas about free labor would gain added import to slave populations, who participated in attempts to gain their freedom.

We would be remiss in leaving the last word of the Enlightenment with slave revolts against ostensibly enlightened overseers. Enlightenment measures helped drive sugar plantations; they also led opposition to them. Thinkers such as Thomas Paine condemned slavery as a barbaric form of unfreedom and coercion; philosophical tendencies to champion reason could influence society in contradictory ways.

TRANSFORMATION OF THE PIETISTS

Ultimately, the new vision of the mutability of human nature, and the prospects of economic growth, would triumph, although such a victory was far from assured even at the end of the eighteenth century. But the trend lines might be seen particularly in the rise and mutation of new religious movements within western religious culture. Such religious movements began in part as opponents of the centralizing forces of economic development, yet many ended championing those same forces.

Independently within and across national boundaries, a pietistic revolution swept a number of Protestant Christian states. These movements could vary dramatically in their theological and cultural specifics, ranging from the Moravians in the German states to Free Church advocates in Sweden and Scotland, and from Nadere Reformatie preachers in the Netherlands to Great Awakening itinerants in the American colonies. The Pietists shared a general conservatism regarding theology, a pessimism about human perfectibility, and a pushback against rationality of state churches in all their forms. In short, they reflected a traditional vision of the world that supported order but resisted any innovations that augured new types of rule.[32] The Pietist movements generally reflected a small property holder revolt against larger conglomerations of church, state, and capital. They rejected Enlightenment ideals about the perfectibility of human nature, or any attempts to glorify consumption and the acquisition of wealth. Some pietistic groups, such as the Moravians, challenged social distinctions created by the accumulation of wealth, coming close to rejecting private property in their tight-knit communities. More groups who were embedded in larger communities simply condemned the effects of the over-accumulation of wealth, as they attacked signs of conspicuous consumption ranging from hair ribbons to leather-bound books. The cultural imperatives of such actions suggest a moral economy in terms of pricing and treatment of laborers.[33]

In Great Britain, the established Church of England retained much of the prestige, and while a tacit toleration allowed followers of other faiths to practice theirs, employment for religious dissenters was often barred, especially access to the universities and therefore to the professions. British dissenters thus lived on a different track from the larger population: clearly a part of British society, but not completely of it. The university emphasis on classical languages was not available to dissenting families, and so such education tended to be more practical and what we might deem vocational. Such an approach complemented the plain style and low-church tendencies of most dissenters, who from years of cultural inheritance practiced thrift naturally, avoiding vain displays of consumption in their dress. Dissenters offered a creed of labor and toil, shunning excess, and valuing practical application of one's efforts.[34] Such habits helped certain tradesmen of dissenting stock grow their businesses beyond the usual limits of guilds and custom. Josiah Wedgwood, the famed potter, built a ceramics empire. Quaker families on both sides of the Atlantic built businesses in pottery and ceramics, mining, banking, and shipping. Some successful dissenters even made their way into Parliament. But as dissenters grew more comfortable in Britain, and shaped British culture and economy, the larger British culture that valued economic risk-taking and consumption also began to affect them. John Wesley, whose Methodists during his lifetime occupied a place between full-on dissenters, such as Quakers and Moravians, on one side and evangelical churchmen on the other, expressed the tension for his people. In a famous passage, he wrote: "For religion must necessarily produce both industry and frugality; and these cannot but produce riches. But as riches increase, so will pride, anger, and love of the world in all its branches." Wesley posed a solution to this dilemma in great acts of charity, giving up the wealth so hard-fought. Historians of Methodism, however, have noted that many Methodists in Britain and the New World followed precisely the path Wesley foretold.[35]

The Methodists, despite their enthusiasm, remained comparatively mainstream and respectable when compared to other groups. The intersection of more radical dissenter groups with the Enlightenment led to the greatest transformative changes regarding wealth and work. Some groups radically desacralized the world, eliminating what remaining pomp and ceremony higher Protestants had retained from the Catholic Church. Further, these groups shared with Enlightenment philosophers a suspicion of traditional Christian doctrines such as the Trinity or the divine status of Christ. Perhaps most significant were the groups who rejected the doctrine of original sin, which held humanity to share in Adam's first fall from grace in the Garden of Eden and human perfectibility to be unattainable in this life. Historian Matthew Kadane has suggested that this rejection of the doctrine was a key factor in transforming economic wealth into a driving social force. In rejecting original sin, groups such as the Unitarians and Quakers unleashed the capitalistic drive for accumulation of wealth, without the fear of corresponding corruption.[36] Thus the creation of dissent, initially reflected in smallholder attempts to resist the accumulation of capital and the marshalling of resources for state and large landholder wealth, came to reflect some aspects of a new worldview. In so doing, labor continued to be praised as virtue-building, but it no longer carried with it the critiques that it necessarily led to hell, when placed above godliness.

The final vision of labor discipline in a new world of endless economic growth was not fully realized in the eighteenth century. Some individuals continued to resist against such innovation. Rural locations might retain traditional patterns that blended work and leisure, and celebrated traditional festival days apart from the fairs of consumption. The seasonal rhythms of agriculture remained, even if fields increasingly became privately owned and more intensively and scientifically farmed. Traditional rights of journeymen and apprentices remained in trades where guilds held sway, and even in places where employers and masters sought technological innovation, the ability of master craftsmen to control quality and output, and of journeymen to rebuff owners' regulations, meant that the daily rhythms of work, and the payment for such, did not inevitably move in one single progressive direction.

Ironically, the attempts of economic reformers to promote new types of labor in the new United States led to a resistance that emphasized forms of labor that, while new, hearkened back to older models more than previously. The Federalist Party of Alexander Hamilton hoped to promote manufacture in a way that disciplined poor and laboring classes into greater market efficiency; their opponents, the Democratic-Republicans of Thomas Jefferson, hailed physiocratic models of agricultural improvement. Allied loosely with the Jeffersonians, but promoting their own vision, were subsistence farmers, small freeholders who toiled on their lands in the aim of achieving competency, or self-sufficiency. Often adopting enthusiastic forms of pietism in religion, and suspicious of market-oriented reforms, such farmers embraced Lockean theories that working and improving the land granted squatters rights of ownership. They therefore rejected the abstract rights of contract that economic innovators held as sacred in terms of land titles, nor did they generally seek agricultural improvement in the way their Jeffersonian allies promoted. In several unconnected rebellions across the American frontier—the Regulator, Shays', Fries', and Whiskey rebellions—they expressed a vision of freeholding independence that acquired the illusion of having ancient roots, and certainly pushed against the elite innovators who held far different views of work. Such an ideology forced concessions from elite Jeffersonianism, and with the rise of the presidency of Andrew Jackson would capture a major part of US politics in the coming century.[37]

CONCLUSION

Intellectual historians might find in the eighteenth century a dualistic struggle between faith and reason, superstition and enlightenment. Economic historians may discern a continual battle between labor and capital, or a transformation from "the world we lost" to a new industrial order. The worlds of work as they related to society in this era cut across both dualities, in part because the culture of work encompassed such opposite categories as faith and reason, labor and capital. On their surface, the social worlds of the eighteenth century appeared to reflect an old order, an *ancien régime* that stretched back to medieval times. Traditional ideas about agricultural and craft labor, gender roles, and poor relief remained throughout the century as brakes on innovation. Many villages and settlements in the countryside hewed to premodern feasts, festivals, and fairs, thus blending leisure and labor. Further, the institution of the household and the social forces of local community remained largely untouched by centralizing forces in the lived experience of many individuals.

However, from beneath this surface major structural changes bubbled forth. As an era without major famine, only intermittent war, and comparatively moderate levels of inflation, the age of Enlightenment demonstrated to some theorists that gradual progress might occur through incremental improvements over time. Consumption increased across social classes and international boundaries, challenging gender roles as well as older prerogatives. Heads of state and philosophers often discerned improvements in central states' attempts to consolidate economic activity, accumulate capital, monetize debt and credit, and break up the very social forms that seemed to be so unchanging.

The division between traditionalists and innovators did not fall neatly along religious or political lines. Not all elites bowed to the new order—some remained deeply skeptical of capital-intensive innovations. Nor did all of the more common sort cling to old traditions, as a few found niches in the new economy that overturned more rigid norms of order in organizing labor. One constant that all sides tended to share in this era was a greater appreciation for the significance of labor, in both individual and aggregate terms. Work built virtue on an individual level; such an observation forced aristocrats out of old modes of languor, even as it prodded the poor into workhouses and increased shop hours. But most traditionalists and innovators also believed that work helped society to cohere, that the act of labor created harmonious relationships and was essential to society's proper functioning. This belief in the value of work helped to usher in the very conflicts between philosophers and the religious, and between management and labor: all sides knew it was valuable, making the stakes higher in determining how labor should be used in the social order.

CHAPTER EIGHT

The Political Culture of Work

BERT DE MUNCK

According to William Sewell in his pathbreaking book *Work and Revolution in France*, work was a central element in the collective identity of the so-called *sans-culottes* during and beyond the French Revolution. Revolutionary workers, artisans, and shopkeepers would have defined themselves as men who worked with their hands—handwork distinguishing them not only from what they considered idle "aristocrats" but also from privileged economic groups who did not work with their hands.[1] On the surface, this view of work is at odds with the common sense conception of labor most of us are familiar with today, in which work has to be imposed because people will only work if stimulated by either necessity or high wages and with an eye on either survival or consumption. This view emerged in the seventeenth and eighteenth centuries, among mercantilist thinkers and such early philosophers of political economy as Adam Smith. While for such seventeenth-century mercantilists as Thomas Mun the stress was on the "utility of poverty" thesis, that is, the idea that workers will work to escape poverty, Adam Smith argued in favor of higher wages for both economic and moral reasons. But they agreed that work was instrumental and "had to be extracted from unwilling workers."[2]

To be sure, these views are not necessarily at odds with those of the *sans-culottes*. While political economy is of course entrenched in utilitarian thinking, the views of the *sans-culottes* as well could be reduced to a utilitarian type of reasoning in which workers demanded political recognition in return for their labor, in addition to a fairer slice of the cake. However, there was more at stake than the distribution of the fruits of labor and capital. Beyond that, work defined membership of the political community for the *sans-culottes*. By the revolution of 1848, labor was conceived of as "the source of popular sovereignty" and "the foundation of political order."[3] Owners of property were meanwhile reduced to acting as trustees of goods (rather than as proprietors), because all resources in the last instance belonged to the people. Thus, rather than being limited to surplus extraction, these discussions revolved around the definition of the political community and the role of labor and skills therein. This urges us to connect the history of work to the history of popular politics.

In order to understand the political dimension of work, we must move beyond the utilitarian framework and reconnect labor and politics on a more fundamental level. The challenge is to analyze the political dimension of the value of work. This chapter specifically connects the conception of work and skills to the conception of the body politic. A political community can be embodied by different groups, and the well-being of the community can be seen as based on different types of work and economic activity.[4] Whose work was considered crucial for the well-being of the collective between, roughly, 1650 and 1800? What type of work was perceived as key and by whom? And above all, how was the collective defined in relation to this?

The focal point is early modern corporative organizations, notably guilds and journeymen associations, which more than any other organization at the time served as a basis for the articulation and defense of workers' rights. These organizations were not only ubiquitous following the urban revolts in the late medieval period, but also depending on the region, they could be rather powerful. Moreover, as this chapter recounts, their members and representatives were inclined to ground their demands in the value of their work. They typically argued in favor of their rights and privileges with reference to the quality of their skills and products. Moreover, their rights and privileges were the major concern of enlightened philosophers and policy makers, who progressively argued in favor of a "modern," deregulated economy and labor market after the mid-seventeenth century.

Inevitably, this choice to focus on corporative organizations will favor cities and regions in which guilds were more ubiquitous, such as northern Italy and northwestern Europe. Moreover, as only powerful guilds really succeeded in connecting their rights and privileges in a sustained way to views and regulations related to product value and skills, such regions as the southern Netherlands and the German lands tended to predominate within these broader regions. The underlying assumption is that the views expressed in the corporative organizations based in these regions had a broader influence but were more effectively smothered elsewhere—including in northern Italy, where corporative organizations were defused long before the mid-seventeenth (and even the mid-fifteenth) century. In both less-urbanized regions, such as eastern Europe, and the oversees colonies, guilds and journeymen associations either never became powerful or did not emerge at all.

WORKING-CLASS CONSCIOUSNESS, MARKET CULTURE, AND SOCIAL STANDING

The idea that working-class consciousness was not straightforwardly determined by transformations on the labor–capital axis, and that factory workers were not the sole harbingers of labor movements, has become commonplace since E. P. Thompson's classic *The Making of the English Working Class* (1963). The main thesis of Sewell's book, published in 1980, was that corporatist idioms and ideals had a strong impact on nineteenth-century revolts, including the 1848 revolution in which Sewell saw not only class distinction but also the incorporation of masters in the workers' movement through terms such as fraternity and reconciliation. In his analysis of around the same period, Iorwerth Prothero has also argued that radicalism should be addressed not from the perspective of either class struggle or the *embourgeoisement* of a certain "labour aristocracy," but from historically deep-rooted artisanal values such as independence and respectability and their connection with elements including exclusivity and the right to a decent living independent from charity and public relief.[5]

Such views are to be situated in debates about the so-called cultural turn, in which the role of class and market forces were questioned. Scholars such as Sewell and Patrick Joyce are steeped in symbolic anthropology and poststructuralism, resulting in the view that the market is not an autonomous force in history but is rather embedded in symbolic systems of meaning.⁶ Markets can of course become "disembedded," as argued by Karl Polanyi in his classic *The Great Transformation* (1944), which implies that social relations and cultural systems of meaning become subject to market forces as history unfolds. Yet this is not, in any case, a linear and straightforward process. In 1984, William Reddy argued, in another classic, *The Rise of Market Culture*, that social conflicts during the Industrial Revolution cannot be understood from the perspective of anonymous market forces alone. While mechanization created the need to concentrate production and control the workforce on the spot, workers did not consider themselves proletarianized. Instead, they continued to see themselves as independent producers who entered into negotiations about the value of their work as if in an early modern marketplace. Nor were their conflicts limited to wages. More often than not they were about independence and dignity and included concerns about customs and traditions related to community ties and family obligations. As summarized by John Smail, in 1992, changes in the "mode of production" were not necessarily and directly accompanied with changes in "social practices" and self-perceptions.⁷

In all, then, late medieval and early modern mentalities and practices appear to have been relatively persistent. Yet the abovementioned debates turn out to be oddly mirrored by the efforts of early modern historians to trace the origins of the labor movement further back in time. As shown in Volume 3 of this series, insubordination and revolts at first were mostly not considered the result of a proper understanding of (class) interest translating in specific demands. They were instead seen as emanating from crowds in defense of customs, as was typically the case in food riots, which would often have been concerned with a certain "moral economy."⁸ Andreas Grießinger argued in 1981 that worker revolts, too, while often being carefully planned, typically revolved around such symbolic aspects as standing and honor.⁹ As far as they concerned access to the group, this moreover materialized in ceremonies which resembled purification rituals in traditional societies as studied by anthropologists including Arnold van Gennep and Victor Turner. Gradually however, class and labor conflict were seen as an early modern phenomenon as well as a modern one. Processes of proletarianization did not fail to pitch workers against masters or merchants in the early modern period. Among others, Catharina Lis and Hugo Soly have shown that early modern journeyman articulated demands and pressed employers not out of a conservative fear for change but starting from a rational understanding of their own interests. Their demands and strategies were not limited to pressing for higher wages and included controlling access to the labor market, but this is explained by the different context of the organization of work—with journeymen not working concentrated in a factory but dispersed in smaller ateliers—rather than by the mind-set of these workers.¹⁰

Ever since, the debate on the "rationality" behind workers' protests has not been settled. This is partly explained by uncertainties about the extent to which a modern labor market existed at all. Lis and Soly have focused on groups of journeymen such as printers and hat makers for whom the labor market was a well-developed and daily reality. As these workers were highly mobile in a geographic sense, they could and did respond to market incentives. Simultaneously, however, work was deeply embedded in paternalistic social relations, with wages, for instance, part of a broader system of reward which included the right to live on the lord's domain for rents below market price, access to communal resources, and flexibility towards seasonal work for women and children, as has for instance been shown for seventeenth-century rural England.¹¹ Unsurprisingly, paternalistic social relations and customary rights also mattered a great deal for urban apprentices. Robert Darnton's account of the so-called cat massacre has famously illustrated that at least apprentices had other concerns than wages and access to the labor market.[12] They were concerned about their food, their sleeping places, and the way they were treated on the shop floor and under the roof of the master. Subsequent work of cultural historians has convincingly shown that apprentices were typically subsumed into the master household and that the multiple frictions and bargaining between masters and apprentices are to be understood from the perspective of the early modern household (Figure 8.1).[13]

Something similar applies to women, who are mostly treated as being dependent on either their father or husband or who else worked in the context of religious communities such as *beguinages*. Nevertheless, women were often seen operating in the vanguard of popular protest, especially in food riots and when a certain "moral economy" was at stake. This has been explained by women's responsibility for nourishing the members of the household and their related sensitivity for rising food prices. In addition, however, women faced specific difficulties in the labor market. As they were often excluded from guilds and, hence, from the more prestigious and privileged positions in the labor market, they typically performed lowly paid jobs such as spinning and lacemaking. These women also actively engaged in protest and riots, displaying a clear consciousness of market mechanisms in general and their own interests in particular. One example is the protest of independent female cotton spinners in Rouen in 1752, which followed a royal ordinance that threatened their autonomy in the yarn market.[14]

In all likelihood, this type of protest increased in number during the seventeenth and eighteenth centuries, as women progressively proletarianized, which implies that they became more dependent on market forces while threatening the patriarchal order. In that sense, their fate resembles that of journeymen. Most journeymen were no longer part of their master's household by the mid-sixteenth century at the latest, but they were not necessarily seen as independent either. Throughout the early modern period employers lamented the fact that journeymen refused to behave like "servants." The journeymen in the Montgolfier paper mill examined by Leonard Rosenband were notoriously referred to, in 1771, as "a sort of little republican state in the midst of the monarchy."[15] This terminology betrays a different conception of the relationship between master and journeymen than one simply regulated by the market, the more so since most journeymen did not consider themselves proletarianized either. A great many of them strove for "independence" and for "liberties" similar to those of guild-based masters. As early as 1966, Natalie Zemon Davis argued, in her analysis of the Company of the Griffarins in the Lyon book printing trade in the first half of the sixteenth century, that journeymen above all refused to be seen and treated as subordinates. While arguing in favor of "mutual and reciprocal love" between masters and journeymen, they drew a contrast with "slavery" and presented themselves as "free men working voluntary at an excellent and noble calling."[16]

All this suggests that both women and journeymen operated in a patriarchal and corporative context in which "masterless" men and women were looked upon with suspicion. A specific problem for journeymen was that they were often themselves husbands responsible for a family while at the same time under the custody of a master. Masters, in turn, also faced tensions between the patriarchal context and the structures of the market. As shown 'Put simply,' in this book, masters were not simply employers. In export industries, they often worked for one or a few large merchants, who bought part or all their produce and perhaps also supplied the raw materials involved. In these

FIGURE 8.1 Tinsmith. In Jan and Caspar Luyken, *Het Menselyk Bedryf. Vertoond in 100 Verbeeldingen van Ambachten, Konsten, Hanteeringen en Bedryven, met Versen*, Amsterdam, 1694.

cases, masters could even be paid partly in raw material or work on machines paid or financed by the merchant. Also, masters could work in subcontracting networks for other masters and thus be paid piece rates similar to those of journeymen. In other words, these masters to a large extent could be proletarianized themselves, as they became increasingly subject to merchant capital and the difference between large and small masters increased. Thus historians have already addressed masters from the perspective of protest and revolt too—albeit mostly in the context of the abolition of the guilds. Michael P. Fitzsimmons argued in his recent book *From Artisan to Worker* that the abolition of the guilds in France at the turn of the eighteenth century was a successful attempt to enable the coming about of a modern industry.[17] Yet here again, discussion about the broader body politic inevitably co emerged.

Although supporters as well as adversaries of the guilds agreed that their abolition would pave the way for the emergence of an unregulated proletariat and, hence, would be a threat to social stability, guilds cannot simply be seen as organizations that guarded the masters from losing control over the means of production. Nor can they be reduced to employers' organizations like those in the late nineteenth and twentieth century. The remarkable thing about the events surrounding the abolition of the guilds at the end of the eighteenth century is that they caused a great deal of despair and disarray notwithstanding the fact that guilds had become empty shells when understood as employers' organizations guaranteeing control over the means of production. What was at stake, in the words of Steven Kaplan, was instead a rival classificatory system, or a different foundation of the social order and taxonomy.[18]

This is not to say that artisanal political attitudes were by definition conservative in nature. Studies on North America have often addressed the political activities of artisans from the vantage point of artisanal radicalism feeding into the American Revolution and in liberal or republican ideas.[19] In comparison, guild-based artisans on the old continent have more often been seen as acting in defense of olden privileges and customs. However, tradesmen in North American cities also defended and secured privileges based upon a corporative social order of sorts. The absence of a guild tradition notwithstanding, they defended freemanship rights, denied outsiders (and slaves) their privileges, and entered into conflict with merchants, for instance in the famous Leisler's Rebellion in late-seventeenth-century colonial New York.[20] Alternatively, guild-based artisans on the continent are no longer seen as conservative either. The last section of this chapter shows that their views also often heralded revolutionary sentiments.

With an eye on a proper understanding of these sentiments, the next section delves deeper into the political rationale behind artisans' labor-related disputes and protests. It shows how they were connected to the perception of skills and product quality. Those who defended the guilds often did so in the name of product quality, arguing that the guilds protected customers from fraud and guaranteed a superior quality. This becomes clear when further fleshing out journeymen's and master's strategies and goals.

POLITICAL STRATEGIES, PRACTICES, AND MOTIVATIONS

The strategies and collective repertoires of working groups ranged from huge strikes and walkouts and large-scale revolts to weekly, monthly, or yearly rituals with a charged symbolic meaning, up to the daily wheeling and dealing on the shop floor. Strikes became more frequent and more violent in the eighteenth century, especially after around 1750.

Historians have counted up to 541 strikes of German journeymen between 1700 and 1806 and 383 strikes of English journeymen between 1717 and 1800, peaking around the early 1790s.[21] But this is only the tip of the iceberg—next to a symptom of growing tensions. Political actions could have a strong ritual bearing as when guild representatives blocked the highly ritualized decision-making procedures, for example by refusing to leave the room where they deliberated or to swear an oath upon a new decree or charter.[22] In extension, guild-based masters symbolically bore out their collective identity in the public sphere during yearly parades and processions, in which they displayed emblems and markers of their group. Nor should we allow juridical strategies to be lacking in this overview. Michael Sonenscher, in particular, has convincingly argued that not only masters but journeymen, too, had frequent recourse to courts to defend their rights and privileges. In fact, the typical form of protest, he argued, was neither the food riot nor the strike but the lawsuit.[23]

The success of most strategies was of course dependent on power relations. The strength of journeymen was typically conditional upon their organizational capacity—which was, in turn, contingent upon the extent to which cooperation was required on the shop floor, their geographic mobility, and the need for an elastic supply of labor, as well as the availability of an infrastructure of inns and other meeting places, next to sheer numbers. In the case of apprentices, on the surface we might assume that they were the weaker party by definition, but here, too, the demand for and supply of apprentices played a role, as did such related factors as the age and social profile of the apprentice. In the case of masters, it becomes even more complicated. While the economic relationship among masters and between masters and merchants or wholesalers could be very diverse and complicated, the political and institutional context also mattered a great deal.[24] Manufacturing masters could have more or less power depending on the autonomy of their guild and the way it was incorporated in the urban political fabric.

Historians have roughly identified two different types of political constellation in early modern cities. The first is a situation in which manufacturing masters enjoyed a great deal of political clout at the urban level for two related reasons. On the one hand, manufacturing masters were in control of their guilds themselves for they could—with varying degrees of autonomy—elect their own representatives from among their own ranks. On the other hand, these guilds guaranteed that manufacturing masters were represented politically up to the urban level because they had often been able to secure a specific number of seats in the local inner and/or outer councils. Notwithstanding myriad local variations, this mostly applies to cities in the southern Netherlands, Sweden, the German imperial cities, and many smaller cities in the empire—including what Mack Walker (1971) called "home towns." This contrasts with most guilds in the northern Netherlands, Britain, and most Italian cities and city-states, where merchants typically held the reins. Deborah Simonton argues for Aberdeen, Scotland, "As the guildry shifted, it became even more men of commerce," that is the burgesses and merchants.[25] In these cases, guilds were largely instruments in the hands of merchants, who used them to control masters and regulate production, while denying them both self-rule and access to local political councils. The situation in France and Spain would seem to have resembled the latter; especially in the heartlands of these more centralized states, guilds, like cities, were mostly far from independent. The most important export sectors were, moreover, likely to be run by large merchants, as was the case in the so-called *Grande Fabrique* (silk weaving) in Lyons.

These differences had a strong bearing on the leverage of the manufacturing master involved. In the southern Netherlands, in principle, merchants could not be involved in production. They were allowed to buy and sell finished products in whatever quantity they thought convenient and even to monopolize access to expert markets, but they could not hire apprentices, journeymen, or impoverished masters themselves. The reverse situation applied in the northern Netherlands, where merchants could mingle in production while manufacturing masters were denied access to export markets or denied the possibility of expanding their businesses.[26] Inevitably, this must have had an impact on the strategies of the artisans concerned. In the southern Netherlands, masters tried all force available to deny merchants access to apprentices and journeymen directly—guarding their monopsony rights on the labor market.[27] Elsewhere, including in large parts of the incorporated trades in northern Italy, masters failed to do so, so that the boundaries between masters and journeymen were often more blurred. In addition, when city-states like Venice and Florence controlled the surrounding countryside and smaller cities in their territory, it was more difficult for master-artisans to guard a boundary between urban manufacturers and rural manufacturers operating in *Kauf* and *Verlag* systems.

The situation in the countryside was mostly similar to one in which merchants held the reins. As the debate on proto industrialization has made clear, local manufacturers could often enjoy a degree of autonomy and control over raw materials and capital goods. But competition and market forces progressively favored situations in which large-scale merchants supplied raw materials and monopolized access to markets. In this context, manufacturing artisans had few opportunities to pressure the merchants or bargain about piece rates and labor conditions, the more so as they were often driven to cottage manufacturing by demographic pressures and the scarcity of land. In this vein, the situation may have been different in settler contexts like rural New England and other American Northeastern regions, where land was abundant and labor (including slave labor and indentures) was scarce.[28] Nor was the establishment of rural guilds successful from the viewpoint of manufacturing artisans. Such guilds were increasingly founded in Hungary from the late eighteenth century, but as they were often mixed (uniting masters of different trades) and often incorporated members from faraway towns, they were mostly unable to control production or defend a monopoly.[29] Not coincidentally, the most famous example of a rural guild is the one studied by Sheilagh Ogilvie in the worsted production in the proto industrial region of the Württemberg Black Forest (southwest Germany). This "guild" was essentially an organization of merchant-entrepreneurs used to monitor and control labor and manufacturing artisans, with the help of privileges obtained from the state.[30]

Nor was the corporative context unimportant for the power and strategies of journeymen. While access to the guilds as a master was typically conditional upon finishing an apprenticeship term and a master piece, these very same regulations could be used to distinguish between free and unfree journeymen. With these terminologies, the journeymen who had finished an apprenticeship term distinguished themselves from those who had not—the latter then being called "unfree." At least in a range of strong guilds on the continent, an apprenticeship term was only mandatory for prospective masters, while journeymen could work for regular masters whether they had finished an apprenticeship term or not. Yet in trades where journeymen could wield enough power, a "right of preference" could be inscribed in the rules, meaning that unfree journeymen were not allowed to work in the trade if there were free journeymen willing to do the job. This was typically connected to a minimum wage, allowing journeymen to refuse to work below the negotiated standard. Masters who did hire unfree journeymen and pay below minimum wages could then be blacklisted, meaning that the unfree journeymen agreed upon refusing to work for him. Unfree journeymen who worked for the master nevertheless risked being molested.[31]

Clearly, then, the power of both guilds and journeymen was very much conditional upon the institutional context, but we should be wary not to reduce the corporative context to something purely institutional. Terms such as "free" and "unfree" betray a broader political attitude. While at present we tend to assume that being "free" equals being free from institutional and political constraints, in the late medieval and early modern context it referred to a positive right, a privilege attributed by a political authority. It equalled being inscribed in the body politic rather than being liberated from it. This privilege was, moreover, gained through apprenticeship, which was seen simultaneously as a procedure through which one gained access to a group by being trained and being socialized into the group. The broader political framework was corporative, which meant that economic and political rights were not awarded on an individual basis but implied membership of a political "body." Early modern cities and other political communities were imagined as "bodies" with different "members." These members were themselves, in turn, conceived of as "bodies" with "members," as was clearly the case with guilds—the members of which were, in turn, "heads" of the households of which they were master.

Obviously, not everybody succeeded in being "incorporated." Notoriously, women mostly struggled to obtain a place in the corporative order. By the eighteenth century, female workers like seamstresses occasionally obtained their own guilds, as was the case in Paris in 1675. Profiting from the mechanisms of the absolute state and the related relative lack of power of the all-male tailor guild, these women defied the male corporative order and existing ideas about womanhood.[32] In a similar vein, journeymen, too, struggled to obtain a place in the corporative social and political order—challenging, in the process, guild-based masters' privileges and authority. From at least the fourteenth century and progressively in the early modern period, employees founded their own "corporations," mostly called "journeymen associations" in the literature.

The incidence of journeymen associations may have correlated with the incidence of conflict between masters and journeymen, if not to the sheer numbers of journeymen in given trades, but this is not to say that they were simple strike organizations.[33] Not only were these journeymen also concerned about their standing and quality, or what could be termed their *état* or *Stand*, like guilds, they also worshipped a patron saint (often the same as their masters), organized collective masses, and obliged members to attend the funeral of a co member.[34] A great number of their rituals, moreover, betray a political sensitivity, directly related to their striving for independence and standing. This is eminently the case with the famous *compagnonnages*, which in eighteenth- and nineteenth-century France refer to an organizational structure in which the so-called *tour de France* of journeymen was embedded. Wandering journeymen could not only revert to specific taverns and inns for boarding and job placement, the *compagnonnages* were also infused with a symbolic repertoire which often referred to the corporative and paternalistic context. Very often the term "devoir" (duty) was used, invoking the duties of single journeymen towards the collective, as expressed in the oath they swore when entering the organization. In return, the journeymen could count on protection, friendship, hospitality, and help in finding a job. A key actor in this was the so-called *mère* (mother), that is, the person who ran the local boarding house (it could also be a *père*—father) and accommodated and supported the journeymen upon arrival.[35]

To be sure, this is not to say that continuity of the corporative tradition reigned supreme. At least north of the Alps, guilds up to the sixteenth century had tried to cultivate and guard a guild ethic and such brotherhood-like ideals as equality, friendship, and mutual aid.[36] Yet these ideals eroded rather drastically from the sixteenth century onwards. While guilds' regulations allowed for ever more variation in firm size, as they gradually relaxed the maxima on the number of journeymen and tools a master could employ, masters refrained from attending collective activities such as funerals of a brethren, masses for the patrons saint, and common meals. This is all the more remarkable as these trends have been recorded also for such regions with strong guilds as the southern Netherlands as well as for trades servicing local rather than export markets.[37] Simultaneously, a new type of civil society emerged, which materialized in organizations such as masonic lodges and friendly societies. Not only was membership of these organizations—in contrast to guilds—voluntary, but they had a more distant relationship with the state and the political sphere.

In the long run, guilds and other corporative organization like chambers of rhetoric not only lost their corporative character but also became perceived, by outsiders, as anachronistic and obsolete. In political thinking, from about the mid-seventeenth century onwards rights and privileges were gradually understood as natural and inherent in individuals, rather than as connected to groups and inscribed in customs. Kaplan has shown that two different views of the social order collided in the eighteenth century. They both refer to their ideal social order as "natural," but while the corporative social order was based on the existing society or orders, physiocratic and enlightened ideas assumed that the natural order results from the fact that everyone has the right "to dispose freely of one's property in oneself" and, hence, to work and employ at one's own discretion.[38] Thus the deregulation and reorganization of the world of work at the end of the eighteenth century was part of a broader transformation in which the corporative order was at stake. This was surely connected to the proletarianization of masters, journeymen, and women, but it was also driven by political transformations and intellectual discourses. In the remaining section, the chapter will shed light on this through a focus on the arguments and the discourses used in discussions related to transformation in the world of work in general and the abolition of guilds in specific.

SKILLS AND THE BODY POLITIC

After the mid-eighteenth century, the deregulation of work and the dismantlement of guilds accelerated. In France, guilds were abolished altogether by the d'Allarde and the Le Chapelier laws in 1791. In subsequent years, the French occupiers of the Low Countries, Switzerland, and parts of the Rhineland and Italy introduced similar measures from 1795. Where the guilds persisted, they often transformed into instruments in the hands of mercantile elites or bureaucratic states who used them to control labor and production. This was not new at the end of the eighteenth century. In France, where cities and guilds had already handed over most of their power and autonomy in the late medieval period, the incorporation of the guilds was further centralized by Colbert in 1673. In the Holy Roman Empire, the Imperial Ordinance on Guilds (*Reichshandwerksordnung*) issued in 1731, in response to a massive strike of Augsburg shoe makers, attempted to subordinate workers by, among other things, prohibiting strikes and assemblies and controlling the movement of workers with the use of a so-called *Kundschaft*, a certificate of leave signed by the previous employer. In Italy, depending on the region, guilds were either further incorporated and instrumentalized (used by the state to control labor and product quality) or bypassed altogether by centralizing policies in the eighteenth and early nineteenth century.³⁹ Overall, guilds' monopolies were undermined and circumvented with the help of the expanding central states. Even states which had been relatively weak before increasingly responded positively to requests from entrepreneurs to set up business outside the corporative structures and exempt from the related labor market regulations.

Territorial states thus accommodated a new economic elite for whom guilds and the privileges of small manufacturers had become a hindrance. Instead of buying finished products from masters, these entrepreneurs henceforth produced them themselves, to subsequently deliver them to shops (*faiseurs de rien, vendeurs de tout*). After the mid-seventeenth century, these political and economic processes were accompanied by a range of new political philosophies, starting with physiocratic thinking, in which it was not only assumed that value added was produced only in the agrarian sector but in which deregulation was favored too. One of the most famous physiocratic thinkers was Anne-Robert-Jacques Turgot (1727–81), who as controller-general of finances under King Louis XVI in France not only deregulated the grain trade but abolished the guilds as well for a short period, in 1776.⁴⁰ Other such thinkers include the Neapolitan Antonio Genovesi and the Piedmontese Giovanni Battista Vasco, who both bore heavily on the debate about free trade and deregulation in Italy. The most famous of all is of course, the Scot Adam Smith, who is renowned for not only his invisible hand theory but also his fierce attacks on guilds' privileges in general and the apprenticeship system (which in England was very rigid owing to the Statute of Artificers prescribing a seven-year term across all trades) in specific. For Smith, indeed, anyone should be entitled to work and to employ workers at his or her own discretion, without any regulation being needed.

Nevertheless, this new type of thinking should not be seen as a mere justification for the increasing power of new political or economic elites. While these philosophical transformations were fundamentally entangled with both economic and political transformations, what transformed in the long run was the very conception of the body politic. Specifically, the connection between the value of work, on the one hand, and membership of the body politic, on the other, had waned. This has emerged from research on apprenticeship, which was traditionally seen as a means of reproducing guilds. Both in regions where guilds were weak and where they were strong, early modern guilds stopped being genuine "corporations." While membership traditionally had been a matter of either being born a member (as the son of a master) or being apprenticed with a master who acted as a surrogate father for some years, this was often no longer the case at the end of the *ancien régime*. Not only did collective rituals wane but apprentices were increasingly perceived as clients in search of skills, resulting in entrance being conceived more in meritocratic and pecuniary terms. French scholars have referred to the phenomenon of the so-called *alloué*, which is an apprentice who had waived his right to become a master and, thus, learned only to acquire skills and access to the labor market.⁴¹ For the German and Austrian contexts, too, historians have pointed at the intrusion of market forces in the relationship between master and apprentice, resulting in the concentration of apprentices per master and a separation of learning from the corporative tradition.⁴² For the southern Netherlands, recent research has, moreover, suggested that master's sons were no longer seen as born in the guild and had to become members similar to outsiders, that is, by finishing an apprenticeship term and master trial, and paying a fee. Simultaneously, masters lost their patriarchal authority or, rather, their patriarchal authority no longer derived from the guild, which had transformed from a type of collective household in which a housefather assumed a public and political role to a set of regulations outside the private sphere of the family (Figure 8.2).⁴³

FIGURE 8.2 William Hogarth, *The Industrious 'Prentice a Favourite, and entrusted by his Master*, Plate IV. In *Industry and Idleness*, 1747.

All this was accompanied by processes of "oligarchization" within (as well as beyond) the guilds, as Kaplan and others have described. But a proper understanding requires connecting this, in turn, to political philosophy and the fundamental transformations related to the discourse on rights, in which rights were gradually thought of as inherent to the individual and to be claimed apart from corporative bodies. Of course, this did not prevent guild masters from adapting to the new situation themselves. In the eighteenth century, smaller masters within guilds reacted to advanced forms of oligarchization and top-down disciplining with claims for more popular forms of internal representation and political participation. In so doing, they invoked "democratic" principles. Harking back to the idea that decisions were to be made by the general assembly of all guild masters, they denounced what they called the "tyranny" or "despotism" of the deans or *jurés*. The latter, in turn, invoked republican arguments about self-rule and autonomy in their attempt to protect their privileges, while the urban magistracy could have recourse to still other arguments, for instance based on authoritarian and more exclusive aristocratic or oligarchic ideas.[44] As such, the conflicts both within guilds and at the defense of guilds may have prepared artisans for their political agitation around 1789 and to their role as *sans-culottes*—as argued by Kaplan.[45]

Nor was this limited to the world of the guilds. In North American cities, too, egalitarian and republican ideals increasingly replaced the support for existing privileges. As has been argued in a case study of New York, artisans incorporated radical English republican ideas and increasingly considered themselves the constituency for legitimate government.[46] On the European continent, radical discourses and ideas found fertile ground among journeymen and (former) masters who increasingly worked outside the corporative framework or in the margins of the regulated economy—either in networks of subcontracting and putting out or

THE POLITICAL CULTURE OF WORK 163

as proletarianized workers. The ever-growing group of unfree journeymen may even have been the first to welcome the fact that natural rights had changed meaning. After all, both so-called false masters and unfree journeymen had an interest in claiming a natural right to work.

What was lost in this process was the connection of political standing to skills and technical knowledge. Both journeymen and guild-based masters when defending their privileges had typically invoked the superior quality of their work as a justification. As to the masters, their argument was that customers would not be cheated by guild members, in contrast to outsiders. This is also visible in their rituals and ceremonies. The guilds' torches and blazons carried along during parades frequently featured their products or instruments, as was the case also in their altarpieces depicting their patron saints (Figure 8.3). The connection between product quality and the political dimension was

FIGURE 8.3 Coat of arms of the Antwerp blacksmiths, Plate XVII 2, and the Antwerp butchers, Plate XVII 9. Both in P. Génard, *Armorial des institutions communales d'Anvers*.

FIGURE 8.3 (*Continued*)

confirmed by the rule that entrance to a guild as a master was typically conditional upon being officially a citizen of the city concerned—or sometimes vice versa. This connection originated in medieval urban revolts, during which the guild-based masters succeeded in gaining a certain degree of political recognition.[47] The chronology and durability of this political recognition strongly differed from region to region and from city to city, but in any case, what was at stake in these struggles was the ability to participate in politics and to be a political subject while at the same time having to work with one's hands. This was not self-evident in the medieval context, given that such highly influential ancient thinkers as Aristotle and Plato had denied the capacity to be involved in politics to manual workers. Both farmers and artisans were considered "slaves of necessity," and thus incapable of acting in a disinterested and rational way in the service of the common good.[48]

References to skills were part of a broader set of discourses and claims about what Werner Sombart has coined "Nahrung." This concept implies that both competition and exclusion should be subject to the wider concern that every member of a community is entitled to a decent living, and, hence, to a fair share of the local production of wealth. According to Sombart and others, this concern for "sustenance" materialized in regulations concerning the grain trade and the price of corn and bread, but it translated also in the right to take part in the local economy as independent housefather.[49] What is nevertheless neglected here is the question of who exactly could claim to contribute to the welfare of the political community concerned—whether a city or a territorial state. When looking at artisans' experiences from this perspective, an interesting paradox emerges after the mid-seventeenth century. On the one hand, production rather than trade was gradually perceived as the source of a state's welfare. This is what physiocrats and the likes of Adam Smith had in common. The hands-on skills of artisans were actually applauded by a great deal of the new philosophers in the eighteenth century. Famous publication projects such as Diderot and D'Alembert's *Encyclopédie ou dictionnaire raisonné des sciences, des arts et des métiers* (edited in France between 1751 and 1772) and the abbé Pluche's *Spectacle de la nature* (first published in 1732) can easily be seen as tributes to what the authors called the "mechanical arts." However, viewed in a long-term perspective, hands-on skills became stripped of *ingenium* and talent. Both historians of labor and historians of science have remarked that while technical knowledge took center stage, the artisans themselves were reduced to a type of sophisticated robot, referred to by Diderot as "automatons" (Figure 8.4).[50] Another much-repeated quote in that respect comes from the famous

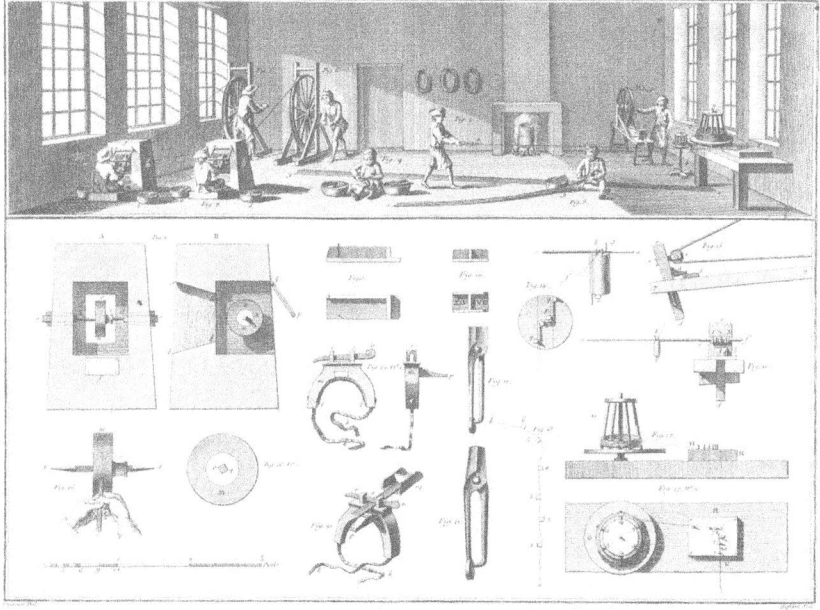

FIGURE 8.4 *Epinglier*, Plate II (Pin Making), engraving of Deferht based upon a design of Goussier. In Denis Diderot and Jean le Rond d'Alembert's, *Encyclopédie, ou dictionnaire raisonné des sciences, des arts et des métiers*, vol. 5, 1751–72.

English entrepreneur Josiah Wedgwood, who referred to his workers as "setts [sic] of hands."[51]

The point here is not only that labor had become a commodity but also that the creation of wealth and value was no longer seen as grounded in the skills and personhood of manufacturing artisans. One expression of it was that the source of the value of products shifted from the value of the raw materials used—guaranteed by the moral quality of the artisans (their honesty and trustworthiness)—to fashionability and novelty, guaranteed by the entrepreneurs or artists who had designed the product and/or the related production process.[52] As such, the power and importance of manufacturing master declined apart from processes of proletarianization too. In the long run, only a small number of the early modern artists and artisans succeeded in escaping the fate of being reduced to trained hands.

Already by the fifteenth and sixteenth centuries, some artisans started to distinguish themselves from what they referred to as "mere handicraft." They started to call their work "art" (or *conste*) and aligned themselves with the so-called "liberal arts," arguing that their work more resembled the work of intellectuals. These artists—in particular, painters, sculptors, and architects—would in the seventeenth and eighteenth centuries assemble in art academies rather than in guilds, but the transformation they pioneered may have had a much greater impact. After all, art academies were soon frequented, at least from the late seventeenth century onwards, by other artisans as well. Moreover, in the eighteenth century, the classical art academies were accompanied by a range of drawing schools, bearing further testimony that drawing became a coveted skill (Figure 8.5). Drawing was

FIGURE 8.5 Gabriel Smith (1724–83) (printmaker) and John Linnell (1729–96) (designer), *A new Book of Ornaments useful for Silversmiths*, 1755. London British Museum, London. © Victoria & Albert Museum, London.

associated with inventiveness and what was called at the time *ingenium*. And *ingenium* was exactly what was denied to most handworkers by the mid-eighteenth century.[53]

It should come as no surprise, then, that Adam Smith justified his attack on guilds and apprenticeship with the idea that artisans did not need *ingenium*. He notoriously argued that:

> Long apprenticeships are altogether unnecessary. The arts, which are much superior to common trades, such as those of making clocks and watches, contain no such mystery as to require a long course of instruction. The first invention of such beautiful machines, indeed, and even that of some of the instruments employed in making them, must, no doubt, have been the work of deep thought and long time, and may justly be considered as among the happiest efforts of human ingenuity. But when both have been fairly invented and are well understood, to explain to any young man, in the compleatest manner, how to apply the instruments and how to construct the machines, cannot well require more than the lessons of a few weeks: perhaps those of a few days might be sufficient.[54]

While Smith's views have often been reduced to a justification of the emergence of the free market, they can also be seen as the culmination of a long-term process in which artisans lost connection with the political sphere. As is well known, artisans had limited access to local political councils by the eighteenth century, owing to processes of state formation and oligarchization. But beyond that, they were also denied the capacity to argue rationally or to even read and understand the charters. So, paradoxically, while work had become connected to natural rights—and with John Locke, the justification of property—the workers themselves were excised from both the intellectual and the political sphere. Work was no longer a basis for political participation or subjectivity. As one scholar working on Adam Smith summarized: "Workers, not citizens, are the inhabitants of the burgeoning industrial age, and the workplace not the *agora*, provides their stage."[55]

CONCLUSION

In sum, it has become clear from this overview that the political culture of work can be reduced to neither a proto class struggle of sorts nor changing discourses on the value of work and skills. On the one hand, market forces and processes of proletarianization were challenging the patriarchal and corporative order, in which work—at least prestigious work—was reserved for male heads of household and connected to a privilege. While increasingly working for a wage throughout their lives, women, journeymen, and impoverished masters escaped the control of masters and housefather and, hence, progressively claimed a right to be incorporated in their own terms. As such, they fostered the emergence of an intellectual and political discourse in which the right to work was a right inherent to each individual rather than a privilege granted by a political entity. On the other hand, enlightened discourses calling for the abolition of guilds and economic privileges, were part of broader political transformations in which territorial states infringed upon the economic and political privileges of cities and guilds.

As a historical process, this was of course neither linear nor unambiguous. The different temporalities of it transcend both the beginning and the end of the period covered in this chapter. While in Italy manufacturing masters had already lost most of their political recognition by the mid-fifteenth century, vestiges of corporative political and economic power continued to influence the discourses, attitudes, and practices of artisans until deep into the nineteenth century. Nevertheless, a focus on the cities and regions in which manufacturing masters had secured firm rights through their guilds up to and including the eighteenth century helps reveal some of the most significant transformations in the political culture of work after the mid-seventeenth century. On the one hand, it sheds light on the political aspirations of manufacturing masters and journeymen, revealing in particular that they grounded their claim for political recognition in the value of their work. On the other hand, it shows that their rights and claims were gradually discredited owing to a combination of economic, political, and cultural transformations.

CHAPTER NINE

Work and Leisure

EMMA GRIFFIN

Leisure, and how much of it workers had, has long been a question of particular interest to historians. In the mid-1960s, the economic historian Sidney Pollard placed the loss of customary leisure time at the heart of his analysis of the rise of the modern, capitalist economy. As he wrote: "Men who were non-accumulative, non-acquisitive, accustomed to work for subsistence, not for maximization of income, had to be made obedient to the cash stimulus."[1] Pollard's suggestion that the early modern worker labored in order to reach a minimum subsistence rather than in order to maximize income has resonated widely throughout many subsequent discussions of work and leisure in the early modern period. As David Levine has more recently summarized, those working the land in preindustrial Britain "worked enough to attain their targeted income and then simply quit."[2]

Not only has the early modern worker been presumed to prefer leisure over surplus income but this preference has been regarded as having significance beyond the purely economic. In his article "Time, Work-Discipline and Industrial Capitalism," E. P. Thompson argued that the task-oriented, rather than clock-based, working patterns of the eighteenth century and earlier contributed to a better overall quality of life. He argued, the "demarcation between 'work' and 'life' was far less sharply drawn" in preindustrial communities, which worked to the task rather than the clock; for such workers, he concluded, "social intercourse and labour are intermingled" in beneficial ways.[3] Similar views concerning the blurring between work and leisure have been echoed by scholars working on premodern communities in continental Europe. William Reddy's work on the spinning industry in eighteenth- and nineteenth-century France, for example, broke down the distinctions between entrepreneur, worker, and consumer, noting that the spinners were all of these at once. Workers neither sought to "maximise purchasing power as consumers [n]or minimize labour time as labourers."[4] Their life was characterized instead by a search to balance the competing demands of work, consumption, and leisure.[5]

In addition to arguing that leisure tended to be more holistically incorporated into working patterns in the preindustrial era, scholars have also suggested that workers enjoyed more of it.[6] Hans-Joachim Voth's study of working hours in Britain found a sharp increase in the period from the late eighteenth century to the middle of the nineteenth, with a correspondingly steep decline in the hours left for leisure.[7] There is also some evidence of increases in working hours in the United States at the turn of the century, as the growth of the nation's cities and industry led to an increase in the number of waged workers.[8]

The wide degree of consensus among scholars concerning the greater availability of leisure to the preindustrial worker can be explained in part by the shared intellectual framework within which much of this work has been situated. Pollard's work was founded upon a concept of the preindustrial moral economy borrowed from Engels, and the same set of working assumptions are also implicit in a wide range of more recent interventions.[9] Thus, despite some disagreement in, for example, the chronology of decline, there is a common belief that preindustrial communities enjoyed a relatively leisured existence, whereas capitalism pushed up working hours and reduced the opportunity for leisure. Surveying the long-term history of work and leisure in the United States, Juliet Schor concluded: "key incentive structures of capitalist economies contain biases towards long working hours [and] dramatically raise work effort."[10] Moreover, there is wide agreement that something important was lost with the decline of older working patterns. As Douglas Reid nostalgically concludes, when the English Black Country workers submitted "to the norms of industrial capitalism" by giving up their Saint Monday (the tradition of staying away from work on Mondays) "the notion of a proper balance between work and leisure was lost."[11]

Clearly, then, thinking about the relationship between work and leisure goes beyond the history of sports and recreations, and takes us to the heart of the nature of working life in preindustrial societies. And in order to assess these various claims about the relatively leisured life of workers in the early modern period, it will be necessary to turn back to the historical record and ask what evidence there is for workers' preferences. Let us start with a definition. The *Oxford English Dictionary* defines leisure as "free or unoccupied time … which one can spend as one pleases." Indeed, it was during the eighteenth century that "leisure," hitherto conceived as an opportunity broadly defined, developed into a concept of time—or an opportunity—that was free from the pressures of work. Did early modern workers have a choice between work and "leisure time," which they were able to spend as they pleased? And if so, what kind of choices did they make?

LABOR VERSUS LEISURE

Part of the difficulty in answering such apparently straightforward questions lies in finding appropriate historical sources. One well-used source has been the writing of the early political economists. It was certainly the belief of many contemporaneous writers that workers exhibited a marked preference for leisure time over work. In their eyes, the poor had a set of expectations for their consumption of food, clothing, and housing, and once they had earned sufficient to meet these expectations they traded labor for leisure. In the 1660s, the economic writer and merchant Sir Josiah Child set out the problem as follows: "In a cheap year they will not work above two days in a week; their humour being such that they will not provide for a hard time; but just work so much and no more, as may maintain them in that mean condition to which they have been accustomed."[12] Similar views were echoed in the early eighteenth century by the Anglo-Dutch political philosopher Bernard Mandeville. He asserted that: "Every Body knows that there is a vast number of Journey-men … who, if by Four Days Labour in a Week they can maintain themselves, will hardly be persuaded to work the fifth; and that there are Thousands of labouring Men of all sorts, who will … put themselves to fifty Inconveniences … to make Holiday."[13] But these, of course, were hardly impartial claims. Child, Mandeville, and other political economists who wrote on the subject had a stake in keeping wages low and were thus eager to assert that high wages simply encouraged indolence and insolence by inducing laborers to turn down available work. Clearly, if we are to make sense of workers' work and leisure preferences in this period, we will need to turn away from the judgments of their employers and search for sources that better reflect the values and outlook of the workers themselves.

Early modern workers have bequeathed a number of autobiographies, which we can use to probe this problem, and although such material is not abundant, it certainly provides an important counterpoint to the writings of upper-class observers. Inevitably, autobiographical material presents us with problems of representation and interpretation. Women very rarely wrote autobiographies and the men who did were, for the most part, unaccustomed to putting pen to paper.[14] Nonetheless, for all their complexity, autobiographies and memoirs represent a unique set of records in which working people set out to describe their lives in their own words and for their own purposes, and as such should form an important element in our attempt to understand the mental horizons and economic choices of the early modern workforce.

Let us start with the example of Edward Barlow. Barlow was born in 1642 in Prestwich, then a village about five miles from Manchester, now physically connected to the city through urban sprawl and subsumed administratively within the metropolitan county of Greater Manchester. As a country dweller, it was not unusual that his first experience of paid work was farm work, but Barlow "never had any great mind to country work." Plowing, sowing, haymaking, reaping, hedging, ditching, thrashing, and dunging among cattle were all, in his opinion, "drudgery."[15] Nonetheless, he was employed in agriculture on a casual basis—"by the day"—for several years until his father found him an opening with a whitester in nearby Manchester. The work involved bleaching yarn for the weaving trade. He went on a "liking," but returned two weeks later informing his parents that he did not in fact like it at all and persuaded them to let him come back. But resettling at home was not straightforward. Returning to his village after refusing to be bound apprentice to a trade he did not like, he faced not only his father's displeasure but also comments from the neighbors, "asking why I could not stay at my place ... [and] hitting me in the teeth."[16] The good folk of Prestwich, it seems, did not take too kindly to the return of a neighbor who turned down work in Manchester and had nothing better to say for himself than that he did not like it.

It is interesting to read Barlow's account of his early working life for clues about early modern understandings of "work" and of "leisure." The most striking feature of work in Barlow's Prestwich is simply that there was not very much work around at all. Prior to his apprenticeship to the whitester, he was clearly not fully employed. He worked "by the day," and only when his neighbors "had any need of me." He described himself as "troublesome" to his parents when "out of work." Even when in work, he earned "but small wages." Yet, despite these small and irregular earnings, he continued in Prestwich for some years as his father was unable to find anyone willing to take on an apprentice—he stayed with his parents until "at last" his father heard of a man "willing to take an apprentice." Indeed, part of the reason that opening had arisen was because the master's mistreatment of his employees ensured an unusually high turnover of workers. Then there was the response of his neighbors when he refused to continue with the whitester and returned to the village. Their hostility to the return of one of their own suggests that Barlow's return signified above all a little less work for themselves—a serious consideration when one day's work buys the next day's meal.

It would also clearly be mistaken to depict the young Edward Barlow as making an active choice between work and leisure. He needed to work, as his parents, being "but poor people," were unable to feed him themselves. Yet, despite this pressing imperative, he was frequently out of work, leaving him "always in want." This was not a man choosing leisure; it was somebody suffering from what we would now term "unemployment." Even if we concede that Barlow's want of employment sometimes left him with time on his hands, it is hard to imagine that he experienced this time as "leisure" in any modern sense of the word, as this lack of work reduced him to a state of severe want.

While unemployment and underemployment were endemic through much of western Europe, the situation in America was rather different. In the first place, many of the early colonial settlers brought with them a deep-seated, Protestant work ethic, which encouraged the principle of working from sunrise to sunset. No less importantly, however, colonial emigrants settled in a land with abundant natural resources ripe for exploitation. In contrast to the densely populated European nations with comparatively limited employment opportunities they left behind, American settlers encountered little difficulty in finding full employment, and their hard labor reaped a tangible and immediate economic reward. This very much wider range of employment opportunities helped to foster longer working hours than were customary in much of western Europe.[17] A study of the seventeenth-century Chesapeake has concluded that the new immigrants worked longer hours at more boring tasks but in return consumed substantially better diets.

We have looked so far at workers who were tied to the work that their master provided, but not all early modern workers were tied into traditional master–servant relationships. This period also witnessed the growth of cottage industry. Sometimes also called domestic manufacture or "proto industry," it refers simply to production that takes place within the home. Small-scale rural industry of this nature had developed in England, the southern Low Countries, and southern Germany in the late Middle Ages, but a second wave of development in the seventeenth and eighteenth centuries greatly increased the number of workers engaged in cottage industries such as spinning, weaving, knitting, metalworking, basketmaking and strawplaiting.[18] Is it possible that these independent workers enjoyed a more favorable situation with regard to leisure than those workers who were bound to an employer?

This certainly has been the view of many historians writing on the subject. The favorable position of weavers was first emphasized in Engels' *Condition of the Working Class in England*. As he explained, the weaver combined his weaving with smallholding, renting "a little piece of land, that he cultivated in his leisure hours, of which he had as many as he chose to take, since he could weave whenever and as long as he pleased."[19] And this view of the domestic workers as independent laborers, dovetailing their industrial avocations with small-scale farming and a healthy amount of leisure, has echoed through the literature ever since Engels' work was translated into English in the late nineteenth century.

It is certainly the case that many of those who worked in cottage industry often did combine small-scale manufacture for the market with farming a small garden for domestic consumption. There is also real substance to the claim that the demarcation between work and leisure was more fluid for these independent workers and that the ability to set working hours was highly valued. Most of the autobiographers engaged in domestic manufacture regarded their work as preferable to agriculture, and the autonomy that came with weaving formed part of its appeal. Weavers and knitters were for the most part self-employed either owning their own looms or renting them in a shop. Either way, they set their own hours, which provided them with the very welcome option of trading work for leisure as they chose. Samuel Bamford approvingly noted that on exchanging his position in a Manchester warehouse for a loom, he became "master of my own time," with the liberty to partake of "country amusements with the other young fellows of the neighbourhood," a liberty which would quickly have led to his dismissal had he tried it at the warehouse.

Yet, on closer reading, it becomes apparent that among many weavers the preference for leisure over labor was less pronounced than Engels proposed. Certainly, when trade was brisk and piece rates were high, some workers did opt to reduce their hours and take leisure instead. George Calladine, for instance, became an apprentice framework knitter in 1805 when the trade was prospering. After two years, he could complete his master's work and also "with ease earn four shillings a day" for himself. With hindsight, Calladine regretted that the custom of paying by the task rather than the hour had encouraged him to become "almost independent of his master … very apt to idle away a day or two at the beginning of the week."[20] Yet Calladine was a young man without dependents at this time; he was barely in his teens, and his preference for "idling" his time might owe as much to his age as much as anything else. Others with a family to raise often made a very different calculation when faced with the same choice. They responded to high piece rates by working longer and maximizing their income. A few of the autobiographers could hardly contain their surprise at the riches that weaving occasionally allowed them to amass. When Ben Brierley and his family took to weaving satin shawls they thought they had "found a silver mine." Ben was earning twenty-four shillings a week and his father thirty: "such an income was enough to turn our heads, We seemed to be rolling in wealth."[21] Clearly, different workers made very different decisions when confronted with the same set of circumstances.

Not only is the evidence of cottage workers' preference for leisure over labor inconclusive, we must also acknowledge that these periods of high wages were exceptional and usually short-lived. Outside a few years of exceptional prosperity, most weavers and knitters were unable to earn a steady year-long income. Indeed, all the autobiographers involved in these cottage industries encountered a recurring difficulty: one moment enjoying the boom times, the next plunged into poverty when demand for their goods fell sharply and rapidly away.[22] Nor was this simply a consequence of the eventual mechanization of the industry during the Industrial Revolution, as Engels had argued. In 1747, many decades before the mechanization of the hosiery industry, William Hutton was forced to look for a new master as a stockinger following the untimely death of his employer. Unfortunately, at this time "trade was dead." The hosiers could not find work sufficient for their own workers, still less take on a newcomer like him. He tried several warehouses, but "all proved a blank," and Hutton was reduced to tears to think he had served seven years as an apprentice to a trade "at which I could not get bread."[23] In all, then, it is highly doubtful that weavers and other cottage workers whether in Britain or elsewhere in Europe enjoyed the favorable working conditions and access to leisure that Engels claimed. The high wage interludes always proved to be short-lived. At some point the bubble burst, and workers were back to working long hours for low wages.

This chapter has argued that it is mistaken to conclude that western workers enjoyed long hours of leisure before 1800. Instead, much of the period between 1650 and 1800 was characterized by underemployment and unemployment, and while these conditions may have sometimes left workers with time on their hands, this was rarely time that they were able to exploit for their own purpose. For agricultural and skilled workers who were bound to their employer by contract, the depressed labor market enabled employers to extract as much labor from their workers as they were able, safe in the knowledge they were unable to seek better conditions elsewhere. The situation for independent cottage workers, such as weavers and knitters, was certainly more favorable when trade was good, though not all workers prized leisure above income, and outside these relatively brief interludes of prosperity, cottage workers by necessity worked long hours simply in order to achieve the income necessary for survival. The only major exception to this pattern was in the North American colonies, where the unusual combination of low population density and abundant natural resources provided workers with meaningful autonomy in the matter of how to divide their time between work and leisure. Towards the end of our period, however, there were the stirrings of economic growth that we now call the "Industrial Revolution," which had the potential to destabilize traditional patterns of work and leisure. It is important to ask, therefore, what impact (if any) the onset of industrialization had on older working patterns.

INDUSTRIALIZATION, WORKING HOURS, AND TIME FOR LEISURE

In order to address this question, let us turn to the work of economic historians that attempts to quantify exactly how long men spent at work in the early modern period and when, if at all, this started to change. Voth's study of court records from the London Old Bailey and the North Assizes between 1760 and 1830 argues for a reduction in leisure time over this period. By using these records to establish whether or not the witnesses of crimes were at work during the time a crime was committed, Voth has demonstrated an increasing working year from the end of the eighteenth century to 1850, accounted for largely by the loss of customary holidays rather than an extension of the working day.[24] Set against this, however, recent work by Gregory Clark and Ysbrand van der Werf has argued against any changes in working hours. Their analysis suggests that working hours remained largely stable between the Middle Ages and 1800, and led them to dismiss the idea of a preindustrial "world of leisure and laughter where people rested often, worked sporadically, and preferred little for material consumption, preferring religion, festivals, love, sport, and war."[25] Why have economic historians' attempts to quantify the amount of time that men spent at work yielded such different answers? Can these very divergent findings be reconciled, both with each other and with the qualitative evidence for high levels of unemployment that we considered above? And how do the experiences of women fit with these patterns?

The key to resolving these problems lies in rejecting totalizing claims about the experiences of *all workers* at any given time, and acknowledging instead the great diversity of experience across the West, particularly with the onset of industrialization—an extended and piecemeal process that occurred in western Europe over a period of well over a hundred years. Even a supposedly *national* study such as Voth's is in reality a *local* study of two English regions—London and the northeast. Not only is Voth's evidence regionally specific, but these two regions were also highly distinctive. Both were urban, and Lancashire was also the crucible of the economic event later described as the "Industrial Revolution." In consequence, his data heavily overrepresents skilled, urban workers and those engaged in manufacturing, while largely omitting those who worked on the land—it included almost no agricultural workers; just 69 of almost 1,000 observations, or 7 percent, were of farm workers.[26] In other words, while Voth has convincingly demonstrated a rise in work intensity in urban and industrial Britain, his evidence is largely silent about the fortunes of workers outside the heartlands of the Industrial Revolution.

Clerk and Van der Werf, by contrast, explicitly sought to analyze labor effort in England over a period of six centuries, and in order to do so looked at two occupations that changed very little throughout this long period—grain threshing and sawing. Their research indicates that not only was there very little technological change in these two occupations over time but so too was there very little change in working patterns or work intensity. But here, again, we run into problems of representativeness. Two traditional sectors of the English economy cannot stand proxy for working experiences as a whole any more than London and Lancashire can. Rather than seeking general answers, it is more helpful to conceive of industrialization as a process which broke down the much more homogeneous preindustrial patterns. Industrial economies were much more complex and divergent than their predecessors, comprising traditional sectors (such as threshing and sawing) and modern sectors based in the industrial regions. As industrialization began to spread across Europe, ever larger numbers were drawn into more intensive working patterns, but even by the very end of the period under consideration here, the process was in its early stages.

The suggestion that traditional working patterns were starting to undergo changes in Britain's industrial regions but remained largely stable in much of the rest of Britain and Europe is further supported by evidence for child labor during the Industrial Revolution. It would clearly be mistaken to construe children's participation in the workforce as a simple choice between labor and leisure, as children rarely exercised any agency over when they started work. However, the extent to which children were employed in the labor market does help us to understand the ways in which that labor market operated insofar as children are more likely to be employed when demand for workers is high, and more likely to be "unemployed" when the demand for labor is low.

In the absence of official records systematically recording the age at which children entered the workforce there has inevitably been some disagreement between historians concerning the extent of child labor throughout this period.[27] However, working-class autobiographies can be used to shed light on children's working patterns in what was an increasingly complex and divergent economy. The autobiographies reveal that the likelihood of being at work was highly contingent upon where a child lived, with those in the industrial districts starting work several years earlier than their rural counterparts. In industrial Britain, the average age at which children started work was just eight and a half years. The situation in the agricultural districts was very different. Children in agricultural districts typically started full-time work around the age of eleven and a half—fully three years later than those living in industrial regions.[28] This relatively late age for starting work was a symptom of the generally low demand for labor in most rural districts that we have already observed. Beyond a small number of seasonal tasks with which small children could help (bird scaring, planting, harvesting, and so forth) children lacked the strength and self-governance necessary to perform useful agricultural work throughout the year. Given the relatively large pool of adolescent and adult workers, employers preferred to select their workforce from these age groups rather than to hire children. The evidence from child labor, therefore, once again suggests that industrialization signified a break with traditional working patterns, albeit a break that was highly localized in nature and, up to 1800, largely confined to Britain. At this date, large parts of Britain and most of western Europe were still unaffected by the Industrial Revolution, and discussions about changing patterns of labor and leisure need to be founded upon a proper appreciation of the fragmented and piecemeal nature of change.

Industrialization tended to increase work intensity for both men and children, but what happened to women? Given the complex and diverse state of the European economy, women's experiences were also inevitably varied. Factories, manufacturing, and (to a lesser degree) mining all offered new employment opportunities to women. As a result, just as the industrial districts witnessed a lengthening of male working hours and a reduction in the ages at which children started work, so did these regions witness an increase in women's participation in the workforce.[29] Outside the industrial regions, female working patterns inevitably changed far less. James B. Collins' work on France, for example, indicates the degree to which women remained clustered in the low-skill, low-pay sectors they had always colonized—laundry work, needlework, and domestic service.[30] In Leiden and Cologne, Martha Howell concludes that women's paid employment was "concentrated in industries that had obvious roots in tasks in which women in subsistence households specialized."[31] It was a pattern repeated across the globe. Furthermore, no matter where women lived or what kind of work they did, suggesting that women could choose between labor and leisure fails to capture the reality of their lives. Middle-class women were less likely to engage in paid employment than their poorer peers, yet this did not mean they followed a life of leisure. All domestic labor was physically arduous in the pre-electric era, and with large families the workload could be considerable. The custom of many skilled workers and apprentices boarding with their masters further increased women's domestic work.[32] Many industries, such as the silk industry centered in Lyon, France, were based in domestic workshops rather than separate mills, so even paid employment did not free women from domestic labor.[33]

The distinction between work and leisure was always more unclear for women than it was for men. After all, young women were rarely permitted to idle away their time within the home. Instead, they were occupied with the endless round of purchasing, preparing, and clearing away meals; cleaning; washing; and minding small children—labor-intensive work, all to be done in an unpaid capacity.[34] For women, life alternated between paid and unpaid work rather than work and leisure, and many women found themselves regularly moving between these two options. From early childhood, girls were put to unpaid work in their family home and typically continued this work into adolescence. This was followed by an interlude between their late teens and early twenties in domestic service, mill work, or some other form of paid work outside the home. With the onset of marriage and motherhood, many women retreated from the labor market once again and were employed in performing unpaid housework inside the home. How long they spent there depended upon how their married life unfolded. Those with reliable breadwinning husbands and large families usually found this marked the end of their participation in the labor market. But women who lost their breadwinner and those with no or few children often re entered the labor market at some point after marriage.[35] Either way, however, it is hard to discern leisure in the lives of women with family responsibilities.

POPULAR LEISURE

There is one final question that we need to address and that concerns leisure itself. We have seen that preindustrial workers often worked less intensively than became common in the industrial districts at the end of our period but suggested that this is much better characterized as underemployment and unemployment than as "leisure." Nonetheless, all workers throughout this period enjoyed some periods away from work. It is necessary to consider both the experience of leisure in the preindustrial world and the ways in which this changed with the onset of industrialization.

Social elites have always regarded popular sports and pastimes with some degree of anxiety, owing to the crowds, gambling, and drunkenness that popular leisure often involves. These anxieties became particularly acute in England and New England with the rise of the Puritans in the sixteenth and seventeenth centuries but entered a period of abeyance during the long eighteenth century.[36] Throughout the eighteenth century, most social elites viewed the people's sports and pastimes as considerably less pernicious than the religious zeal which had recently persecuted them. As William Stukeley explained: "the last age had discourag'd the innocent and useful sports of the common people, by an injudicious zeal for religion, which has drove them into worse amusements."[37] Generally, Catholic Europe had always exhibited greater tolerance towards popular customs, viewing them as valued traditions that slotted into a conservative and unchanging social order.[38] As a result, during most of the period under consideration, there was little elite interference with popular pastimes. William Borlase, eighteenth-century Cornish antiquary, marshalled all the traditional arguments in favor of popular recreation when he described parish celebrations as an occasion for "civilising the people, for composing differences by the mediation and meeting of friends, for increase of love and unity by these feasts of charity, and for the relief and comfort of the poor."[39] Such views played a powerful role in protecting popular pastimes from unwelcome elite interference throughout the long eighteenth century.

But although popular recreations were generally free from attack during this period, this did not straightforwardly translate into a vibrant recreational calendar for most working people. The reality for workers throughout most of preindustrial Europe was that opportunities for recreation were limited, in both nature and extent.[40] Although workers did not work intensively, owing to generally low levels of employment, they were not always able to use their free time engaged in activities that we would recognize as "leisure."

Let us return, once more, to our disgruntled farm worker from England, Edward Barlow. Despite frequently being out of work, Barlow just once refers to something that corresponds to our modern understanding of leisure and that was on a Sunday evening, after evening prayers. At this time, he used to meet "with some of our neighbours' children, for we were used to resort together upon a holiday for to play together and discourse." Throughout the following century, writers agreed that leisure could only be enjoyed outside the expected hours of work and prayer. "Winter Sundays," for example, were the time that the Northamptonshire poet John Clare named as available for recreation. Clare, characteristically, preferred leaving his neighbors to play football, while he "stuck to [his] corner stool poring over a book."[41] Other writers indicated that the light summer evenings could also be exploited for recreation. "As the days lengthened, in the evening after our work was done, we assembled on our village-green to spend our time in some rustic amusements, such as wrestling, football, etc.," wrote one small farmer.[42] Leisure, so far as these laborers experienced it, was not something that could be snatched during the working week, even if work happened to be slack. And although Sundays were generally kept free of work, leisure still had to be fitted around the demands of church.

These restrictions on popular leisure were even more pronounced in the lives of women, as Andreas Gestrich's study of the central European practice of *Lichtstuben* reveals. Gestrich has looked at the different ways in which young men and women spent their evenings in two rural villages in Württemberg in southwestern Germany. The boys rented rooms in the locality where they could meet in the winter months. They spent their evenings together and at leisure. Women also rented rooms to meet in the evenings, but in contrast to their male peers, their use of these rooms was not completely free from work. Their *Lichtstuben* were, literally, "lighted rooms"—that is, rooms that were lit and heated so that women could save on fuel costs as they sat and worked, at spinning or needlework, together.[43]

Eighteenth-century writers not only testified that most leisure was something which occurred outside ordinary working hours but also indicated that it was often very simple in form, requiring next to nothing in terms of space or resources. Across Europe a host of outdoor recreations—wrestling, boxing, football, cricket, and other now forgotten ball games—prevailed. High levels of interpersonal violence were tolerated in all of these sports, and although they were bound by certain rules and conventions, these rules were not codified at a national, still less, international level.

Football was among the most widely enjoyed athletic sports of early modern Europe. It was played in all regions and in many different forms: sometimes by large unequal teams traversing wide stretches of public land, sometimes through the streets of towns and cities, and sometimes in a more recognizably modern form, confined to pitches of fixed size. This variability was typical of early modern sports. No matter how football was played, however, it remained firmly rooted in the lower ranks of society. It was not unknown for social elites to participate in or promote the game, but in general they turned to sports such as hunting, coursing, and cricket for exercise, and the game of football was left largely in the hands of the common people.

It has been widely argued that popular football in the eighteenth century and earlier was unruly and unstructured, and that it was not until the public schools redeveloped the game—introducing teams, pitches, and goals of fixed size—in the nineteenth century that the modern game was born.[44] Yet the traditional form of "folk football" upon which this account is based was never widespread. There certainly are examples across Europe of great set football matches, linked to a certain date in the calendar, and played out between neighboring settlements or parishes. In such games, the teams were composed of all the willing men from each community, so they were inevitably frequently of uneven size. Matches were played without identifiable positions or pitch, and local landmarks—the market cross, the village well, or the church porch—might serve as goals. Such games were clearly very different from football in its modern form. Yet annual set matches of this kind have been recorded in no more than a handful of towns and villages.[45] It is precisely owing to their exceptional nature that these kinds of matches have left a mark on the historical record. Most football was played on a much smaller scale and usually in a form much closer to the modern game than standard accounts allow. The early modern game was not played according to nationally agreed rules: the size of goals, pitches, and teams might all vary; so too might the length of play. But the absence of national regulations should not be confused with an absence of rules of any kind. Decisions about the nature of play were agreed before the start of the game, and where matches were played competitively, these rules were carefully enforced. In Britain there is evidence of such games being advertised, along with their rules, in the provincial newspapers.[46] The advertising of such games suggests that football may also have had some appeal as a spectator sport at this time, though there is no evidence of large crowds being drawn to such events. For the most part, men enjoyed games of football as participants rather than as spectators.

The only athletic sport to rival football in popularity was cricket. The sport was enjoyed by aristocrats in the late seventeenth century and it grew steadily in popularity throughout this period.[47] Eighteenth-century newspapers advertising matches between gentlemen testify to the ongoing involvement of social elites, and the private diaries of parsons, millers, farmers, craftsmen, and shopkeepers indicate that cricket extended steadily to the middle ranks of society during the eighteenth century.[48] How far the game extended down the social scale is more difficult to establish on the basis of the evidence that has survived. There certainly was some involvement of the rural poor in the game of cricket, but the timing of many cricket matches—weekday afternoons—would clearly do much to restrict the involvement of those who needed to work for a living (Figure 9.1).

The only early modern sports which routinely drew in large crowds of spectators were those involving hand-to-hand combat, which we can subsume for convenience under the heading of "boxing." All western nations had their own versions of interpersonal combat sports (as well as others, such as cock fighting and bull baiting, involving combats between animals), in which very high levels of violence were tolerated.[49] A manual from early-eighteenth-century Britain, for example, provided instruction for techniques such as head butting, punching, eye gouging, and choking.[50] The largely unrestrained violence that was permitted may have helped to provide entertainment but it also meant that organized fights had an unfortunate tendency to end in death, resulting in manslaughter charges for the victorious fighter. It was undoubtedly this which provided the spur for reform of the sport's rules. The first set of boxing rules were introduced by the champion fighter Jack Broughton in 1743 and known as Broughton's rules. Broughton also encouraged the use of "mufflers," a form of padded glove, though their use remained optional for over a hundred years. Broughton's rules were further revised and consolidated in the nineteenth century, when the use of gloves was mandated. But boxing was clearly well ahead of the curve in the matter of the codification of its rule. Most sports did not adopt a set of nationally agreed rules at any point before 1800. Indeed, even the newly codified sport

FIGURE 9.1 Bull-baiting. In Henry Alken, *The National Sports of Great Britain… with Descriptions, in English and French*, 1823.

of boxing coexisted with a very wide range of non codified combat sports, each played according to local tradition (Figure 9.2).

In addition to sports that were organized and took place out-of-doors were a host of more informal recreational activities that took place inside the home. Through the colder winter months, families spent their evenings indoors—wiling away their free hours socializing with neighbors, reading aloud, singing, and storytelling. As we have seen in the case of Germany, some villagers rented rooms so that they could socialize with friends and neighbors as well as family. Indeed, these pastimes formed the mainstay of most people's leisure activities in rural areas well into the nineteenth century. Much of the reason for this is simply because incomes were so low that most people did not have money to spend on leisure. Despite the occasional large-scale spectator events, such as prize-fighting and horseracing, most forms of leisure had to be accessed for free. Even many adult males lacked the spare income to spend on leisure and women and children certainly did. This did not entirely close down the workers' opportunities for leisure, but it did help to circumscribe the form that they took.

The major exception to this came in the form of annual festivals, carnivals, fairs, and parish celebrations. For most of the year, leisure activities were a somewhat desultory affair, but all European communities enjoyed an annual cycle of fairs, carnivals, and revels. More than any other occasion in the recreational calendar, these events provided laborers a day or more of holiday. In the colder climates of northern Europe, fairs and parish feasts predominated. Fairs were complex occasions, typically spanning several days, and mixing both recreational and commercial functions. In smaller settlements, parish dedication feasts took the place of the trading fairs found in large towns. But at fairs both large and small, a recognizable set of entertainments—plays, freak shows,

FIGURE 9.2 *Rural Sports. Cudgel Playing.* In *The Sporting Magazine; or, Monthly Calendar of the Transactions of the Turf, the Chace, and Every Other Diversion Interesting to the Man of Pleasure, Enterprize, and Spirit,* 1799.

games, and races—could be found. Workers were accustomed to travelling several miles in order to enjoy the feasts and fairs that were celebrated in neighboring communities and employers were expected to allow time off so their workers could attend. Few other events came around with such regularity to enliven the existence of the laboring classes (Figure 9.3).

Fairs and parish celebrations were enjoyed in much of southern and Mediterranean Europe, too, but in these regions, the Carnival season provided the greatest popular festival of the year. Carnival was located in towns and involved drinking, the eating of luxuries such as meat and pancakes in advance of the arrival of Lent, masks, fancy dress, processions, and plays—all performed in the open air in public, civic spaces. Pre-Lenten carnival traditions were much weaker in the colder northern climates of Britain and Scandinavia, but here a condensed day of activities took place on Shrove Tuesday, making that day among the most widely celebrated in early modern Europe. William Fitzstephen's late-twelfth-century history of St. Thomas Becket included an account of cockfighting and football on Shrove Tuesday and repeated prohibition orders throughout following centuries suggest a continuous history of these customs throughout medieval and early modern Europe. There is some evidence of the withdrawal of social elites from carnival and Shrovetide customs during the early modern period, with the celebrations becoming more plebeian and youthful in character. As the season's (or day's) activities sometimes involved masks and dressing up, and as celebrations occasionally got out of hand, it has sometimes been described as a time of licensed misrule (Figure 9.4).[51]

There were in addition a host of other dates punctuating the year that brought festivity and the cessation of work. Some, such as harvest celebrations, were tied to the

FIGURE 9.3 David Teniers the Younger, *Landscape with Peasants Playing Bowls Outside an Inn*, c. 1660. Los Angeles, David Teniers the Younger, LACMA.

FIGURE 9.4 Etienne Jeaurat (1699–1789), *Carnival in the streets of Paris*, 1757. Paris Musée Carnavalet. Photo: DeAgostini / Getty Images.

agricultural year; others, Christmas and Easter, for example, were rooted in the Christian calendar. By the eighteenth century, many countries also had their own local celebrations, such as the newer anniversary of Guy Fawkes celebrated in Britain. Coronations and royal birthdays were also celebrated in ever more lavish style as the eighteenth century progressed (Figure 9.5).

Although some scholars have discerned a withdrawal of social elites from once shared popular customs over the early modern period, the more significant disruption to traditional leisure patterns came with the Industrial Revolution. As ever, the industrializing regions in the north of England were in the vanguard of change. Although industrialization forced up working hours, this increase in work intensity did not have the negative effect on recreation that we might presume. Indeed, quite the reverse. By the end of the period under discussion in this volume, workers in the urban and industrial regions enjoyed greater access to leisure than they did anywhere else. Here workers not only relaxed with such traditional activities as ball games and storytelling with neighbors, they also engaged in a raft of activities—alehouses, theaters, boxing matches, libraries, clubs, and societies—much of which had previously been the domain of social elites. How might this counterintuitive outcome be explained? Why were longer working hours also accompanied by greater access to the world of leisure?

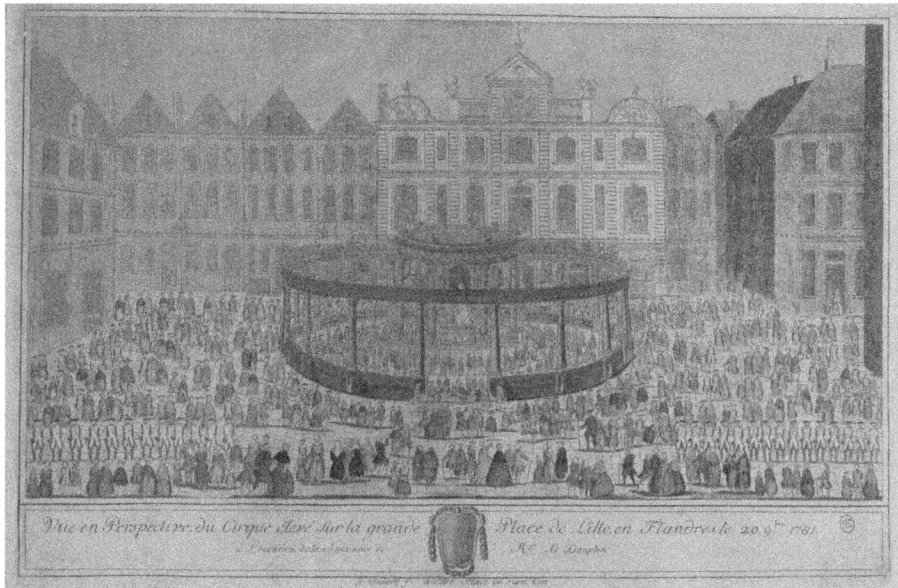

FIGURE 9.5 *Celebrations at Lille in honour of the birth of the Dauphin*, 1781. Paris, Bibliotheque des Arts Decoratifs, Archives Charmet. Photo: Bridgeman Images.

The reasons are inevitably complex, but two factors stand out. First, industrial workers were able to command higher wages than those who worked on the land, which enabled them to engage in activities that had previously been beyond their means. Even such an apparently timeless activity as visiting the alehouse in reality required spare income that many eighteenth-century rural workers simply did not have. Money was also needed to access such varied entertainments as plays, books, boxing matches, and cockfights, and workers could start to engage in these activities on a regular basis only when their earnings outstripped their basic needs.

The growth of clubs and associational activity that occurred at this time was also assisted by higher wages, but here a second, quite different, force was also at work. Engagement in the public sphere required workers to enjoy a degree of independence from their employers, and this independence was only attained when work became more abundant during the era of industrialization. The cities permitted men to spend their evenings at night schools, in reading groups or book clubs, or in political clubs, where they could discuss ideas that might directly challenge the interests of their employers and social superiors. It was no accident that associational activity, trade unionism, and political activism had emerged in Britain's urban and industrial centers by 1800 while many such activities did not penetrate large swathes of rural Europe until well into the second half of the nineteenth century. These forms of recreational activity required a relatively autonomous and independent workforce of the kind only to be found in the high-wage industrial sector. By the same token, it is also no accident that women were for the most part excluded from such activities, for although young, unmarried women did find work in the new factories and mills, the experience often proved to be transitory. Once married with children, the mills girls traded their factory work for the unpaid work of the home—a role that had little of the social potential of well-paid work outside the home.

CONCLUSION

From the evidence presented here, it is clear that we have to reject the suggestion that workers enjoyed a high degree of leisure in the early modern period. In spite of the powerful hold of these claims on generations of historians, the evidence simply does not support this rose-tinted view. Working-class writers suggest, instead, that what has often been regarded as "leisure" is better understood as unemployment and underemployment, and that this did not facilitate leisure in helpful ways. The low demand for labor made workers highly dependent upon whoever could provide work, and left them vulnerable to long hours and exploitation. This gradually changed with the onset of industrialization at the end of the eighteenth century. In the factory and mining districts, more work was available and although this resulted in an increase in working hours it was also accompanied by an extension in their opportunities for leisure. Higher incomes and greater autonomy permitted workers to engage in a raft of new leisure activities which had previously been the preserve of social elites. As a result, although industrialization did not, initially, increase the workers' free time, it did enhance their ability to spend free time "as one pleases."

NOTES

Introduction

1. Alexander Pope, "Epitaph Intended for Sir Isaac Newton," in *The Poems of Alexander Pope*, ed. John Butt (New Haven, CT: Yale University Press, 1965), 808.
2. Mary Wollstonecraft, *Vindication of the Rights of Woman* (London: J. Johnson, 1792), 286.
3. Jean-Jacques Rousseau, *Discourse on Inequality* (1754; repr. Whitefish, MN: Kessinger Publishing, 2004), 15.
4. An excellent analysis of the economic Enlightenment is Emma Rothschild, *Economic Sentiments: Adam Smith, Condorcet, and the Enlightenment* (Cambridge, MA: Harvard University Press, 2013). Josef Ehmer and Catharina Lis, eds, *The Idea of Work in Europe from Antiquity to Modern Times* (Farnham: Ashgate, 2009); Cynthia J. Koepp and Steven Laurence Kaplan, eds, *Work in France: Representations, Meaning, Organization, and Practice* (Ithaca, NY: Cornell University Press, 1986).
5. Catharina Lis and Hugo Soly, *Worthy Efforts: Attitudes to Work and Workers in Pre-Industrial Europe* (Leiden: Brill, 2012), *passim*.
6. Adam Smith, *An Inquiry into the Nature and Causes of the Wealth of Nations* (London: T. Cadell, 1776), bk. 1, 140.
7. John Locke, *Two Treatises of Government*, 1690, Second Treatise, §40, see §§25–51 for his argument about the property of labor, §§123–6.
8. Ibid., §27.
9. David Hume, *Essays, Moral, Political, Literary*, ed. Eugene F. Miller (Indianapolis, IN: Library of Economics and Liberty, 1987). Available online: http://www.econlib.org/library/LFBooks/Hume/hmMPL24.html; Smith, *Wealth of Nations*, 58–9.
10. Anne Robert Jacques Turgot, "Six Projects of Edicts," in *The Turgot Collection*, ed. David Goerdon (Auburn, AL: Ludwig von Mises Institute, 2011), 278.
11. Ibid., 277.
12. Corinne Maitte, "Travail," in *Dictionnaire de l'historien*, eds Claude Gauvard and Jean-François Sirinelli (Paris: Presses universitaires de France, 2015), 714–17; Philippe Minard and Anne Jollet, "Le travail dans son histoire: les fils renoués," *Cahiers d'histoire. Revue d'histoire critique* 83 (2001): 47–65; Wolfgang Asholt and Walter Fähnders, "Travail," in *Dictionnaire européen des Lumières*, ed. Michel Delon (Paris: Presses universitaires de France, 1997), 1065–8; Yannick Fonteneau, "Penser le travail à l'époque moderne (XVIIe–XIXe siècles): introduction et perspectives," *Cahiers d'histoire. Revue d'histoire critique* 110 (2010): 1–23.
13. Katrina Honeyman and Jordan Goodman, "Women's Work, Gender Conflict, and Labour Markets in Europe, 1500–1900," *The Economic History Review* 44, no. 4 (1991): 608–28.
14. Ehmer and Lis, eds, *The Idea of Work*, 23; Deborah Simonton, *A History of European Women's Work* (London: Routledge, 1998).
15. Jordan Goodman and Katrina Honeyman, *Gainful Pursuits: The Making of Industrial Europe, 1600–1914* (London: Edward Arnold, 1988), 27–9.
16. Peter Borsay, *The English Urban Renaissance: Culture and Society in the Provincial Town 1660–1770* (Oxford: Clarendon Press, 1991).

17 James T. Lemon, "Colonial America in the Eighteenth Century," in *Colonial British America: Essays in the New History of the Early Modern Era*, eds Jack P. Greene and J. R. Pole (Baltimore: Johns Hopkins University Press, 1984), 125, 133.
18 Alan S. Milward and Samuel B. Saul, *Development of the Economies of Continental Europe* (London: George Allen and Unwin, 1973), 41.
19 Sheilagh Ogilvie, *Institutions and European Trade: Merchant Guilds, 1000–1800* (Cambridge: Cambridge University Press, 2011). See also Chapters Four and Eight in this volume.
20 Geraldine Sheridan, *Louder than Words: Ways of Seeing Women Workers in Eighteenth-century France* (Lubbock: Texas Tech University Press, 2009), *passim*.
21 Clare Crowston, *Fabricating Women: The Seamstresses of Old Regime France, 1675–1791* (Durham, NC: Duke University Press, 2001).
22 Smith, *Wealth of Nations*, bk. 2, 139–40.
23 See especially the discussion in S. R. Epstein and Maarten Prak, eds, *Guilds, Innovation and the European Economy, 1400–1800* (Cambridge: Cambridge University Press, 2008).
24 Fernand Braudel, *The Identity of France, Vol. 2: People and Production*, trans. Siân Reynolds (London: Fontana Press, 1990), 505–8.
25 Ibid., 511.
26 Adrienne D. Hood, "The Material World of Cloth: Production and Use in Eighteenth-century Rural Pennsylvania," *William and Mary Quarterly* 53, no. 1 (1996).
27 Milward and Saul, *Economies of Continental Europe*, 85.
28 Braudel, *Identity of France*, vol. 2, 518.
29 Gay Gullickson, *Spinners and Weavers of Auffay* (New York: Cambridge University Press, 1986).
30 See Deborah Simonton, "Earning and Learning: Girlhood in Pre-Industrial Europe," *Women's History Review* 11, no. 3 (2004): 363–85, especially, 374–5; and "Bringing Up Girls: Work in Pre-Industrial Europe," in *Secret Gardens, Satanic Mills: Placing Girls in Modern European History*, eds Christina Benninghaus, Mary Jo Maynes, and Brigitte Söland (Bloomington: Indiana University Press, 2004), 23–37.
31 Sarah C. Maza, *Servants and Masters in Eighteenth-century France* (Princeton, NY: Princeton, 1983), 64.
32 Sébastien Locatelli, *Voyage de France: Mœurs et coutumes françaises (1664–1665)* (Paris: Picard, 1905), 45; Anne Montenach, "Legal Trade and Black Markets: Foodtrades in Lyon in the Late Seventeenth and Early Eighteenth Centuries," in *Female Agency in the Urban Economy, Gender in European Towns, 1640–1830*, eds Deborah Simonton and Anne Montenach (New York: Routledge, 2013), 17–34. See also Arlette Farge, *Fragile Lives: Violence, Power and Solidarity in Eighteenth-century Paris* (Cambridge, MA: Harvard University Press, 1993).
33 John Gibson, *History of Glasgow, from the Earliest Accounts to the Present Time* (Glasgow: R. Chapman and A. Duncan, 1777), 151.
34 Two important studies, with further bibliography, are Epstein and Prak, eds, *Guilds, Innovation and the European Economy*; Jan Lucassen, Tine De Moor, and Jan Luiten van Zanden, eds, *The Return of the Guilds: International Review of Social History Supplements* (Cambridge: Cambridge University Press, 2008).
35 Olwen Hufton, *The Prospect before Her: A History of Women in Western Europe, 1500–1800* (New York: Alfred A. Knopf, 1996), 174–5.
36 Laurence Fontaine, *Le marché: Histoire et usages d'une conquête sociale* (Paris: Gallimard, 2014); Laurence Fontaine and Jürgen Schlumbohm, eds, *Household Strategies for Survival 1600–2000: Fission, Faction and Cooperation, International Review of Social History Supplements* (Cambridge: Cambridge University Press, 2000).

37 Crowston, *Fabricating Women*, 408–9; Deborah Simonton, "'Sister to the Tailor': Guilds, Gender and the Needle Trades in Eighteenth-century Europe," in *Early Professional Women in Northern Europe, c. 1650 to the 1850s*, eds Johanna Ilmakunnas, Marjatta Rahikainen, and Kirsi Vainio-Korhonen (Abingdon: Routledge, 2017), 149–51; Dora Dumont, "Women and Guilds in Bologna: The Ambiguities of 'Marginality'," *Radical History Review* 70 (1998): 4–5.
38 *Johnson's Oxford Journal*, September 28, 1771.
39 Smith, *Wealth of Nations*, bk. 2, 488.
40 Michael Sonenscher, "Mythical Work: Workshop Production and the *Compagnonnages* of Eighteenth-century France," in *The Historical Meanings of Work*, ed. Patrick Joyce (Cambridge: Cambridge University Press, 1989), 50.
41 See Jean Quataert, "The Shaping of Women's Work in Manufacturing Guilds, Households and the State in Central Europe, 1648–1870," *American Historical Review* 90 (1985): 1134–5.
42 Franklin Mendels, "Proto-Industrialization: The First Phase of the Industrialization Process," *Journal of Economic History* 32 (1972): 241–61.
43 Hans Medick, "The Proto-Industrial Family Economy: The Structural Function of Household and Family during the Transition from Peasant Society to Industrial Capitalism," *Social History* 3 (1976): 296.
44 For the debate see L. A. Clarkson, *Proto-Industrialisation: The First Phase of Industrialisation?* (London: Macmillan, 1985); Maxine Berg, Pat Hudson, and Michael Sonenscher, eds, *Manufacture in Town and Country Before the Factory* (Cambridge: Cambridge University Press, 1983); Rab Houston and K. D. M. Snell, "Proto-industrialization? Cottage Industry, Social Change, and Industrial Revolution," *Historical Journal* 27, no. 2 (1984): 473–92. See also D. C. Coleman, "Protoindustrialisation: A Concept Too Many," *The Economic History Review* 36, no. 3 (1983): 435–48; Peter Kreidte, Hans Medick, and Jürgen Schlumbohm, eds, *Industrialization before Industrialization: Rural Industry in the Genesis of Capitalism* (Cambridge: Cambridge University Press, 1981).
45 John A. Davis, "Industrialization in Britain and Europe before 1850: New Perspectives, Old Problems," in *The First Industrial Revolutions: The Nature of Industrialization*, eds Peter Mathias and John A. Davis (Oxford: Basil Blackwell, 1989), 63.
46 Jürgen Schlumbohm, "Seasonal Fluctuations and Social Division of Labour: Rural Linen Production in the Osnabrück and Bielefeld Regions and the Urban Woollen Industry in the Niederlausitz, c. 1770–c. 1850," in Berg, Hudson, and Sonenscher, eds, *Manufacture in Town and Country*, 92–123; Gullickson, *Spinners and Weavers*. See also Pat Hudson, "Proto-Industrialisation: The Case of the West Riding Wool Textile Industry in the 18th and early 19th Centuries," *History Workshop Journal* 12 (1982): 34–61.
47 Jan de Vries, "The Industrial Revolution and the Industrious Revolution," *The Journal of Economic History*, Papers Presented at the Fifty-Third Annual Meeting of the Economic History Association 54, no. 2 (1994): 249–70 and *The Industrious Revolution: Consumer Behaviour and the Household Economy, 1650 to the Present* (Cambridge: Cambridge University Press, 2008).
48 De Vries, *Industrious Revolution*, 10.
49 Ibid., x.
50 Deborah Valenze, "Review of *The Industrious Revolution and the Household Economy*, by Jan de Vries," *Journal of Interdisciplinary History* 40, no. 3 (2010): 443–4.
51 Neil McKendrick, "The Consumer Revolution in Eighteenth-Century England," in *The Birth of a Consumer Society*, eds Neil McKendrick, John Brewer, and J. H. Plumb (London: Hutchinson, 1982), 9.
52 Maxine Berg, *Luxury and Pleasure in Eighteenth-century Britain* (Oxford: Oxford University Press, 2005).

53 John Komlos, "Review of *The Industrious Revolution and the Household Economy*, by Jan de Vries," *The Journal of Modern History* 82, no. 2 (2010): 436; see also Charles Feinstein, "Pessimism Perpetuated: Real Wages and the Standard of Living in Britain during and after the Industrial Revolution," *Journal of Economic History* 58 (1998): 625–58.

54 Elise van Nederveen Meerkerk, "Couples Cooperating? Dutch Textile Workers, Family Labour and the 'Industrious Revolution', c. 1600–1800," *Continuity and Change* 23, no. 2 (2008): 237–66. See also Michael Kwass, "Review," *American Historical Review* (June 2009): 705–8, here 706; and Frank Trentmann, *Empire of Things: How We Became a World of Consumers, from the Fifteenth Century to the Twenty-First* (New York: Harper Collins, 2016), 74–5.

55 Valenze, "Review of *The Industrious Revolution*," 443.

56 Corinne Maitte and Didier Terrier, eds, *Les temps du travail: normes, pratiques, évolutions (XIVe-XIXe siècle)* (Rennes: Presses universitaires de Rennes, 2014).

57 See E. P. Thompson, "Time, Work-Discipline, and Industrial Capitalism," *Past & Present* 38 (December 1967): 56–97.

58 David Landes, *Revolution in Time: Clocks and the Making of the Modern World* (Cambridge, MA: Harvard University Press, 1983), 231, 442.

59 M. Dorothy George, *London Life in the Eighteenth Century* (Harmondsworth: Penguin Books, 1965), 173; Laurence Fontaine, "The Circulation of Luxury Goods in Eighteenth-century Paris: Social Redistribution and an Alternative Currency," in *Luxury in the Eighteenth Century: Debates, Desires, and Delectable Goods*, eds Maxine Berg and Elizabeth Eger (Basingstoke: Palgrave, 2003), 89–102.

60 Lorna Weatherill, *Consumer Behaviour and Material Culture in Britain 1660–1760* (London: Routledge, 1988), 26–7, 184, 188, see also 169.

61 Thompson, "Time, Work-discipline," 73.

62 Henri Lefebvre, *Critique de la vie quotidienne* (Paris: l'Arche, 1958), ii, 52–6; Lucien Febvre, "Le temps vécu et le temps-mesure," in *Le problème de l'incroyance au XVIe siècle* (Paris: Albin Michel, 1942), 431.

63 See Thompson, "Time, Work-discipline," 42–3, 55.

64 "Some regulations and rules made for this manufactory more than 30 years back," c. 1810, Wedgwood MSS. (Keele University), 4045.5.

65 *Aberdeen Journal*, August 20, 1781.

66 Benjamin Franklin, "Advice to a Young Tradesman, Written by an Old One," in *The American Instructor: or, Young Man's Best Companion*, ed. George Fisher, 9th ed. (Philadelphia, PA: B. Franklin and D. Hall, 1748), 375–7.

67 Catharine Cappe, *Observations on Charity Schools* (London: J. Hatchard, 1805), 23, 32.

68 Rev. J. Clayton's *Advice to the Friendly Poor*, written and published at the Request of the late and present Officers of the Town of Manchester, 1755.

69 Richard Saunders [Benjamin Franklin], *Poor Richard, 1735. An Almanack For the Year of Christ 1735* (Philadelphia, PA: B. Franklin, 1735).

70 Historians are at odds about what "leisure" meant in eighteenth-century society. See Peter Burke, "The Invention of Leisure in Early Modern Europe," *Past & Present* 146 (1995): 136–50; Joan-Lluís Marfany, "The Invention of Leisure in Early Modern Europe," *Past & Present* 156 (1997): 174–91; and Burke's Reply, "The Invention of Leisure in Early Modern Europe: Reply," *Past & Present* 156 (1997): 192–7.

71 Jacques-Louis Ménétra, *Journal de ma vie*, ed. Daniel Roche (Paris: Montalba, 1982), 159. *Guinguettes* are open-air cafés with dancing and music.

Chapter One

1. Jutta Bolt and Jan Luiten van Zanden, "The First Update of the Maddison Project: Re-Estimating Growth Before 1820," Maddison-Project Working Paper WP-4 (2013): 3–5.
2. Mark Overton, "Re-establishing the English Agricultural Revolution," *Agricultural History Review* 44, no. 1 (1996): 3.
3. E. Anthony Wrigley, "Urban Growth and Agricultural Change: England and the Continent in the Early Modern Period," *Journal of Interdisciplinary History* 15, no. 4 (1985): 683–728.
4. See also Chapter Seven in this volume.
5. Franklin Mendels, "Proto-Industrialization: The First Phase of the Industrialization Process," *Journal of Economic History* 32 (1972): 241–61; Peter Kriedte, Hans Medick, and Jürgen Schlumbohm, *Industrialization before Industrialization: Rural Industry in the Genesis of Capitalism* (Cambridge: Cambridge University Press, 1981).
6. Daniel Defoe, *A Journal of the Plague Year* (London: A. Dodd without Temple-Bar; and J. Graves, 1722).
7. Joan Thirsk, *Economic Policy and Projects: The Development of Consumer Society in Early Modern England* (New York: Oxford University Press, 1978).
8. Jan de Vries, "The Industrial Revolution and the Industrious Revolution," *The Journal of Economic History* 54, no. 2 (1994): 255.
9. Osamu Saito, "Who Worked When: Life-Time Profiles of Labour Force Participation in Cardington and Corfe Castle in the Late Eighteenth and Mid-nineteenth Centuries," *Local Population Studies* 22 (1979): 14–29; Maxine Berg, "What Difference did Women's Work Make to the Industrial Revolution?," *History Workshop Journal* 35 (1993): 22–44.
10. For an overview, see Jane Humphries and Carmen Sarasúa, "Off the Record: Reconstructing Women's Labor Force Participation in the European Past," *Feminist Economics* 18, no. 4 (2012): 39–67.
11. Beatrice Zucca Micheletto, "Reconsidering Women's Labor Force Participation Rates in Eighteenth-century Turin," *Feminist Economics* 19, no. 4 (2013): 212.
12. Carmen Sarasúa, "Women's Work and Structural Change: Occupational Structure in 18th century Spain," *The Economic History Review* (2018), Early View, DOI: 10.1111/ehr.12733. Ricardo Hernández, "Women's Labor Participation Rates in the Kingdom of Castilla in the Eighteenth Century," *Feminist Economics* 19, no. 4 (2013): 181–99.
13. Ariadne Schmidt and Elise van Nederveen Meerkeek, "Reconsidering The 'First Male-Breadwinner Economy': Women's Labor Force Participation in the Netherlands, 1600–1900," *Feminist Economics* 18, no. 4 (2012): 69–96.
14. Danielle van den Heuvel, *Women and Entrepreneurship: Female Traders in the Northern Netherlands c. 1580–1815* (Amsterdam: Aksant, 2007), 271–3.
15. Humphries and Sarasúa, "Off the Record," 20.
16. Nancy Folbre, "Patriarchy in Colonial New England," *Review of Radical Political Economics* 12, no. 2 (1980): 4–13. See also Chapter Nine in this volume.
17. Cristina Borderías, Pilar Pérez-Fuentes, and Carmen Sarasúa, "Gender Inequalities in Family Consumption: Spain 1850–1930," in *Gender Inequalities, Households and the Production of Well-Being in Modern Europe*, eds Tindara Addabbo et al. (Burlington, VT: Ashgate 2010), 179–95.
18. Carmen Sarasúa, "Technical Innovations at the Service of Cheaper Labour in Pre-industrial Europe: The Enlightened Agenda to Transform the Gender Division of Labour in Silk Manufacturing," *History and Technology* 24, no. 1 (2008): 23–39.

19 Sheilagh Ogilvie, "The European Economy in the Eighteenth Century," in *The Short Oxford History of Europe*, vol. XII: *The Eighteenth Century: Europe 1688–1815*, ed. T. C. W. Blanning (Oxford: Oxford University Press, 2000), 124.
20 Berg, "What Difference," 23. Deborah Simonton, *A History of European Women's Work, 1700 to the Present* (London: Routledge, 1998), 73.
21 Olwen Hufton first used this concept in *The Poor of Eighteenth Century France 1750–1789* (Oxford: Clarendon Press, 1974). Steven King and Alannah Tomkins, eds, *The Poor in England, 1700–1850: An Economy of Makeshifts* (Manchester: Manchester University Press, 2003). See also Chapter Six in this volume.
22 For Lyon's silk production, see Daryl Hafter, ed., *European Women and Pre-industrial Craft* (Bloomington: Indiana University Press, 1995); and *Women at Work in Preindustrial France* (University Park: Pennsylvania State University Press, 2007).
23 Joel Mokyr, *A Culture of Growth: The Origins of the Modern Economy* (Princeton, NJ: Princeton University Press, 2015), 1.
24 Ibid. For the scientific revolution, see Margaret Jacob, *The Cultural Meaning of the Scientific Revolution* (Philadelphia, PA: Temple University Press, 1988).
25 Clorinda Donato and Robert M. Maniquis, eds, *The Encyclopédie and the Age of Revolution* (Boston, MA: G. K. Hall, 1992), 12.
26 Annie Jacob, *Le Travail, reflet des cultures: Du sauvage indolent au travailleur productif* (Paris: Presses universitaires de France, 1994).
27 Paul J. McNulty, *The Origins and Development of Labor Economics: A Chapter in the History of Social Thought* (Cambridge, MA: MIT Press, 1984).
28 Adam Smith, *An Inquiry into the Nature and Causes of the Wealth of Nations*, eds R.H. Campbell and A. S. Skinner (Oxford: Clarendon Press, 1976. First published London,1776), 387.
29 Josefa Amar y Borbón, *Discurso en defensa del talento de las mujeres y otros cargos en que se emplean los hombres* (1786).
30 Olympe de Gouges, *The Declaration of the Rights of Woman* (September 1791), XIII.
31 Louis-Sébastien Mercier, *Le Tableau de Paris* (Paris: Éditions La Découverte, 1998. First published Amsterdam, 1781–8), 261–2.
32 Smith, *Wealth of Nations*, 7.
33 See also Chapter Eight in this volume.
34 Mercier, *Le Tableau de Paris*, 154.
35 Carmen Sarasúa, "Una política de empleo antes de la Industrialización: Paro, estructura de la ocupación y salarios en la obra de Campomanes," in *Campomanes y su obra económica*, eds Francisco Comín and Pablo Martín Aceña (Madrid: Instituto de Estudios Fiscales, 2004), 171–91.
36 Pedro Rodríguez de Campomanes, *Las cinco clases de pobres* (The five classes of Poor people), 1778, quoted in Sarasúa, "Technical innovations," 16.
37 "Real Cédula of 12 of January, 1779 by which is ordered that with no pretext be prohibited or obstructed, by the Guilds of these Kingdoms or other persons, the teaching to women and girls of all those works and artefacts that are proper of their sex, despite the regulations that in their Ordinances may the Masters of the respective Guilds have."
38 The dates for Spain, in Sarasúa, "Una política de empleo antes de la Industrialización," 185; for Italy, Paola Massa Piergiovanni, "Technological Typologies and Economic Organisation of Silk Workers in Italy, from the XVIth to the XVIIIth Centuries," *The Journal of European Economic History* 22, no. 3 (1993): 543–64, here 559.
39 Antonio Meijide Pardo, "La emigración gallega intrapeninsular en el siglo XVIII," *Estudios de Historia Social de España* 4, no. 2 (1960): 463–606, here 532–3 (the "female exodus").

40 Ibid., 534. For more on this migratory flow and for European women dressing in men's clothing to enlist in the army or to sign up to the fleet, see Carmen Sarasúa, "Leaving Home to Help the Family? Temporary Migrants in Eighteenth and Nineteenth Century Spain," in *Women, Gender and Labour Migration: Historical and Global Perspectives*, ed. Pamela Sharp (London: Routledge, 2000), 29–59.

41 Craig Muldrew, "'Th' ancient Distaff' and 'Whirling Spindle': Measuring the Contribution of Spinning to Household Earnings and the National Economy in England, 1550–1770," *The Economic History Review* 65 (2012): 498–526; Jane Humphries and Jacob Weisdorf, "The Wages of Women in England, 1260–1850," *Oxford Economic and Social History Working Papers*, no. 127 (2015); Jane Humphries and Benjamin Schneider, "Spinning the Industrial Revolution," *The Economic History Review* (forthcoming), DOI: 10.1111/ehr.12693.

42 Smith, *Wealth of Nations*, 16.

43 Lars Magnusson, "Proto-industrialization in Sweden," in *European Proto-industrialization*, eds Sheilagh Ogilvie and Markus Cerman (Cambridge: Cambridge University Press, 1996), 210.

Chapter Two

1 Voltaire, *Candide or Optimism*, trans. John Butt (Harmondsworth: Penguin Books, 1947), 143–4.
2 Musée du Louvre, Paris.
3 Museo del Prado, Madrid.
4 Musée du Louvre, Paris.
5 Andrea Bayer, ed., *Painters of Reality: The Legacy of Leonardo and Caravaggio in Lombardy* (New Haven, CT: Yale University Press; New York: Metropolitan Museum of Art, 2004), 218–19, 227.
6 Christopher Brown, *Scenes of Everyday Life: Dutch Genre Painting of the Seventeenth Century* (London: Faber and Faber, 1984), 89, 90–3, 149.
7 Rijksmuseum, Amsterdam; Wallace Collection, London; National Gallery, London.
8 Hunterian Art Gallery, University of Glasgow.
9 National Gallery of Art, Washington.
10 Musée du Louvre, Paris.
11 Ronald Paulson, *Hogarth, Vol II, High Art and Low, 1732–1750* (Cambridge: Lutterworth Press, 1991), 289.
12 See also Chapter Seven in this volume.
13 National Galleries of Scotland, Edinburgh.
14 Cincinnati Art Museum, Ohio.
15 Kay Dian Kriz, *Slavery, Sugar, and the Culture of Refinement: Picturing the British West Indies 1700–1840* (New Haven, CT: Yale University Press, 2008), 37–69.
16 Musée de l'Histoire de Nantes.
17 Denis Diderot, *Encyclopédie, ou Dictionnaire raisonné des sciences, des arts et des métiers, par une société de gens de lettres* (Paris: Briasson,1751–72; Paris: Panckoucke, 1777), vol. 1, 714.
18 Steven Laurence Kaplan and Cynthia J. Koepp, *Work in France: Representations, Meaning, Organization, and Practice* (Ithaca, NY: Cornell University Press, 1986), 278.
19 Ibid., 241.

20 Celina Fox, *The Arts of Industry in the Age of Enlightenment* (New Haven, CT: Yale University Press, 2009), 274.
21 Geraldine Sheridan, *Louder than Words: Ways of Seeing Women Workers in Eighteenth-century France* (Lubbock: Texas Tech University Press, 2009), *passim*.
22 Ibid., 15.
23 Ibid., 218–9, 223. See also Chapter One in this volume.
24 Nationalmuseum, Stockholm.
25 Françoise Dehousse et al., *Léonard Defrance: L'Œuvre Peint* (Liège: Éditions du Perron et Eugène Wahle, 1985), 167.
26 Ibid., 155.
27 National Galleries of Scotland, Edinburgh.
28 Cytharfa Castle Museum and Art Gallery, Merthyr Tydfil, Wales.
29 Yale Center for British Art, New Haven, CT.
30 Science Museum, London.
31 Tate Britain, London.
32 Francis D. Klingender, *Art and the Industrial Revolution*, ed. Arthur Elton (Chatham: Evelyn, Adams and Mackay, 1968. First published London, 1947), 51.
33 Fox, *The Arts of Industry*, 428.
34 Manchester Art Gallery, UK.
35 Elizabeth E. Barker and Alex Kidson, *Joseph Wright of Derby in Liverpool* (New Haven, CT: Yale University Press, 2007), 67.
36 The Hermitage, St. Petersburg.
37 Judy Egerton et al., *Wright of Derby* (London: Tate Gallery, 1990), 99–104.
38 Judy Egerton, *George Stubbs, Painter: Catalogue Raisonné* (New Haven, CT: Yale University Press, 2007), 468–77.
39 Christiana Payne, *Toil and Plenty: Images of the Agricultural Landscape in England, 1780–1890* (New Haven, CT: Yale University Press, 1993), 83–4.
40 The British Museum, London; Yale Center for British Art, New Haven, CT.
41 Victoria and Albert Museum, London.
42 James Thomson, *The Seasons* (1746), "Autumn," lines 153–61.
43 Ibid., lines 141–3.
44 John Dyer, *The Fleece: A Poem in Four Books* (London: R. and J. Dodsley, 1757), bk. III.
45 Isabelle Baudino, "Eighteenth-century Images of Working Women," in *Aspects of Women's Work in Eighteenth-century Britain*, eds Isabelle Baudino et al. (Aldershot: Ashgate, 2005), 173, 176.
46 Vincent Milliot, *Les cris de Paris ou le peuple travesti: Les représentations des petits métiers parisiens (XVIe-XVIIIe siècle)* (Paris: Sorbonne, 2014. First published 1995).
47 Martin Postle, *Angels and Urchins: The Fancy Picture in 18th-century British Art* (Nottingham: Djanogly Art Gallery / Lund Humphries, 1998), 85.
48 Wallace Collection, London.
49 Holburne Museum, Bath, UK.
50 Postle, *Angels and Urchins*, 83–4.
51 Giles Waterfield, Anne French, and Matthew Craske, *Below Stairs: 400 Years of Servants' Portraits* (London: National Portrait Gallery, 2004), 17–18.
52 Tate Britain, London.
53 Waterfield and French, *Below Stairs*, 64–5.
54 Musée du Louvre, Paris.
55 Metropolitan Museum of Art, New York.

56 Respectively, National Gallery, London and Goodwood House, West Sussex, UK.
57 Metropolitan Museum of Art, New York.
58 National Gallery, London.
59 Musée du Louvre, Paris.
60 Martin Postle, ed., *Johann Zoffany RA: Society Observed* (New Haven, CT: Yale University Press, 2011), 227–8.

Chapter Three

1 Proponents of this narrative included E. P. Thompson, *The Making of the English Working Class* (London: Victor Gollancz, 1963); Peter Linebaugh, *The London Hanged: Crime and Civil Society in the Eighteenth Century* (Cambridge: Cambridge University Press, 1992); Howard B. Rock, Paul A. Gilje, and Robert Asher, eds, *American Artisans: Crafting a Social Identity, 1750–1850* (Baltimore: Johns Hopkins University Press, 1995); Peter Linbaugh and Marcus Rediker, *The Many-Headed Hydra: The Hidden History of the Revolutionary Atlantic* (New York: Verso, 2002).
2 For a direct critique of the idea of the immiserated worker, see Emma Griffin, *Liberty's Dawn: A People's History of the Industrial Revolution* (New Haven, CT: Yale University Press, 2013).
3 Maxine Berg, *The Age of Manufactures* (London: Fontana Press, 1985); Maxine Berg, "Small Producer Capitalism in Eighteenth Century Britain," *Business History* 35, no. 1 (1993): 17–39.
4 Trevor Burnard, *Planters, Merchants, and Slaves: Plantation Societies in British America, 1650–1820* (Chicago: University of Chicago Press, 2015); Richard S. Dunn, *A Tale of Two Plantations: Slave Life and Labor in Jamaica and Virginia* (Cambridge, MA: Harvard University Press, 2014); Justin Roberts, *Slavery and Enlightenment in the British Atlantic: 1750–1807* (New York: Cambridge University Press, 2013).
5 Keith Wrightson, *Earthly Necessities: Economic Lives in Early Modern Britain* (New Haven, CT: Yale University Press, 2000), 335.
6 Jan de Vries, *The Industrious Revolution: Consumer Demand and the Household Economy, 1650 to the Present* (Cambridge: Cambridge University Press, 2008).
7 Jan de Vries, *European Urbanization, 1500–1800* (London: Methuen and Co., 1984).
8 On farm size and productivity in England, see Leigh Shaw Taylor, "The Rise of Agrarian Capitalism and the Decline of Family Farming in England," *The Economic History Review* 65, no. 1 (2012): 26–60; Olwen Hufton, "Social Conflict and the Grain Supply in Eighteenth-Century France," *Journal of Interdisciplinary History* 14, no. 2 (1983): 303–31.
9 Lucy Simler, "Tenancy in Colonial Pennsylvania: The Case of Chester County," *William and Mary Quarterly*, 3rd ser., no. 4 (1986): 542–69.
10 On Henry Laurens, see S. Max Edelson, *Plantation Enterprise in Colonial South Carolina* (Cambridge, MA: Harvard University Press, 2006). On aristocratic estates in Britain and France, see Patrick O'Brien and Caglar Keyder, *Economic Growth in Britain and France 1780–1914: Two Paths to the Twentieth Century* (London: George Allen & Unwin, 1978), 102–45.
11 For life on a remote northern English farm, see John Styles, "Clothes and the Non-Elite Consumer in the North of England, 1660–1800," in *Échanges et cultures textiles dans l'Europe pré-industrielle*, eds Jacques Bottin and Nicole Pellegrin (Lille: Villeneuve d'Ascq, 1996), 295–308. On early modern Alpine dairying, see Barbara Orland, "Alpine Milk: Dairy Farming as Pre-modern Strategy of Land Use," *Environment and History* 10, no. 3 (2004):

327–64; D. A. Baker, "The Marketing of Corn in the First Half of the Eighteenth Century: North-East Kent," *Agricultural History Review* 18, no. 2 (1970): 126–50.

12 For discussion of the gendered and racial aspects of field work in colonial British America, see Kathleen Brown, *Good Wives, Nasty Wenches, and Anxious Patriarchs: Gender, Race, and Power in Colonial Virginia* (Chapel Hill: University of North Carolina Press, 1996), 212–46.

13 On rural women and manufacturing work, see Sheilagh Ogilvie, *State Corporatism and Proto-Industry: The Württemberg Black Forest, 1580–1797* (Cambridge: Cambridge University Press, 1997); Pat Hudson and W. Robert Lee, *Women's Work and the Family Economy in Historical Perspective* (Manchester: Manchester University Press, 1990); Gay Gullickson, "The Sexual Division of Labor in Cottage Industry and Agriculture in the Pays de Caux 1750–1850," *French Historical Studies* 12, no. 2 (1981): 177–99; Pamela Sharpe, "Literally Spinsters: A New Interpretation of Local Economy and Demography in Colyton in the Seventeenth and Eighteenth Centuries," *The Economic History Review* 44, no. 1 (1991): 46–65.

14 Adrienne D. Hood, "The Material world of Cloth: Production and Use in Eighteenth-Century Rural Pennsylvania," *William and Mary Quarterly* 53, no. 1 (1996): 43–66.

15 Paul S. Seaver, *Wallington's World: A Puritan Artisan in Seventeenth Century London* (Stanford: Stanford University Press, 1995).

16 Adam Smith, "Of the Division of Labour," in *The Wealth of Nations* (London: W. Strahan and T. Cadell, 1776), vol. 1, bk. 1 "Of the Causes of Improvement in the productive Powers of Labour, and of the Order according to which its Produce is naturally distributed among the different Ranks of the People."

17 Shena Mason, *Matthew Boulton: Selling What all the World Desires* (New Haven, CT: Yale University Press, 2009); Neil McKendrick, "Josiah Wedgwood and Factory Discipline," in *The Rise of Capitalism*, ed. David S. Landes (New York: Macmillan, 1966), 65–81; Sidney Pollard, "The Factory Village in the Industrial Revolution," *The English Historical Review* 79, no. 312 (1964): 513–31.

18 John Smail, "Manufacturer or Artisan? The Relationship between Economic and Cultural Change in the Early Stages of the Eighteenth-Century Industrialization," *Journal of Social History* 25, no. 4 (1992): 791–814.

19 On Swedish iron and its overseas markets, see Göran Rydén, "Skill and Technical Change in the Swedish Iron Industry, 1750–1860," *Technology and Culture* 39, no.3 (July 1998): 383–407; Chris Evans, Owen Jackson, and Göran Rydén, "Baltic Iron and the British Iron Industry in the Eighteenth Century," *The Economic History Review* 55, no. 4 (2002): 642–65.

20 Berg, "Small Producer Capitalism"; Helen Clifford, "Concepts of Invention, Identity and Imitation in the London and Provincial Metal-Working Trades, 1750–1800," *Journal of Design History* 12, no. 3 (1999): 241–56; Emma Hart, "Charleston and The British Industrial Revolution," in *Global Perspectives on the Industrial Transformation in the American South*, eds Susanna Delfino and Michele Gillespie (Columbia: University of Missouri Press, 2005), 26–49.

21 Daryl M. Hafter, *Women at Work in Preindustrial France* (University Park: Pennsylvania State University, 2010).

22 Daniel Defoe, "Of the Tradesman Letting His Wife be Acquainted with His Business," in *The Complete English Tradesman: In Familiar Letter; Directing him in all the several Parts and Progressions of Trade* (London: Charles Rivington, 1726), 348–67.

23 Julie Hardwick, *Family Business: Litigation and the Political Economies of Daily Life in Early Modern France* (New York: Oxford University Press, 2009).

24 James Schmiechen and Kenneth Carls, *The British Market Hall: A Social and Architectural History* (New Haven, CT: Yale University Press, 1999); Danielle van den Heuvel, "Partners in Marriage and Business? Guilds and the Family Economy in the Urban Food Markets in the Dutch Republic," *Continuity and Change* 23, no. 2 (2008): 217–36.

25 Sydney Watts, *Meat Matters: Butchers, Politics and Market Culture in Eighteenth-Century Paris* (Rochester, NY: University of Rochester Press, 2006); Emma Hart, "From Field to Plate, The Early Modern Livestock Trade and the Development of an American Economic Culture," *William and Mary Quarterly* 73 (2016): 107–40.

26 On families and guild membership, see Danielle van den Heuvel and Elise van Nederveen Meerkerk, "Introduction: Partners in Business? Spousal Cooperation in Trades in Early Modern England and the Dutch Republic," *Continuity and Change* 23, no. 2 (2008): 209–16; Watts, *Meat Matters*, 123–42.

27 Janine Lanza, *From Wives to Widows in Early Modern Paris: Gender, Economy, and the Law* (Aldershot: Ashgate, 2007).

28 Anne Montenach, "Creating a Space for Themselves on the Urban Market: Survival Strategies and Economic Opportunities for Single Women in French Provincial Towns (Seventeenth-Eighteenth Centuries)," in *Single Life and the City, 1200–1900*, eds Julie De Groot, Isabelle Devos, and Ariadne Schmidt (Basingstoke: Palgrave, 2015).

29 Watts, *Meat Matters*, 46–58.

30 See Chapter Six in this volume.

31 Danielle van den Heuvel, "Policing Peddlers. The Prosecution of Illegal Street Trade in Eighteenth-century Dutch Towns," *The Historical Journal* 58, no. 2 (2015): 367–92; Laurence Fontaine, *History of Pedlars in Europe* (Durham, NC: Duke University Press, 2012); Jeroen Salman, *Pedlars and the Popular Press: Itinerant Distribution Networks in England and the Netherlands, 1600–1850* (Leiden: Brill, 2013); Robin Myers, Michael Harris, and Giles Mandelbrote, eds, *Fairs, Markets, and the Itinerant Book Trade* (London: British Library, 2007).

32 "The Custom of going to the town before a fair begins, and exposing goods to sale at any inn, &c. it is expected will be put a stop to, as it hath been very prejudicial to the shopkeepers. If the laws for regulating pedlars and auctioneers should be amended, it is expected that the revenue will be benefited and the resident trader protected from the depredations of itinerants": *Newcastle Journal*, April 23, 1774.

33 Lorna Mui and Hoh-Cheung Mui, *Shops and Shopkeeping in Eighteenth-Century England* (London: Routledge, 1989).

34 J. A. Chartres, "The Marketing of Agricultural Produce, 1640–1750," in *Agrarian History of England and Wales: Volume 4*, ed. Joan Thirsk (Cambridge: Cambridge University Press, 1964), 406–510; S. R. H. Jones, "The Country Trade and the Marketing and Distribution of Birmingham Hardware, 1750–1810," *Business History* 26, no. 1 (1984): 24–42.

35 Catherine Cangany, *Frontier Seaport: Detroit's Transformation into an Atlantic Entrepôt* (Chicago: University of Chicago Press, 2014), 41–70.

36 On the increase in shipping and the experiences of sailors, see Ian K. Steele, *The English Atlantic, 1675–1740: An Exploration of Communication and Community* (Oxford: Oxford University Press, 1986); Daniel Vickers and Vince Walsh, *Young Men and the Sea: Yankee Seafarers in the Age of Sail* (New Haven, CT: Yale University Press, 2005); W. Jeffrey Bolster, *Black Jacks: African American Seamen in the Age of Sail* (Cambridge, MA: Harvard University Press, 1998).

37 Olaudah Equiano, *The Interesting Narrative of the Life of Olaudah Equiano, Or Gustavus Vassa, The African* (London: T. Wilkins, 1789); James Walvin, *An African's Life, 1745–1797: The Life and Times of Olaudah Equiano* (New York: Continuum, 1998).

38 Denver Brunsman, *The Evil Necessity: British Naval Impressment in the Eighteenth-Century Atlantic World* (Charlottesville: University of Virginia Press, 2013); Nathan Pearl-Rosenthal, *Citizen-Sailors: Becoming American in the Age of Revolution* (Cambridge, MA: Harvard University Press, 2015).
39 Christopher Iannini, "'An Itinerant Man': Crèvecoeur's Caribbean, Raynal's Revolution, and the Fate of Atlantic Cosmopolitanism," *William and Mary Quarterly* 61 (2004): 201–34.
40 Ira Berlin, *Many Thousands Gone: The First Two Centuries of Slavery in North America* (Cambridge, MA: Harvard University Press, 2000); Philip Morgan, *Slave Counterpoint: Black Culture in the Eighteenth-Century Chesapeake and Lowcountry* (Chapel Hill: University of North Carolina Press, 1998).
41 Edelson, *Plantation Enterprise*; Morgan, *Slave Counterpoint*.
42 Burnard, *Planters*; Dunn, *A Tale of Two Plantations*; Roberts, *Slavery*.

Chapter Four

1 William Sewell, *Work and Revolution in France: The Language of Labor from the Old Regime to 1848* (Cambridge: Cambridge University Press, 1980).
2 Marta V. Vicente, "Crafting the Industrial Revolution: Artisan Families and the Calico Industry in Eighteenth-Century Spain," in *Reconceptualizing the Industrial Revolution*, eds Jeff Horn, Leonard Rosenband, and Merritt Roe Smith (Cambridge, MA: MIT Press, 2010), 156.
3 For descriptions of the vast array of work performed by artisans see René de Lespinasse, *Les Métiers et corporations de Paris*, 3 vols. (Paris: Imprimerie Nationale, 1886–94); a limited picture of the statutes that organized Roman craft guilds can be found in "Gli statute delle università Romane di arti e mestiere conservati nell'archivo storico capitolino," *Roma moderna e contemporanea* 6, no. 3 (1998): 257–90.
4 James Farr, *Artisans in Europe, 1300–1914* (Cambridge: Cambridge University Press, 2000), 3.
5 Steven L. Kaplan, *La fin des corporations* (Paris: Fayard, 2001), especially chap. 2.
6 Steven L. Kaplan, "Social Classification and Representation in the Corporate World of Eighteenth-Century France: Turgot's 'Carnival'," in *Work in France: Representations, Meaning, Organization, and Practice*, eds Steven L. Kaplan and Cynthia Koepp (Ithaca, NY: Cornell University Press, 1986), 183.
7 Regina Grafe and Oscar Gelderblom, "The Rise and Fall of Merchant Guilds: Re-thinking the Comparative Study of Commercial Institutions in Premodern Europe," *Journal of Interdisciplinary History* 40, no. 4 (1990): 486.
8 Michael Sonenscher, *Work and Wages: Natural Law, Politics and the Eighteenth-Century French Trades* (Cambridge: Cambridge University Press, 1989); Kaplan, "Social Classification."
9 Michael Berlin, "'Broken All in Pieces': Artisans and the Regulation of Workmanship in Early Modern London," in *The Artisan and the European Town, 1500–1900*, ed. Geoffrey Crossick (Aldershot: Ashgate, 1997), 75.
10 Sonenscher, *Work and Wages*, 113–15.
11 Lars Edgren, "Craftsmen in the Political and Symbolic Order: The Case of Eighteenth-century Malmo," in Crossick, ed., *The Artisan*, 141–3.
12 Joseph Ward, *Metropolitan Communities: Trade, Guilds, Identity, and Change in Early Modern London* (Stanford: Stanford University Press, 1997), 57–60.
13 The most influential critique of Darnton's book was written by Roger Chartier, "Text, Symbols, and Frenchness," *Journal of Modern History* 57 (1985): 685.

14 Sonenscher, *Work and Wages*, 11.
15 Robert Darnton, *The Great Cat Massacre and Other Episodes in French Cultural History* (New York: Vintage, 1984), 75.
16 Sonenscher, *Work and Wages*, 12.
17 Philip R. Hoffmann, "In Defence of Corporate Liberties: Early Modern Guilds and the Problem of Illicit Artisan Work," *Urban History* 34, no. 1 (2007): 77.
18 Simona Cerutti, "Travail, mobilité et légitimité: Suppliques au roi dans une société d'Ancien Régime (Turin, XVIIIe siècle)," *Annales. Histoire, Sciences Sociales* 65, no. 3 (2010): 573–4; Norah Carlin, "Liberty and Fraternities in the English Revolution: The Politics of London Artisans' Protests, 1635–1659," *International Review of Social History* 39 (1994): 229–30.
19 Jan de Vries, *The Industrious Revolution: Consumer Behaviour and the Household Economy, 1650 to the Present* (Cambridge: Cambridge University Press, 2008), 10. See also Chapters One and Five in this volume.
20 Farr, *Artisans in Europe*, 50–1.
21 Der-Yuan Yang, "The Evolution of Craftsmen Guilds: A Coordination Perspective," *Proceedings of the 42nd Annual Meeting of the Canadian Economic Association* (June 2008), 17. See also Chapter Eight in this volume.
22 Edward J. Shephard, Jr., "Social and Geographic Mobility of the Eighteenth-Century Guild Artisan: An Analysis of Guild Receptions in Dijon, 1700–1790," in *Work in France. Representations, Meaning, Organization, and Practice*, eds Steven Laurence Kaplan and Cynthia J. Koepp (Ithaca, NY: Cornell University Press, 1986), 99.
23 René de Lespinasse, *Les métiers et corporations de la ville de Paris XIVe–XVIIIe siècles* (Paris: Imprimerie Nationale, 1843–1922), vol. 3, 168; Patrick Wallis, "Labour, Law and Training in Early Modern London: Apprenticeship and the City's Institutions," *London School of Economics, Working Papers* 11, no. 154 (2011): 38.
24 Farr, *Artisans in Europe*, 4.
25 Peter Sahlins, *Boundaries: The Making of France and Spain in the Pyrenees* (Berkeley: University of California Press, 1989), 270.
26 Haim Burstin, "Unskilled Labor in Paris at the End of the Eighteenth Century," in *The Workplace Before the Factory: Artisans and Proletarians, 1500–1800*, eds Thomas Safley and Leonard Rosenband (Ithaca, NY: Cornell University Press, 1993), 63.
27 Catharina Lis, *Social Change and the Labouring Poor: Antwerp, 1700–1860* (New Haven, CT: Yale University Press, 1986), 42–3.
28 Eleonora Canepari, "Who Is Not Welcome? Reception and Rejection of Migrant in Early Modern Italian Cities," in *Gated Communities? Regulating Migration in Early Modern Cities*, eds Bert De Munck and Anne Winter (London: Routledge, 2016), 102; and Chapter Six in this volume.
29 Lis, *Social Change*, 13–14; Kathryn Norberg, *Rich and Poor in Grenoble, 1600–1814* (Berkeley: University of California Press, 1985), 224; *Household Strategies for Survival 1600–2000: Fission, Faction and Cooperation*, eds Laurence Fontaine and Jürgen Schlumbohm (*International Review of Social History*, supplement 8, 2000), 4.
30 See also Chapter Six in this volume.
31 Among the many criticisms of the family economy model of female work, see Clare Crowston's *Fashioning Women: The Seamstresses of Old Regime France, 1675–1791* (Durham, NC: Duke University Press, 2001), 183–4.
32 See, for example, the information about wages for female workers in haberdashers' shops in Michael Sonenscher, *The Hatters of Eighteenth-Century France* (Berkeley: University of California Press, 1987).

33 Janine M. Lanza, *From Wives to Widows in Early Modern Paris: Gender, Economy and Law* (Aldershot: Ashgate, 2007).
34 Archives Nationales, Y 15352, August 1, 1753.
35 Merry Wiesner, "Having Her Own Smoke: Employment and Independence for Singlewomen in Germany, 1400–1750," in *Singlewomen in the European Past, 1250–1800*, eds Judith Bennett and Amy Froide (Philadelphia: University of Pennsylvania Press, 1999), 195; Olwen Hufton, *The Prospect Before Her: A History of Women in Western Europe* (New York: Knopf, 1995), 253; Pamela Sharpe, "Literally Spinsters: A New Interpretation of Local Economy and Demography in Colyton in the Seventeenth and Eighteenth Centuries," *The Economic History Review* 44, no. 1 (1991): 46–65.
36 Archives Nationales, LL 839, 1717–19.
37 Hilary McD. Beckles, *White Servitude and Black Slavery in Barbados, 1627–1715* (Knoxville: University of Tennessee Press, 1989), 13, 38.
38 John J. Navin, "Intimidation, Violence, and Race in British America," *The Historian* 77, no. 3 (2015): 471.
39 Historian Michael Ignatieff estimates that 70 percent of all criminals convicted of a capital crime opted instead for transport to the English colonies. Navin, "Intimidation, Violence, and Race," 473.
40 Matthew Mason, "Slavery, Servitude and British Representations of Colonial North America," *Southern Quarterly* 43, no. 4 (2006): 110.
41 Ibid., 112.
42 Beckles, *White Servitude and Black Slavery*, 39.
43 Lois Green Carr and Lorena S. Walsh, "Economic Diversification and Labor Organization in the Chesapeake, 1650–1820," in *Work and Labor in Early America*, ed. Stephen Innes (Chapel Hill: University of North Carolina Press, 1988), 155.
44 Navin, "Intimidation, Violence, and Race," 473.
45 Ibid., 474.
46 Ira Berlin, *Many Thousands Gone: The First Two Centuries of Slavery in North America* (Cambridge, MA: Harvard University Press, 1998), 9.
47 Berlin, *Many Thousands Gone*, 96.
48 Ira Berlin and Philip D. Morgan, "Labor and the Shaping of Slave Life in the Americas," in *Cultivation and Culture: Labor and the Shaping of Slave Life in the Americas*, eds Ira Berlin and Philip D. Morgan (Charlottesville: University Press of Virginia, 1993), 1. See also Chapters Three and Seven in this volume.
49 Laura Croghan Kamoie, "Planters' Exchange Patterns in the Colonial Chesapeake: Toward Defining a Regional Domestic Economy," in *The Atlantic Economy during the Seventeenth and Eighteenth Centuries: Organization, Operation, Practice, and Personnel*, ed. Peter A. Coclanis (Columbia: University of South Carolina Press, 2005), 323.
50 Berlin and Morgan, "Labor and the Shaping of Slave Life," 44.
51 Peter Kolchin, *American Slavery, 1619–1877*, 2nd edn. (New York: Hill & Wang, 2003), 101.
52 Steven F. Miller, "Plantation Labor Organization and Slave Life on the Cotton Frontier: the Alabama-Mississippi Black Belt, 1815–1840," in Berlin and Morgan, ed., *Cultivation and Culture*, 165.
53 Miller, "Plantation Labor," 163.
54 Jeremy Popkin, *A Concise History of the Haitian Revolution* (Malden, MA: Wiley-Blackwell, 2011), 10.
55 Ibid., 11.
56 Laurent Dubois, *A Colony of Citizens: Revolution and Slave Emancipation in the French Caribbean, 1787–1804* (Chapel Hill: University of North Carolina Press, 2004), 50–1.

Chapter Five

1. Quoted in Leonard N. Rosenband, *Papermaking in Eighteenth-Century France: Management, Labor, and Revolution at the Montgolfier Mill, 1761–1805* (Baltimore: Johns Hopkins University Press, 2000), 46.
2. On this intersection, see Cathy Matson, ed., *The Economy of Early America: Historical Perspectives and New Directions* (University Park: Pennsylvania State University Press, 2006); Sidney Pollard, *The Genesis of Modern Management: A Study of the Industrial Revolution in Great Britain* (Cambridge, MA: Harvard University Press, 1965); Michael Sonenscher, *Work and Wages: Natural Law, Politics and the Eighteenth-Century French Trades* (Cambridge: Cambridge University Press, 1989); E. P. Thompson, *The Making of the English Working Class* (New York: Vintage Books, 1963); Mack Walker, *German Home Towns: Community, State, and General Estate, 1648–1871* (Ithaca, NY: Cornell University Press, 1971).
3. Thomas S. Ashton, *The Industrial Revolution, 1760–1830* (Oxford: Oxford University Press, 1948).
4. N. F. R. Crafts, *British Economic Growth during the Industrial Revolution* (Oxford: Clarendon Press, 1985). See also Robert C. Allen, *Global Economic History: A Very Short Introduction* (Oxford: Oxford University Press, 2011), 27.
5. William J. Ashworth, *Customs and Excise: Trade, Production, and Consumption in England, 1640–1845* (Oxford: Oxford University Press, 2003).
6. Quoted in Keith Thomas, ed., *The Oxford Book of Work* (Oxford: Oxford University Press, 1999), v.
7. Benjamin Franklin, *The Autobiography of Benjamin Franklin*, ed. Leonard Labaree et al. (New Haven, CT: Yale University Press, 1964. First published 1791), 99–101.
8. Robert Darnton, *The Great Cat Massacre and Other Episodes in French Cultural History* (New York: Basic Books, 1984), 75–104.
9. Angus Maddison, *The World Economy* (Paris: Development Centre of the Organisation for Economic Co-operation and Development, 2007), 232, Table B-2.
10. Quoted in Jan de Vries, "The Industrial Revolution and the Industrious Revolution," *Journal of Economic History* 54 (1994): 259.
11. Quoted in Hans-Ulrich Thamer, "On the Use and Abuse of Handicraft: Journeyman Culture and Enlightened Public Opinion in 18th and 19th Century Germany," in *Understanding Popular Culture: Europe from the Middle Ages to the Nineteenth Century*, ed. Steven L. Kaplan (Berlin: Mouton, 1984), 275.
12. Adam Smith, *An Inquiry into the Nature and Causes of the Wealth of Nations*, ed. Edwin Cannan (New York: Modern Library, 1937. First published 1776), 128.
13. Quoted in Jaume Torras, "Craft Guilds and Rural Industries in Early Modern Spain," in *Guilds, Economy and Society*, eds S. R. Epstein et al. (Seville: Secretariado de Publicaciones de la Universidad de Sevilla, 1998), 25.
14. Walker, *German Home Towns*, 98–9.
15. Sonenscher, *Work and Wages*, 104.
16. Quoted in John Rule, *The Experience of Labour in Eighteenth-Century English Industry* (New York: St. Martin's Press, 1981), 55.
17. Quoted in ibid., 51.
18. Robert Darnton, *The Literary Underground of the Old Regime* (Cambridge, MA: Harvard University Press, 1982), 152.
19. Sonenscher, *Work and Wages*, 95.

20 Reinhold Reith, "Wage Conflicts and Wage Formation in Early Modern German Guilds," in Epstein et al., eds, *Guilds, Economy and Society*, 83.
21 Reinhold Reith, "Wage Forms, Wage Systems and Wage Conflicts in German Crafts during the Eighteenth and Earlier Nineteenth Centuries," in *Experiencing Wages: Social and Cultural Aspects of Wage Forms in Europe since 1500*, eds Peter Scholliers and Leonard Schwarz (New York: Berghahn Books, 2004), 124.
22 Quoted in Pollard, *Genesis*, 182.
23 David Landes, "What Do Bosses Really Do?" *Journal of Economic History* 46 (1986): 603.
24 "État des moulins à papier," Archives Départementales de l'Hérault, C2676.
25 On the Montgolfiers' program of time discipline, see Rosenband, *Papermaking*, 108–10.
26 Quoted in Peter Mathias, *The Transformation of England: Essays in the Economic and Social History of England in the Eighteenth Century* (New York: Columbia University Press, 1979), 148.
27 Quoted in ibid., 151.
28 Smith, *Wealth of Nations*, 82–3.
29 Jan de Vries, *The Industrious Revolution: Consumer Behavior and the Household Economy, 1650 to the Present* (Cambridge: Cambridge University Press, 2008). Compare Leonard N. Rosenband, "The Industrious Revolution: A Concept Too Many?," *International Labor and Working Class History* 90 (2016): 213–43. See also Corine Maitte and Didier Terrier, eds, *Les temps du travail: Normes, pratiques, évolutions (XIVe-XIXe siècle)* (Rennes: Presses universitaires de Rennes, 2014).
30 Quoted in Darnton, *Great Cat Massacre*, 134.
31 Frank Trentmann, *Empire of Things: How We Became a World of Consumers, from the Fifteenth Century to the Twenty-First* (New York: Harper Collins, 2016), 74–5.
32 Quoted in Rosenband, *Papermaking*, 108.
33 Justin Roberts, *Slavery and the Enlightenment in the British Atlantic, 1750–1807* (Cambridge: Cambridge University Press, 2013), 1–25, quote is on p. 5.
34 Bernardino Ramazzini, *Diseases of Workers*, trans. Wilmer Cave Wright (Chicago: University of Chicago Press, 1940. Second enlarged edition first published 1713), 291. The first edition of Ramazzini, *De morbis artificum* was published in Modena in 1700. Wright "revised" Ramazzini's text and added "notes," but the present author cannot evaluate her efforts.
35 *Encyclopaedia Britannica*, "Art," 3d ed. (Edinburgh, 1797), 709.
36 Ramazzini, *Diseases*: gilders, 33; timepieces, 327; glassworkers, 61–3.
37 Quoted in David Levine and Keith Wrightson, *The Making of an Industrial Society: Whickham, 1560–1765* (Oxford: Clarendon Press, 1991), 272.
38 Quoted in Steven L. Kaplan, "The Luxury Guilds in Paris in the Eighteenth Century," *Francia* 9 (1982): 260.
39 Gail Bossenga, "Capitalism and Corporations in Eighteenth-Century France," in *Naissance des libertés économiques*, ed. Alain Plessis (Paris: Institut d'histoire et de l'industrie, 1993), 13–31, quote is on p. 15.
40 Quoted in ibid., 14.
41 James Farr, *Artisans in Europe, 1300–1914* (Cambridge: Cambridge University Press, 2000), 203.
42 Quoted in ibid., 207.
43 Landes, "Bosses," 604.
44 Pierre Deyon and Philippe Guignet, "The Royal Manufactures and Economic and Technological Progress in France before the Industrial Revolution," *Journal of European Economic History* 9 (1980): 611–32, quote on p. 626. The number of French royal manufactories steadily increased during the eighteenth century.

45 Philippe Minard, "La fin de l'inspection des manufactures: Premières hypothèses sur le dérèglement d'une institution du commerce," in *État, finances et économie pendant la Révolution* (actes du colloque de Bercy, octobre 1989), ed., Comité pour l'histoire économique et financière de la France, (Paris: Imprimerie Nationale, 1991), 295–303.
46 Sheilagh Ogilvie, "The Economics of Guilds," *Journal of Economic Perspectives* 28 (2014): 171.
47 Robert Duplessis, *Transitions to Capitalism in Early Modern Europe* (Cambridge: Cambridge University Press, 1997), 230.
48 Quoted in William Sewell, Jr., *Work and Revolution in France: The Language of Labor from the Old Regime to 1848* (Cambridge: Cambridge University Press, 1980), 87.
49 For a useful overview, see Seth Rockman, "Review Essay: What Makes the History of Capitalism Newsworthy?" *Journal of the Early Republic* 34 (2014): 439–66.
50 On the *Encyclopédie* plates, see William Sewell, Jr., "Visions of Labor: Illustrations of the Mechanical Arts before, in, and after Diderot's *Encyclopédie*," in *Work in France: Representations, Meaning, Organization, and Practice*, eds Steven L. Kaplan and Cynthia Koepp (Ithaca, NY: Cornell University Press, 1986), 258–86. See also Robert Darnton, *The Business of Enlightenment: A Publishing History of the* Encyclopédie, *1775–1800* (Cambridge, MA: Harvard University Press, 1979), 242–3, esp. n. 98.
51 Joel Mokyr, *The Lever of Riches: Technological Creativity and Economic Progress* (New York: Oxford University Press, 1990); *The Gifts of Athena: Historical Origins of the Knowledge Economy* (Princeton, NJ: Princeton University Press, 2002); *The Enlightened Economy: An Economic History of Britain, 1700–1850* (New Haven, CT: Yale University Press, 2009).
52 For his explanation of this term, see Mokyr, *Gifts of Athena*, 34–5, and *Economic Enlightenment*, 56.
53 Mokyr, *Enlightened Economy*, 60.
54 Ibid., 54–5.
55 For his explanation of "useful knowledge," see Mokyr, *Gifts of Athena*, chap. 2, and *Enlightened Economy*, chap. 3.
56 Mokyr, *Enlightened Economy*, 60.
57 Quoted in E. P. Thompson, *Customs in Common: Studies in Traditional Popular Culture* (New York: New Press, 1991), 384.
58 For the Montgolfiers' purposes and measures of their success, see Rosenband, *Papermaking*.
59 Quoted in Neil McKendrick, "Josiah Wedgwood and Factory Discipline," *Historical Journal* 4 (1961): 34.
60 Ibid., 31.
61 Ibid., 46.
62 Ibid., 33.
63 Harry Braverman, *Labor and Monopoly Capital: The Degradation of Work in the Twentieth Century* (New York: Monthly Review Press, 1974); Karl Marx, *Capital, Volume 1: A Critique of Political Economy*, trans. Ben Fowkes (London: Penguin Books, 1992. First published 1867).
64 McKendrick, "Wedgwood," 33.
65 Ibid., 42.
66 Quoted in ibid., 46.
67 On the perspective of the lesser manufacturers, see Pollard, *Genesis*, 192.
68 Robert C. Davis, "Arsenal and *Arsenalotti*: Workplace and Community in Seventeenth-Century Venice," in *The Workplace before the Factory: Artisans and Proletarians, 1500–1800*, eds Thomas Max Safley and Leonard N. Rosenband (Ithaca, NY: Cornell University Press, 1993), 180–203.
69 Rule, *Experience of Labour*, 63.

70 Quoted in Peter Linebaugh, *The London Hanged: Crime and Civil Society in the Eighteenth Century* (Cambridge: Cambridge University Press, 1992), 397.
71 William J. Ashworth, "'System of terror': Samuel Bentham, Accountability, and Dockyard Reform during the Napoleonic Wars," *Social History* 23 (1998): 68.
72 Quoted in Linebaugh, *London Hanged*, 397.
73 Ibid., 394.
74 Ibid., 400.
75 Ibid., 399.
76 Mathias, *Transformation of England*, 22.
77 Christine MacLeod, "The European Origins of British Technological Predominance," in *Exceptionalism and Industrialisation: Britain and Its European Rivals, 1688–1815*, ed. Leandro Prados de la Escosura (Cambridge: Cambridge University Press, 2004), 113.
78 Walt W. Rostow, *The Stages of Economic Growth; a Non-Communist Manifesto* (Cambridge: Cambridge University Press, 1960).
79 Thompson, *Customs in Common*, 382.

Chapter Six

1 Eleonora Canepari and Beatrice Zucca Micheletto, *Le travail comme ressource, Mélanges de l'École française de Rome—Italie, Méditerranée* 123 (2011).
2 Wolfgang Kaiser, ed., *La loge et le fondouk: Les dimensions spatiales des pratiques marchandes en Méditerranée* (Aix-en-Provence: Karthala-MMSH, 2014).
3 Wilbur Zelinsky, "The Hypothesis of the Mobility Transition," *The Geographical Review* 61 (1971): 219–49.
4 Jan Lucassen and Leo Lucassen, eds, *Migration, Migration history, History: Old Paradigms and New Perspectives* (Berne: Peter Lang, 1999), 8.
5 Jan Lucassen and Leo Lucassen, "The Mobility Transition Revisited, 1500–1900: What the Case of Europe Can Offer to Global History," *Journal of Global History* 4, no. 3 (2009): 371.
6 Laurence Fontaine, "Gli studi sulla mobilità in Europa nell'età moderna: Problemi e prospettive di ricerca," *Quaderni storici* 93 (1996): 739–56.
7 Robert Park, Ernest W. Burgess, and Roderick D. Mc Kenzie, *The City* (Chicago: University of Chicago Press, 1925).
8 Norbert Elias and John L. Scotson, *The Established and the Outsiders* (London: F. Cass, 1965).
9 Angiolina Arru, "Reti locali, reti globali: il credito degli immigrati (secoli XVII–XIX)," in *L'Italia delle migrazioni interne: Donne, uomini, mobilità in età moderna e contemporanea*, eds Angiolina Arru and Franco Ramella (Rome: Donzelli editore, 2003), 77–110.
10 Simona Cerutti, Robert Descimon, and Maarten Prak, eds, *Cittadinanze, Quaderni storici* 89 (1995); Angiolina Arru, Franco Ramella, and Joseph Ehmer, eds, *Migrazioni, Quaderni storici* 106 (2001).
11 Simona Cerutti, *Étrangers: Étude d'une condition d'incertitude dans une société d'Ancien Régime* (Paris: Fayard, 2012).
12 *Statuta Almae Urbis Romae* (1580).
13 Bernard Lepetit, "La ville: Cadre, objet, sujet," *Enquête* 4 (1996). Available online: http://enquete.revues.org/663.
14 Lucassen and Lucassen, "The Mobility Transition Revisited," 349.
15 On mobility *within* the early modern city, see Jeremy Boulton, *Neighbourhood and Society: A London Suburb in the Seventeenth Century* (Cambridge: Cambridge University Press, 1987); Olivier Zeller, "La mobilité résidentielle de François Valesque, épicier en gros

et échevin de Lyon: 1706–1791," *Cahiers d'histoire* 44 (1999). Available online: http://ch.revues.org/383.

16 Jean-Yves Grenier, *L'économie d'Ancien Régime: Un monde de l'échange et de l'incertitude* (Paris: Albin Michel, 1996); Giovanni Levi, *Inheriting Power: The Story of an Exorcist* (Chicago: University of Chicago Press, 1988).

17 Carmen Sarasúa, "Leaving Home to Help the Family? Male and Female Temporary Migrants in Eighteenth- and Nineteenth-century Spain," in *Women, Gender, and Labour Migration: Historical and Global Perspectives*, ed. Pamela Sharpe (London: Routledge, 2001), 48–78.

18 Jan Lucassen, "The Other Proletarians: Seasonal Labourers, Mercenaries and Miners," *International Review of Social History* 39, supplement (1994): 173.

19 Jelle Van Lottum and Aske Laursen Brock, "Rural to Urban Migration in Eighteenth- century Scandinavia: Evidence from the Maritime Sector," *Mems Working Paper* no. 3 (2014).

20 Ibid., 7.

21 Lucassen, "The Other Proletarians."

22 Donald Woodward, *Men at Work: Labourers and Building Craftsmen in the Towns of Northern England, 1450–1750* (Cambridge: Cambridge University Press, 1995); regarding women laborers, see Woodward, p. 108.

23 Ibid.,103–5.

24 Ibid., 115.

25 Christian Simon, "Labour Relations at Manufactures in the Eighteenth Century: The Calico Printers in Europe," *International Review of Social History* 39, supplement (1994) supplement: 122.

26 In particular, the "life-cycle servants": Peter Laslett, "Characteristics of the Western Family Considered over Time," *Journal of Family History* 2 (1977): 89–115.

27 Raffaella Sarti, "Historians, Social Scientists, Servants, and Domestic Workers: Fifty Years of Research on Domestic and Care Work," *International Review of Social History* 59 (2014): 279–314.

28 Sarasúa, "Leaving Home," 48–78.

29 Josef Ehmer, "Migration of Journeymen as Nineteenth-century Mass Migration," in *Migrations et migrants dans une perspective historique: Permanences et innovations / Migrations and Migrants in Historical Perspective. Permanencies and Innovations*, ed. René Leboutte (Bruxelles: Peter Lang, 2000), 98–9.

30 Josef Ehmer, "Worlds of Mobility: Migration Patterns of Viennese Artisans in the 18th Century," in *The Artisan and the European Town, 1500–1900*, ed. Geoffrey Crossick (Aldershot: Ashgate, 1997), 181. See also Sylvia Hahn, "Inclusion and Exclusion of Migrants in the Multicultural Realm of the Habsburg State of Many Peoples," *Histoire sociale / Social History* 33 (2000): 307–24; and Sigrid Wadauer, "Journeymen's Mobility and the Guild System: A Space of Possibilities Based on Central European Cases," in *Guilds and Association in Europe, 900–1900*, eds Ian A. Gadd and Patrick Wallis (London: Centre for Metropolitan History, 2006), 169–86.

31 Archivio Storico del Vicariato di Roma (ASVR), Parrocchia di Santa Maria ad MArtyres, Stati d'anime, 1677, 1682.

32 Manuel Arranz Herrero and Ramon Grau Fernandez, "Problemas de inmigración y asimilación en la Barcelona del siglo XVIII," *Revista de Geografia* 4 (1970): 71–80.

33 Ibid., 71.

34 Montserrat Carbonell-Esteller, "Using Microcredit and Restructuring Households: Two Complementary Survival Strategies in Late Eighteenth-Century Barcelona," *International Review of Social History* 45, no. 8 (2000): 71–92.

35 Robert Darnton, *The Great Cat Massacre and Other Episodes in French Cultural History* (New York: Basic Books, 1984); Michael Sonenscher, *Work and Wages: Natural Law, Politics and the Eighteenth-century French Trades* (Cambridge: Cambridge University Press, 1989).
36 William J. Sewell, *Work and Revolution in France: The Language of Labor from the Old Regime to 1848* (Cambridge: Cambridge University Press, 1980), 52, 106.
37 Daniel Roche, *Le peuple de Paris* (Paris: Fayard, 1998), 95.
38 Laurence Fontaine, *Histoire du colportage en Europe (XVe–XIXe siècle)* (Paris: Albin Michel, 1993); Arlette Farge, *Vivre dans la rue à Paris au XVIIIe siècle* (Paris: Gallimard-Julliard, 1979).
39 David Montgomery, "The Working Classes of the Pre-Industrial American City 1780–1830," *Labor History* 9 (1968): 3–22.
40 Stephen Innes, ed., *Work and Labor in Early America* (Chapel Hill: University of North Carolina Press, 1988), 223; John K. Alexander, "Poverty, Fear, and Continuity: An Analysis of the Poor in Late Eighteenth-century Philadelphia," in *Peoples of Philadelphia, 1790–1940: A History of Ethnic Groups and Lower Class Life*, eds Allen F. Davis and Mark H. Haller (Philadelphia, PA: Temple University Press, 1973), 13–37; Gary B. Nash, "Poverty and Poor Relief in Pre-Revolutionary Philadelphia," *William and Mary Quarterly* 33 (1976): 3–30.
41 Jeanne Cuillier, "Mobility and the Social Organization of Urban Space in the United States, 1760–1820," *International Journal of Urban and Regional Research* 2 (1978): 271.
42 Douglas L. Jones, "The Strolling Poor. Transiency in Eighteenth-century Massachusetts," *Journal of Social History* 53 (1974): 28–53.
43 Sigrid Wadauer, Thomas Buchner, and Alexander Mejstrik, eds, *The History of Labour Intermediation Institutions and Finding Employment in the Nineteenth and Early Twentieth Centuries* (New York: Berghahn Books, 2015).
44 Jacques-Louis Ménétra, *Journal de ma vie*, ed. Daniel Roche (Paris: Montalba, 1986).
45 Ehmer, *"Worlds of Mobility,"* 172.
46 Ibid.
47 Ibid., 173.
48 Ibid., 174.
49 See also Wadauer, "Journeymen's Mobility and the Guild System."
50 Laurence Fontaine, *Le marché: Histoire et usages d'une conquête sociale* (Paris: Gallimard, 2013).
51 Ibid.
52 Corine Maitte, *Les chemins de verre: Les migrations des verriers d'Altare et de Venise (XVIe–XIXe siècles)* (Rennes: Presses universitaires de Rennes, 2009).
53 Arru, "Reti locali, reti globali"; Eleonora Canepari, "Keeping in Touch: Migrant Workers' Translocal Ties in Early Modern Italy," in *Micro-Spatial Histories of Global Labour*, eds Christian De Vito and Anne Gerritsen (London: Palgrave Macmillan, 2018).
54 Peggy Levitt and Nina Glick Schiller, "Conceptualizing Simultaneity: A Transnational Social Field Perspective on Society," *International Migration Review* 38 (2004): 1004; Paul-André Rosental, "Maintien/rupture: Un nouveau couple pour l'analyse des migrations," *Annales ESC* 45, no. 6 (1990): 1408.
55 Margareth Grieco, *Keeping It in the Family: Social Networks and Employment Chance* (London: Tavistock Publications, 1987).
56 Louis-Sébastien Mercier, *Tableau de Paris* (Paris: Virchaux & Compagnie, 1782), 291.
57 Raul Merzario, *Adamocrazia: Famiglie di emigranti in una regione alpina (Svizzera italiana, XVIII secolo)* (Bologne: il Mulino, 2000).

58 Ibid., 58.
59 Sarasúa, "Leaving Home," 35.
60 Emilio J. Castilla et al., "Social Networks in Silicon Valley," in *The Silicon Valley Edge: A Habitat for Innovation and Entrepreneurship*, eds Lee Chong-Moon et al. (Stanford, CA: Stanford University Press, 2000), 218–47; Marc Granovetter, *Getting a Job: A Study of Contacts and Careers* (Chicago: University of Chicago Press, 1974).
61 Bronisław Geremek, *Le salariat dans l'artisanat aux XIIIe-XVe siècles: Étude sur le marché de la main-d'œuvre au Moyen Âge* (Paris and La Haye: Mouton, 1968).
62 *Teatro social del siglo XIX*, vol. II, Madrid 1846, quoted in Sarasúa, "Leaving Home," 56.
63 Mercier, *Tableau de Paris*, 381.
64 Lucassen, "The Other Proletarians," 166.
65 Jones, "The Strolling Poor," 34.
66 Carbonell-Esteller, "Using Microcredit," 81.
67 Michael Mitteraurer, *Why Europe? The Medieval Origins of its Paths* (Chicago: University of Chicago Press, 2010), 67.
68 Jürgen Schlumbohm, "Labour in Proto-Industrialization: Big-Questions and Micro-Answers," in *Early Modern Capitalism: Economic and Social Change in Europe, 1400–1800*, ed. Maarten Prak (London: Routledge, 2001), 129.
69 Mark Merry and Philip Baker, "'For the House Herself and One Servant': Family and Household in Late Seventeenth-century London," *The London Journal* 34 (2009): 205–23.
70 Ibid., 206.
71 Jane Humphries, "Household Economy," in *The Cambridge Economic History of Modern Britain, Vol. I: Industrialization 1700–1860*, eds Roderick Floud and Paul Johnson (Cambridge: Cambridge University Press, 2004), 238–67.
72 Thomas Sokoll, *Household and Family Among the Poor: The Case of two Essex Communities in the Late Eighteenth and Early Nineteenth Centuries* (Bochum: Brockmeyer, 1993), and "The Pauper Household Small and Simple? The Evidence from Listings of Inhabitants and Pauper Lists of Early Modern England Reassessed," *Ethnologia Europaea* 17 (1987): 25–42.
73 Robert Jütte, *Poverty and Deviance in Early Modern Europe* (Cambridge: Cambridge University Press, 2004), 87.
74 Carbonell-Esteller, "Using Microcredit," 83.
75 Monica Chojnacka, *Working Women of Early Modern Venice* (Baltimore: Johns Hopkins University Press, 2001), 98.
76 Joanne McEwan, "The Lodging Exchange: Space, Authority and Knowledge in Eighteenth-Century London," in *Accommodating Poverty: The Housing and Living Arrangements of the English Poor, c. 1600–1850*, eds Joanne McEwan and Pamela Sharpe (Basingstoke: Palgrave Macmillan, 2011), 54.
77 Chojnacka, *Working Women*, 98.
78 Elizabeth Blackmar, "Re-walking the 'Walking City': Housing and Property Relations in New York City, 1780–1840," *Radical History Review* 21 (1979): 375.
79 Ibid., 376.
80 Fontaine, *Le marché*.
81 ASC, *Camera capitolina*, cabinet. XI, vol. 66, *Statuto dell'università et arte dei fornari e panettieri dell'alma città di Roma*, chap. 33.
82 Ibid., t. 60, *Statuti dell'università et arte de pescivendoli di Roma*, 1636, 3rd part, chap. 14. See also ibid., t. 77, *Statuti dell'università e mercanti dell'arte dei vaccinari di Roma*, 1676, chap. 43.

83 Ibid., t. 53, *Statuti, ordini e costitutioni dell'università, e collegio de' barbieri di Roma*, 1713, chap. 29.
84 Ibid., t. 79, *Statuta universitatis carpentariorum almae urbis*, 1624, chap. 48.
85 Ibid., t. 69, *Statuto dell'università de mastri di sellari di Roma*, chap. 29. Ibid., t. 38, *Statuti nuovi dell'università dell'arte de pellicciari di Roma*, 1706, chap. 12.
86 Ibid., t. 67, *Statuti e capitoli dell'università de' regattieri di Roma*, chap. 15. See also the example of the guild of merchants and wine warehousemen: ibid., t. 71, *Statuti dell'Università de mercanti di vini detti magazinieri*, 1731, chap. 24.

Chapter Seven

1 The division between traditional-progressive views I have adapted, in part, from the typology found in Forrest McDonald, *Novus Ordo Seclorum: The Intellectual Origins of the Constitution* (Lawrence: University of Kansas, 1986), 98–107.
2 A literary-influenced version of this image can be found in E. M. W. Tillyard, *The Elizabethan World Picture* (London: Chatto and Windus, 1943).
3 Paolo Malanima, "The Italian Economy Before Modern Growth," Institute of Studies on Mediterranean Economies, 2011. Available online: http://www.paolomalanima.it/default_file/Papers/The_Italian_Economy_Before_Modern_Growth.pdf; Carlos Alvarez-Nogal and Leandro Prados de la Escosura, "The Rise and Fall of Spain (1270–1850)," *The Economic History Review* 66, no. 1 (2013): 1–37.
4 Thomas Malthus, *An Essay on the Principle of Population* (Oxford: Oxford University Press, 2003. First published 1798). In this edition, editor Geoffrey Gilbert provides a useful introduction to Malthus's thought.
5 Jerome Blum, *The End of the Old Order in Rural Europe* (Princeton, NJ: Princeton University Press, 1978); Peter M. Jones, *Agricultural Enlightenment: Knowledge, Technology, and Nature, 1750–1840* (Oxford: Oxford University Press, 2016).
6 This image is sketched in broad terms in Isser Woloch, *Eighteenth-Century Europe: Tradition and Progress, 1715–1789* (New York: Norton, 1982), 79–82.
7 On Hogarth's prints generally, see Ronald Paulson, *Hogarth: His Life, Art, and Times* (New Haven: Yale University Press, 1971). Benjamin Franklin, *Poor Richard's Almanac* (Lexington, KY: Renaissance Classics, 2012), 8, 13; 'Wit and Wisdom' from *Poor Richard's Almanac* (Mineola, NY: Dover, 1999), 8.
8 George Wittkowsky, "Swift's *Modest Proposal*: The Biography of an Early Georgian Pamphlet," *Journal of the History of Ideas* 4, no. 1 (1943): 75–104.
9 Ole Peter Grell and Andrew Cunningham, eds, *Health Care and Poor Relief in Counter-Reformation Europe* (London: Routledge, 1999).
10 Thomas Max Safley, ed., *The Reformation of Charity: The Secular and the Religious in Early Modern Poor Relief* (Leiden: Brill, 2003); Robert E. Cray, Jr., *Paupers and Poor Relief in New York City and its Rural Environs, 1700–1830* (Philadelphia, PA: Temple University Press, 1988).
11 Sheilagh Ogilvie, *Institutions and European Trade: Merchant Guilds, 1000–1800* (Cambridge: Cambridge University Press, 2011). See also Chapters Four and Eight in this volume.
12 Carlo Poni, "Norms and Disputes: The Shoemakers' Guild in Eighteenth-Century Bologna," *Past & Present* 123 (1989): 80–108; Leonard Rosenband, *Papermaking in Eighteenth-century France: Management, Labor, and Revolution at the Montgolfier Mill, 1761–1805* (Baltimore: Johns Hopkins University Press, 2000).
13 Rosemary O'Day, "Matchmaking and Moneymaking in a Patronage Society: The First Duke and Duchess of Chandos c.1712–35," *The Economic History Review* 66, no. 1 (2013): 273–96; Amanda Vickery, *Behind Closed Doors: At Home in Georgian England* (New Haven, CT:

Yale University Press, 2009); *The Gentleman's Daughter: Women's Lives in Georgian England* (New Haven, CT: Yale University Press, 1998).

14 Deborah Simonton, *A History of European Women's Work: 1700 to the Present* (New York: Routledge, 1998).

15 Deborah Simonton, "Widows and Wenches: Single Women in Eighteenth-century Urban Economies," in *Female Agency in the Urban Economy: Gender in European Towns, 1640–1830*, eds Deborah Simonton and Anne Montenach (New York: Routledge, 2013), 109, 112.

16 Timothy Gilfoyle, *City of Eros: New York City, Prostitution, and the Commercialization of Sex, 1790–1920* (New York: Norton, 1992); Paul Langford, *A Polite and Commercial People: England 1727–1783* (New York: Oxford University Press, 1998), 144–5.

17 On the Physiocrats, see Elizabeth Fox-Genovese, *The Origins of Physiocracy: Economic Revolution and Social Order in Eighteenth-century France* (Ithaca, NY: Cornell University Press, 1976).

18 Drew McCoy, *The Elusive Republic: Political Economy in Jeffersonian America* (Chapel Hill: University of North Carolina Press, 1980), 44–5; McDonald, *Novus Ordo Seclorum*, 106–8.

19 P. G. M. Dickson, *The Financial Revolution in England: A Study in the Development of Public Credit, 1688–1756* (London: Macmillan, 1967).

20 Poni, "Norms and Disputes," 106–8.

21 McCoy, *The Elusive Republic*, 25–7.

22 Langford, *Polite and Commercial People*, 68–71. On rising consumption in the American colonies, see T. H. Breen, *Marketplace of Revolution: How Consumer Politics Shaped American Independence* (New York: Oxford University Press, 2004).

23 The following are representative but not exhaustive examples. On Native Americans, see Richard White, *The Middle Ground: Indians, Empires, and Republics in the Great Lakes Region, 1650–1815* (New York: Cambridge University, 1984), 94–141; on journeymen's privileges, see Rosenband, *Papermaking*; on laborers' income in Italy, see Malanima, "The Italian Economy"; on moralist critiques, see Breen, *Marketplace of Revolution*, 171–7.

24 Rosemary O'Day, *The Professions in Early Modern England: Servants of the Commonweal* (London: Longman, 2000).

25 The noble Chandos family, which used finance to preserve traditional kinship ties through marriage, also included new investments in finance; see O'Day, "Matchmaking and Moneymaking."

26 Julian Hoppit, *Risk and Failure in English Business, 1700–1800* (New York: Cambridge University Press, 1987).

27 Karen Halttunen, "Humanitarianism and the Pornography of Pain in Anglo-American Culture," *American Historical Review* 100 (1995): 303–34.

28 Laura Rodriguez, "The Spanish Riots of 1766," *Past and Present* 59 (1973): 117–46.

29 See also Chapters Three and Four in this volume.

30 Justin Roberts, *Slavery and Enlightenment in the British Atlantic, 1750–1807* (Cambridge: Cambridge University Press, 2013); see also Eric Otremba, "Enlightened Institutions: Science, Plantations, and Slavery" (PhD diss., University of Minnesota, USA, 2012).

31 Ira Berlin, *Many Thousands Gone: The First Two Centuries of Slavery in North America* (Cambridge, MA: Harvard University Press, 1998).

32 The chief interpreter of pietism as an international movement was William R. Ward. His three major works on it are *The Protestant Evangelical Awakening* (Cambridge: Cambridge University Press, 1992); *Christianity under the Ancien Régime, 1648–1789* (Cambridge: Cambridge University Press, 1999); *Early Evangelicalism: A Global Intellectual History, 1670–1789* (Cambridge: Cambridge University Press, 2006).

33 For an explication of this impulse on the American frontier, see Charles Sellers, *The Market Revolution: Jacksonian America, 1815–1846* (New York: Oxford University Press, 1991), 8–14, 29–31.
34 On dissenter plain style, see Leigh Eric Schmidt, "'A Church-going People are a Dress-Loving People': Clothes, Communication, and Legal Culture in Early America," *Church History* 58 no. 1 (1989): 36–51.
35 Langford, *Polite and Commercial People*, 665–6; David Brion Davis, *The Problem of Slavery in the Age of Revolution* (New York: Oxford University Press, 1975), chap. 5; Wesley's quote appears reproduced in numerous works; see, among others, E. P. Thompson, *The Making of the English Working Class* (New York: Random House, 1963), 355.
36 Matthew Kadane, "Anti-Trinitarianism and the Republican Tradition in Enlightenment Britain," *Republics of Letters: A Journal for the Study of Knowledge, Politics, and the Arts* 2, no. 1 (2010); see also Matthew Kadane and Margaret C. Jacob, "Missing, Now Found in the Eighteenth Century: Weber's Protestant Capitalist," *American Historical Review* 108, no. 1 (2003): 20–49.
37 Alan Taylor, *Liberty Men and Great Proprietors: The Revolutionary Settlement on the Maine Frontier* (Chapel Hill: University of North Carolina Press, 1990).

Chapter Eight

1 For a critique, see Lynn Hunt and George Sheridan, "Corporatism, Association, and the Language of Labor in France, 1750–1850," *Journal of Modern History* 58 (1986): 822–5.
2 David A. Spencer, *The Political Economy of Work* (London: Routledge, 2009), 9.
3 William H. Sewell, *Work and Revolution in France: The Language of Labor from the Old Regime to 1848* (Cambridge: Cambridge University Press, 1980), 263, 265.
4 For example, Thomas Buhner, "Perceptions of Work in Early Modern Economic Thought: Dutch Mercantilism and Central European Cameralism in Comparative perspective," in *The Idea of Work in Europe from Antiquity to Modern Times*, eds Josef Ehmer and Catharina Lis (Aldershot: Ashgate, 2009), 191–213.
5 Iorwerth Prothero, *Artisans and Politics in Early Nineteenth-century London: John Gast and His Times* (London: Methuen, 1981).
6 Patrick, Joyce, ed. *The Historical Meanings of Work* (Cambridge: Cambridge University Press, 1987).
7 John Smail, "Manufacturer or Artisan? The Relationship between Economic and Cultural Change in the Early Stages of the Eighteenth-century Industrialization," *Journal of Social History* 25, no. 4 (1992): 791–814.
8 For recent views and references, see John Rule, "Industrial Disputes, Wage Bargaining and the Moral Economy," in *Moral Economy and Popular Protest. Crowds, Conflict and Authority*, eds Adrian Randall and Andrew Charlesworth (London: Macmillan, 2000), 166–85.
9 Andreas Grießinger, *Das symbolische Kapital der Ehre: Streikbewegungen und kollektives Bewusstsein deutscher Handwerksgesellen im 18. Jahrhundert* (Frankfurt: Ullstein, 1981).
10 Catharina Lis and Hugo Soly, "De macht van 'vrije arbeiders': Collectieve acties van hoedenmakersgezellen in de Zuidelijke Nederlanden (zestiende-negentiende eeuw)," in *Werken volgens de regels: Ambachten in Brabant en Vlaanderen, 1500–1800*, eds Catharina Lis and Hugo Soly (Brussels: VUB-Press, 1994), 15–50; "'An Irresistible Phalanx': Journeymen Associations in Western Europe, 1300–1800," in *Before the Unions: Wage Earners and Collective Action in Europe, 1300–1850*, eds Catharina Lis, Jan Lucassen, and Hugo Soly (*International Review of Social History* Supplement 2; Cambridge: Cambridge University Press, 1994).

11 For example, Buchanan Sharp, *In Contempt of All Authority: Rural Artisans and Riot in the West of England, 1586–1660* (Berkeley: University of California Press, 1980); Steve Hindle, "Work, Reward and Labour Discipline in Late Seventeenth-century England," in *Remaking English Society: Social Relations and Social Change in Early Modern England*, eds Steve Hindle, Alexandra Shepard, and John Walter (Woodbridge: Boydell Press, 2013), 255–79.

12 Robert Darnton, *The Great Cat Massacre and Other Episodes in French Cultural History* (New York: Vintage, 1984). See also Chapters Four and Five in this volume.

13 For a synthesis and references, see Maarten Prak, "Moral Order in the World of Work: Social Control and the Guilds in Europe," in *Social Control in Europe. Vol. 1, 1500–1800*, eds Herman Roodenburg and Pieter Spierenburg (Columbus: Ohio State University Press, 2004), 176–99.

14 William M. Reddy, *The Rise of Market Culture: The Textile Trade and French Society, 1750–1900* (Cambridge: Cambridge University Press, 1984), 31–4.

15 Quoted in Leonard N. Rosenband, *Papermaking in Eighteenth-century France: Management, Labor, and Revolution at the Montgolfier Mill, 1761–1805* (Baltimore: Johns Hopkins University Press, 2000), 51.

16 Natalie Zemon Davis, "A Trade Union in Sixteenth-century France," *The Economic History Review*, 2nd ser., 19 (1966): 48–69, quote on 52–3; also cited in Lis and Soly, "'An Irresistible Phalanx'," 18 and Catharina Lis and Hugo Soly, *Worthy Efforts: Attitudes to Work and Workers in Pre-Industrial Europe* (Leiden: Brill, 2012), 533.

17 Michael P. Fitzsimmons, *From Artisan to Worker: Guilds, the French State, and the Organisation of Labor, 1776–1821* (Cambridge: Cambridge University Press, 2010).

18 Steven L. Kaplan, "Social Classification and Representation in the Corporate World of Eighteenth-century France: Turgot's 'Carnival'," in *Work in France: Representations, Meaning, Organization, and Practice*, eds Steven L. Kaplan and Cynthia Koepp (Ithaca, NY: Cornell University Press), 176–228.

19 For example, Gary B. Nash, *The Urban Crucible: The Northern Seaports and the Origins of the American Revolution* (Cambridge, MA: Harvard University Press, 1986); Gordon Wood, *The Radicalism of the American Revolution* (New York: A. A. Knopf, 1992); Alan Tully, *Forming American Politics: Ideas, Interests, and Institutions in Colonial New York and Pennsylvania* (Baltimore: Johns Hopkins University Press, 1994).

20 Nash, *The Urban Crucible*, 24–8, 54–7; Simon Middleton, *From Privileges to Rights: Work and Politics in Colonial New York City* (Philadelphia: University of Pennsylvania Press, 2006), 7, 41–2, 88–95, 145–9.

21 References in Lis and Soly, *Worthy Efforts*, 537–8.

22 Myriad examples in Karin Van Honacker, *Lokaal verzet en oproer in de 17de en 18de eeuw: Collectieve acties tegen het centraal gezag in Brussel, Antwerpen en Leuven* (Heule: UGA, 1994).

23 Michael Sonenscher, "Journeymen, the Courts and the French Trades, 1781–1791," *Past & Present* 114 (1987): 77–109.

24 See Chapter Four in this volume.

25 Deborah Simonton, "'… to Merit the Countenance of the Magistrates': Gender and Civic Identity in Eighteenth-century Aberdeen," in *Gender in Urban Europe: Sites of Political Activity and Citizenship 1750–1900*, eds Nina Koefoed, Åsa Karlsson-Sjögren, and Krista Cowman (London: Routledge, 2014), 20.

26 Catharina Lis and Hugo Soly, "Different Paths of Development: Capitalism in the Northern and Southern Netherlands during the Middle Ages and the Early Modern Period," *Review* 20 (1997): 211–42; "Craft Guilds in Comparative Perspective: The Northern and the Southern Netherlands, a Survey," in *Craft Guilds in the Early Modern Low Countries: Work, Power and Representation*, eds Maarten Prak et al. (Aldershot: Ashgate, 2006), 1–31, esp. 14–17.

27 For example, Bert De Munck, "La qualité du corporatisme: Stratégies économiques et symboliques des corporations anversoises du XVe siècle à leur abolition," *Revue d'histoire moderne et contemporaine* 54, no. 1 (2007): 116–44; "Skills, Trust and Changing Consumer Preferences: The Decline of Antwerp's Craft Guilds from the Perspective of the Product Market, ca. 1500–ca. 1800," *International Review of Social History* 53, no. 2 (2008): 197–233.

28 See, for example, Christopher Clark, "Social Structure and Manufacturing before the Factory: Rural New England, 1750–1830," in *The Workplace before the Factory: Artisans and Proletarians, 1500–1800*, eds Thomas Max Safley and Leonard N. Rosenband (Ithaca, NY: Cornell University Press, 1993), 11–36.

29 Vera Bácskai, "Artisans in Hungarian Towns on the Eve of Industrialization," in *The Artisan and the European Town, 1500–1900*, ed. Geoffrey Crossick (Aldershot: Scolar Press, 1997), 203.

30 Sheilagh Ogilvie, *State Corporatism and Proto-Industry: The Württemberg Black Forest, 1580–1797* (Cambridge: Cambridge University Press, 1997).

31 Details and references in Bert De Munck, "One Counter and Your own Account. Redefining Illicit Labour in Early Modern Antwerp," *Urban History* 37, no. 1 (2010): 26–44, esp. 29–34.

32 Clare H. Crowston, *Fabricating Women: The Seamstresses of Old Regime France, 1675–1791* (Durham, NC: Duke University Press, 2001).

33 Cynthia M. Truant, "Independent and Insolent: Journeymen and their 'Rites' in the Old Regime Workplace," in Kaplan and Koepp, ed., *Work in France*, 162; Arnd Klüge, *Die Zünfte* (Stuttgart: Franz Steiner Verlag, 2009), 199–227.

34 Alfons K. L. Thijs, "Religion and Social Structure: Religious Rituals in Pre-Industrial Trade Associations," in Prak et al., ed., *Craft Guilds*, 157–73.

35 Truant, "Independent and Insolent."

36 See the influential work of Antony Black, *Guild and State: European Political Thought from the Twelfth Century to the Present* (New Brunswick, NJ: Transaction Publishers, 2009 . First published 1984).

37 For example, Alfons K. L. Thijs, *Van "werkwinkel" tot "fabriek": De textielnijverheid te Antwerpen (einde 15de–begin 19de eeuw)* (Brussels: Gemeentekrediet, 1987), 219–57; Klüge, *Die Zünfte*, 172–3; De Munck, "One Counter," 31–2.

38 Kaplan "Social," 186. See also Chapters One and Seven in this volume.

39 For the state-of-the-art and references in Heinz-Gerhard Haupt, ed., *Das Ende der Zünfte. Ein europäischer Vergleich* (Göttingen: Vandenhoeck & Ruprecht, 2002); and Alberto Guenzi et al., eds, *Guilds, Markets and Work Regulations in Italy, 16th–19th Centuries* (Aldershot: Ashgate, 1998).

40 See also Chapter Seven in this volume.

41 Steven L. Kaplan, "L'apprentissage au XVIIIe siècle: Le cas de Paris," *Revue d'histoire moderne et contemporaine* 40, no. 3 (1993): 459–66.

42 Andreas Grießinger and Reinhold Reith, "Lehrlinge im deutschen Handwerk des ausgehenden 18: Jahrhunderts. Arbeitsorganisation, Sozialbeziehungen und alltägliche Konflikte," *Zeitschrift für Historische Forschung* 13 (1986): 149–99; Reinhold Reith, "Apprentices in the German and Austrian Crafts in Early Modern Times—Apprentices as Wage Earners?" in *Learning on the Shop Floor: Historical Perspectives on Apprenticeship*, eds Bert De Munck, Steven L. Kaplan, and Hugo Soly (London: Berghahn Books, 2007), 179–202.

43 Bert De Munck, "From Brotherhood Community to Civil Society? Apprentices Between Guild, Household and the Freedom of Contract in Early Modern Antwerp," *Social History* 35, no. 1 (2010): 1–20.

44 For example, Steven L. Kaplan, "Idéologie, conflits et pratiques politiques dans les corporations parisiennes au XVIIIe siècle," *Revue d'histoire moderne et contemporaine* 49, no. 1 (2002): 5–55; Maïka De Keyzer, "Opportunisme, corporatisme en progressiviteit: Conflicten en vertogen van corporatieve belangengroepen in het stedelijk milieu van het achttiende-eeuwse Mechelen," *Tijdschrift voor sociale en economische geschiedenis* 7, no. 4 (2010): 3–26.
45 Kaplan, "Idéologie," 53.
46 Middleton, *From Privileges to Rights*, 6.
47 For a summary, see James R. Farr, *Artisans in Europe, 1300–1914* (Cambridge: Cambridge University Press, 2000), 170–89.
48 Lis and Soly, *Worthy Efforts*, chap. 1, 14–16.
49 For recent views, see Robert Brandt and Thomas Buchner, eds, *Nahrung, Markt oder Gemeinnutz: Werner Sombart und das vorindustrielle Handwerk* (Bielefeld: Verlag für Regionalgeschichte, 2004).
50 See, for example, Simon Schaffer, "Enlightened Automata," in *The Sciences in Enlightened Europe*, eds William Clark, Jan Golinski, and Simon Schaffer (Chicago: University of Chicago Press, 1999), 126–65.
51 Quoted in Neil McKendrick, "Josiah Wedgewood and Factory Discipline," *Historical Journal* 4, no. 1 (1961), 46; and Farr, *Artisans in Europe*, 144.
52 De Munck, "Skills"; Barbara Bettoni, "Usefulness, Ornament and Novelty: The Debate on Quality in Button and Buckle Manufacturing in Northern Italy (XVIII–XIX century)," in *Concepts of Value in Material Culture, 1500–1900*, eds Bert De Munck and Dries Lyna (Aldershot: Ashgate, 2016), 171–206.
53 For a synthesis and references, see Lis and Soly, *Worthy Efforts*, chap. 6.
54 Adam Smith, *An Inquiry into the Nature and Causes of the Wealth of Nations* (London: T. Cadell, 1776), bk. I, chap. 10, part 2, §71.
55 Craig Carson, "Adam Smith and Economic Citizenship," *Postmodern Culture* 22 (2012): 3.

Chapter Nine

1 Sidney Pollard, *The Genesis of Modern Management: A Study of the Industrial Revolution in Great Britain* (Cambridge, MA: Harvard University Press, 1965), 106.
2 David Levine, *Reproducing Families: The Political Economy of English Population History* (Cambridge: Cambridge University Press, 1987), 21.
3 Edward P. Thompson, "Time, Work-Discipline and Industrial Capitalism," *Past and Present* 38 (1967): 60.
4 Maxine Berg, Pat Hudson, and Michael Sonenscher, eds, *Manufacture in Town and Country Before the Factory* (Cambridge: Cambridge University Press, 1983), 9–10; Deborah Simonton, *A History of European Women's Work: 1700 to the Present* (London: Routledge, 1998).
5 William Reddy, *The Rise of Market Culture: The Textile Trade and French Society, 1750–1900* (Cambridge: Cambridge University Press, 1984), 33.
6 Douglas Reid, "The decline of Saint Monday, 1766–1876," *Past and Present* 71 (1976): 76–101.
7 Hans-Joachim Voth, *Time and Work in England 1750–1830* (Cambridge: Cambridge University Press, 2000).
8 David Roediger and Philip Foner, *Our Own Time: A History of American Labor and the Working Day* (New York: Verso, 1989).

9   Friedrich Engels, *The Condition of the Working Class in England*, ed. D. McLellan (Oxford: Oxford University Press, 1993), 15–17.
10 Juliet Schor, *The Overworked American: The Unexpected Decline of Leisure* (New York: Basic Books, 1992), 7.
11 Reid, "Decline of Saint Monday," 101.
12 Sir Josiah Child, *A New Discourse of Trade, Wherein are Recommended Several Weighty Points...*, 5th edn., (Glasgow: Robert and Andrew Foulis, 1751), 12.
13 Bernard Mandeville, *The Fable of the Bees: or, Private Vices, Publick Benefits* (London: 1724), 21.
14 For a rare example, however, see: Mary Saxby, *Memoirs of a Female Vagrant Written by Herself*, ed. Samuel Greathead (London: J. W. Morris, 1806).
15 Edward Barlow, *Barlow's Journal of his Life at Sea in King's Ships... from 1659 to 1703*, ed. Basil Lubbock (London: Hurst & Blackett, 1934), 21.
16 Ibid., 19–20.
17 Lois Green Carr, "Emigration and the Standard of Living: The Seventeenth-century Chesapeake," *Journal of Economic History* 52, no. 2 (1992): 271–91.
18 Franklin F. Mendels, "Proto-Industrialization: The First Phase of the Industrialization Process," *The Journal of Economic History* 32, no. 1 (1972): 241–61. See also Charles Sabel and Jonathan Zeitlin, "Historical Alternatives to Mass Production," *Past & Present* 108 (1985): 133–76; Pat Hudson, "Industrial Organisation and Structure," in *The Cambridge Economic History of Modern Britain: Industrialisation, 1700–1860*, eds Roderick Floud and Paul Johnson (Cambridge: Cambridge University Press, 2004).
19 Engels, *Condition of Working Class*, 15–16.
20 George Calladine, *The Diary of Colour-Serjeant George Calladine, 19th Foot, 1793–1837*, ed. Major M. L. Ferrar (London: E. Fisher & Co, 1922), 2.
21 Benjamin Brierley, *Home Memories: The Autobiography of a Handloom Weaver* (Manchester, 1886; repr. Bramhall, 2002).
22 William Hutton, *The Life of William Hutton, F.A.S.S., Including a Particular Account of the Riots at Birmingham in 1791* (London, 1816), 63–4; Nottinghamshire Archives, Nottingham: Moss, Joseph, "Recollections of Joseph Moss, a journeyman stockinger, 1817," DD148/1, n.p.
23 Hutton, *Life of Hutton*, 63–4.
24 Voth, *Time and Work*; Hans-Joachim Voth, "The Longest Years: New Estimates of Labor Input in England, 1760–1830," *The Journal of Economic History* 61, no. 4 (2001): 1065–82; E. Hopkins, "Working Hours and Conditions during the Industrial Revolution: A Reappraisal," *The Economic History Review* 35, no. 1 (1982): 52–66.
25 Gregory Clark and Ysbrand van der Werf, "Work in Progress: The Industrious Revolution?" *Journal of Economic History* 55, no. 3 (1998): 830–43.
26 Voth, "Longest Years," table 7, 1076.
27 See the debates in Hugh Cunningham, "The Employment and Unemployment of Children in England c. 1680–1851," *Past & Present* 126 (1990): 115–50; and Peter Kirby, "How Many Children Were 'Unemployed' in Eighteenth- and Nineteenth-century England?" *Past & Present* 187, no. 1 (2005): 187–202.
28 Figures taken from Emma Griffin, *Liberty's Dawn: A People's History of the British Industrial Revolution* (New Haven, CT: Yale University Press, 2013), 57–83, 64–5, 81–2.
29 Mary Jo Maynes, "In Search of Arachne's Daughters: European Girls, Economic Development and the Textile Trade, 1750–1880," in *Secret Gardens, Satanic Mills: Placing Girls in European History, 1750–1960*, ed. Marie Jo Maynes, Brigitta Søland, and Christina

Benninghaus (Bloomington: Indiana University Press, 2005), 38–53; Maxine Berg, "What Difference Did Women's Work to the Industrial Revolution?" *History Workshop Journal* 35, no. 1 (1993): 22–44.

30 James B. Collins, "The Economic Role of Women in Seventeenth-century France," *French Historical Studies* 16, no. 2 (1989): 436–70. See also Daryl M. Hafter and Nina Kushner, eds, *Women and Work in Eighteenth-century France* (Baton Rouge: Louisiana State University Press, 2015).

31 Martha C. Howell, *Women, Production, and Patriarchy in Late Medieval Cities* (Chicago: University of Chicago Press, 1990).

32 Emma Hart, "Work, Family, and the Eighteenth-century History of a Middle Class in the American South," *Journal of Southern History* 78 (2012): 551–78.

33 For the French silk industry, see Jeff Horn, *The Path Not Taken: French Industrialization in the Age of Revolution, 1750–1830* (Cambridge, MA: MIT Press, 2006).

34 Deborah Simonton, "Bringing up Girls: Work in Pre-industrial Europe," in Maynes, S.land, and Benninghaus, eds, *Secret Gardens*, 23, 27.

35 Griffin, *Liberty's Dawn*, 84–106; Deborah Simonton, "'Birds of Passage' or 'Career' Women? Thoughts on the Life Cycle of the Eighteenth-century European Servant," *Women's History Review* 20, no. 2 (2011): 207–25.

36 Hanspeter Wagner, *Puritan Attitudes towards Recreation in Early Seventeenth-century New England, With Particular Consideration of Physical Recreation* (Bern: Peter Lang, 1982).

37 William Stukeley, *Itinerarium Curiosum* (London: William Stukeley, 1724), 91.

38 Peter Burke, *Popular Culture in Early Modern Europe* (London: Maurice Temple Smith, 1978).

39 William Borlase, *The Natural History of Cornwall* (Oxford: W. Jackson, 1758), 300.

40 See, in particular, Robert W. Malcolmson, *Popular Recreations in English Society, 1700–1850* (Cambridge: Cambridge University Press, 1973).

41 John Clare, *Clare: Selected Poems and Prose*, eds Eric Robinson and Geoffrey Summerfield (Oxford: Oxford University Press, 1966).

42 John Denson, *A Peasant's Voice to Landowners, on the Best Means of Benefiting Agricultural Labourers, and of Reducing Poor Rates* (Cambridge, W.H. Smith, 1830).

43 Andreas Gestrich, "After Dark: Girls' Leisure, Work and Sexuality in Eighteenth- and Nineteenth-century Rural Southwest Germany," in Maynes, Søland, and Benninghaus, eds, *Secret Gardens*, 54–68.

44 For the most thoroughgoing analysis of this kind, see Eric Dunning and Kenneth Sheard, *Barbarians, Gentlemen and Players: A Sociological Study of Rugby Football* (New York: New York University Press, 1979), 2, 29–34, 65. See also James Walvin, *The People's Game* (Edinburgh: Mainstream, 1984), 9–30.

45 R. Pearse Chope, "Football on Good Friday," *Devon and Cornwall Notes and Queries* 10 (1918–19): 113–14.

46 *Ipswich Journal*, August 21, 1741, September 8, 1750, September 30, 1752. Adrian Harvey, "Football's Missing Link: The Real Story of the Evolution of Modern Football," *European Sports History Review* 1 (1999): 92–116.

47 Derek Birley, *A Social History of English Cricket* (London: Aurum, 1999); David Underdown, *Start of Play: Cricket and Culture in Eighteenth-century Britain* (Harmondsworth: Penguin Books, 2000).

48 For example, James Woodforde, *The Diary of a Country Parson, 1758–1802*, ed. John Beresford, 5 vols. (Oxford: Oxford University Press, 1924–31), April 29, 1760, May 14, 1760, 14; William Cole, *The Blecheley Diary of the Rev. William Cole, 1765–1767*, ed.

Francis Griffin Stokes, with an introduction by Helen Waddell (London: Constable, 1931), October 30, 1766, 143.

49 For more detail see Emma Griffin, *England's Revelry: A History of Popular Sports and Pastimes, 1660–1800* (Oxford: Oxford University Press, 2005).

50 See Sir Thomas Parkyns, of Bunny Baronet, *The Inn-Play or Cornish-Hugg Wrestler. Digested in a Method with Teacheth to break all Holds, and throw most Falls mathematically* (London: Thomas Weekes, 1727). Malissa Smith, *A History of Women's Boxing* (Lanham, MD: Rowman & Littlefield, 2014).

51 See Ronald Hutton, *The Rise and Fall of Merry England: The Ritual Year, 1400–1700* (Oxford: Oxford University Press, 1994), 244; and *The Stations of the Sun: A History of the Ritual Year in Britain* (Oxford: Oxford University Press, 1996), 155–6.

FURTHER READINGS

Alexander, John K. "Poverty, Fear, and Continuity: An Analysis of the Poor in Late Eighteenth-Century Philadelphia." In *Peoples of Philadelphia, 1790–1940: A History of Ethnic Groups and Lower Class Life*, edited by Allen F. Davis and Mark H. Haller, 13–37. Philadelphia: Temple University Press, 1973.

Allen, Robert C. *Global Economic History: A Very Short Introduction*. Oxford: Oxford University Press, 2011.

Alvarez-Nogal, Carlos, and Leandro Prados de La Escosura. "The Rise and Fall of Spain (1270–1850)." *The Economic History Review* 66, no. 1 (2013): 1–37.

Archer, John E. *Social Unrest and Popular Protest in England, 1780–1840*. Cambridge: Cambridge University Press, 2000.

Arranz Herrero, Manuel, and Ramon Grau Fernandez. "Problemas de inmigración y asimilación en la Barcelona del siglo XVIII." *Revista de Geografia* 4 (1970): 71–80.

Arru, Angiolina, Franco Ramella, and Joseph Ehmer, eds *Migrazioni*, Issue of *Quaderni storici* 106 (2001).

Arru, Angiolina. "Reti locali, reti globali: il credito degli immigrati (secoli XVII–XIX)." In *L'Italia delle migrazioni interne: Donne, uomini, mobilità in età moderna e contemporanea*, edited by Angiolina Arru and Franco Ramella, 77–110. Rome: Donzelli editore, 2003.

Ashton, Thomas S. *The Industrial Revolution, 1760–1830*. Oxford: Oxford University Press, 1948.

Ashworth, William J. *Customs and Excise: Trade, Production, and Consumption in England, 1640–1845*. Oxford: Oxford University Press, 2003.

Barker, Elizabeth E., and Alex Kidson. *Joseph Wright of Derby in Liverpool*. New Haven, CT: Yale University Press, 2007.

Baudino, Isabelle, et al. *Aspects of Women's Work in Eighteenth-century Britain*. Aldershot: Ashgate, 2005.

Bayer, Andrea, ed. *Painters of Reality: The Legacy of Leonardo and Caravaggio in Lombardy*. New Haven, CT: Yale University Press; New York: Metropolitan Museum of Art, 2004.

Beckles, Hilary McD. *White Servitude and Black Slavery in Barbados, 1627–1715*. Knoxville: University of Tennessee Press, 1989.

Berg, Maxine. "Small Producer Capitalism in Eighteenth Century Britain." *Business History* 35, no. 1 (1993): 17–39.

Berg, Maxine. "What Difference did Women's Work Make to the Industrial Revolution?" *History Workshop Journal* 35 (1993): 22–44.

Berg, Maxine, Pat Hudson, and Michael Sonenscher, eds *Manufacture in Town and Country before the Factory*. Cambridge: Cambridge University Press, 1983.

Berg, Maxine. *The Age of Manufactures*. London: Fontana Press, 1985.

Berlin, Ira. *Many Thousands Gone: The First Two Centuries of Slavery in North America*. Cambridge, MA: Harvard University Press, 1998.

Berlin, Ira, and Philip D. Morgan, eds *Cultivation and Culture: Labor and the Shaping of Slave Life in the Americas*. Charlottesville: University Press of Virginia, 1993.

Biernacki, Richard. *The Fabrication of Labor: Germany and Britain, 1640–1914*. Berkeley: University of California Press, 1995.

Birley, Derek. *A Social History of English Cricket*. London: Aurum, 1999.

Blum, Jerome. *The End of the Old Order in Rural Europe*. Princeton, NJ: Princeton University Press, 1978.

Bolster, W. Jeffrey. *Black Jacks: African American Seamen in the Age of Sail*. Cambridge, MA: Harvard University Press, 1998.

Borsay, Peter, and Jan Hein Furnee. *Leisure Cultures in Urban Europe, c.1700–1870: A Transnational Perspective*. Manchester: Manchester University Press, 2015.

Bossenga, Gail. "La Révolution française et les corporations: Trois exemples lillois." *Annales ESC* 43, no. 2 (1988): 405–26.

Bossenga, Gail. "Protecting Merchants. Guilds and Commercial Capitalism." *French Historical Studies* 15, no. 4 (1989): 693–703.

Bossenga, Gail. "Capitalism and Corporations in Eighteenth-Century France." In *Naissance des libertés économiques*, edited by Alain Plessis, 13–31. Paris: Institut d'histoire de l'industrie, 1993.

Boulton, Jeremy. *Neighbourhood and Society: A London Suburb in the Seventeenth Century*. Cambridge: Cambridge University Press, 1987.

Breen, Timothy H. *Marketplace of Revolution: How Consumer Politics Shaped American Independence*. Oxford: Oxford University Press, 2004.

Brierley, Benjamin. *Home Memories: The Autobiography of a Handloom Weaver*. Manchester: A. Heywood & son, 1886; repr. Bramhall, 2002.

Brown, Christopher. *Scenes of Everyday Life: Dutch Genre Painting of the Seventeenth Century*. London: Faber and Faber, 1984.

Brown, Kathleen. *Good Wives, Nasty Wenches, and Anxious Patriarchs: Gender, Race, and Power in Colonial Virginia*. Chapel Hill: University of North Carolina Press, 1996.

Brunsman, Denver. *The Evil Necessity: British Naval Impressment in the Eighteenth-Century Atlantic World*. Charlottesville: University of Virginia Press, 2013.

Burke, Peter. *Popular Culture in Early Modern Europe*. London: T. Smith, 1978.

Burnard, Trevor. *Planters, Merchants, and Slaves: Plantation Societies in British America, 1650–1820*. Chicago: University of Chicago Press, 2015.

Calladine, George. *The Diary of Colour-Serjeant George Calladine*. London: E. Fisher & Co., 1922.

Canepari, Eleonora. "Who Is Not Welcome? Reception and Rejection of Migrant in Early Modern Italian Cities." In *Gated Communities? Regulating Migration in Early Modern Cities*, edited by Bert De Munck and Anne Winter, 101–16. London: Routledge, 2016.

Canepari, Eleonora. "Keeping in Touch: Migrant Workers' Translocal Ties in Early Modern Italy." In *Micro-Spatial Histories of Global Labour*, edited by Christian De Vito and Anne Gerritsen. London: Palgrave Macmillan, 2018, 203–22.

Canepari, Eleonora, and Beatrice Zucca Micheletto. *Le travail comme ressource*. Issue of *Mélanges de l'École française de Rome – Italie, Méditerranée* 123 (2011).

Cangany, Catherine. *Frontier Seaport: Detroit's Transformation into an Atlantic Entrepôt*. Chicago: University of Chicago Press, 2014.

Carbonnel-Esteller, Montserrat. "Using Microcredit and Restructuring Households: Two Complementary Survival Strategies in Late Eighteenth-Century Barcelona." *International Review of Social History* 45, no. 8 (2000): 71–92.

Carlin, Norah. "Liberty and Fraternities in the English Revolution: The Politics of London Artisans' Protests, 1635–1659." *International Review of Social History* 39 no. 2 (1994): 223–54.

Carr, Lois Green. "Emigration and the Standard of Living: The Seventeenth Century Chesapeake." *Journal of Economic History* 52, no. 2 (1992): 271–91.

Carr, Lois Green, and Lorena S. Walsh. "Economic Diversification and Labor Organization in the Chesapeake, 1650–1820." In *Work and Labor in Early America*, edited by Stephen Innes, 144–88. Chapel Hill: University of North Carolina Press, 1988.

Cerutti, Simona, Robert Descimon, and Maarten Prak, eds *Cittadinanze*. Issue of *Quaderni storici* 89 (1995).

Cerutti, Simona. "Travail, mobilité et légitimité: Suppliques au roi dans une sociéte d'Ancien Régime (Turin, XVIIIe siècle)." *Annales. Histoire, Sciences Sociales* 65, no. 3 (2010): 571–611.

Cerutti, Simona. *Étrangers. Étude d'une condition d'incertitude dans une société d'Ancien Régime*. Paris: Fayard, 2012.

Chartres, J. A. "The Marketing of Agricultural Produce, 1640–1750." In *Agricultural History of England and Wales: Volume 4*, edited by Joan Thirsk. Cambridge: Cambridge University Press, 1964.

Chojnacka, Monica. *Working Women of Early Modern Venice*. Baltimore: Johns Hopkins University Press, 2001.

Clark, Gregory, and Ysbrand van der Werf. "Work in Progress? The Industrious Revolution." *Journal of Economic History* 58 (1998): 830–43.

Cole, William. *The Blecheley Diary of the Rev. William Cole, 1765-1767, edited by Francis Griffin Stokes, with an introduction by Helen Waddell*. London: Constable, 1931.

Cray, Robert E., Jr. *Paupers and Poor Relief in New York City and its Rural Environs, 1700–1830*. Philadelphia: Temple University Press, 1988.

Crossick, Geoffrey, ed. *The Artisan and the European Town, 1500–1900*. Aldershot: Scolar Press, 1997.

Crowston, Clare Haru. *Fabricating Women: The Seamstresses of Old Regime France, 1765–1791*. Durham, NC: Duke University Press, 2001.

Cuillier, Jeanne. "Mobility and the Social Organization of Urban Space in the United States, 1760–1820." *International Journal of Urban and Regional Research* 2 (1978): 270–86.

Cunningham, Hugh. "The Employment and Unemployment of Children in England c. 1680–1851." *Past & Present* 126 (1990): 115–50.

Cunningham, Hugh. *Time, Work and Leisure: Life Changes in England Since 1700*. Manchester: Manchester University Press, 2014.

Darnton, Robert. *The Literary Underground of the Old Regime*. Cambridge, MA: Harvard University Press, 1982.

Darnton, Robert. *The Great Cat Massacre and Other Episodes in French Cultural History*. New York: Vintage, 1984.

Davis, David Brion. *The Problem of Slavery in the Age of Revolution*. Ithaca, NY: Cornell University Press, 1975.

De Munck, Bert. "Corpses, Live Models, and Nature. Assessing Skills and Knowledge before the Industrial Revolution (case: Antwerp)." *Technology and Culture* 51, no. 2 (2010): 332–56.

De Munck, Bert. "Artisans, Products and Gifts: Rethinking the History of Material Culture in Early Modern Europe." *Past & Present* 224 (2014): 39–74.

De Vries, Jan. "Between Purchasing Power and the World of Goods: Understanding the Household Economy in Early Modern Europe." In *Consumption and the World of Goods*, edited by John Brewer and Roy Porter, 85–132. London: Routledge, 1993.

De Vries, Jan. "The Industrial Revolution and the Industrious Revolution." *The Journal of Economic History* 54, no. 2 (1994): 249–70.

De Vries, Jan. *The Industrious Revolution: Consumer Behavior and the Household Economy, 1650 to the Present.* Cambridge: Cambridge University Press, 2008.

Dubois, Laurent. *A Colony of Citizens: Revolution and Slave Emancipation in the French Caribbean, 1787–1804.* Chapel Hill: University of North Carolina Press, 2004.

Dunn, Richard. *A Tale of Two Plantations: Slave Life and Labor in Jamaica and Virginia.* Cambridge, MA: Harvard University Press, 2014.

Edelson, S. Max. *Plantation Enterprise in Colonial South Carolina.* Cambridge, MA: Harvard University Press, 2006.

Ehmer, Josef, and Catharina Lis, eds *The Idea of Work in Europe from Antiquity to Modern Times.* Aldershot: Ashgate, 2009.

Epstein, Stephan R., and Maarten Prak, eds *Guilds, Innovation, and the European Economy, 1400–1800.* Cambridge: Cambridge University Press, 2008.

Erickson, Amy. "Married Women's Occupations in Eighteenth-Century London." *Continuity and Change* 23, no. 2 (2008): 267–307.

Farge, Arlette. *Vivre dans la rue à Paris au XVIIIe siècle.* Paris: Gallimard-Julliard, 1979.

Farr, James R. *Hands of Honor: Artisans and their World in Dijon, 1550–1650.* Ithaca, NY: Cornell University Press, 1988.

Farr, James R. *Artisans in Europe, 1300–1914.* Cambridge: Cambridge University Press, 2000.

Fitzsimmons, Michael P. *From Artisan to Worker: Guilds, the French State, and the Organisation of Labor, 1776–1821.* Cambridge: Cambridge University Press, 2010.

Floud, Roderick, and Paul Johnson, eds *The Cambridge Economic History of Modern Britain*, vol. 1, *Industrialisation, 1700–1860.* Cambridge: Cambridge University Press, 2004.

Fontaine, Laurence, and Jürgen Schlumbohm. "Household Strategies for Survival: An Introduction." In *Household Strategies for Survival 1600–2000: Fission, Faction and Cooperation*, edited by Laurence Fontaine and Jürgen Schlumbohm, 1–18. International Review of Social History, Supplement 8. Cambridge: Cambridge University Press, 2000.

Fontaine, Laurence. *History of Pedlars in Europe*, translated by. Vicki Whittaker. Durham, NC: Duke University Press, 2012.

Fontaine, Laurence. *Le marché: Histoire et usages d'une conquête sociale.* Paris: Gallimard, 2013.

Fox, Celina. *The Arts of Industry in the Age of Enlightenment.* New Haven, CT: Yale University Press, 2009.

Fox-Genovese, Elizabeth. "Women and Work." In *French Women and the Age of Enlightenment*, edited by Samia L. Spencer, 111–27. Bloomington: Indiana University Press, 1984.

Fox-Genovese, Elizabeth. *The Origins of Physiocracy: Economic Revolution and Social Order in Eighteenth-Century France.* Ithaca, NY: Cornell University, 1976.

Glennie, Paul, and Nigel Thrift. *Shaping the Day: A History of Timekeeping in England and Wales 1300–1800.* Oxford: Oxford University Press, 2009.

Grenier, Jean-Yves. *L'économie d'Ancien Régime: Un monde de l'échange et de l'incertitude.* Paris: Albin Michel, 1996.

Grießinger, Andreas. *Das symbolische Kapital der Ehre: Streikbewegungen und kollektives Bewusstsein deutscher Handwerksgesellen im 18. Jahrhundert.* Frankfurt: Ullstein, 1981.

Griffin, Emma. *England's Revelry: A History of Popular Sports and Pastimes, 1660–1800.* Oxford: Oxford University Press, 2005.

Griffin, Emma. *Liberty's Dawn: A People's History of the Industrial Revolution.* New Haven, CT: Yale University Press, 2013.

Griffin, Emma. "'Wholesome Recreations and Cheering Influences': Popular Recreation and Social Elites in Eighteenth-century Britain." In *British Sporting Culture: The Literature and Culture of Sport in the Long Eighteenth Century*, edited by Sharon Harrow and Peter Radford, 19–34. Burlington: Ashgate, 2015.

Guenzi, Alberto, Paola Massa, and Fausto Piola Caselli, eds *Guilds, Markets and Work Regulations in Italy, 16th–19th Centuries*. Aldershot: Ashgate, 1998.

Gullickson, Gay. "The Sexual Division of Labor in Cottage Industry and Agriculture in the Pays de Caux 1750–1850." *French Historical Studies* 12 (1981): 177–99.

Hafter, Daryl M., ed. *European Women and Pre-Industrial Craft*. Bloomington: Indiana University Press, 1995.

Hafter, Daryl M. *Women at Work in Pre-Industrial France*. University Park: Pennsylvania State University Press, 2012.

Hafter, Daryl M., and Nina Kushner, eds *Women and Work in Eighteenth-Century France*. Baton Rouge: Louisiana State University Press, 2015.

Hardwick, Julie. *Practice of Patriarchy: Gender and the Politics of Household Authority in Early Modern France*. University Park: Pennsylvania State University Press, 1998.

Hardwick, Julie. *Family Business: Litigation and the Political Economies of Daily Life in Early Modern France*. New York: Oxford University Press, 2009.

Hart, Emma. "Charleston and the British Industrial Revolution." In *Global Perspectives on the Industrial Transformation in the American South*, edited by Susanna Delfino and Michele Gillespie, 26–49. Columbia: University of Missouri Press, 2005.

Hart, Emma. "From Field to Plate, The Early Modern Livestock Trade and the Development of an American Economic Culture." *William and Mary Quarterly* 73 (2016): 107–40.

Hatcher, John. "Labour, Leisure and Economic Thought before the Nineteenth Century." *Past & Present* 160 (1998): 64–115.

Heuvel, Danielle van den. "Policing Peddlers: The Prosecution of Illegal Street Trade in Eighteenth-century Dutch Towns." *The Historical Journal* 58, no. 2 (2015): 367–92.

Heuvel, Danielle van den, and Elise van Nederveen Meerkerk. "Introduction: Partners in Business? Spousal Cooperation in Trades in Early Modern England and the Dutch Republic." *Continuity and Change* 23, no. 2 (2008): 209–16.

Hoffmann, Philip R. "In Defense of Corporate Liberties: Early Modern Guilds and the Problem of Illicit Artisan Work." *Urban History* 34, no. 1 (2007): 76–88.

Hudson Pat, and W. Robert Lee. *Women's Work and the Family Economy in Historical Perspective*. Manchester: Manchester University Press, 1990.

Hufton, Olwen. *The Prospect Before Her: A History of Women in Western Europe*. New York: Knopf, 1995.

Humphries, Jane, and Benjamin Schneider. "Spinning the Industrial Revolution." *Economic History Review* (forthcoming) DOI: 10.1111/ehr.12693.

Humphries, Jane, and Carmen Sarasua. "Off the Record: Reconstructing Women's Labor Force Participation in the European Past." *Feminist Economics* 18, no. 4 (2012): 39–67.

Hunt, Lynn, and George Sheridan. "Corporatism, Association, and the Language of Labor in France, 1750–1850." *Journal of Modern History* 58 (1986): 813–44.

Hutton, Ronald. *The Rise and Fall of Merry England: The Ritual Year, 1400–1700*. Oxford: Oxford University Press, 1994.

Hutton, Ronald, *The Stations of the Sun: A History of the Ritual Year in Britain*. Oxford: Oxford University Press, 1996.

Innes, Stephen, ed. *Work and Labor in Early America*. Chapel Hill: University of North Carolina Press, 1988.

Jacques-Louis Ménétra, compagnon vitrier au XVIIIe siècle. Journal de ma vie, ed. Daniel Roche. Paris: Albin Michel, 1998.

Jones, Peter M. *Agricultural Enlightenment: Knowledge, Technology, and Nature, 1750–1840*. Oxford: Oxford University Press, 2016.

Joyce, Patrick, ed. *The Historical Meanings of Work*. Cambridge: Cambridge University Press, 1987.

Kaplan, Steven L. "Réflexions sur la police du monde du travail, 1700–1815." *Revue historique* 261, no. 1 (1979): 17–77.

Kaplan, Steven L. "Les corporations, les 'faux-ouvriers' et le faubourg St. Antoine au XVIIIe siècle." *Annales ESC* 43, no. 2 (1988): 353–78.

Kaplan, Steven L. *La fin des corporations*. Paris: Fayard, 2001.

Kaplan, Steven L., and Cynthia Koepp, eds *Work in France: Representations, Meaning, Organization, and Practice*. Ithaca, NY: Cornell University Press, 1986.

Kirby, Peter. "How Many Children Were 'Unemployed' in Eighteenth- and Nineteenth-century England?" *Past & Present* 187, no. 1 (2005): 187–202.

Klingender, Francis D. *Art and the Industrial Revolution*, edited and revised by Arthur Elton. Chatham: Evelyn, Adams and Mackay, 1968. First published 1947 by Noel Carrington (London).

Klüge, Arnd. *Die Zünfte*. Stuttgart: Franz Steiner Verlag, 2009.

Kolchin, Peter. *American Slavery, 1619–1877*. New York: Hill & Wang, 2003.

Kriedte, Peter, Hans Medick, and Jurgen Schlumbohm, *Industrialization Before Industrialization*. Cambridge: Cambridge University Press, 1982.

Kriz, Kay Dian. *Slavery, Sugar, and the Culture of Refinement: Picturing the British West Indies 1700–1840*. New Haven, CT: Yale University Press, 2008.

Lanza, Janine. *From Wives to Widows in Early Modern Paris: Gender, Economy and Law*. Aldershot: Ashgate, 2007.

Levine, David, and Keith Wrightson. *The Making of an Industrial Society: Whickham, 1560–1765*. Oxford: Clarendon Press, 1991.

Lis, Catharina, and Hugo Soly. *Worthy Efforts: Attitudes to Work and Workers in Pre-Industrial Europe*. Leiden: Brill, 2012.

Lis, Catharina, Jan Lucassen, and Hugo Soly, eds *Before the Unions: Wage Earners and Collective Action in Europe, 1300–1850*. International Review of Social History, Supplement 2. Cambridge: Cambridge University Press, 1994.

Lis, Catharina. *Social Change and the Labouring Poor: Antwerp, 1700–1860*. New Haven, CT: Yale University Press, 1986.

Lucassen, Jan, and Leo Lucassen, eds *Migration, Migration History, History. Old Paradigms and New Perspectives*. Berne: Peter Lang, 1999.

Lucassen, Jan, and Leo Lucassen. "The Mobility Transition Revisited, 1500–1900: What the Case of Europe Can Offer to Global History." *Journal of Global History* 4, no. 3 (2009): 347–77.

Lucassen, Jan, Tine De Moor, and Jan Luiten van Zanden, eds *The Return of the Guilds*. International Review of Social History, Supplement 16. Cambridge: Cambridge University Press, 2009.

Lucassen, Jan. "The Other Proletarians: Seasonal Labourers, Mercenaries and Miners." *International Review of Social History* 39, Supplement (1994) 171–94.

Maitte, Corine, *Les Chemins de verre: Les migrations des verriers d'Altare et de Venise (XVIe-XIXe siècles)*. Rennes: Presses universitaires de Rennes, 2009.

Maitte, Corine, and Didier Terrier, eds *Les Temps du travail: Normes, pratiques, évolutions (XIVe-XIXe siècle)*. Rennes: Presses universitaires de Rennes, 2014.

Malcolmson, Robert W. *Popular Recreations in English Society, 1700–1850*. Cambridge: Cambridge University Press, 1973.

Mason, Matthew. "Slavery, Servitude and British Representations of Colonial North America." *Southern Quarterly* 43, no. 4 (2006): 109–25.

Maynes, Mary Jo, Birgitte Søland, and Christina Benninghaus, eds *Secret Gardens, Satanic Mills: Placing Girls in European History, 1750–1960*. Bloomington: Indiana University Press, 2005.

Mendels, Franklin F. "Proto-Industrialization: The First Phase of the Industrialization Process." *The Journal of Economic History* 32, no. 1 (1972): 241–61.

Milliot, Vincent. *Les cris de Paris ou le peuple travesti: Les représentations des petits métiers parisiens (XVIe-XVIIIe siècle)*. Paris: Sorbonne, 2014 [1995].

Mokyr, Joel. *The Lever of Riches: Technological Creativity and Economic Progress*. New York: Oxford University Press, 1990.

Mokyr, Joel. *The Gifts of Athena: Historical Origins of the Knowledge Economy*. Princeton, NJ: Princeton University Press, 2002.

Mokyr, Joel. *The Enlightened Economy: An Economic History of Britain, 1700–1850*. New Haven, CT: Yale University Press, 2009.

Muldrew, Craig. "'Th' ancient Distaff' and 'Whirling Spindle': Measuring the Contribution of Spinning to Household Earnings and the National Economy in England, 1550–1770." *The Economic History Review* 65 (2012): 498–526.

Norberg, Kathryn. *Rich and Poor in Grenoble, 1600–1814*. Berkeley: University of California Press, 1985.

O'Day, Rosemary. *The Professions in Early Modern England: Servants of the Commonweal*. London: Longman, 2000.

O'Day, Rosemary. *Women's Agency in Early Modern Britain and the American Colonies*. London: Longman, 2007.

Ogilvie, Sheilagh. *State Corporatism and Proto-Industry: The Württemberg Black Forest, 1580–1797*. Cambridge: Cambridge University Press, 1997.

Ogilvie, Sheilagh. *A Bitter Living: Women, Markets, and Social Capital in Early Modern Germany*. Oxford: Oxford University Press, 2003.

Ogilvie, Sheilagh. "The Economics of Guilds." *Journal of Economic Perspectives* 28 (2014): 169–92.

Ogilvie, Sheilagh, and Markus Cerman, eds *European Proto-Industrialization*. Cambridge: Cambridge University Press, 1996.

Overton, Mark. "Re-establishing the English Agricultural Revolution." *Agricultural History Review* 44, no. 1 (1996): 1–20.

Pollard, Sidney. *The Genesis of Modern Management: A Study of the Industrial Revolution in Great Britain*. Cambridge, MA: Harvard University Press, 1965.

Prak, Maarten, et al., eds *Craft Guilds in the Early Modern Low Countries. Work, Power and Representation*. Aldershot: Ashgate, 2006.

Roberts, Justin. *Slavery and the Enlightenment in the British Atlantic, 1750–1807*. New York: Cambridge University Press, 2013.

Roberts, Lissa, Simon Schaffer, and Peter Dear, eds *The Mindful Hand: Inquiry and Invention from the late Renaissance to Early Industrialisation*. Amsterdam: KNAW, 2007.

Roche, Daniel. *Le peuple de Paris*. Paris: Fayard, 1998.

Rock, Howard B., Paul A. Gilje, and Robert Asher, eds *American Artisans: Crafting a Social Identity, 1750–1850*. Baltimore: Johns Hopkins University Press, 1995.

Roediger, David, and Philip Foner. *Our Own Time: A History of American Labor and the Working Day*. New York: Verso, 1989.

Rosenband, Leonard N. "The Industrious Revolution: A Concept Too Many?" *International Labor and Working Class History* 90 (2016): 213–43.

Rosenband, Leonard N. *Papermaking in Eighteenth-Century France: Management, Labor, and Revolution at the Montgolfier Mill, 1761–1805*. Baltimore: Johns Hopkins University Press, 2000.

Rule, John, ed. *British Trade Unionism, 1750-1850: The Formative Years*. New York: Longman, 1988.

Rule, John. *The Experience of Labour in Eighteenth-Century English Industry*. New York: St. Martin's Press, 1981.

Safley, Thomas Max, and Leonard N. Rosenband, eds *The Workplace before the Factory: Artisans and Proletarians, 1500–1800*. Ithaca, NY: Cornell University Press, 1993.

Sarasúa, Carmen. "The Role of the State in Shaping Women's and Men's Entrance into the Labour Market. Spain, 18th and 19th Centuries." *Continuity and Change* 12, no. 3 (1997): 347–71.

Sarasúa, Carmen. "Technical Innovations at the Service of Cheaper Labour in Pre-Industrial Europe: The Enlightened Agenda to Transform the Gender Division of Labour in Silk Manufacturing." *History and Technology* 24, no. 1 (2008): 23–39.

Sarti, Raffaella. "Historians, Social Scientists, Servants, and Domestic Workers: Fifty Years of Research on Domestic and Care Work." *International Review of Social History* 59 (2014): 279–314.

Schlumbohm, Jürgen. "Labour in Proto-Industrialization: Big-Questions and Micro-Answers." In *Early Modern Capitalism: Economic and Social Change in Europe, 1400–1800*, edited by Maarten Prak, 123–32. London: Routledge, 2001.

Schmidt, Ariadne, and Elise van Nederveen Meerkeek. "Reconsidering The 'First Male-Breadwinner Economy': Women's Labor Force Participation in the Netherlands, 1600–1900." *Feminist Economics* 18, no. 4 (2012): 69–96.

Scholliers, Peter, and Leonard Schwarz. *Experiencing Wages: Social and Cultural Aspects of Wage Forms in Europe since 1500*. New York: Berghahn Books, 2004.

Schwarz, Leonard. "Custom, Wages and Workload in England during Industrialization." *Past & Present* 197, no. 1 (2007): 143–75.

Sewell, William. *Work and Revolution in France: The Language of Labor from the Old Regime to 1848*. Cambridge: Cambridge University Press, 1980.

Sharpe, Pamela. *Women, Gender, and Labour Migration: Historical and Global Perspectives*. London: Routledge, 2001.

Sheridan, Geraldine. *Louder than Words: Ways of Seeing Women Workers in Eighteenth-century France*. Lubbock: Texas Tech University Press, 2009.

Simon, Christian. "Labour Relations at Manufactures in the Eighteenth Century: The Calico Printers in Europe." *International Review of Social History* 39, supplement (1994): 115–44.

Simonton, Deborah. *A History of European Women's Work, 1700 to the Present*. London: Routledge, 1998.

Simonton, Deborah, "'Birds of Passage' or 'Career' Women? Thoughts on the Life Cycle of the Eighteenth-Century European Servant." *Women's History Review* 20, no. 2 (2011): 207–25.

Simonton, Deborah, and Anne Montenach, eds *Female Agency in the Urban Economy: Gender in European Towns, 1640–1830*. New York: Routledge, 2013.

Smail, John. "Manufacturer or Artisan? The Relationship between Economic and Cultural Change in the Early Stages of the Eighteenth-Century Industrialization." *Journal of Social History* 25, no. 4 (1992): 791–814.

Sonenscher, Michael. "Les sans-culottes de l'An II: Repenser le langage du travail dans la France révolutionnaire." *Annales ESC* 40, no. 5 (1985): 1087–108.

Sonenscher, Michael. *The Hatters of Eighteenth-Century France*. Berkeley: University of California Press, 1987.

Sonenscher, Michael. *Work and Wages: Natural Law, Politics and the Eighteenth century French Trades*. Cambridge: Cambridge University Press, 1989.

Sutton, William. *Journeymen for Jesus*. University Park: Pennsylvania State University, 1998.

Taylor, Leigh Shaw. "The Rise of Agrarian Capitalism and the Decline of Family Farming in England." *The Economic History Review* 65, no. 1 (2012): 26–60.

Thomas, Keith, ed. *The Oxford Book of Work*. Oxford: Oxford University Press, 1999.

Thompson, Edward P. *The Making of the English Working Class*. London: Victor Gollancz Ltd, 1963.

Thompson, Edward P. "Time, Work-Discipline and Industrial Capitalism." *Past & Present* 38 (1967): 59–97.

Thompson, Edward P. *Customs in Common: Studies in Traditional Popular Culture*. New York: New Press, 1991.

Tilly, Louise, and Joan Scott. *Women, Work, and Family*. London: Routledge, 1987.

Truant, Cynthia M. *The Rites of Labour: Brotherhoods of Compagnonnage in Old and New Regime France*. Ithaca, NY: Cornell University Press, 1994.

Underdown, David. *Start of Play: Cricket and Culture in Eighteenth-century Britain*. Harmondsworth: Penguin Books, 2000.

Vicente, Marta V. "Crafting the Industrial Revolution: Artisan Families and the Calico Industry in Eighteenth-century Spain." In *Reconceptualizing the Industrial Revolution*, edited by Jeff Horn, Leonard N. Rosenband, and Merritt Roe Smith, 151–68. Cambridge, MA: MIT Press, 2010.

Vickers, Daniel, and Vince Walsh. *Young Men and the Sea: Yankee Seafarers in the Age of Sail*. New Haven, CT: Yale University Press, 2005.

Voth, Hans-Joachim. "Time and Work in Eighteenth-century London." *Journal of Economic History* 58 (1998): 29–58.

Voth, Hans-Joachim. *Time and Work in England 1750–1830*. Oxford: Oxford University Press, 2000.

Wallis, Patrick. "Labour, Law and Training in Early Modern London: Apprenticeship and the City's Institutions." *London School of Economics, Working Papers* 11, no. 154 (2011): 1–38.

Walsh, John. "'The Bane of Industry'? Popular Evangelicalism and Work in the Eighteenth Century." In *The Use and Abuse of Time in Christian History*, edited by Robert Swanson, 223–41. Rochester, NY: Boydell Press, 2002.

Ward, William R. *Early Evangelicalism: A Global Intellectual History, 1670–1789*. Cambridge: Cambridge University Press, 2006.

Waterfield, Giles, and Anne French. *Below Stairs: 400 Years of Servants' Portraits*. London: National Portrait Gallery, 2004.

Weisner, Merry. "Having Her Own Smoke: Employment and Independence for Singlewomen in Germany, 1400–1750." In *Singlewomen in the European Past, 1250–1800*, edited by Judith Bennett and Amy Froide, 192–216. Philadelphia: University of Pennsylvania Press, 1999.

Woodward, Donald. *Men at Work: Labourers and Building Craftsmen in the Towns of Northern England, 1450–1750*. Cambridge: Cambridge University Press, 1995.

Wrightson, Keith. *Earthly Necessities: Economic Lives in Early Modern Britain*. New Haven, CT: Yale University Press, 2000.

Zucca Micheletto, Beatrice. "Reconsidering Women's Labor Force Participation Rates in Eighteenth-century Turin." *Feminist Economics* 19, no. 4 (2013): 200–23.

INDEX

Note: Page references with letter "n" followed by locators denote note numbers.

abbé Pluche 165
abolition of the guilds. *See* guilds; abolition
agriculture 2, 4–6, 19–20, 107, 132, 138, 145, 148
   commercialization 62–4, 70, 73–4, 91
   images 51–2
   labor 21, 29, 34, 36, 124, 171–6
   seasons 27, 148, 182
allegory 40, 42
alloué 80, 104, 161
Americas 4, 6, 56, 64, 70, 74, 88, 102, 148, 158
   American cities 118, 156, 162, 169
   American colonies 8, 20, 62, 66, 89, 135–6, 139, 146, 174
   American Revolution 1, 72, 133, 144, 156
   immigrants 14, 63, 73, 158, 172
apprentices 117–19, 121, 126, 171, 173
   conflict 81, 82, 86, 88, 96, 104, 154 (*see also* employer–employee relations)
   demand for 157, 158
   and household 65, 97, 124–5, 136, 154, 176
   imagery 14, 44, 51, 58–9, 133
apprenticeship
   critique 3, 8, 161, 167
   decline and abolition 82–3, 105–6, 126
   system 80, 83, 97, 104, 109, 116, 148, 158–9, 161
   training 13, 97, 110
artisans 8, 12, 16, 29, 75, 82–3, 93
   artisanal values 23, 66, 78–81, 91
   trades 6, 47, 64–6, 81, 86

Bentham, Samuel 107, 108, 109, 110
Birmingham 12, 65, 66
Black Forest, The 64, 158, 177
blacksmiths 40, 49–53, 55, 98, 163
body politic 156, 159, 160–1
Boulton, Matthew 12, 65, 66, 75, 110
boxing 178, 179–80, 182, 183
brickmakers 116, 124

Britain 6, 45, 70, 72, 82, 99, 131, 132, 136, 139, 144–5
   agriculture 4–5, 132, 138, 169
   England 10, 12, 17, 48, 55, 56, 63, 66, 88, 101, 125, 139, 153
   guilds 6, 157, 161
   industry 36, 79, 95, 106, 110, 172, 173, 174–5, 182
   leisure 177–9, 181, 182
   religion 146–7
   Scotland 4, 17, 20, 146, 157
   urbanization 4, 5, 21, 62, 67, 158
brotherhood 104, 160

Caribbean, The 4, 45, 62, 73, 74, 92
carnivals 180, 181, 182
casual labor 13, 118, 128, 171
charity 23, 26, 45, 59, 80, 86, 135, 147, 152, 177
   schools 17, 144, 145
Charleston 63, 69, 73
Chesapeake, The 73, 74, 91, 146, 172
chiaroscuro 41, 47, 48, 49, 61
children 17, 20, 32, 106, 133, 177, 180
   child labor 13, 24, 34, 36, 39, 59, 74, 145, 153, 175–6
   and family 9, 10, 20, 72, 86, 104, 133, 136
   as family labor 24, 33, 62, 105
   imagery 40, 42–3, 44–5, 47, 48–9, 54–5
   industrious revolution 15–16, 23, 101, 145
cities 4, 62
   American 156, 162
   European 19, 21, 22, 63, 68
   growth 5–6, 21, 35, 67, 84, 169
   leisure 178, 183
   mobility 25, 32, 36, 85, 113–29
   poor 33, 37, 145
   work 27, 80, 84, 99, 110, 136, 152, 156–62, 167
class struggle 152, 167
clothing 25, 34, 45, 53, 89, 146, 170, 191 n.40
clothworking 13, 33, 45, 64, 66

cohabitation 113, 124, 125, 126, 129
collective
   identity 83, 151, 157
   repertoires 96, 105, 152, 156
   strategies 159, 160, 161
colonies 6, 20, 22, 24, 26, 36, 62, 63, 66, 88–92, 145, 152. *See also specific countries*
   colonial trade 21, 87, 88
   colonization 4–5, 19, 29, 32, 72–3
compagnonnages 98, 104, 159
concentrated production 9, 93, 98, 107–10, 153
consumption 5, 99, 131–3, 136, 139, 149, 169, 170, 174
   consumer goods 15–16, 24–5, 32, 34, 82, 101
   consumer revolution 15, 22, 26
   consumerism 4, 22, 23, 65–7, 72, 74, 83, 105, 139, 141, 144, 147
corporations 6, 12, 80, 97, 119, 152, 158–61
   corporatist ideals 104–6, 154, 156, 167
cottage industry. *See* domestic industry; proto-industry
craft guilds. *See* guilds
custom 13, 37, 71, 89, 98, 102, 104, 107–10, 132, 147
customary rights 62, 135, 144, 153
   spaces 67, 69
customs 23, 91, 96, 153, 156, 160, 176, 177, 181, 182

d'Alembert, Jean le Rond 1, 29, 106, 165
Detroit 71, 72
Diderot, Denis 1, 29, 46, 55, 106, 165
dishonor. *See* honor
domestic industry 8, 13, 14, 17, 23, 26, 105, 158, 172–4, 176, 177. *See also* proto-industry
domestic servants 5, 9, 27–8, 34, 42, 53, 55, 69, 77, 116, 118, 125, 136, 154, 172. *See also* indentured labor

education 2, 17, 31, 37, 42, 43, 144, 147
egalitarianism 24, 31, 59, 162
employers 6, 55, 66, 80, 82, 84, 88, 102, 117, 123–4, 153–6, 175, 181
   employer–employee relations 12, 77, 79, 82, 87, 93, 131, 145, 148, 165, 172–3, 183
Encyclopaedia Britannica 1, 102
Encyclopédie 1, 3, 6, 58, 165
   impact 29, 39, 46–8, 106–7

Engels, Friedrich 170, 172, 173
Enlightenment 1–2, 29, 61–2, 64, 72, 149
   enlightened ideas 8, 29, 37, 42, 99, 144, 146
   individuals 26, 47, 48, 97, 139, 148, 152, 160, 167
   and work 2–3, 12, 18, 31–3, 46, 73–5, 99, 106–7, 131, 146, 147
Equiano, Olaudah 72

fairs 69, 148, 180–1
farming 5, 10, 19, 21, 24, 62–4, 69, 172
feminism 1, 3, 31, 42
food riots 37, 145, 153–4, 157
   Esquilache Riots, Spain 145
France 3, 15, 21, 33, 79, 92, 97, 101, 132
   agriculture 5, 165
   art and artists 42, 53, 56
   Enlightenment 2, 138–40, 161 (*see also* physiocracy)
   guilds 3, 12, 85, 97, 105–6, 156, 157–60
   manufacturing 9–10, 27, 32, 64, 66, 169, 176
Franklin, Benjamin 1, 14, 17–18, 63, 96, 104, 133
French Revolution 6, 37, 91–2, 96, 97, 105, 144, 151
friendship and mutual aid 97, 159, 160

gender. *See also* masculinity; women
   division of labor 9, 13, 59, 63, 69
   ideology 3, 11, 15, 64, 148–9
   imagery 39–40, 56, 59
   labor market segregation 33–6, 66
   skill and status 13, 14, 78, 85 (*see also* skill)
Germany 5, 8, 32, 64, 115–16, 132, 146, 180
   artisans and guilds 79, 82, 98, 105, 152, 157–8
   rural industry 172, 177
Great Cat Massacre 81–2, 88, 96, 154
guilds 6–8, 12, 18, 36, 135–6, 147. *See also* apprenticeship; corporations; honor; journeymen; masters; oligarchization; unfree labor
   critique 3, 97
   dissolution 33, 106, 156, 160–1, 167
   guild system 78–84, 157–9
   politics 156–7, 161–4
   quality 70, 156, 163–4
   rights 148, 152, 156, 168
   skill 13, 163, 166, 167

tensions 98, 104–5, 139, 154
and women 12, 13–14, 34, 64, 85–6, 116, 154, 159

Haiti 91, 92
Hamilton, Alexander 139, 148
hiring place 113, 121, 123, 124, 128
Hogarth, William 14, 18, 44, 45, 51, 55, 58, 133, 138
holidays 18, 80, 98, 170, 174, 177, 180–2
honor 13, 18, 79, 83, 110, 153
  guild 6, 12, 80, 83
hours of work 17, 18, 25, 96, 107, 149, 174, 175, 177, 178, 180, 184
  increase in 16, 23, 24, 98–9, 101–2, 169–70, 172, 176, 182

illness and mortality 20, 26, 91, 98, 102, 135, 136, 179
indentured labor 3, 10, 86, 87–9, 90, 93, 158
indigenous peoples. *See* Native Americans
industrious revolution 15, 22–4, 64, 95, 101
industriousness 14, 17–18, 44, 53, 74, 99
industry 8–9, 12, 21, 32, 70. *See also* proto-industry
  imagery 40, 47–51, 56, 59
  industrial development 8–9, 12, 173
  industrial organization 5–6, 14–17, 26, 65–6, 75, 107–8
  industrial production 33, 75, 85
  industrial revolution, narrative of 15, 22, 29, 36, 61–6, 75, 77, 95
  industrialization 36, 40, 79, 101, 110–11, 174–6, 182
Industry and Idleness 14, 44–5, 51, 58, 133
insubordination 88, 153. *See also* employer–employee relations
Italy 12, 32, 82, 120, 132, 135, 136, 142, 160, 161, 167
  northern 5, 42, 152, 158
itinerant sales 70, 72, 119–20, 121, 126, 128–9. *See also* peddlers

Jefferson, Thomas 1, 2, 139, 148
journeymen 102, 104, 118, 136, 160, 167–8. *See also* Great Cat Massacre; employer–employee relations; tramping
  associations 80, 104, 105, 119, 152, 159
  mobility 114, 115, 116, 117, 119, 124, 126
  "right of preference" 158

rights/interests 97–8, 109, 110, 142, 148, 153–4, 156–9, 163
tensions 77, 82–3, 88, 97, 105, 107
labor
  demand 8, 10, 19, 82, 84, 85, 89
  discipline 9, 16–17, 36, 89, 101, 107–10, 144–6, 148, 169
  division of labor 3, 5, 9, 12–15, 17, 25, 32–3, 37, 56, 59, 65, 69, 108–9, 139
  markets 113–21, 126, 128, 131, 153–4, 158, 160–1, 174–6
  supply 5, 22–4, 32–5, 64, 89, 157
  value 3, 14, 30–1, 39–40, 42, 83, 90, 147–8, 151, 166
lace making 23, 24, 41, 42, 56, 59
Laurens, Henry 63, 73
leisure 5, 15, 16, 18, 24–5, 102, 131, 143, 148, 169–84. *See also* sports; fairs; carnivals
  imagery 42, 54
liberal 3, 31, 95, 133, 145, 156
  arts 46, 166
Lichtstuben 177–8
Locke, John 3, 39, 138, 167

Malthus, Thomas 20, 132, 138–9
Mandeville, Bernard de 139–41, 170
markets 8, 21, 26, 31, 36, 95, 97, 99, 101, 104, 108, 136, 138, 144. *See also* labor, markets
  marketplace 4, 10, 15, 23, 45, 67–9, 72, 82
masculinity 12, 13, 44, 85, 135. *See also* gender
masters 8, 9, 28, 32, 34, 45, 102, 110, 148, 176. *See also* employer–employee relations; slavery
  master artisans 6, 64, 66, 79–83, 96–8, 117–19, 125–6, 135–6, 152–68, 171–3
  under pressure 8, 12–13, 104–7
  property owners 55, 61, 73–5, 85, 88–91, 93
meat 19, 69, 181
mechanical arts 46, 96, 106, 165
metal working 47, 61, 65–6, 105–6, 172
migration 4–5, 10, 26, 32, 34, 85, 113–21, 123, 126, 128
  mobility 10, 24–5, 27, 36, 70, 72, 113–16, 118–21, 123, 125–6, 128–9, 157
monopolies 80, 106, 161

Montgolfier, Étienne de 99, 101, 107–10, 136, 154
Montgolfier, Pierre de 95, 99, 101, 107–10, 136, 154
moral economy 61, 147, 153–4, 170
Morice, Margaret 136
Mun, Thomas 151

Nahrung/sustenance 165
Native Americans 6, 16, 20, 62, 63, 71–2, 142
natural rights 163, 167
needlework 43, 56, 176, 178
Netherlands, The 9, 19, 40, 70, 116, 131, 144, 146
   agriculture 4, 5
   guilds 152, 157–8, 160, 161
   urbanized 62, 67
networks 4, 8–9, 17, 63, 66, 85, 113–14, 118–21, 123, 128–9, 136, 142, 156, 162

oligarchization 162, 167

paid work 3, 23, 31, 171, 176, 183
papermaking 95, 98–102, 107, 110, 136, 154
Paris 5, 21, 47, 53, 63, 69, 80, 83, 86, 96–8, 118, 123, 128, 138, 159
participation rates (women's/men's) 23
paternalistic relations 45, 153, 159
patriarchal authority 61, 135, 154, 161, 167
peasantry 14, 131, 138
peddlers 70, 72, 119–20, 126, 128
physiocrats 2–3, 29, 138–9, 160–1, 165
plantations 4, 45, 63, 73–4, 91–2, 145–6
Polanyi, Karl 153
poor relief 85, 135, 144–5, 148
population growth 15, 20–1, 32, 36, 117, 138
porcelain 4, 32
porters 116, 118, 121–2
portraiture 43, 55
Portugal 5, 132, 135
privileges 6, 9, 80, 83, 119, 144, 152, 156–63, 167
product quality 156, 160, 163
proletarianization 118, 128, 153, 160, 166–7
prostitution 24, 31, 55, 138
protest 82, 93, 153–4, 156–7. *See also* food riots; riot; revolts
proto-industry 21, 26, 63, 64, 65, 125, 158, 172

radicalism 110, 152, 156
Ramazzini, Bernardino 102

regulation 17, 148, 152, 154, 156
   civic 10, 34–5, 37, 67, 105, 123, 146, 178
   guild 6, 62, 64, 69, 70, 80, 82, 85–6, 116, 126, 135, 157–63
   mercantile 2–3
religion 1, 14, 16, 17, 70, 80, 86, 110, 131, 135, 146–9, 154, 177
republican ideas 31, 139, 148, 154, 156, 162
resistance 34, 88–9, 93, 105, 148
revolts 146, 152–3, 156, 164
riot 37, 145, 153–4, 157
rural manufactures 27, 33. *See also* domestic industry; proto-industrialization

sailors 70, 72
Saint-Domingue 91, 92
sans-culottes 110, 151, 162
seasonal workers 116, 123
service sector 116–18
shipyards 9, 108
simultaneity 121, 128
skill 6, 12–14, 35, 93, 95–9, 104, 106–11, 151–2, 156, 160–1, 163, 165–7
   imagery, 6, 47, 49, 55–6
   skilled workers 3, 6, 8, 13, 61, 77, 79–80, 83, 93, 95, 102, 117, 135, 174, 176
   unskilled workers 6, 13, 34, 78, 80, 83, 84–5
slavery 4, 18, 31, 36, 45, 72–3, 87–92, 145–6, 154
   slave rebellions 146
Smith, Adam 1, 13, 165
   consumption 100–1, 139, 141–2
   critique of apprenticeship and guilds 3, 8, 97, 161, 167
   labor 3, 8, 30–2, 37, 39, 53, 65, 139, 146, 151
Soho works. *See* Boulton, Matthew
Spain 5, 8, 24, 116, 132, 135, 139, 142, 145
   industry 32–4, 110
sports 177–9, 181
street sellers. *See* peddlers
strife. *See* employer-employee relations
strike 49, 107, 156–7, 159–60
sugar 4, 9, 21, 45, 62, 73–5, 91, 101, 146
Sweden 32, 37, 66, 146, 157

technology 13, 95, 111
   technical knowledge 34, 163, 165
textile manufactures 24, 33–4
time 3, 9, 15–18
tobacco 4–5, 9, 24, 44, 47, 73, 75, 91, 146

trades 3, 5, 6, 8, 10–11, 16, 25, 34, 95–6, 118–19, 138
   artisanal 47, 66–7, 98, 101, 109–10, 126, 135–6, 142, 148, 158–61
   provisioning 69, 136
tramping system 18, 104, 110, 118, 128, 159
transients 78, 118, 124, 128
Turgot, Anne-Robert-Jacques, Baron de l'Aulne 3, 8, 97, 106, 161

unfree labor 78, 86–8, 93, 118, 158–9, 163
unsettled 97, 113–15, 118
urban growth 5–6, 21, 35, 67, 84, 169. *See also* cities
utility 16, 23, 97, 151

vegetables 42, 68

Wedgwood, Josiah 107–8, 110, 147, 166
wet-nurses 116, 121, 123–4
women 20, 78, 92–3, 123–5, 136, 145, 153–4, 171, 177–83
   Enlightenment 1–2, 31, 33
   guilds 6–8, 12, 85–6, 159–60, 167
   imagery 39–43, 45–7, 53, 55–6, 59
   married women's work 15, 17, 24, 31, 62, 66, 69, 85–6, 176, 183
   single women 64, 66, 69, 86, 124, 183
   widows 69, 85–6, 125, 129, 135–6
   women's work 3, 8–13, 16–17, 23–4, 33–7, 63–4, 67, 72, 95, 97, 99, 101–2, 105–7, 116, 120–3, 176
work. *See also* labor
   as degrading 39, 45, 89
   as spectacle 39, 47, 59
   unpaid work 3, 173, 183
   value 14, 40, 42, 55–6, 149, 151, 161, 167
workers' rights. *See* guilds; journeymen; masters; *and specific countries*
working hours. *See* hours of work
workshops 6–9, 12, 17, 24, 26, 64–7, 79–82, 95–102, 106, 117, 120–3, 126, 176
   imagery 40, 42, 47, 56